Racism in the 21st Century

Racism in the 21st Century

An Empirical Analysis of Skin Color

Ronald E. Hall
Editor

Michigan State University, Lansing, MI, USA

 Springer

Editor
Ronald E. Hall
Michigan State University
School of Social Work
254 Baker Hall
East Lansing, MI 48824, USA
hallr@msu.edu

ISBN: 978-0-387-79097-8   e-ISBN: 978-0-387-79098-5
DOI: 10.1007/978-0-387-79097-8

Library of Congress Control Number: 2008932551

Printed on acid-free paper

springer.com

In memory of my loving parents,
Judge B. and Doris B. Hall
and to Robert L. Green, Ph.D.,
Dean/Professor Emeritus, Urban
Affairs Program, Michigan
State University

Preface

People of color the world over manifest the impacts of a racism originating in a distant era in history. Among Americans, there nonetheless remain professionals who are trained with hardly any reference at all to the biological, social and economic implications of skin color among an increasingly diverse population. Furthermore, those who teach at some of our most prestigious universities have not been exposed to the implications of skin color as a 21st century manifestation of racism.

Throughout my career, I have puzzled over the manner in which racism has evolved and continues to impose consequences upon society. I am constantly surprised by the fact that our obsession with racism gives hardly any consideration of the social and cultural gaps perpetuated by skin color. In fact, most Americans go about their daily affairs without ever mentioning a word about it. It should therefore come as no surprise that Americans have not understood the role of skin color in the conduct of racist social and economic interactions. For many reasons, the topic has remained an unspeakable taboo in practically every sector of the academy and the society at-large. This, I see as dangerous. It serves the tenets of racism and preserves the colonial status quo. In the aftermath, people of color define their worth by their proximity to Caucasian social and biological characteristics.

Racism via race or skin color can be neither understood nor assessed for its impact without a logical frame of reference. The chapters in this book will give readers some insight to the implications of skin color among people of color who may have idealized Western phenotypes as a consequence of the historical influences of colonization. We characterize the secret notion of hierarchy and quality of life perpetrated on the basis of skin color. The contributing authors have illustrated this perpetuation by first giving account of the biology of skin color and its manifestation of racism in the 21st century. Subsequent chapters address the penalties exacted upon society by racism and its pervasiveness. In the final chapter, I close with a summation of the skin color phenomenon.

In multiple respects, this book is unique. It takes readers beyond the black/white racial dichotomy by exposing a manifestation of racism that appears among those who would be otherwise considered victims. This is not an attempt to minimize white racism, or any other social ills. It is not a criticism or judgment of people of color, but merely a mirror in which our society may view a surprising reflection of itself. We do not presume to be complete or flawless in our presentation. Rather, we hope to promote dialogue about all forms and manner of societal denigration. We engage in this dialogue despite the real danger of stereotyping and cultural misrepresentation, or even worse, misuse for racist purposes.

Some of my colleagues argue that writing about skin color will do more harm than good because it is so provocative. But it is my opinion that confronting a provocative topic is a healthy and socially appropriate way to benefit American society and humanity in general. This book is only a start, but a start is where solutions begin.

In conclusion, I believe the problem for any author who attempts comment upon such a charged topic as racism by skin color may make errors of interpretation. When that interpretation reaches publication, we run the risk of doing disservice to all. In the grist of self worth, the following authors engage in their attempt at discussion under the assumption of dignity and respect for all people. Solution will result to the extent that we maintain openness and a willingness to consider new ideas. Furthermore, those of us stained by the rumors of inferiority associated with skin color indulge an extremely dangerous luxury. By virtue of victimization in modern circles of scholarship there is a tendency to portray ourselves as simultaneously the embodiment of quintessential virtue and cultural piety. Social denigration may be claimed to provide an unchangeable cloak of integrity and an innate nobility that sets one morally apart from oppressors. Victims of racism often feel that they have earned the right to cast a moral stone at the racists among them! There is a tendency to take no responsibility for its social injustice and to delude ourselves into ignoring the implications of skin color because white racism seems worse. I believe it is much better to discuss the very real racist taboos of skin color despite the dangers of discomfort, inaccuracy or misinterpretation.

In the final analysis, humanity, of whatever gender, race or skin color cannot deny the dignity and worth of another without diminishing some measure of its own. For in the image of one's victim, is a reflection of one's self. Study of racism in the 21st century may be an accurate revelation of what we've become. Believing that, it is my sincerest hope and that of the contributing authors that those who read this book move past stereotypes or misinterpretations. They should focus instead on the dynamics of our existence as closely linked members of a common genetic family.

East Lansing, MI   Ronald E. Hall

Acknowledgements

Thanks to these giants,
who let me stand on their shoulders and glimpse the impossible:

Elaine Baker, Ph.D.
Creigs C. Beverly, Ph.D.
Nan Elizabeth Casey, Attorney Counselor at Law
Kenneth Corcy, Ph.D.
Mamie R. Darlington, Ph.D.
Marilyn Flynn, Ph.D.
Robert J. Griffore, Ph.D.
Richard Lyle, Ph.D.
Lillian A. Phenice, Ph.D.
George T. Rowan, Ph.D.

Contents

Part I The Biology of Race and Today's Manifestations of Racism

1 Demystifying Skin Color and "Race"   3
   Keith C. Cheng

2 Manifestations of Racism in the 21st Century   25
   Ronald E. Hall

Part II What are the Costs of Racism?

3 Skin Color Bias in the Workplace: The Media's Role and Implications
   Toward Preference   47
   Matthew S. Harrison, Wendy Reynolds-Dobbs, and Kecia M. Thomas

4 The Cost of Color: What We Pay for Being Black and Brown   63
   Margaret Hunter

5 Skin Color, Immigrant Wages, and Discrimination   77
   Joni Hersch

Part III The Pervasivences of Racism

6 Racial Characteristics and Female Facial Attractiveness Perception
   Among United States University Students   93
   Nicole E. Belletti and T. Joel Wade

7 Lifetime Prevalence and Quality of Interracial Interactions on Color
   Consciousness Among White Young Adults 125
   Alfiee M. Breland-Noble, Joy King, Stacy Young, Brea Eaton,
   Melissa Willis, Keri Hurst, and Chastity Simmons

**8   Skin Color Biases: Attractiveness and Halo Effects in the Evaluation of
      African Americans**   135
      T. Joel Wade

9   The Latin Americanization of Racial Stratification in the U.S.   151
      Eduardo Bonilla-Silva and David R. Dietrich

**10   Skin Color and Latinos with Disabilities: Expanding What We Know
      About Colorism in the United States**   171
      Keith B. Wilson and Julissa Senices

11   Brown Outs: The Role of Skin Color and Latinas   193
      Christina Gómez

**12   "There Is No Racism Here": Understanding Latinos'
      Perceptions of Color Discrimination Through Sending-Receiving
      Society Comparison**   205
      Wendy D. Roth

13   Conclusion   235
      Ronald E. Hall

Author Biographies   247

Index   253

Contributors

Nicole E. Belletti
Department of Psychology, Bucknell University, Walnut Port, PA, USA,
nicole.belletti@gmail.com

Eduardo Bonilla-Silva
Department of Sociology, Duke University, Durham, NC, USA,
ebs@soc.duke.edu

Alfiee M. Breland-Noble
Department of Psychiatry, Duke University, Durham, NC, USA,
abreland@psych.duhs.duke.edu

Keith C. Cheng
Jake Gittlen Cancer Research Foundation, Pennsylvania State University
College of Medicine, Hershey, PA, USA,
Kcheng76@gmail.com

David R. Dietrich
Department of Sociology, Duke University, Durham, NC, USA,
david.dietrich@duke.edu

Christina Gómez
Department of Sociology, Northeastern Illinois University, Chicago, IL, USA,
cgomez@neiu.edu

Ronald E. Hall
School of Social Work, Michigan State University, East Lansing, MI, USA,
hallr@msu.edu

Matthew S. Harrison
Department of Applied (Industrial/Organizational) Psychology, The University
of Georgia, Athens, GA, USA,
msharris@uga.edu

Joni Hersch
Department of Law and Economics, Vanderbilt University, Nashville,
TN, USA,
joni.hersch@vanderbilt.edu

Margaret Hunter
Department of Sociology, Mills College, Oakland, CA, USA,
mhunter@mills.edu

Wendy Reynolds-Dobbs
Department of Applied (Industrial/Organizational) Psychology,
The University of Georgia, Athens, GA, USA,
gaps@uga.edu

Wendy D. Roth
Department of Sociology, University of British Columbia, Vancouver, BC,
Canada,
wroth@interchange.ubc.ca

Julissa Senices
Department of Counselor Education, Counseling Psychology and
Rehabilitation Services, The Pennsylvania State University, State College, PA,
USA,
jisll2@psu.edu

Kecia M. Thomas
Institute for African American Studies, The University of Georgia, Athens,
GA, USA,
kthomas@uga.edu

T. Joel Wade
Department of Psychology, Bucknell University, Walnut Port, PA, USA,
jwade@bucknell.edu

Keith B. Wilson
Department of Counselor Education, Counseling Psychology
and Rehabilitation Services, The Pennsylvania State University, State College,
PA, USA,
kbw4@psu.edu

Part I
The Biology of Race and Today's Manifestations of Racism

Chapter 1
Demystifying Skin Color and "Race"

Keith C. Cheng

Abstract Historical confusion in thinking about skin color and race derives from the state of science at the time human classifications were proposed, and from our incomplete understanding of the genetics of human pigmentation and human ancestry. The pervasiveness of racism reflects the universal human desire for kinship, in settings of competition for resources, where it is common to devalue and harm other groups for the benefit of the group with which one identifies. To gain insight into the biological basis of skin color, scientists have studied the structure of pigmented tissues, hundreds of pigment variants in vertebrates, and a range of enzymes and molecules that affect melanin formation. We have learned that most population-specific traits can be explained by evolutionary chance, and that a small minority of traits, including skin color, have exerted a selective advantage during evolution. The selective advantages of dark and light skin color in the equatorial and more polar geographic regions, respectively, antedate sun screen and Vitamin D supplementation. Since modern technology has largely rendered these evolutionary advantages irrelevant, skin color has become a sociological issue that is amenable to reason. Education can play a central role in work toward a society free of racism, as long as that education is firmly grounded in critically evaluated science and is free of tribalism.

This work is written from my perspective as a geneticist and physician whose curiosity led to unexpected insight into the genetic basis of skin color. Until our discovery of the zebrafish *golden* gene, I had no professional intent to study either skin color or race. The presented considerations are informed and motivated by issues faced by minorities.

K.C. Cheng
Jake Gittlen Cancer Research Foundation, Division of Experimental Pathology,
Pennsylvania State University College of Medicine, Hershey, PA, USA
e-mail: kcheng76@gmail.com

Introduction

Scientific advances profoundly affect our worldviews. Advances in physics allowed us to realize that the earth is not flat. The discovery of microbes allowed us to abandon beliefs in spirits and humors as the cause of human disease. Similarly, as argued in this chapter, knowledge of the biological and genetic basis of skin color and ancestry will allow humanity to correct misconceptions about skin color and race that have contributed to some of the greatest injustices in human history.

In deciding upon specifics to include in this chapter, I asked what aspects of scientific understanding and thinking about the concept of race might, most likely, suggest solutions to the problems of racism. It was clearly important to address the concerns of today's scientists about even using the term "race." This concern is based on the poorly defined sociological components and violence-laden history of race (Marks 1995, Sankar & Cho 2002, Bamshad et al.2004, Mountain & Risch 2004, Sternberg et al. 2005, Gould & Lewontin 1979). Awareness of the historical, anthropological, and philosophical aspects of "race" and racism are also essential to attain any real understanding of the complexities of race and racism.

After a brief historical overview of human classifications and racism, we will cover some of the basic cell biology, genetics and medical implications of skin color as it affects our thinking about ancestry and race. In order to add insight into the mechanisms of modern science, I will share the story of the recent discovery of a likely genetic mechanism underlying the evolution of light skin in peoples of European ancestry (Lamason et al. 2005). I will then explain how the issues raised by this discovery, combined with the awareness of issues associated with being part of an ethnic minority, led me to believe that scientists, while justified in their avoidance of the use of race in scientific investigation, do not need to avoid the issue of race. A main point of this chapter is that a healing process is critical to diminishing racism, that scientists can help this process by active engagement in calm, logical and scientifically accurate discussions of race and ancestry with the lay public.

Historical Context

Much of the confusion in thinking about skin color and race derives from the state of science at the time human classifications were proposed and from our incomplete understanding of the genetics of human pigmentation and human ancestry. Classifications of humans from the 18th and 19th centuries were created by physicians with minimal knowledge about the biology of skin color. The practice of medicine was based more on humors and spirits than current concepts of pathophysiology. The idea that all living things are composed of cells was only beginning to be understood. The idea that cells contained organelles (such as those containing pigment) would only be possible with advances in microscopy that came in the 20th century. Although thoughts about inheritance were postulated, DNA and genes were unknown concepts. The first classifications of humans were based on the available small samples of people. Within this context, it is not surprising that the founder of today's form of biological taxonomy, Carolus Linnaeus (Linné 1767), and the founder of anthropology, Johann Friedrich Blumenbach (1865) wrote classifications that contained concepts typical of their era, but known to be incorrect today. Linnaeus succumbed to the assignment of negative personality features to human groups. Blumenbach, despite his prominent and positive role in the Enlightenment, unscientifically assigned aesthetic value to the physical features of skulls. These mistakes, which fed ethnocentric assumptions about intelligence, carried on through Western scientific history even into the 20th century and were unfortunately used to justify bad science (reviewed by Gould 1996) and centuries of human atrocities across the globe.

Modern scientists, armed with modern knowledge and education in modern philosophies of equality, are finally able to distance themselves from the evils of racism. However, we still have a large distance to travel. Even in this modern day, many people, including at times notable scientists, forget that there are two primary and separate determinants of the state of any living thing: the genetic and the environmental, otherwise known as "nature" and "nurture". Whenever both roles are not simultaneously considered, or distinctions clouded, erroneous conclusions are drawn. Hence today's continuing struggle with race and racism.

Whence Racism?

Racism has been a pervasive form of tribalism in human societies of all times and places. Why this is the case is the subject of abundant and vociferous debate. To provide a starting point for discussion, I offer a personal perspective on this question that is based on reading of scientific literature, personal experience, and discussions with psychologists and anthropologists. The pervasiveness of racism is consistent with the human desire for kinship that, in settings of competition for resources, leads to the practice of actively devaluing and harming other groups for the benefit of the group with which one identifies. Tribalism is associated with all manner of distinctions, ranging from skin color to religion to regional/ethnic groups to sport team allegiance. Since parts of tribalism have evolutionary benefit, it is also reflected in other animals (Lorenz 1966). Any solution to racism must therefore acknowledge our instincts, and use the power of reason to teach ourselves how related we actually all are. There is reason to believe that greater understanding of skin color, ancestry, genetics, and the sociology of race will lead to greater tolerance and equality.

A conclusion of overriding importance for public policy is that the *social environment, not the genetics*, of underprivileged peoples must be the relentless focus of successful governments and societies—good societies will provide opportunity for every human regardless of ancestry, thereby allowing everyone in their society the opportunity to reach his or her full potential. It is the *social environment*—not the genetics—that is the primary variable that determines human achievement and development of intelligence by learning. What we now know about what it takes to achieve excellence, together with what we now know about the neurobiology of learning, converge on this conclusion. If this writing accomplishes its purpose, it will contribute in some manner to increasing acceptance between peoples regardless of color, thereby facilitating the equitable distribution of opportunity.

The Cell Biology of Pigmentation

In all humans, regardless of "race," skin is colored by a mixture of pigments called melanin (Jablonski 2004, 2006, Sturm 2006, Barsh 2003). The predominant form of melanin is black eumelanin, and the body's factories for generating melanin are pigmented cells called melanocytes—G. *melas*, black; G. *kytos*, cell. The study of pigmented tissues under the electron microscope showed that melanin is packaged within melanocytes in membrane-bound subcellular structures called melanosomes—G. *soma*, body. As more melanin is generated by the cell, the number, size, pigment density, and elongation of these melanosomes increase. The melanocytes of human skin, which are approximately equal in number regardless of the degree of skin pigmentation, are responsible for generating all of the melanosomes in human skin. Most of human skin is comprised of keratinocytes—G. *keras*, horn. The melanocytes deliver melanosomes to the keratinocytes by packing their fingerlike cellular projections with melanosomes, and then "feeding" them to the keratinocytes. The melanosomes we see in keratinocytes thus derive from melanocytes, rather than the keratinocytes themselves. For reasons we do not yet understand, the greater melanin production seen in darker skin is associated with larger, darker, longer, and more numerous melanosomes. A key point to learn here is that the most common differences in pigmentation appear to be due to differences in the level of activity of the involved genes or proteins, rather than their presence or absence.

To gain insight into the biological and genetic basis of pigmentation, scientists have studied the structure of pigmented tissues, hundreds of pigment variants in mice and other organisms, dozens of genetic abnormalities that diminish pigmentation in all vertebrates (including humans), and a range of enzymes and molecules that affect melanin formation (Sturm 2006). The cellular and molecular mechanisms of biological processes, including pigmentation, have shown remarkable conservation in evolution. Despite vast amounts of work, the genes determining the key skin color differences between races had been elusive (Barsh 2003). In the last decade, we have begun to identify genes underlying the largest difference in human skin color—that between peoples of African versus European descent. The discovery of this key to understanding skin color differences between people of West African and European ancestry came from the study of a light-skinned variant of a popular pet, the zebrafish (Lamason et al. 2005, Sturm 2006).

Zebrafish and the Genetics of Human Skin Color

Our new insight into the genetics of human skin color was serendipitous, coming from two seemingly unlikely sources—cancer research (Lamason et al. 2005) and zebrafish, a common pet store fish that has become a favorite of researchers interested in the biology of vertebrates (Lieschke & Currie 2007). In brief, since mutations in body cells are responsible for turning normal cells into cancer cells, we were interested in finding genes involved in the process of mutation. We used a powerful scientific tool for finding genes that are involved in any biological process—making and studying mutants in the context of what are called genetic screens. For our genetic screen in zebrafish, we used a lightly colored variant of zebrafish, called *golden*, which the founder of the field, George Streisinger, had found in a pet store in Oregon. What Dr. Streisinger did was to develop a visual test to detect mutation in which mutant cells appear as light cells on a dark background in the eye (Streisinger 1984)—figuratively "stars in the sky." We used that test in our genetic screen to find genes involved in susceptibility to cancer (Moore et al. 2006). Now that we have indicated our original reason for our use of *golden* fish, we can focus back on the nature of the variation itself. The populations of zebrafish from pet stores are derived from companies in warm parts of the country, such as Florida, that raise them by the tens of thousands—in populations that represent to some degree the variation in nature. We know from a multitude of DNA studies and photographic studies that humans vary in a multitude of subtle ways. The fact is that the continent with, by far, the greatest variation of any population is Africa. That variation includes variation in a large number of characteristics, such as shapes and lengths of noses, ears, limbs, and pigmentation. Zebrafish populations also vary in many ways, including patterns of pigmented cells, lengths of fins, and pigmentation; *golden* zebrafish may be viewed as one might view a lighter-skinned individual in Africa. For our research, we wanted to find the sequence of the *golden* gene because it would potentially help us to characterize the mutants we had derived from our cancer project. But beyond cancer research, this work would yield an unexpected insight into the evolution of human skin color variation.

The central finding leading to our discovery about human skin color derived from curiosity about the *cellular process* affected in *golden* zebrafish. To satisfy

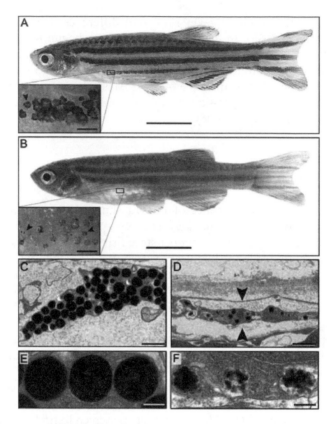

Fig. 1.1 Phenotype of *Golden* Zebrafish
Lateral views of adult wild-type (**A**) and *golden* (**B**) zebrafish. Insets show melanophores
(arrowheads). Scale bars: 5 mm (inset 0.5 mm). *gol*^{b1} mutants have smaller melanophores with
fewer, dysmorphic melanosomes. Transmission electron micrographs of skin melanophore
from 55 hpf wild-type (**C and E**) and *gol*^{b1} (**D and F**) larvae. *gol*^{b1} skin melanophores (arrowheads show edges) are thinner and contain fewer melanosomes than wild-type. Melanosomes
of *gol*^{b1} larvae are smaller, less pigmented and irregular compared to wild-type. Scale bars:
(**C, D**) 1000 nm; (**E, F**) 200 nm. (Reprinted with permission from *Science* magazine.)

that curiosity, we first studied adult *golden* fish under a light microscope to look
closely at their skin. We noted that the pigmented *cells* in the dark stripes are
present in the most common number and pattern, but lighter in color and often
smaller in size (Fig. 1.1, A and B)—the pigmented cells were just smaller in size
and lighter in color. But why were the pigment cells lighter in color? We used the
electron microscope to determine what might have happened to the melanosomes (Fig. 1.1, C and E) in the skin cells of *golden* fish. The light color of *golden*
pigmented cells could be due to one or more of three changes—a reduction in
the number of melanosomes per cell, in the average size of the melanosomes, or
in the amount of pigment deposited in the average melanosome. As a rule of

thumb in biology, individual gene functions are frequently quite specific, so we expected only *one* feature (number *or* size *or* pigment intensity) of melanosomes to be changed in *golden* fish. Thus, it was to my great surprise that *all three* of these features were diminished in the melanosomes of *golden* zebrafish (Fig. 1.1, C–F). Nothing in my entire career in science was more striking than the moment in which I came to understand that these *same three qualitative changes* had long been known to be associated with the differences between light and dark *human* skin (Bolognia & Orlow 2003)! This finding directly suggested that whatever gene or mechanism is involved in causing the light skin of golden zebrafish would also prove to be important in humans—this motivated our subsequent studies.

In everyday life, the lay public has historically developed its views of the world based on single types of "evidence"—if a source we consider authoritative tells us that the sun goes around the earth, or that the earth is flat, we are apt to accept the contention as fact without looking at alternative explanations that are just as or even more possible, especially if it is said to dictate our fate or otherwise serves our interests. If we are taught that everyone in another "race" or political party is inferior we tend to accept that too. If we are taught that humans have nothing to do with global warming we may listen more to individuals with no scientific training and clear conflicts of interest. We must even look harder at falsified documents by politicians and non-scientists than at evidence generated by scientists who understand the dangerous trends and who suggest positive and responsible courses of action. In good science, however, we make models based on evidence, and then test as many predictions of those models as possible in such a way that the evidence can *support or contradict* each model. As applied to skin color, we began from an observation—that cellular changes associated with light skin in both zebrafish and humans are similar, I asked what multiple forms of evidence could be found that support or eliminate the idea that a mutation in the human gene corresponding to the zebrafish *golden* gene played an important role in the light skin of one or more human populations. That would first require finding the zebrafish gene and then the human gene.

We identified the gene responsible for the color of *golden* zebrafish after years of molecular analyses, whose specifics are not important to this discussion. What you do need to know, however, is that genes can be thought of as segments of DNA that, from bacteria to humans, most frequently encode the sequences of amino acid subunits in the corresponding proteins (which include the structural units that hold us together, make up our hair, and facilitate all of the biochemical reactions that make life possible). After finding the sequence of the zebrafish gene, we searched on-line databases, and found a single human gene whose amino acid sequence was 68% identical to that of the zebrafish gene. Similar genes *within* a species, molecular cousins, if you will, are called members of gene families, or *paralogs*. Genes of similar structure and function *between* different species, typically of the most identical function, are called "*orthologues.*" The 500 amino-acid human *golden* gene, also called *SLC24A5*, encodes what is called a "sodium, calcium exchanger," based upon similarity with its similarly named paralogs. The presence of one corresponding human orthologue to the zebrafish *golden* gene reflects its strong evolutionary conservation in at least all vertebrates. The next task was to find evidence for or against conserved function of the human protein in pigmentation. Since there is a large evolutionary distance between fish and humans, a stringent test would be to determine whether the human protein could function in zebrafish. The *golden* mutant in this gene allowed us to test that possibility. To do this test, we could inject the RNA or DNA that would be expected to be made into protein, and see whether the pigmented cells in *golden* embryos would become as dark as those in zebrafish without the mutation in the *golden* gene. Strikingly, we found that the human homologue can cause the light *golden* cells of zebrafish to darken. In fact, *both* European and African versions of the gene caused *golden* cells to darken. Upon studying the new "HapMap" database (HapMap 2007) of human genetic variation (a catalogue of single letter changes commonly found in human DNA), we discovered in a particular place in this gene, a guanine, or "G" is present in nearly all African and East Asian (Chinese and Japanese) sample populations, and that adenine, or "A" was present in every individual in the European HapMap population (from Utah, derived from northwestern Europe). Among the ten places where there was known variation between populations in this gene, this change was the *only* one causing a change in the genetic code resulting in a change in amino acid in the corresponding gene—the 111th amino acid, alanine, which is invariant in vertebrate evolution, was changed into a threonine in all of the European individuals tested (Lamason et al. 2005). Since *Ala* is the abbreviation for alanine (pronounced "al′—a—neen") and *Thr* the abbreviation for threonine (prounounced "three—o—neen"), this amino acid change is abbreviated *Ala111Thr*. This nomenclature is common in genetics.

A Key Role for SLC24A5 in the Lightening of Skin Color in Europeans

Using the zebrafish, we had discovered an important gene that affects the number, size, and depth of staining of melanosomes. We also found that the human gene could contribute to pigmentation by replacing the corresponding gene's function in zebrafish. After noting the similarity between the skin of *golden* zebrafish and the skin of Europeans, we searched for and found a one-letter change in the DNA sequence in the human version of the zebrafish gene that changed amino acid 111. But for what fraction of measured skin color differences between Africans and Europeans does the *Ala111Thr* change in *SLC24A5* account? In our collaboration, anthropologist Mark Shriver and colleagues used DNA and quantitative machine-based measurements of skin color to correlate the presence of this change in people with so-called "admixed" European-African ancestry to corresponding skin color measurements. To have admixed European-African ancestry is to have both European and

African parentage. From this work, we were able to calculate that the *Ala111Thr* change accounts for 25–38% of the skin color difference between West African and northern European skin (Lamason et al. 2005). This range of effect was subsequently confirmed by studying the skin and DNA of populations from South Asia (the Indian subcontinent) (Stokowski et al. 2007).

We then looked for specific evidence of selection for light skin in the population of European ancestry by studying the patterns of variation across the pages of our genetic code book—our DNA. Here, we are looking to see whether evidence exists for biological selection for a DNA change corresponding to lighter skin color conveyed by a variation in a very specific point in a specific gene on a specific chromosome. We know that most variation in DNA is due to genetic variation within groups, and has no biological effect (Collins 2004). In the case of the *Ala111Thr* change in *SLC24A5* in Europeans, however, we have a very rare situation—a wide constellation of evidence consistent with selection. To understand this evidence you need to know that we have one set of chromosomes from our mothers and a second set from our fathers. In the case of the *golden* gene, for both zebrafish and humans, two copies of the mutant chromosome are necessary for the lighter skin color. If we expect that there is selection for light skin color, *both* copies of the gene will be mutant, and *nearby variations* present on the original mutated chromosome will be indirectly selected for—a genetic "hitch-hiking," if you will. This leads directly to less variation in the region around *SLC24A5*. The size of the region showing decreased variation around *SLC24A5* is larger than anywhere else in the genome, and only for the European population. This is the strongest evidence one could have expected, in support of the idea that there was *selection* for light skin color in the northern latitudes of Europe.

If there is selection for lighter skin as humans move to northerly latitudes, there has to be some *biological reason* for having light skin in those regions. There exist two types of complementary evidence that have to do with essential nutrients and sunlight (Jablonski 2004, 2006). Sunlight is needed for one essential nutrient (vitamin D). However, sunlight is less intense and less lengthy in northern latitudes—it would therefore be predicted that light skin is favored in those latitudes. But why is there darker skin in Africa? Since intense sunlight destroys another nutrient (folate) that is essential for proper fetal development, darker skin is favored for survival in equatorial regions. If there is selection for light skin, the European allele of *SLC24A5* should also be found across all of Europe. That is indeed the case and is consistent with selection for light skin within Europeans peoples (Lamason et al. 2005, Norton et al. 2007), perhaps after the last glacial retreat some 15,000 years ago (Fig. 1.2). *When* the mutation arose is an open question—existing evidence is consistent with a model in which the mutation was present in Africa long before humans migrated into Europe. The mutation in the human *golden* gene may have been a naturally occurring variant in Africa. Similarly, in zebrafish, we find *golden* mixed in with populations of zebrafish. In humans there was selective pressure for the lighter variant, but not in zebrafish.

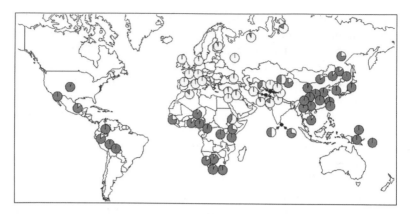

Fig. 1.2 World Distribution of the *Ala111Thr* Allele of *SLC24A5*
World distribution of the *Ala111Thr* allele of *SLC24A5*. This representation is derived from data from a collaboration with Ken Kidd (Yale University), combined with data from Norton et al. (2007), and from Soejima & Koda (2007). The proportion of alleles in each population is represented by a pie chart in which the ancestral allele is represented in grey, and the new, derived allele is represented in white. It is readily apparent that the *Ala111Thr* derived allele of *SLC24A5* becomes more predominant in Europe as the population is further northwest. Notably, the derived allele is nearly absent in East Asia, where the evolution of light skin was derived by other genetic mechanisms, in a process called convergent evolution. The small proportion of this allele in Mexican and Vietnamese populations might be accounted for by admixture with European (Spanish/Portuguese and French populations, respectively). When the DNA variations associated with light skin color in East Asians are found, we expect the corresponding diagram to show white circles in East Asia and the Americas, grey circles in Africa, and unpredicted proportions among European populations. Figure generated with Jason Mest and Victor Canfield. (Figure courtesy of the author.)

What other genetic variations are associated with light skin color in Europeans? Pigment variants in animals helped scientists to find another gene important in the evolution of human light skin: *MATP* ("membrane-associated transporter protein," also called *SLC45A2* or *AIM1*—"antigen in melanoma 1"). Among the animals informing us about the pigmentary function of this gene were the so-called *underwhite* mutation in mice (Newton et al. 2001) and the "b" mutation in the medaka fish (Fukamachi et al. 2001). In humans, a specific mutation in this gene, *Leu374Phe* mutation (the ancestral amino acid leucine is replaced in the variant by phenylalanine at amino acid 374) is present in most but not all Europeans (less frequent than the *SLC24A5* mutation) and contributes about an equal amount to skin color as the European *Ala111Thr* variant in *SLC24A5*. But what relative contribution did the variations in *golden* and *MATP* play in selection for skin color? Compared with the 150,000 base-pair region of diminished variation in *SLC24A5*, *MATP* is associated with a smaller, 40,000 base-pair region of diminished variation in Europeans. This smaller region may be evidence of lesser selection for this mutation in *MATP* compared with that in *SLC24A5*, or simply that the *golden* variant is necessary to see a significant effect on skin color mediated by *MATP*. This question remains to be resolved. Nonetheless, the single-letter changes in *SLC24A5* and *MATP* alone are estimated to contribute to half or more of the difference in skin color between Africans and Europeans—two single-letter changes among the three billion in our DNA. These changes influence skin color, but have no other known implications—in particular, implications about intelligence.

At the time of publication of our work with *golden*, there were no published data on the frequency of the European allele among individuals on the Indian subcontinent. In their pursuit of genetic markers of European versus Sri Lankan populations, however, Soejima and Koda showed that the European allele of *SLC24A5* can be found at frequencies of about 50 and 30% in the lighter Sinhalese and darker Tamil populations, respectively (Soejima & Koda 2007). The focus of their chapter was on the fact that the northern European allele of *MATP* discussed below is nearly absent in Sri Lankans. Their work suggests the possibility that Europeans originated in South Asia, becoming lighter in skin color through adaptive mutations such as that in MATP, as descendants moved into the more northerly latitudes. A monumental study of thousands of Icelanders published late in 2007 identified other mutations, presumably subsequent to that in *SLC24A5* that seem to have contributed to the extra-light skin of Scandinavian peoples (Sulem et al. 2007). Together the data suggest the possibility that the gradation of light skin toward that of Scandinavians required a genetic foundation laid by *SLC24A5,* upon which additional mutations may be added to further lighten the skin.

We have learned from the above that when a trait is selected for, it can be expected that the amount of genetic variation around the selected variation will show less change around it. While this diminished variation applies to *SLC24A5* in Europeans, there is no diminished variation in the region around *SLC24A5* in the light-skinned East Asians of Beijing and Tokyo, both of whom are light peoples. This indicates that variation in *SLC24A5* has nothing to do with their lighter skin color. East Asians (Chinese, Japanese, and Koreans) evolved light skin independently from Europeans, via mutations in different genes that remain to be identified (Lamason *et al.* 2005, Norton *et al.* 2007). This finding of "convergent evolution" for light skin color in northern latitudes by different genetic mechanisms comprises compelling evidence that, during the migration of humans into northerly latitudes, light skin color is biologically necessary.

Health Implications of Light Skin Color

Light skin in Europeans is associated with skin cancer susceptibility (SEER 2004). Skin cancer is of several types corresponding to the cell types normally present in the epidermis—the layer of skin covering our entire bodies.

Squamous cell carcinoma of the skin arises from its predominant cell type, the keratinocytes. Basal cell carcinoma arises from the cells at the bottom layer of the epidermis, the basal cells. Melanoma arises from the cells making all the pigment of skin, the melanocytes. The incidence of all of these types of skin cancers is increased in Europeans. All are thought to arise from lack of protection of the DNA of the skin cells from the sun, which is known to cause specific types of mutations. The cancer of pigmented cells, melanoma, is one of the most deadly human cancers. After it spreads, it kills four out of five patients within five years due to a dearth of effective treatments (Terando et al. 2007). One of the greatest hopes in melanoma treatment is immunotherapy, in which antibodies or specialized "killer" cells are directed to attack proteins on the cancer cell (Terando et al. 2007). Once development from the egg to adult is complete, pigmented cells are no longer essential for life (other than for protection from the sun and to enhance vision). Proteins that are particularly abundant in pigmented cells are potentially good targets for immunotherapy. In support of the use of this protein for targeting, we were able to show that the *SLC24A5* protein is expressed primarily in pigmented cells and at levels thousands of times higher in melanoma than in non-pigmented cells (Lamason et al. 2005). By attaching fluorescent "flags" into the protein, we determined that it likely sits in the melanosome membrane or its precursor. Work primarily by others has since revealed that some 1500 other proteins are associated with melanosomes (Chi et al. 2006). Which of these are specific to melanosomes and common in most or all melanomas will have to be determined to help choose the best target. An important unanswered question is why East Asians (e.g. Chinese, Japanese, and Koreans) have lighter skin but do not show the degree of increase in the risk of skin cancer that is characteristic of people of European ancestry. Finding the genes underlying the light color of East Asian skin, and comparing the mechanisms of decreased pigmentation with that of Europeans, will be key to understanding skin cancer susceptibility. We might also mention that European ancestry is associated with the most common form of acquired blindness in humans, age-related macular degeneration (Yates & Moore 2000), suggesting that *SLC24A5* might contribute to this disease (Cheng & Canfield 2006).

The field of pharmacogenomics studies how variations in our DNA cause variations in our responsiveness to drugs. The Race, Ethnicity, and Genetics Working Group (2005) is part of the National Human Genome Research Institute (NHGRI) at the National Institutes of Health, dedicated to ensuring proper consideration of the connections between race, ethnicity, and genetics (Race, Ethnicity, and Genetics Working Group 2005), such as those associated with the finding of the *golden* gene. At the time of publication of our work in 2005, we met them in part to discuss the question of whether the group agreed or disagreed with the idea that discussing the finding about *golden* with the public would derive the best societal benefit by presenting it as *demystifying* skin color and race (primarily associated with skin color). In short, the committee agreed. Now for the details.

Part of the inspiration for our discussion was the publicity around BiDil, the first medication tailored for a specific racial group—in this case African Americans with heart failure. BiDil had been approved because black patients frequently respond inadequately to beta-blockers and ACE inhibitors, both of which are used to treat heart disease (Kahn 2005). However, the drug may work better in African Americans not because of skin color but because, it is said, heart failure is more commonly due to hypertension in African Americans, while, in people of European ancestry, ischemic damage associated with atherosclerosis is more frequently responsible. It has thus been argued that the drug should be prescribed for heart failure secondary to hypertension, regardless of skin color. It is of course important to develop drugs that work most effectively in subpopulations. In Africans, or any subpopulation, genetic variations affecting specific disease susceptibility or drug responsiveness variations may be unique or common. It is important to note that African Americans are partly European in genetic background. The fraction of European ancestry in African Americans can be estimated to be between 9 and 27%, as suggested by the frequency of European alleles of *SLC24A5* or *MATP* in three African American populations in the Single Nucleotide Polymorphism database (dbSNP) database found in the HapMap website (http://www.hapmap.org/). Gene variations associated with drug responsiveness have no reason to be particularly associated with skin-color genes. Rather, such traits would be expected, most of the time, to be inherited independently from skin-color genes, making skin color, and therefore race, an unreliable substitute for knowing the real gene variations that correlate with drug responsiveness. Only after we know what specific sequences correlate with drug responsiveness can we begin to measure the strength of correlations between skin color and drug responsiveness. Unless a skin-color gene variant is directly responsible for drug responsiveness, skin color will never be a guarantee of such an association. These arguments apply to variations associated with disease susceptibility as well. A similar view has been stated by *New England Journal of Medicine* editor Robert Schwartz (Schwartz 2001).

Psychological and psychiatric issues are also associated with skin color. Lighter skin color has become so desirable among non-European peoples that self-esteem and social behavior are significantly impacted by skin color (Hall 1995, Butts 2003). This phenomenon is so strong that in essentially all non-European societies, and particularly among women, the use of skin-lightening creams has become commonplace, even when such use is known to be harmful to both the skin, and also to other organs (Ntambwe 2004). For example, more than half of women in Nigeria and Senegal have been reported to use harmful skin-lightening creams (Ofili et al. 2006, Ajose 2005, Mahé et al. 2003). Even more tragic is the fact that darker-skinned individuals *within* families are *not* given the same respect or opportunities as siblings who are born with lighter skin (Rangel 2007).

Perhaps the most important health implications of skin color have to do with race-associated health care disparities. These disparities are in turn related largely to income, education, job opportunity and access to health care, and are well-known to be associated with skin color (James et al. 2007). The relationship between skin color, race, and racism is discussed elsewhere in this book. The complex interplay between demographics, generations of racism, socioeconomics, and human behavior are separate issues that require additional study, long-term planning, and implementation if we are to ameliorate race-determined health care disparities. We should take pause to realize that the social consequences of negative attitudes toward skin color *alone* have had, and will continue to have, a huge and largely adverse global impact on human health.

Sociology of the SLC24A5 Story

Discussion of any gene change that helps to define the light skin color of Europeans can be expected to elicit controversy. Accordingly, before the *golden* story even appeared, several scientific colleagues warned me that discussing race would amount to walking a minefield—that I should stick with the science and avoid discussions of race. Many expressed the viewpoint that race is a social construct with no scientific merit (Tishkoff & Williams 2002, Bamshad et al. 2004, Sternberg et al. 2005, Gould & Lewontin 1979).

Ancestry is a much more specific and useful scientific term than race. As confirmed by continuing work on human variation (HapMap 2007), there exists far more variation between individuals within most populations than between traditional major population groups. However, there is no denying that variation is greatly diminished in small inbred populations, or that *SLC24A5* is a gene clearly associated with a key physical feature associated with the traditional concept of race. I felt it would not be helpful to deny a direct answer to the public's most frequently asked question—the implications of the finding with regard to race an area in which society must have help from scientists.

Given that discussion of race is inherently controversial, there is wisdom in avoiding hurtful controversy. However, as a member of an ethnic minority affected by racism, were I to deny discussion of the relevance of the new science to race I would be disingenuous—denying inherently social implications of this knowledge in order to stay comfortable in my ivory tower. Furthermore, I strongly sensed that this was an unusual opportunity for the public to gain a deeper understanding of the problems of thinking and acting in terms of "race." At best, a positive new perspective and even a redefinition of race could then be shared with others and possibly contribute to increasing understanding and diminishing racism. Initially, a convincing way of dealing with the issue of race and skin color was not evident. In my search for the best path to follow, I was fortunate to find the work of Stephen Oppenheimer, who is known for his scholarly exposition of the scientific basis of human origins in Africa (Oppenheimer 2004). Dr. Oppenheimer kindly corresponded with me by email as a complete stranger. He validated my discomfort about denial, saying that, in his opinion, self-censure is often worse than addressing difficult issues. He shared an approach that had worked well for him: Before engaging in a discussion about human differences, determine the purpose of the discussion. Enhancing understanding of diversity is acceptable; whereas racism, which devalues a group by being competitive, exclusive, or derogatory, is unacceptable (Oppenheimer 2004). Melanoma researcher John Pawelek shared with me words of his son, Unitarian Universalist minister, Joshua Pawelek (Pawelek 2006), "...the denial of race will not work, for it leads to a denial of racism—and you can't address a problem if you don't think it exists." These ideas supported my decision to stand behind the notion that informed discussion about the genetics of human skin color could clarify our thinking about race, and diminish racism among our youth. These discussions laid the foundation for using the *golden* story to demystify skin color and race during my travels to present our work.

Among the more challenging questions were, "Is *SLC24A5* the 'race' gene?" and "Is this the 'white' gene?" My answer was that *SLC24A5* is neither the "race" nor "white" gene because it is only one factor in both race and skin color. One of my scientific colleagues has pointed out that "Skin color does not equal race" (Schneider *et al.* 2002). *As traditionally used, race is a sociological concept with both genetic and non-genetic components.* The inclusion of these two different components contributes greatly to making the term so controversial. The obvious physical (and therefore most commonly genetic) features of race include skin color, facial features, hair and eye color; the sociological aspects of race, or tribe, include nationality, language culture, and social advantage/disadvantage—and are not genetically determined. It is also simplistic to call *SLC24A5* gene the "white" gene since the *SLC24A5* protein is present and active in the pigment cells of all races. The European variant is simply less active. Since the different type of mutation in *golden* zebrafish is most likely to result in lack of any function, and the fish still develop some pigment, it is most likely that *SLC24A5* acts by modifying the degree, rather than determining the presence or absence, of pigmentation.

Demystifying Skin Color and Race

In discussions with the Race, Ethnicity and Genetics Working Group of the National Human Genome Research Institute and with Institute Director Francis Collins on the day of release of the *Science* magazine story on 16 December 2005 (Lamason et al. 2005), I suggested, on the basis of the above arguments, the possibility that the most responsible thing for us to do, as scientists, would be to face the challenge of the relationship between race and skin color, rather than to avoid it. After discussion, we all agreed that we could use this type of molecular understanding to begin, as Dr. Collins put it, to "demystify" skin color for the lay public. This viewpoint began to be conveyed that very afternoon during interviews that appeared in the next 24 hours on the television programs, ABC's *World News Tonight* and *Good Morning America*, and in radio and newspaper coverage. Theodore Shaw, President of the NAACP Legal Defense and Educational Fund, said in the *Good Morning America* segment that the average person would not care about the finding, or fundamentally change his behavior even if he did learn about it (Shaw 2005). While this is likely true of adults, *our children, before they learn tribal attitudes, are more likely to be receptive to learning that skin color is determined by just a few letters out of the instruction book of life*. While this hypothesis remains to be proven, there is reason to believe that teaching our youth to recognize tribalism, and to distinguish between genetic and environmental impacts on human outcomes, will diminish the systematic injustices of racism perpetrated on the basis of skin color. In the face of a vast potential benefit of pursuing this course of action and no significant negative consequences, such a course of action, as long as it responsibly managed and polished along the way, would seem wise to follow.

Skin Pigmentation, Science, and Race

At this point in human and scientific history, it is clear that human pigmentation is determined by a finite number of genes that affect one or more aspects of how melanin pigments are formed, the morphology of the organelles containing that pigment, and the transport of those organelles to the bulk of our skin cells (*keratinocytes*), resulting in the color of our hair and eyes. The evidence suggests that the most extreme natural differences in pigmentation may be due to biological advantages of dark skin in habitats with extreme sun exposure, and the advantages of diminished pigmentation in habitats of limited sun exposure. Skin color may be one of just a small number of specific human traits that differ between traditional racial groups, and are associated with clear genetic mechanisms and genomic evidence of selection.

In contrast to the selective forces apparent for skin color, most—perhaps all—other physical and biochemical traits characteristic of each group exist solely on the basis of random genetic variation within large populations, followed by population bottlenecks—that is, the small number of individuals (the "founder population") who gave rise to each group outside of Africa. Within human tribes that have historically been limited to specific regions, distinguishing physical characteristics of each population are stronger, not because of selection but rather because of the limited range of genetic variation that is associated with small founder populations. Other traits for which there are both biological mechanisms for and genomic signatures of selection, such as the sickle cell trait based on resistance to malaria, are common within individual populations (Tishkoff & Williams 2002) but far from universal within those groups. No matter how many variations are eventually found to determine physical traits, such as pigmentation, we already know that there will be but a small minority of traits that exist by evolutionary chance within each major human population.

Education

There are at least three reasons as to why education serves as an antidote to racism. First, by educating our youth about the biological basis of skin color and the genetic components of race, and the environmental determination of values, cultures and habits of mind, it becomes obvious that social advantages associated with light skin are based on biologically false assumptions that are grounded in tribal emotions. Students can become aware of the complex but well-documented history of social prejudice-driven pseudo-science (Gould 1996) that underlies our heritage of discrimination, and learn to recognize the associated fallacies.

The second major reason is that education is now necessary for success in our new information-based society. Less educated populations are marginalized in modern society. No matter what importance we may place on more traditional forms of social or cultural education, functioning in modern society requires a minimum set of knowledge and habits of mind that are facilitated by education in problem-solving fields such as science, mathematics, and engineering, together with the acquisition of self-management and people management skills required for handling of today's volumes of data and personnel—these skills are required for smoothly functioning modern societies to be built and maintained. Societies, from the national level to local communities to the family, must work together to fulfill the compelling responsibility for educating the currently underprivileged. It is of equal importance that the leaders of the underprivileged stir up an unwavering commitment to education—an education that plays an important role in the acquisition of knowledge and skills that increases the likelihood of success. It is important to note a key responsibility that only the underprivileged can control, and that must be fulfilled in every location where educational solutions are developed. This responsibility is to inculcate positive attitudes toward education. The motivation for consistency in such an attitude is especially great, since academic success is the single best way to put to rest claims that lack of achievement is due to genetically determined intellectual ability.

The third reason education is so important is something that is obvious to any musician: the so-called "intelligence" that matters—the ability to solve problems—is created by opportunity, a commitment to solving those problems, learning functional habits of mind, and making a commitment to disciplined practicing of learned and creative ways to solve those problems. The biological basis of this view is our knowledge that learning creates new neural circuits (Gase & Schlaug 2003) and may even increase neuronal volume (Schneider *et al.*

2002). Lack of education deprives people of knowledge needed for the best jobs and impedes development of the ability to solve problems; therefore, depriving people of education is an effective manipulation to keep people down. Even with the highest possible motivation, a potential Einstein cannot make contributions without proper education and academic opportunity. Thus, anyone not blinded by competitive tribalism can see that a sweeping range of abilities is present in all populations, and that discussion about the genetics of intelligence has been a poor excuse for not taking responsibility for providing opportunity for subjugated peoples. It is heartening to see that there is significant motion today toward making education possible for everyone. Our very survival may depend upon our ability, across the globe, to choose modes of education that are dedicated to universal, not tribal, interests.

Conclusions

The term *race* derives from a natural human interest in categorizing the components of our world. From the beginning, the concept of race has been contaminated by scientifically incorrect assumptions that seem to have been motivated by our tribal tendencies to justify how "us" is better than "them." As used today, race refers to both physical features that are genetically determined and other features that are environmentally determined. Racism is now deeply and insidiously embedded within our societies. It seems reasonable to act on the possibility that resolving the societal problems of racism will benefit from a direct and open acknowledgement of our natural tendency toward tribal motivations and the irrational justifications that follow. Scientists can help discredit racism by teaching about the depth of fundamental biological similarities between all humans, breaking down the construct of race into components that are more precise and less burdened by tribalism, such as "ancestry," "genetics," and "environment." To further the equal treatment of humans regardless of ancestry, scientists can persistently remind society that genetics and race are invalid excuses for not attending to the social inequalities stemming from racism. Education can play a central role in work toward a society free of racism if it includes a firm grounding in the method and practice of the sciences and is freed of misanthropic expressions of tribalism. For this approach to succeed, we must work hard toward ensuring that education is accorded the importance it deserves, and that non-tribal, evidence-based education becomes the ideal sought by all. Furthermore, education can and should cultivate habits of mind that improve the capacity to exploit opportunity and achieve self-fulfillment, while promoting greater harmony in the societies of the future. There is reason for optimism: when in the last 1000 years might we have imagined a discussion of such a touchy topic as race, put together by scholars of globally diverse ancestry, dedicated to the common good?

Acknowledgments I thank my colleagues around the world for valuable discussions about skin color and race, my family and lab for tolerating this obsession for the past two years. Many colleagues generously shared their time, knowledge, and perspectives. I am particularly indebted to Stephen Oppenheimer, Robert Jones, Scott Thompson, Jonathan Weker, and Philip Wilson. Lindsay Rush and Shou Ling Leong made valuable suggestions across multiple drafts, as did Anthony Cheng, who also helped by researching tribalism and the evolution of scientific perceptions of human variation. I thank Ken Kidd for generously generating data, Victor Canfield and Jason Mest for producing Fig. 1.2, and Sarah Frey for editorial assistance.

References

Ajose, F. O. A. (2005). Consequences of skin bleaching in Nigerian men and women. *International Journal of Dermatology*, 44, 41–43.

Bamshad, M., Wooding, S., Salisbury, B. A., & Stephens. J. C. (2004). Deconstructing the relationship between genetics and race. *Nature Reviews Genetics*, 5, 598–609.

Barsh, G. S. (2003). What controls variation in human skin color? *PLoS Biology*, 1, 019–022.

Blumenbach, J. F. (1865) The anthropological treatises of Johann Friedrich Blumenbach and the inaugural dissertation of John Hunter, M.D. on the varieties of man, translated by T. Bendyshe. London: Longman, Green, Longman, Roberts, & Green.

Bolognia, J. L., & Orlow, S. J. (2003). Chapter 65: Melanocyte biology. In Bolognia, J. L., Jorizzo, J. L., & Rapini, R. P. (Eds.). *Dermatology* (p. 935). London (UK): Mosby.

Butts, H. (2003). Skin color perception and self-esteem. *The Journal of Negro Education*, 32, 122–128.

Cheng, K. C., & Canfield, V. A. (2006). The role of SLC24A5 in skin color. *Investigative Dermatology*, 16, 836–838.

Chi, A., Valencia, J. C., Hu, Z.-Z., Watabe, H., Yamaguchi, H., Mangini, N. J., Huang, H., Canfield, V. A., Cheng, K. C., Yang, F., Abe, R., Yamagishi, S., Shabanowitz, J., Hearing, V. J., Wu, C., Appella, E., & Hunt, D. F. (2006). Proteomic and bioinformatic characterization of the biogenesis and function of melanosomes. *Journal of Proteome Research*, 5, 3135–3144.

Collins, F. S. (2004). What we do and don't know about 'race', 'ethnicity', genetics, and health at the dawn of the genome era. *Nature Genetics*, 36, S13–S15.

Fukamachi, S., Shimada, A., & Shima, A. (2001). Mutations in the gene encoding B, a novel transporter protein, reduce melanin content in medaka. *Nature Genetics*, 28, 381–385.

Gase, C., & Schlaug, G. (2003). Brain structures differ between musicians and non-musicians. *The Journal of Neuroscience*, 23, 9240–9245.

Gould, S. J. (1996). *The mismeasure of man*. New York: Norton.

Gould, S. J., & Lewontin, R. C. (1979). The spandrels of San Marco and the Panglossian paradigm: A critique of the adaptationist programme. *Proceedings of the Royal Society of London. Series B, Biological Sciences*, 205 (No. 1161, *The Evolution of Adaptation by Natural Selection*), 581–598.

Hall, R. (1995). The bleaching syndrome: African Americans' response to culture domination vis-à-vis skin color. *Journal of Black Studies*, 26, 172–184.

[HapMap] (2007). The International HapMap Project, a database of human genetic variation. Available at http://www.hapmap.org/.

Jablonski, N. G. (2004). The evolution of human skin and skin color. *Annual Review of Anthropology*, 33, 585–623.

———. (2006). *Skin: A natural history*. Berkeley, CA: University of California Press.

James, C., Thomas, M., Lillie-Blanton, M., & Garfield, R. (2007). Key facts: Race, ethnicity and medical care, 2007 update. Menlo Park, CA: J. Kaiser Family Foundation. Available at http://www.kff.org/minorityhealth/6069.cfm.

Kahn, J. (2005). Misreading race and genomics after BiDil. *Nature Genetics*, 37, 655–656.

Lamason, R. L., Mohideen, M.-A. P. K., Mest, J. R., Wong, A. C., Norton, H. L., Aros, M. C., Jurynec, M. J., Mao, X., Humphreville, V. R., Humbert, J. E., Sinha, S., Moore, J. L., Jagadeeswaran, P., Zhao, W., Ning, G., Makalowska, I., McKeigue, P. M., O'Donnell, D., Kittles, R., Parra, E. J., Mangini, N. J., Grunwald, D. J., Shriver, M. D., Canfield, V. A., & Cheng, K. C. (2005). SLC24A5, a putative cation exchanger, affects pigmentation in zebrafish and humans. *Science*, Dec. 16, 310, (5755)1782–1786.

Lieschke, G. J., & Currie, P. D. (2007). Animal models of human disease: Zebrafish swim into view. *Nature Reviews Genetics*, 8, 353–367.

Linné, C. (1767). Systema naturae (13th Ed.) Vindobonae [Vienna]: Ioannis Thomae.

Lorenz, K. (1966). On aggression. M. K. Wilson (Trans.). New York: Harcourt, Brace & World.

Mahé, A., Ly, F., Aymard, G., & Dangou, J. M. (2003). Skin diseases associated with the cosmetic use of bleaching products in women from Dakar, Senegal. *British Journal of Dermatology*, 148, 493–500.

Marks, J. (1995). *Human biodiversity: Genes, race, and History*. New York: Walter de Gruyter.

Moore, J. L., Rush, L. M., Breneman, C., Mohideen, M.-A. P., & Cheng, K. C. (2006). Zebrafish genomic instability mutants and cancer susceptibility. *Genetics*, 174, 585–600.

Mountain, J. L., & Risch, N. (2004). Assessing genetic contributions to phenotypic differences among "racial" and "ethnic" groups. *Nature Genetics*, 36, S48–S53.

Newton, J. M., Cohen-Barak, O., Hagiwara, N., Gardner, J. M., Davisson, M. T., King, R. A., & Brilliant, M. H. (2001). Mutations in the human orthologue of the mouse *underwhite* gene (*uw*) underlie a new form of oculocutaneous albinism, OCA4. *American Journal of Human Genetics*, 69, 981–988.

Norton, H. L., Kittles, R. A., Parra, E., McKeigue, P., Mao, X., Cheng, K. C., Canfield, V. A., Bradley, D. G., McEvoy, B., Shriver, M. D. (2007). Genetic evidence for the convergent evolution of light skin in Europeans and East Asians. *Molecular Biology and Evolution*, 24, 710–722.

Ntambwe, M. (2004). Mirror mirror on the wall, who is the FAIREST of them all? *Science in Africa*, www.scienceinafrica.co.za/2004/march/skinlightening.htm.

Ofili, A. N., Eze, E. U., Onunu, A. N. (2006). Prevalence of use of skin lightening agents amongst University of Benin undergraduates in Benin City, Nigeria, *Nigerian Medical Practitioner*, 49, 24–27.

Oppenheimer, S. (2004). *Out of eden*. London (UK): Constable & Robinson.

Pawelek, J. M. (2006). *Racism and spiritual death in the United States of America,* Sermon, 15 January 2006, the Unitarian Universalist Society: East, Manchester, CT. Available at http://www.uuse.org/html/past_services/2006/01/15_racism_spiritual_death.htm.

Race, Ethnicity, and Genetics Working Group. (2005). The use of racial, ethnic, and ancestral categories in human genetics research. *The American Journal of Human Genetics*, 77, 519–532.

Rangel, M. A. (2007). Is parental love colorblind? Allocation of resources within mixed families. *Harris School Working Paper Series*, 07.14.

Sankar, P., & Cho, M. K. (2002). Toward a new vocabulary of human genetic variation. *Science*, 298, 1337–1338.

Schneider, P., Scherg, M., Dosch, H. G., Spect, H. J., Gutschalk, A., & Rupp, A. (2002). Morphology of Heschl's gyrus reflects enhanced activation in the auditory cortex of musicians. *Nature Neuroscience*, 5, 688–694.

Schwartz, R. S. (2001). Editorial: Racial profiling in medical research. *New England Journal of Medicine*, 344, 1392–1393.

[SEER] Surveillance Epidemiology and End Results. National Cancer Institute website, providing information on cancer. Available at http://seer.cancer.gov/csr/1975_2004 sections.html.

Shaw, T. (2005). Theodore Shaw interview, on ABC Television program, *Good Morning America*, 17 December 2005.

Soejima, M., & Koda, Y. (2007). Population differences of two coding SNPs in pigmentation-related genes *SLC24A5* and *SLC45A2*. *International Journal of Legal Medicine*, 121, 36–39.

Sternberg, R. J., Grigorenko, E. L., & Kidd, K. K. (2005). Intelligence, race, and genetics. *American Psychologist*, 60, 46–59.

Stokowski, R. P., Krishna Pant, P. V., Dadd, T., Fereday, A., Hinds, D. A., Jarman, C., Filsell, W., Ginger, R.S., Green, M. R., van der Ouderaa, F. J., & Cox, D. R. (2007). A genomewide association study of skin pigmentation in a South Asian population. *American Journal of Human Genetics*, 81, 1119–1132.

Streisinger, G. (1984). Attainment of miminal biological variability and measurements of genotoxicity: Production of homozygous diploid zebrafish. *National Cancer Institute Monograph*, 65, 53–58.

Sturm, R. A. (2006). A golden age for human pigmentation genetics. *Trends in Genetics*, 22, 464–468.

Sulem, P., Gudbjartsson, D. F., Stacey, S. N., Helgason, A., Rafnar, T., Magnusson, K. P., Manolescu, A., Karason, A., Palsson, A., Thorleifsson, G., Jakobsdottir, M., Steinberg, S., Pálsson, S., Jonasson, F., Sigurgeirsson, B., Thorisdottir, K., Ragnarsson, R., Benediktsdottir, K. R., Aben, K. K., Kiemeney, L. A., Olafsson, J. H., Gulcher, J., Kong, A., Thorsteinsdottir, U., & Stefansson, K. (2007). Genetic determinants of hair, eye, and skin pigmentation in Europeans. *Nature Genetics*, 39, 1443–1452 (2007).

Terando, A. M., Faries, M. B., Morton, D. L. (2007). Vaccine therapy for melanoma: Current status and future directions. *Vaccine*, 25S, B4–B16.

Tishkoff, S. A., & Williams, S. M. (2002). Genetic analysis of African populations: Human evolution and complex disease. *Nature Review Genetics*, 3, 611–621.

Yates J. R., & Moore, A. T. (2000). Genetic susceptibility to age related macular degeneration. *Journal of Medical Genetics*, 37, 83–87.

Chapter 2
Manifestations of Racism in the 21st Century

Ronald E. Hall

Abstract For people of color (African-, Asian-, Latino-, and Native-American descent) in Western countries, the important attributes of the social system are ideals, which they internalize. According to James Baldwin, the root of American difficulty is directly related to skin color ideals. All matters considered necessitate the construction of the Bleaching Syndrome to acknowledge and comprehensively organize what is otherwise obvious, i.e., issues involving skin color. Much of what the Bleaching Syndrome involves is pathological to people of color and could not be imposed because it is contrary to their physical, emotional, and psychological well-being. In the aftermath, people of color and the social scientists among them, including Whites, must aspire to more conducive, somatic norms to escape the pathological influences of the Bleaching Syndrome or risk manifestation of racism in the 21st century and beyond.

Introduction

For people of color (eg., African-, Asian-, Latino-, and Native-American descent) in Western countries, the most important attributes of their social system are its ideals, which they internalize. Those ideals that reach the level of institutionalization become in effect standards of personal consequence. Such standards do not require, although they often have, the support of law; standards help persons organize their universes by determining what is appropriate and what is not. In conjunction, internalized ideals and societal institutions are the principal vehicles in the manifestation of racism in the 21st century. Racism caused by internalized ideals and societal institutions can be essentially one and the same in the absence of an equal distribution of power, which people of color do not have.

The ideals of a society are also important in holding it together. That includes the implied or expressed, the formal or informal agreements instilled

R.E. Hall
School of Social Work, Michigan State University, East Lansing, MI, USA
e-mail: hallr@msu.edu

R.E. Hall (ed.), *Racism in the 21st Century*, DOI: 10.1007/978-0-387-79097-8_2,
© Springer Science+Business Media, LLC 2008

in a nation's citizenry. The ideals internalized by people of color in Western countries eventually become synonymous with expectations. When the expectations of the citizen and the larger society are conducive, normal development will ensue. Conflict occurs for people of color who must assimilate into alien societies. The normal process of development is interrupted in such a way as to cause psychological pain, a product of their denigration through having or experiencing conflicting ideals. The pain is associated with an attempt on the part of people of color to adjust to what is, in fact, an inconducive or oppressive environment for them. The immediate solution would be to alter the environment, which their lack of power does not permit them to do.

Western ideals can be internalized by people of color either as a matter of choice through achieving their aspirations or by coercion in a White-dominated environment. The worth of any set of ideals is in the stability and order they bring to the psyche. Characteristic of most social phenomena, ideals are not static but are fluid entities constantly responding to social pressures during the assimilation process. The inability of people of color, both at home and abroad, to recognize this process and interrupt it at the appropriate point is an obstacle to their escape from the effects of racism, which then denigrates their native identity.

According to Linda Acupanda McGloin (1992), under racist circumstances the issue of identity is relevant to both men and women of color. But unlike oppressed Whites in such circumstances, the minority psyche has experienced decades of historical assaults by more than one colonial power. Each experience that may be manifested today originated from the brutalities of societal oppression and various forms of hierarchical subjugation that is long past but no less apparent. No doubt problems in the Americas existed prior to Western colonization. However, in the aftermath of colonial social, economic, and political control identity and other psychic phenomena for people of color have been complicated to a pathological extent. Thus, given the importance of social and historical events, the following questions are posed where racism in the 21st century and people of color are concerned: Can assimilation contribute to the repair of a denigrated self? Will awareness of the newest forms of racism enable the dissipation of self-denigrating fantasies? Under healthy circumstances, assimilation has played a key role in the liberation and psychological well-being of a people. For people of color, health will be contingent upon their ability to obtain organized glimpses into the psychological damage that has been incurred over time from racism and post-colonial oppression. In the wake of oppression are images that have been fashioned from Western dominant-group fantasies.

Upon their arrival in the Philippines, Spanish colonials had visualized a Filipina prototype that would best serve the exploitation and subjugation of Filipino people. They required that the Filipina be demure, modest, patient, devoutly religious, cultured, submissive, and virginal. Her status would be valued commensurate with the quantity of Western blood that ran through her veins. Spanish ancestry was important because it would vary the color of her skin accordingly, making her increasingly lighter as a result of a lineage of sexual contact with the dominant colonial male. The major portion of this dynamic is repressed in the Filipina psyche, making her for the most part like all people of color who are unaware of its significance, ultimately becoming an accessory to her own victimization.

Spanish colonial fantasies of the Filipina ideal are still upheld today, enabling impediments to Filipina liberation and psychological health. Colonial fantasies served the purpose of Spanish males whose Western counterparts reinforced the continuation of domination in more sophisticated ways. Perhaps some very minor progress might be evident in that the indigenous people of the Philippines who were once embarrassed being called "indios" (an ethic reference assigned to them by colonial Spaniards) now insist upon being known as "Filipino," while the descendants of colonizers now prefer to call themselves "Spanish" (McGloin 1992).

The implication of post-colonial assimilation has been captured for all people of color theoretically by W.E.B. DuBois. Early on, DuBois wrote of the "Double Consciousness" aspect of the African-American experience—a no less colonized Western minority (Myrdal 1944). DuBois supported this assumption by making reference to the fact that dark-skinned African-Americans who socialized in a post-colonial culture maintained one set of behaviors that were appropriate within the group and another set composed of assimilation norms that were preferred by the dominant group mainstream, into which they were required to assimilate. The purpose of assimilating was to realize their aspirations and ultimately the "American Dream." In some cases light-skinned African-Americans "passing" for white—where an African-American would assume the identity of a white American in order to take advantage of the privileges and opportunities brought about by successful assimilation—was used as a strategy to circumvent racism and other forms of societal oppression. These light-skinned Black Americans were frequently the descendants of African slaves and slave masters. The act of passing in brief does not necessarily represent a desire on the part of such African-Americans to denigrate themselves, but is rather a necessity of survival. It allows for a degree of function to the extent that victims assume another identity, but the longevity of that identity is ultimately pathological because it requires the host to accept and indeed value the denigration of self. It reinforces psychological pain, in that it is a game, which requires those who play to be constantly on guard. It may also require separation from family to affect the colonial role, which to members of a family-oriented culture is the most painful act of all. As pathology the act is potent and destructive to the psyche because family is where the sense of identity originates. L. Chestang (1995) referred to this as the "nurturing environment." The "nurturing environment" may be compared to Erik Erikson's (1968) "significant others," those who are closest and most involved in the determination of an individual's sense of who they are. The individual's experiences and sense of identity growing out of his or her relationship with "significant others" play an important part in socialization and the ability of the individual to live a sane, productive life, and most importantly to escape the ill-effects of racism for a healthy life experience.

Regarding racism in the 21st century, George Mead's (1934) concept of the "generalized other" may also be used to understand people of color who, by assimilation, internalize conflicting Western ideals. Mead (1934) defined the "generalized other" as taking on the attitude of the dominant (Western) society in regard to the self. In this way one learns to become an object to the self, to have an identity, to know the self through role- taking and from the reflection of others. In acting out the roles of Western others, people of color take others' roles into their own nature and begin to alienate themselves from all that is in their best interest. From the many roles assumed, there gradually arises a generalized other. This attitude of the generalized other or alien Western self is intended to unify the self, as people of color incorporate society's responses and react accordingly.

Mead spoke only of one generalized other. However, people of color in Western cultures who assume the images of Western fantasy have a strong possibility of seeing themselves stigmatized, as in fact they often are. The more they incorporate a negative image of themselves into their identity, the more they will be stigmatized in their perception of who they are. Yet it is apparent that people of color do attain a good sense of self despite the challenges. That sense of self can be assumed as an alternative generalized other, to which Dolores Norton refers in her notion of the "Dual Perspective," where people of color unlike whites experience the social environment as a "twoness" (sustaining and nurturing) (Norton 1978).

The alternative generalized other, as Norton would contend, is the attitude of the family and immediate community environment, the "nurturing environment" of Chestang, the "significant others" of Erikson. If people of color receive love and care from their families as children, this can instill a positive sense of self and effectively combat racism. Since many are reasonably isolated from the dominant community physically and socially—at least early on—the attitude of the more immediate generalized other, the family, can develop, restore, or help them maintain self-esteem. People of color can use that esteem as a buffer against the effects of the attitude of the generalized other from the larger Western society as they experience the wider community. This cannot be accomplished totally though, for even as youth people of color are very much aware of the biased, race-based attitude of the Western mainstream. Especially in today's age of advanced media technology and urban living, the attempt is made more difficult. If the mechanisms of socialization in the nurturing environment or the more immediate generalized other are positive, this may help children of color balance the racist images that may come from the environment of post-colonial populations, else the consequences may impair the individual for a lifetime.

Regarding people of color in the 21st century, Abraham Maslow (1971) perceived individuals as having a wide range of potential for personal development. He thought it natural and universal for human beings to want to develop to their fullest capacity. For people of color, the problem starts in how they define their fullest capacity. By nature human beings are basically fit. Without prompting, they will strive to develop themselves for the benefit of society. Maslow referred to this as "self-actualization" (1971) and is the highest possible stage of human development. In fact those who reach such a stage are indeed rare. Once a stage is attained, by satisfying the needs of the prior stage, the individual is prepared to move on to the next level. In the West, unfortunately, most persons are in a state of constant struggle to realize aspirations for a particular stage of the Western hierarchy: At the base of the hierarchy are physiological needs such as food and water. At the next level are safety needs such as security, stability, and freedom from fear. At the level following is the satisfaction of belongingness and love needs provided by friends, family, and significant others. Self-esteem needs include self-respect, attention, and appreciation. The final stage, self-actualization, is reached by the highest developed individual as pertains to morality, etc. All but the very exceptional members of humanity tend to stagnate for different reasons just at or below the third stage of development. People of color may stagnate because of complications extended from racism and colonization. Members of the Western mainstream stagnate because of the spoils extended from racism and colonization. While Maslow does admit to the relevancy of age for progression through the various stages, the dynamics associated with Western assimilation are also a strong factor. As per the aforementioned theoretical constructs, that assimilation has become exceedingly complicated by the impact of post-colonial norms, in particular for people of color who reside in Western countries today.

The ethnic landscape of Western civilization today comprises one of the most diverse populations of humankind ever (Kitano 1985). The descendants of Europeans, Africans, Asians, and others have made significant contributions to its wealth. However, all have not shared equally in its prosperity. Despite such racial and ethnic diversity, being referred to as a person of color remains an obstacle to full or structural assimilation into Western society, because being a person of color has strong implications for stress levels. It may also limit opportunities for any members within the group and aspirations for the quality of life so aptly desired (Burke, Divinagracia, & Mamo 1998). Is it any wonder that African- and Euro-Americans are obviously similar in genetic structure? Both frequent a common existential space and both rely upon nourishment from that space to evolve. However, their evolution within that space may differ significantly. For African-Americans, skin color is critical. For Euro-Americans, skin color though relevant is almost completely inconsequential as a disadvantage (Frost 1989). In human genes, as in social experiences, people may have much in common yet may have evolved from distinct social and genetic heritages.

Thus, analysis of commonality in some respects may co-exist with contrasts in others. In regard to people of color, any observer would be in error to categorize by race, independent of skin color, in this 21st century millennium. The most significant consequence of this error has been a tendency to underestimate the impact of skin color, because there is no analogous impact on Euro-Americans, i.e.: Eurocentrism. As a result, understanding African-Americans in the context of theories designed by and for Euro-Americans is less effective because it misses an essential component of the African-American assimilation experience. In the hyper-utilization of white constructs, people of color are poorly portrayed, and such poor portrayal is an outgrowth of Euro-centrism and the accompanying trivialization of skin color. In the context of racism, it ultimately sustains pathologies among dark-skinned populations who become social and societal failures in their subjection to racist oppression (Arroyo 1996).

There are a few methods to circumvent Eurocentrism and to correct this methodological flaw. The first is the utilization of the democratic process: to incorporate a variety of demographic tools and settle upon the most popular tool. This approach would prove fitting in a democratic sovereignty, but not necessarily as an effective one. Demographic tools that rely on popularity run the risk of collapsing into an intellectual solipsism that is unproductive and no less hegemonic than the Eurocentrism of race. The second alternative suggests a more encompassing and universal approach, which must accommodate a meaningful effort and knowledgeable sensitivity to a diverse population that now comprises the world. Although African- and Euro-Americans have a distinct evolutionary heritage, they also have a common genetic variation in skin color. The boundary of their color exceeds racial demarcation, which has no biological significance. Consequently, the use of skin color by social scientists will prove less biased in a time when Western racial homogeneity will have all but completely diminished (Lee 1991).

Skin Color: African-Americans

In studying the theoretical dynamics of skin color among African-Americans, relative to racism in the 21st century, a dramatic demonstration may be seen by examining stereotypes seen in film and litigation. In film, the "tragic mulatto" stereotype represented light-skinned African-Americans who were born into a world that defined them as Black if they had any known African heritage. Donald Bogle (1989), in a well-researched effort, offers a detailed chronology beginning with a 1912 film called *The Debt*: set in the old South, a White man's wife and his Black octoroon mistress bear him children simultaneously. After growing up together, his white son and light-skinned, African-American daughter become romantically involved and decide to get married. Eventually, it is revealed to them at a crucial moment that they are, in fact, brother and sister. Their lives are thus ruined, not only because they are kin but also because the young woman has Black blood. She has white skin and blue eyes, which would otherwise define her as white, but here they are irrelevant. Her societal identification must be that of an African-American.

In reality, many light-skinned African-Americans left the South for the North, where they could pass as white. *Pinky*, a film released in 1949 (Bogle 1989, Kazan 1949), featured a light-skinned nurse who returns to the South after having passed as white in the North. Pinky is depressed by the Black Southern life of daily threats and insults, and plans to return North to her white fiancé and to her life as a white woman in a free society. However, her African-American grandmother convinces her to stay with her people. Pinky confides to her white fiancé, "Tom, you can change your name . . . . I'm a Negro. I can't deny it." And so, as was true of all African-Americans, Pinky's life meets tragedy by the racist standards of color.

True to life, actress Dorothy Dandridge exemplified the ultimate metaphor of the "tragic mulatto" in the failings of her film career (Bogle 1989). The African-American attributes that enabled her professionally may have forced her to live out a screen image that eventually destroyed her. *Carmen Jones* was the celebrated film that established her as the definitive Tragic Mulatto. In the film, her love interest was a "good-colored boy," portrayed by Harry Belafonte. Carmen convinces him to desert the army and run away with her, after which they end up in a Chicago hotel. Then she leaves him for a prizefighter, and is later strangled for her unfaithfulness. Dandridge appeared to experience the racism of skin color not only through her film characters but also in her real life, as a light-skinned, African-American woman. She eventually succumbed to alcoholism, drugs, and destructive love affairs. Finally in 1965, at the age of forty-one, Dorothy Dandridge was found dead following an overdose of anti-depression pills. The catastrophe in Dandridge's life was that, as a light-skinned African-American, color more than race denied her the possibility of fulfillment, either as completely African- or completely Euro-American. That is because the most significant but seldom acknowledged attribute for people of color is their skin color. Accounts of such oppression are not limited to film, and are apparent in recent litigation.

Perhaps the first case brought to trial by African-Americans on the basis of skin color was that of Tracy Walker versus the Internal Revenue Service (IRS). It was tried in the Atlanta Federal District Court in 1989. The plaintiff was a permanent clerk typist, a light-skinned African-American, in the IRS's Atlanta office. Her supervisor—employee of the defendant—was Ruby Lewis, a dark-skinned African-American. Employees of the office in which the plaintiff and the defendant worked were predominantly African-American. In fact, following her termination, the plaintiff was replaced by another African-American. According to the record, the working relationship between the plaintiff and the defendant was strained from the very beginning, since approximately November of 1985. The plaintiff contends that the defendant singled her out for close scrutiny and reprimanded her because of her light skin for many things that were false or unsubstantial. In the summation expert testimony by Dr. Ronald E. Hall was heard, and the court determined the plaintiff's case to have merit. At the conclusion of the trial, though, the federal court ruled in favor of the IRS. The charges were deemed poorly documented, and Walker's claims of skin color harassment could not be supported by witness testimony. It was allowed, however, that skin color prejudice could exist between Blacks (similar to racism among whites), although perhaps the case before the judge was not the best test of the issue. At present, the plaintiff is considering higher court (*Walker v. IRS* 1989).

Skin Color: Hispanic Americans

Travel brochures for the island of Puerto Rico aptly profess the rich variation in skin color and other physical attributes of its people. Vacationing tourists are impressed by the apparent lack of color prejudice that the residents proudly proclaim. Unmentioned, however, is the blatant discrimination against dark-skinned Puerto Ricans. Its existence is invisible to the casual observer, but substantiated as fact by documented litigation similar to that of African-Americans Lewis and Walker. This case is important, in that it accounts for charges of skin color discrimination, both across and within group and gender lines. The Latino-American case of Felix versus Manquez in fact preceded that of the African-American case of *Walker v. the IRS*.

The U.S. District Court of the District of Columbia litigated the case of the dark-skinned Felix versus the lighter-skinned Manquez in 1981. Both the plaintiff and the defendant were Latino-American employees of the Office of the Commonwealth of Puerto Rico in Washington, D.C. (OCPRW). The plaintiff alleges that the defendant did not promote her on the basis of skin color discrimination. At trial, the plaintiff introduced the personnel cards of twenty-eight of her former fellow employees. She testified that, among them, only two were as dark, or darker, in color than her. All of the other employees in the office, according to the plaintiff, were light-skinned. In summation, the court determined that the plaintiff was not promoted in grade for legitimate business reasons, having nothing whatever to do with her skin color (*Felix v. Manquez* 1980).

In a more recent case brought by Latino-Americans, the U.S. District Court of the District of Puerto Rico litigated Falero versus Stryker Corporation in 1998. Falero, the plaintiff, is a dark-skinned male while Rigoberto, the corporation defendant, is a light-skinned male. The plaintiff claims he was terminated from his job because of his dark skin. Rigoberto contends that Falero did not establish that he was replaced by someone who was not within the protected class. He further stated that the plaintiff's job had not been filled by anyone, but admits one of his areas of work was assigned to another employee. Thus, direct evidence of skin color discrimination was lacking.

Although part of the case rationale had been accepted, the court decided that no reasonable judge of the facts could conclude from the evidence in the record, when viewed in the light most favorable to plaintiff, that the defendant discriminated against the plaintiff on the basis of his skin color. Therefore, the court granted the defendant's motion for summary judgment. Additionally, after dismissing the plaintiff's foundational federal claims, the court reassessed its jurisdiction over the supplemental state claims. Thus, in the exercise of its discretion, and after balancing the competing factors, the court declined to exercise jurisdiction over the plaintiff's supplemental claims. The plaintiff's state law claims were then dismissed without prejudice (*Falero v. Stryker Corporation* 1998). However, the inability of African- and Latino-Americans to prevail in a court of law should not imply that the issue of racist skin color discrimination is without merit. Regardless of the outcome, the mere filing of litigation makes the importance of skin color among African- and Latino-Americans obvious.

Skin Color: Asian-Americans

The issue of skin color among Asian-Americans conforms to White racism and has a long, established history (Banerjee 1985). It determines their manifestation of racism in the 21st century. When Japanese migrate to the U.S., they bring with them their notions about light skin, which include the denigration of dark-skinned persons (Washington 1990). When they begin the assimilation process, the belief that light skin is superior and dark skin is inferior negatively affects their ability to interact socially with darker-skinned Americans (1990). It may even have contributed to the recent tensions between African and Korean American communities in Los Angeles, and various other parts of the nation (Kim 1990). It is a reflection of Western assimilation whereby Asians from India, Pakistan, Bangladesh, and Sri Lanka who constantly seek, once settled in the U.S., ways to prove themselves "White" (Mazumdar 1989).

The most dramatic illustration of skin color issues among Asian-Americans pertains to marital patterns. Free and uninhibited assimilation would view the selection of marriage partners as an indicator that color would not be a barrier (Aguirre, Saenz, & Hwang 1995). An alternate approach would infer that marrying outside of one's race was a function of inequality in dominant, stratified societies. For Asian-Americans who participate in out-marriage, that marriage becomes a means to exchange status characteristics (Shinagawa & Pang 1988). The result is "Eurogamy," a racist social phenomenon defined by a predisposition to the selection of spouses on the basis of skin color (Hall 1997). On that basis, dark-skinned persons are presumed to be ineligible for ideal marriage, even if they are of equal or higher socioeconomic status. Eurogamy among Asian-Americans is therefore influenced by skin color discrimination. While some do marry people of color, Asian-American men who marry "out," or Eurogamously, are apparently less likely to do so than Asian women (Rhee 1988).

Eurogamy is a universally obvious but previously undocumented aspect of the Asian-American social environment. It is used as an assimilation strategy under the social rules of Western domination and racism. It is the preferred marital pattern of a darker-skinned group (by fact or metaphor, Asian-Americans) into a lighter-skinned group (by fact or metaphor, Euro-Americans). In acquiring Euro-American genes via marriage, the stigma of Asian skin color is lessened in their children. The phenomenon is most frequent among Asian-Americans who settle in large urban centers.

In New York City, Asians who practice Eurogamy tend to be second generation Americans or later, female, older, better educated, of higher occupational status, and have higher incomes (Sung 1990). These urbanized citizens are associated less with the customarily closed Asian community. Whether or not Eurogamy adversely affects their children has not been substantiated, but their children do appear to have problems (1990).

Perhaps the most spectacular manifestation of racism in the 21st century among Asian-Americans is referred to as "brown racism." According to Robert Washington (1990), brown racism is perpetrated by Chinese, Filipino, and Southeast-Asian-Americans against persons of African descent. It is a variation of discrimination that probably occurred as a result of Western colonization. The behaviors are obvious but seldom addressed given the Eurocentrism of racism as a purely black/white racial issue.

Skin Color: Native Americans

Dark-skinned Native-Americans are well aware of their African roots and are not ashamed to make reference thereto (Hooks 1992):

> Speaking primarily to the folks who have always denied the many truths of U.S. history that tell of imperialist expansion, cultural genocide, and racism, Katz makes it seem that it is important to convince his audience that 'black Indians' never even existed.

William Katz (1986), the author of *Black Indians*, is criticized by hooks for not acknowledging the Eurocentrism that has made the African-mixed Native-American "invisible." Furthermore, the invisibility of such persons has been made easier by the social discourse of "full-blooded" Native-Americans and their lighter-skinned Euro-mixed counterparts particularly in urban locations. Arguably, that discourse contributes to racist discrimination against dark-skinned Native-Americans of whatever parentage by those who are light-skinned, "full-blooded" or otherwise. Thus, "full-blooded" Native-Americans and Native-Americans of mixed Euro-American parentage, by virtue of being light-skinned, have allowed for the alienation of dark-skinned Native-Americans on the basis of the "one-drop" theory (Russell, Wilson, & Hall 1992). In fact, according to V. Dominguez (1997) it may be that a substantial number of African-Americans have at least 25% Euro-American ancestry and perhaps 80% Native-American ancestry. Were those same persons citizens of some South American countries, they would undoubtedly be considered "mestizo," or of mixed-blood.

For various reasons irrespective of urbanization and "blood quantum," scholars contend that the Native-American population appears to be experiencing significant growth (Snipp 1989). Unfortunately, their research has ignored the implications of skin color and its effect upon the Native-American perception of dark skin. Some, such as J. Nagel (1997), have acknowledged it in their research, but this acknowledgment has been all too subtle. Perhaps similar to the Latino-American community, there is a feeling in the Native community that the acknowledgement of intragroup discrimination would invite group disjuncture at a time when unity is imperative (Jarvenpa 1985). However, scholars, in their hesitation, may actually contribute to group disjuncture. In Avery F. Gordon's (1997) *Haunting and the Sociological Imagination*, discrimination can be banished from the literature but not wholly from reality of the people. Such banishment contributes to tension in the absence of dialogue, making it even more offensive and less likely the subject of healthy intellectual debate. Those who prefer to define Native-American identity on the basis of skin color then worsen that disjointedness. Conversely, in opting for a purely color-based prerequisite, scholars realize that authentic Native-American identity may be questioned by other Native-Americans, tribes, and governments (Wilson 1992). Thus, on the basis of skin color, the perception of a Native-American population growth is arguably a manifestation of personal beliefs.

As for identity, the prevalence of racial constructs validate blood quantum by skin color, which impairs the ability of African-mixed Native-Americans to be accepted as authentic and to circumvent racism. For example, claiming their Native-American identity may be problematic for reasons including: (a) African-mixed Native-Americans may be seen as wanting to escape the social stigma associated with being "Black;" and (b) discrimination on the basis of their dark skin may disqualify them because in appearance, unlike their lighter-skinned, Euro-mixed counterparts, they are more physically similar to African-Americans, for example the Lumbee, Pequot, Seminole, and others.

Under the circumstances it is plausible to suggest that Native-Americans, especially those who have been urbanized, have been encouraged to discriminate against their own through African blood quantum (dark skin). In the outcome, dark-skinned Native-Americans, regardless of their parentage, have been denied legitimate acceptance into the fold of group nationhood. That denial is racist in essence because the Native-American psyche, like others among oppressed populations of color, has been shaped, transformed, and constructed in such a way as to create a hierarchy that validates dominant race category and diminishes the significance of color. The acceptance of light-skinned Native-Americans into the fold as archetypical has resulted in their assimilation through "white" ways, "white" culture, and on occasion "white" racism, as in the case of Chris Simon.

Chris Simon, a professional hockey player and member of the Ojibwa tribe, was fined $36,585 and suspended three games for apparently directing racial slurs at a "Black" player named Mike Grier (National Hockey League 1997). In

arguably the most "white" and homogeneous of major sports, the behavior of modern-day Native-Americans is analogous to that of their slave-owning ancestors. What is more, Native-Americans have criticized African-Americans for playing on sports teams that degrade them by the use of such mascots as the NFL's Washington "Red Skins" and the major league baseball team the Cleveland "Indians." Yet no African-American has ever degraded Native-Americans in their use of mascots for professional sports teams, as their ownership is all but nonexistent. Criticism by Native-Americans of team ownership is all too tacit. This oversight on their part is arguably a manifestation of racism in the 21st century indicated by all people of color (1997).

Beauty and Women of Color

Perhaps the most insidious manifestation of racism in the 21st century is the impact upon women of color, who under colonial influence have internalized beauty ideals that are alien to their dark skin. In Pakistan, women of color aspire to light skin by bleaching themselves. One such woman is a well-educated, 23-year-old named Nasim Jamil (IRIN 2004). While she is young and attractive she is not at all satisfied with the way she looks. "I am not fair enough," she commented to a local news organization. She further maintains that, "white is best. When you ask Pakistani ladies what their idea of an ideal woman is, they will tell you that she should have fair skin." This is a fact, according to Fozia Yasmin, who works for the Pakistani nongovernmental organization who reported to the IRIN news organization. At least 50% of women Yasmin has encountered have sought her business for concerns about their skin color. Her company has three practitioners in its employ, who offer workshops at colleges for building self-esteem in the lives of women who dislike their skin color. "You see advertisements for skin creams everywhere you go in this country," which is not at all uncommon. As women who reside in an Islamic nation they are expected to look their best without exception while simultaneously required to be subservient to men (2004).

"Fair skin is considered an asset in India," says Rachna Gupta, a 38-year-old, part-time interior designer (Leistikow 2003). Considering this, about once a month she visits her local beauty salon in south Delhi for an application of Jolen Creme Bleach. The package states, "lightens excess dark hair," but Rachna has it applied to her face to effect lighter skin. "It's not good for the skin," she insists, "but I still get it done because I am on the darker side and it makes me feel nice. Aesthetically, it looks nice" (2003).

In Canada, a student named Grace, a 16-year-old woman of color, gets up in the morning and while standing in front of the mirror is hurt by what she sees of herself (Obaahema Network 2002). The image that is reflected in the mirror is one that causes her to be severely depressed. She does not like her kinky-permed-straight African hair, in a world where almost all hair is straight. Her

nose is broad and her lips are thick, in a world where noses are keen and lips are thin. Her dark brown eyes suggest she is ugly and, having no way to escape, resorts to applying bleaching creams to her skin. Each time she resorts to the bleaching creams is an opportunity to escape her ugliness. With each application she can get closer to the idealized light-skinned Western beauty. When the cream wears off, Grace is forced to acknowledge the fact that she is Black. She must admit that she is undesirable to men and only by bleaching to lighten her skin can she be rescued from her fate. She believes her failure to bleach will sentence her to a life of horror and shame in her dark skin (2002).

A similar woman of color named Latoya is a 17-year-old Jamaican who is determined to bleach her skin, which the locals call "brownin" (Obaahema Network 2002). "Brownin" is a Jamaican term used all over the island in reference to Blacks who have light skin. Latoya applies thick layers of bleaching creams to her face despite the fact that some may contain dangerous steroids. She is aware that the warning labels advise her that the practice of bleaching could damage her skin. Without concern she goes about daily bleaching because she is pleased with what she sees of herself. "When I walk on the streets you can hear people say, 'Hey, check out the 'brownin.' It is cool. It looks pretty." This is what Latoya wants more than anything else. "When you are lighter, people pay more attention to you. It makes you more important" (2002).

Selina Margaret Oppong is a 50-year-old African woman who started bleaching her skin "with the aim to brighten up the skin." Her counterpart hairstylist, Maama Adwoa, is against the idea of bleaching as a practice for beautifying ugly dark African skin. She contends that fading, as it is called, does little good. African women fade "because they think they might look beautiful." Another woman named Cecilia Animahh is inclined to be even more frank: "In Ghana," according to her, "some of the men want bleaching girls." That being so, it appears that getting a light skin that glows is all but impossible for naturally dark-skinned African women. "I started bleaching two years ago, but stopped because I started developing very bad stretch marks," according to Diana Gyaamfua, who is 28 years old. Added to the incidence of stretch marks is the fact that those who bleach their skin usually eventually begin to look like they have been sunburned. Their faces develop a brick red and puffy look associated with black, grotesque-looking splotches (Chisholm 2002).

In more extreme reactions to skin bleaching, African women incur increased risks to their health leading to the disruption of internal organ function. "There is suspicion of an increased risk of renal failure as a result of the mercury contained in some of the products that people use for bleaching," according to African physician, Dr. Doe (Opala 2001). Unfortunately, too many women who bleach do not seek medical help until it is too late. This has spurred an effort on the part of doctors to promote public service announcements in hopes of educating the public to the dangers of bleaching. Doe confides that Maama Adwoa has encountered the "stop bleaching" announcements in the media. "They say we should stop bleaching because of skin cancer and skin disease. But people don't want to listen because they don't know . . . ." (2001). In the end they develop such bad skin problems that they can no longer go out into the sun without risking more problems. The extent of such persons in Africa is becoming so widespread that some women are beginning to exercise caution. Unfortunately, other women are applying additional creams in hopes of getting their skin back to its natural state of color. But for women who are uneducated about bleaching and who have relied on Western beauty products, various West African nations continue to object to bleaching. For example, in Gambia, the government has decided to outlaw all skin bleaching products including Bu-Tone, Madonna Cream, Glo-Tone, and the American-made Ambi. The government decided to be lenient on those who were caught with bleached skin. Furthermore, officials in Europe have also begun to take issue with the practice as Denmark has also banned skin bleaching creams and soaps. Danish officials have traveled to a number of local African shops and collected the products. Unfortunately, Tura, a product outlawed by the Danes, is still popular in Ghana and other African countries. While the business community may find these actions extreme, doctors concur that they are not without reason.

> Some of these products were banned sometime in the past, but somehow, some of them still find their way onto the local markets where most of these bleachers get their products ... There, you don't need a prescription to buy anything, Dr. Doe explains (2001).

Thus, despite the absence of skin color issues from the mainstream literature it prevails among the most critical manifestations of racism among people of color who are yet to be counted. Notwithstanding the fact that people of color have filed litigation to combat what they feel is skin color discrimination and regardless of the fact that Black film stars are hurt by color stereotypes on screen and in reality, mainstream scholarship has not found reason to document their strife. In addition, the fact that women of color find it necessary to lighten their skin despite the emotional and health risks it poses is no less racist than when mainstream scholars ignore their strife. Their version is a manifestation of racism in the 21st century and a motivation to increasingly resort to the phenomenon called the Bleaching Syndrome in an effort to rescue themselves.

The Bleaching Syndrome

According to James Baldwin, the root of American difficulty is directly related to skin color (Jones 1966; Robinson & Ward 1995). This would contradict much of the rhetoric of race and suggest skin color as the manifestation of racism in the 21st century. But as this author (1995) notes, the issue of skin color has never been subjected to rigorous debate. Thus, the well-known phenomenon of racism via race has obliged distortions in the truth. It is evident among people of color whereby light-skinned African-Americans such as Dorothy Dandridge commit suicide. African- and Latino-Americans file litigation such as *Walker v. the IRS*. Latino-Americans in both Puerto Rico and on the U.S. mainland have sought redress through litigation before and after cases were filed by African-Americans. Asian-Americans exposed to the dominant influences of Western culture and its racism have aspired to marital patterns that associate status and marriage potential with skin color. Despite the location of some Native-Americans on reservations, the issue of skin color as a manifestation of racism in the 21st century is no less apparent among them. As a group subjected to a culture of cruelty that parallels the antebellum South, Native-Americans have resorted to authentication of identity by skin color and racist slurs characteristic of "white supremacists." But perhaps the most potent manifestation of racism in the 21st century is the impact of white beauty standards upon women of color who want little more than to be thought of as beautiful. Their pain is constant without the benefit of being acknowledged by mainstream social scientists because issues pertaining to women of color do not rise to a level of significance. Mainstream scholars such as Maslow and Mead have not accounted for people of color in the design and application of their theoretical constructs. Furthermore, scholars of color including Norton and Chestang similarly have been less than enthused about giving an account of racism as it might manifest in the 21st century—a no less racist act, however, subtle and/or unintended. All matters considered necessitate the construction of the Bleaching Syndrome to acknowledge and comprehensively organize what is otherwise obvious.

The genesis of the Bleaching Syndrome is historically rooted in old "beauty" creams and folk preparations used by people of color to make their skin lighter. According to *Webster's Dictionary*, "bleach" is a verb that means to remove color or to make white (Mish 1989). A "syndrome" consists of a grouping of symptoms, i.e.: behaviors that occur in conjunction and make up a recognizable pattern (1989). In combination, historical folklore and English terminology literally define the Bleaching Syndrome. Because of its universality, it is also a metaphor. Its relevance to people of color in the aftermath of colonialism is universal because its application is limitless. However, when applied to people of color, its existence is substantiated in a most dramatic fashion. For, it is they who have had to idealize norms, which are often radically inconsistent with outward appearances (Levine & Padilla 1980).

In addition, the psychological pain they suffer is exacerbated by Western culture's overt and covert forms of racism and general lack of tolerance for its growing diversity. The effort on the part of people of color to assimilate and simultaneously bring about a reduction in psychological pain is made possible by their obsession with the "bleached" ideal, which is manifested in their perception of preferred white norms and rootedness in white culture. No other aspect of self-denigration is more revealing.

The Bleaching Syndrome is a self-denigrating process of orientation that requires a disparity in power. Were it not for the differential in power between people of color and their Western mainstream hosts, the Syndrome could not exist. Much of what the Bleaching Syndrome involves is pathological to people of color and could not otherwise be imposed because it is contrary to their physical, emotional, and psychological well-being. The Bleaching Syndrome may be manifested by people of color in their values, interaction styles, behavioral responses, language use, and so forth. It is a distortion of Maslow's hierarchy of needs (Zastrow & Kirst-Ashman 1990). Such impositions are not only denigrating but are initially painful. The intensity of the pain may subside over time, but the ultimate ill-effects are not lessened.

The Bleaching Syndrome is an essential fact of human experience regardless of where it is acted out or applied. Anywhere in the world, at any point in history, it has been a factor—particularly in post-colonized societies, including the West. As long as less powerful groups must assimilate into more powerful cultures to increase their quality of life, oppressed populations will continue to avail themselves to various forms of self-denigration. To the extent that people of color are willing to engage in self-denigration, the Bleaching Syndrome can become a factor in seemingly unrelated social ills, such as depression, spouse abuse, and poverty. However, not every person of color exhibits the Bleaching Syndrome to stave off the pain. Many diseases among those who succumb can be traced to experiences with Western domination. Social ills are merely one manifestation of their difficulties. It is this fact that Western society has yet to readily acknowledge in the policy or treatment process involving people of color. That is because self-indictment is not an attribute of the powerful. It then makes the Bleaching Syndrome uniquely suited for enabling the exploitation of people of color because its existence is not subject to the social, political, or philosophical indictment of any Western faction.

Focusing on the Bleaching Syndrome in the context of skin color, people of color who migrate to the U.S. are regarded as "minorities" (Kitano 1985). Their most salient feature is their darker skin, which immediately assigns them to an outgroup (Hall 1990). In the U.S., skin color may have an effect upon every phase of life, including job placement, earnings, and most importantly self-concept (Vontress 1970). It is a "master status," which distinguishes people of color from the lighter-skinned Western mainstream. So potent is this "master status" that it has recently become the grounds for legal action between persons of relative light and dark skin color but of the same ethnic group, i.e.: Latino- and African-Americans (*Morrow v. the IRS* 1990). A resort to legal tactics is an indication that, for people of color, experiences with Western culture have been particularly painful, given the psychologically conflicting ideals of Western society. That is, they have internalized Western norms, but, unlike members of the dominant population, they are prohibited from structural or full assimilation into the population (Rabinowitz 1978). Their willingness to submit reflects an effort to improve their quality of life and live out their dreams. In doing so, people of color may develop a disdain for dark skin because the disdain is culturally reinforced. It is regarded by the various Western institutions as an obstacle, which might otherwise afford them the opportunity to realize their aspirations. However, the contradiction between dark skin and ideal light skin has resulted in psychological pain and their various attempts at self-denigration in order to cope. To minimize the consequences and at the same time enable assimilation, people of color have aspired to light skin despite the pathology. Furthermore, since the degree of Western assimilation closely correlates with the phenotype of the dominant population, i.e.: light skin, light skin has emerged as one of the most critical prerequisites relative to the Western quality of life (Reuter 1969). To facilitate the process, people of color rely heavily upon various concoctions and social strategies to fit in. Thus, light skin has come to be utilized as a reference point in the decision-making process for whatever life-choices are considered.

Initiating the use of skin color via the Bleaching Syndrome must begin at the academic level. One suggestion is to radically address the contents of the social science literature. While skin color is less relevant to a Eurocentric mainstream for African-Americans and other people of color, it may define the reality of their existential experience (Hall 2003). A cursory review of social science literature such as *Social Work* attests to a lack of attention to skin color as an issue that is significant to people of color, and which could be used as a viable assessment tool. Skin color is in fact relevant across the entire lifespan, as is known by all African-American social workers who are informed of issues significant to people of color. Despite this fact, according to the *Social Work Abstracts* database 1977–2007, a minimum of articles have been published on "skin color" in the last thirty years. In leading social work journals, skin color content has been all but totally omitted in that time period, accommodating Eurocentric frames of reference. In leading textbooks such as *Understanding Human Behavior in the Social Environment* (Zastrow & Kirst-Ashman 2006), the issue of skin color as it pertains to people of color is omitted from the index and the 300-plus pages of lexis that comprise the work in toto. The fact that both authors are of European descent cannot be dismissed as irrelevant to their Eurocentric perspective. While they may be cognizant of critical issues, they, as social work authors, determine the priority of what reaches publication. The information they disseminate then determines the realities of what people of color encounter. This results in pathological complications that are otherwise unnecessary (Bogolub 2006). Thus, modifying social work literature to equate the significance of skin color with mainstream Eurocentric content is conducive to the global elimination of racism.

Acknowledging skin color as a manifestation of racism in the future will require a new direction for social workers, psychologists, sociologists, and others. In fact, such a critical issue has been trivialized by the prevalence of racial constructs. The Eurocentric intelligentsia, which via the Bleaching Syndrome includes people of color, would argue that any accusations of trivialization are little more than disputes between one faction trying to bring about an objective conclusion and another opposing group, for reasons of intellectual discourse. Since the beginning of the 21st century, an effort to accommodate diversity intellectually and otherwise has never been more critical for Western civilization. Prior to the emergence of diversity as a valued social concept, scholars did not generally equate skin color with race as it pertains to racism. They disagreed about many things, but they shared a commitment to racial constructs in differentiating one group from another and their potential to be racist. Subsequently, scholarly agreement on the trivialization of skin color had not been subjected to intellectual debate. Thus, social scientists in general, who might have disagreed with racial constructs as being the foundation of racism, were relegated to the fringes of the academy. What followed is the trivialization of skin color despite its obvious pathological influence, resulting in the Bleaching Syndrome.

The facts about people of color leave no doubt as to the significance of skin color in their lives. In business professions, in the arts, at the university, and the norms of society it is obvious that most in America as well as the entire West are of a similar mindset—among whom, skin color is a less salient issue (Bonila-Silva 1991). Whatever the root of our differentiation, be it race, nationality, socialization, or a simple lack of exposure to skin color issues, in the aftermath social science is rendered less effective.

To better educate the public about the significance of skin color for manifestations of racism in the 21st century will require an acknowledgement of its formidable potential. Skin color as a significant issue has, up to the present, been overlooked on the basis of cultural taboos and maintaining polite professional discourse. Some of the taboos include assumed differences between people, which are little more than myth. By disqualifying these myths from polite conversation, in fact, sustains the difficulty encountered by oppressed populations worldwide.

Acknowledgement of the Bleaching Syndrome minimizes the potential for conflict as introduced by racist motivations. Study of the Bleaching Syndrome has the potential to address current matters of assimilation, such as "passing" and repairing a denigrated self. This will accommodate awareness of a newer more insidious manifestation of racism, which cannot be limited to racial boundaries. It is increasingly evident that, at least among people of color, this racism based on skin color is pertinent to the study of their self-image, their self-esteem, their family dynamics, and so forth. Its acknowledgement is a necessity in a world that is fast becoming not only racially indistinct but ethnically and culturally indistinct as well. This subsequent diversity has facilitated assertions on the part of people of color to then redefine themselves, i.e.: to bleach their skin. Their efforts have validated the importance of skin color as having a direct correlation to their overall well-being. In the aftermath, people of color and the social scientists among them, including Whites, must aspire to more conducive, somatic norms to escape the pathological influences of the Bleaching Syndrome, or risk jeopardizing the 21st century and beyond.

References

Aguirre, B., Saenz, R., & Hwang, S. (1995). Remarriage and intermarriage of Asians in the United States of America. *Journal of Comparative Family Studies*, 26(2), 207–215.
Arroyo, J. (1996). Psychotherapist bias with Hispanics: An analog study. *Hispanic Journal of Behavioral Sciences*, 18(1), 21–28.

Banerjee, S. (1985). Assortive mating for color in Indian population. *Journal of Biosocial Science*, 17, 205–209.

Bogle, D. (1989). *Toms, Coons, Mulattoes, Mammies and Bucks: An interpretative history of Blacks in American films*. New York: Viking, 1973; new expanded edition, New York: Continuum, 1989.

Bogolub, E. (2006). The impact of recruitment-generated bias on qualitative research interviews with foster children. *Families in Society*, 87(1), 140–143.

Bonila-Silva, E. (1991). The essential social fact of race. *American Sociological Review*, 64(6), 899–906.

Burke, R., Divinagracia, L., & Mamo, E. (1998). Supervisors' support received by women managers: Country and sex supervisors. *Psychological Reports*, 83(1), 12–14.

Chestang, L. (1995). Is it time to rethink affirmative action? No! *Journal of Social Work Education*, 32(1), 12–18.

Chisholm, N. (2002). Skin bleaching and the rejection of blackness: Fade to white. *The Village Voice*, January 23–29, 2002.

Dominguez, V. (1997). *White by definition: Social classification in Creole*. New Brunswick, NJ: Rutgers University Press.

Erikson, Erik H. (1968). *Identity: youth and crisis*. New York: Norton.

Falero v. Stryker Corporation, 10 F.Supp.2d 93 (D. Puerto Rico 1998).

Felix v. Manquez, 24EPD 279 (D.C.D.C. 1980).

Frost, P. (1989). Human skin color: a possible relationship between its sexual dimorphism and its social perception. *Perspectives in Biology and Medicine*, 32(1), pp. 38–58.

Gordon, Avery F. (1997). *Ghostly matters: Haunting and the sociological imagination*. Minneapolis, MN: University of Minnesota Press.

Hall, R. (2003). *Skin color as a post-colonial issue among Asian-Americans*. Lewiston, NY: Mellen Press.

Hall, R. E. (1990). The projected manifestations of aspiration, personal values, and environmental assessment cognates of cutaneo-chroma (skin color) for a selected population of African Americans (Doctoral dissertation, Atlanta University, 1989). Dissertation Abstracts International, 50, 3363A.

———. (1997). Eurogamy among Asian Americans: A note on Western assimilation. *Social Science Journal*, 34(3), pp. 403–408.

hooks, bell. (1992). Revolutionary renegades: Native Americans, African Americans and Black Indians. In *Black looks: Race and representation*. Boston: South End Press.

[IRIN] IRINNEWS.ORG. (2004). Pakistan focus on skin bleaching. UN Office of Humanitarian Affairs.

Jarvenpa, R. (1985). The political economy and political ethnicity of Indian adoption and identities. *Ethnic and Racial Studies*, 8, 29–48.

Jones, B. F. (1966). James Baldwin: The struggle for identity. *British Journal of Sociology*, 17, 107–121.

Katz, William L. (1986). *Black Indians: A hidden heritage*. New York: Atheneum.

Kazan, Elia. (1949). *Pinky* (director: Elia Kazan; 20th Century Fox, screenwriters: Philip Dunne, Dudley Nichols.) A film based on the 1946 novel *Pinky*, by Cid Ricketts

Kim, K. (1990). Blacks against Korean merchants: An interpretation of contributory factors. *Migration World Magazine*, 18(5), 11–15.

Kitano, H. (1985). *Race relations*. Englewood Cliffs, NJ: Prentice-Hall.

Lee, Y. (1991). Stereotypes, silence, and threats: The determinants of perceived group homogeneity. Dissertation Abstracts International, 52(6-B), 3342.

Leistikow, N. (2003). Indian women criticize "Fair and Lovely" ideal. 28 April 2003. http://www.womensenews.org/article.cfm/dyn/aid/1308/context/archive. Accessed 23 January 2007.

Levine, E. S., & Padilla, A. M. (1980). *Crossing cultures in therapy*. Monterey, CA: Brooks/ Cole.

Maslow, A. H. (1971). Self-actualizing and beyond. In *The farther reaches of human nature*. (pp. 41–53). New York: Viking, 1971.

Mazumdar, S. (1989). Racist response to discrimination: The Aryan myth and South Asians in the United States. *South Asian Bulletin*, 9(1), 47–55.

McGloin, L. (1992). Colonization: Its impact on self-image. *FFP Bulletin*, Spring/Summer.

Mead, G. (1934). *Mind, self and society*. Chicago: University of Chicago Press.

Mish, F. C. (Ed.). (1989). *Webster's ninth new collegiate dictionary*. Springfield, MA: Merriam Webster.

Morrow v. the Internal Revenue Service, 742 F. Supp. 670 (N.D. Ga. 1990).

Myrdal, G. (1944). *An American dilemma*. New York: Harper & Row.

Nagel, J. (1997). *American Indian ethnic renewal: Red power and the resurgence of Identity and Power*. New York and Oxford (UK): Oxford University Press.

National Hockey League. (1997). NHL suspends Simon for slur. *Times Fax*.

———. (1983). Black family life patterns, the development of self and cognitive development of Black children. In G. J. Powell (Ed.), *The psychosocial development of minority group children* (pp. 181–193). New York: Brunner/Mazel, 1983.

Obaahema Network. (November, 2002). Effects of skin bleaching. http://www.obaahema. com/Channels/health_fitness/article.cfm?ArticleID = 7. Accessed 23 January 2008.

Opala, K. (2001). Cosmetics ban: Did standards body err? http://allafrica.com/stories/ printable/200105290458.html. Accessed 12 April, 2003.

Rabinowitz, H. (1978). *Race relations in the urban south*. New York: Oxford University Press.

Reuter, E. (1969). *The mulatto in the United States*. New York: Haskell House.

Rhee, S. (1988). Korean and Vietnamese outmarriage: Characteristics and implications. Los Angeles: UCLA, DSW Dissertation.

Robinson, T., & Ward, J. (Aug. 1995). African American adolescents and skin color. *Journal of Black Psychology*, 21(3), 256–274.

Russell, K., Wilson, M., & Hall, R. (1992). *The color complex: The politics of skin color among African Americans*. New York: Harcourt Brace Jovanovich.

Shinagawa, L., & Pang, G. (1988). Intraethnic, and interracial marriages among Asian-Americans in California, 1980. *Berkeley Journal of Sociology*, 33, 95–114.

Snipp, C. Matthew. (1989). *American Indians: The first of this land*. New York: Russell Sage Foundation.

Sung, B. (1990). Chinese American intermarriage. *Journal of Comparative American Studies*, Fall, 21(3), 337–352.

Vontress, C. (1970). Counseling Black. *Personnel and Guidance Journal*, 48, 713–719.

Walker v. the IRS, 713 F Supp. 403. (U.S. Dist. Ga. 1989).

Washington, Robert. (1990). Brown discrimination and the formation of a world system of racial stratification. *International Journal of Politics, Culture, and Society*, 4(2), 209–227.

Wilson, M. (1992). What difference could a revolution make? Group work in the new Nicaragua. *Social Work with Groups*, 15(2/3), pp. 301–314.

Zastrow, C., & Kirst-Ashman, K. (1990). *Understanding human behavior and the social environment*. Chicago, IL: Nelson Hall.

Part II
What Are the Costs of Racism?

Chapter 3
Skin Color Bias in the Workplace: The Media's Role and Implications Toward Preference

Matthew S. Harrison, Wendy Reynolds-Dobbs, and Kecia M. Thomas

Abstract Racial discrimination is a widely studied topic in the areas of sociology and psychology. A common negligence of several studies concerning this issue is that many disregard the subject of skin tone stratification, and present an analysis of discrimination based upon the treatment of Blacks and Whites (both as collective units); thereby overlooking a prevalent issue that has long existed in western culture-colorism. This particular chapter examines the influence of colorism in today's society with a specific look at the role the media plays and how, in turn, this has potential implications in the workplace. Given the variability amongst the images the media presents us with in regards to Blacks (depending upon whether or not the individual is light- or dark-skinned), the favorability of a Black applicant can be highly dependable on not necessarily their race (as often assumed), but perhaps more so, their complexion.

Introduction

"I have a dream that my four little children will one day live in a nation where they will not be judged by the color of their skin but by the content of their character." This quote, found in Dr. Martin Luther King's famous *I Have a Dream* speech (King 1963), resonates with individuals from all races and ethnicities. Dr. King's choice of wording, however, is most interesting in that he says "color of their skin." Most often it is inferred that his meaning by this statement is that he hopes his children will not be discriminated against because they are Blacks. Whether or not this was Dr. King's sole meaning by this declaration, one does not fully know, but it is not surprising that American society immediately assumes that the issue of skin color is a Black versus White

M.S. Harrison
Department of Applied (Industrial/Organizational) Psychology, The University of Georgia, Athens, GA, USA
e-mail: msharris@uga.edu

R.E. Hall (ed.), *Racism in the 21st Century*, DOI: 10.1007/978-0-387-79097-8_3,
© Springer Science+Business Media, LLC 2008

issue. Given the longstanding history of the relationship between Blacks and Whites in America, race relations in the U.S. are most commonly thought of in this dichotomous manner. Ultimately, each race is generalized and homogenized into one grouping (Celious & Oyserman 2001).

Even racial-identity theories follow this same inexplicit categorization, where race is viewed as a simple binary relationship between Blacks and Whites, and any potential diversity within each race is simply ignored or overlooked. Because race is a social construction, these theories are accurate in their assumption that similarities do exist within racial groups (Celious & Oyserman 2001); however, it is important to note that the potential for differences to exist within races is even greater. These individuals may be of a different gender, socioeconomic status, (and for purposes of this chapter) skin color—all of which play a substantial role in the life they lead and the treatment they receive from others.

Black Americans may very well live in the same society, but their life experiences may vary greatly depending on whether or not one is light- or dark-skinned. O. L. Edwards (1973) claims that of the many characteristics into which people of America are divided, none has greater significance than one's skin color. Skin color is so divisive in America, and in most other western cultures, because whiteness and blackness are (and have always been) in binary opposition to one another. Whiteness is most often associated with beauty, purity, and graciousness, while blackness symbolizes ugliness, evilness, and incivility (Hunter 2002). These disparate views of what "black" and "white" represent are extremely powerful and have even been extended into the symbolic differences between "dark" and "light," respectively. Thus, this dichotomy between Blacks and Whites has been expanded into a stratification system within the Black race itself, where light-skinned Blacks take on the aforementioned characteristics associated with Whites, while dark-skinned Blacks are ascribed the negative characteristics commonly associated with blackness. It is therefore not farfetched to presume that lighter-skinned Blacks receive preferential treatment over their darker-skinned counterparts (Thompson & Keith 2001).

Thus, as our title suggests, this chapter will focus on issues of preferential treatment due to skin tone as it relates to the workplace. More specifically, we will discuss the role media plays in our development of perceptions and overall expectations of individuals. Given that individuals are often depicted in the media very differently based upon their race, gender, ethnicity, and even skin color, the assessments we ultimately have of others is heavily shaped by these often stereotypical portrayals. Because much of society generally accepts these untrue representations, they have major implications in all areas of life—including work. This chapter will discuss how these false images—specifically as they relate to skin color—manifest themselves in the workplace and ultimately lead to disparaging biases between light- and dark-skinned applicants and employees.

Colorism/Skin Color Bias

Issues of partisan behavior due to skin tone dates back to the chattel system of slavery in America, where the division of work chores among slaves was based on skin color (Hunter 2002). Slaves who were dark-skinned, or of pure African ancestry, typically worked in the fields and were viewed as having the more physically demanding tasks; while slaves who were lighter (due to mixed parentage—as it was common for slave masters to have nonconsensual and consensual sexual relationships with their slaves) were given the more "desirable" and prestigious positions within the chattel system (Keith & Herring 1991). These work chore divisions not only engulfed a great deal of bitterness between slaves, but it also reinforced the notion that the lighter one's complexion, "the better off he or she was in the eyes of the majority group members" (Ross 1997, p. 555).

What is most shocking is that this statement still holds true nearly 200 years later. According to the findings of researchers Hughes and Hertel, lighter-skinned Blacks are more likely to have completed more years of schooling, have higher salaries, and have more prominent jobs than their darker-skinned counterparts (1990). Even more compelling, perhaps, is that they found that skin color has such a profound effect that the gap in educational attainment and socioeconomic status between light- and dark-skinned Blacks is equivalent to the gap between Whites and Blacks in general. These findings, combined with studies juxtaposing socioeconomic attainment between mulattoes (i.e., Blacks from mixed heritage) and Blacks, clearly detail the importance and prevalence of colorism, and further illustrate the prominence of color-based stratification in American society (Hill 2000). Thus, lighter-skinned Blacks tend to be more advantaged educationally, economically, and are more likely to experience status advancement than those with darker skin (Seltzer & Smith 1991; Udry et al. 1971). These social advantages that are allotted to this group of lighter-skinned Blacks emphasize and reinforce a system in our society that privileges light skin over dark skin—this classification structure and system of preference is the general definition and forms the building blocks of colorism (Hunter 2002).

Role of the Media in Shaping Our Perceptions

The issue of colorism not only stems from the longstanding history of skin-color bias in our society, but is also reinforced in the everyday images we are bombarded with via the media. Since the 19th century, mass media has been a major part of American culture. Whether it comes in the form of magazines, television, movies, or the ever-growing internet, mass media plays an important role in our daily lives. Media, unlike any other form of communication, has been able to keep us connected and informed about world issues, struggles, and politics. It has been able to entertain us and take us to places that are beyond our physical reach. Most importantly, media gives us the opportunity to learn about other people, cultures, and environments to which we may not have immediate access. Therefore, media provides us with a quick and easy way to access information about various topics.

Although there are many positive attributes to mass media, there are some drawbacks to its system. Since the media can sometimes be our first introduction to the unknown, media representations and images are extremely important to our understanding of others. In addition, media also tends to present us with images that are supposed to define normalcy and essentially inform us of how we should live our lives. Even though this may seem positive, our ideas about not just others but also ourselves are oftentimes based on mass media representations, which are controlled by a minute group of individuals where some scholars and critics feel that limited social themes are used to represent or characterize ethnic minorities (Bogle 2001; Dixon & Linz 2000b). Therefore, the images in mass media may not accurately represent individuals, especially ethnic minority individuals, thus leaving us with a false impression of others and essentially ourselves. Most importantly, these images reinforce stereotypes, which inaccurately shape viewers' perceptions of others and the social world (Givens & Monahan 2005; Potter 1999).

Media's Representation of African Americans

African American portrayals in the media are oftentimes based on negative stereotypes that do not accurately portray reality (Rada 2000). Dating back to the slavery era, images such as the Mammy, Coon, Sambo, and Brute not only justified a system of oppression for African Americans, but these images were also extremely negative, offensive, and blatantly untrue. Although in today's society, these images are not as obvious and apparent as they were in the past, many of these stereotypical images encountered in early media have now been replaced with new, subtler representations of African Americans. For example, in regard to news media, a number of recent studies have shown that news television programs often misrepresent Black Americans as perpetrators of crime and violence while Whites are often viewed as innocent victims. For instance, in a study that examined the portrayal of Blacks and Whites in news programs in the Los Angeles area, researchers found that Blacks were over-represented as perpetrators of crime in television news reports (37%) compared to arrest reports, which were 21% (Dixon & Linz 2000a, 2000b). In addition, they were also underrepresented as innocent victims in news reports (23%) compared to crime reports (28%). These results were quite different from Whites who were underrepresented as perpetrators of crime and overrepresented as victims in crime in news reports (Dixon & Linz 2000a, 2000b).

These studies along with other research (e.g., Entman 1992, 1994, Entman & Rojecki 2000) reveal how media depicts African Americans in a negative light where they are oftentimes associated with criminality on television news, particularly when juxtaposed to Whites.

These negative portrayals, regardless of their accuracy, may affect African Americans' perceptions about themselves as well as members of their own group (Fujioka 1999). In addition, these same images of African Americans may exert some influence on viewers' perceptions of this group (Fujioka 1999). For instance, in a 1991 nationwide opinion poll on ethnic images in the United States, researchers found that out of all other ethnic groups (i.e., Whites, African Americans, Latino Americans, and Asian Americans) Whites received the most positive scores in regard to traits such as having a good work ethic, being dependable, and being intelligent, while African Americans received lower scores, revealing that Blacks were perceived as being undependable, more violent, and lazy (Smith 1991). Furthermore, McAney (1993) found that more than 37% of both African American and White adults perceived African Americans as being more likely to commit crimes than members of other ethnic groups. These opinion polls suggest that stereotypical media representations of Blacks *do* affect people's perceptions of African Americans. In addition to the role of one's race in social judgments, scholars are now beginning to focus on the potential for within-race differences as it relates to how society judges individuals (Dixon 2005). Thus, the color of one's skin may also play a significant factor in how African Americans are perceived by not just themselves but by others.

Media's Representation and Colorism

As stated earlier, colorism (or skin-tone bias) has always been an issue for the African American community. According to Maddox and Gray (2002), anecdotal and experimental evidence suggests that both Blacks and Whites engage in discriminatory behavior based on an individual's skin color. Researchers have found that African Americans with more Afrocentric features (e.g., full lips, wide nose, kinky hair, darker skin) are usually more associated with negative and/or stereotypical evaluations than African Americans with more Eurocentric features (e.g., thinner lips, slender noses, straighter hair, lighter skin) (Maddox & Gray 2002; Oliver et al. 2004). Furthermore, Maddox and Gray (2002) have argued that darker skin tone is more likely than lighter skin tone to be associated with Blacks and, therefore, dark skin is more likely to conjure up stereotypical images of African Americans. Considering this theory, how then does the media reflect colorism for African Americans? Does the media influence our social and professional judgments of dark skin versus light skin in African Americans?

Media's Representation and Colorism for African American Women

Historically, the ideas of colorism suggest that African Americans with lighter skin tone are more intelligent and attractive than their darker-skin toned counterparts. Regarding media, most of the research that has examined colorism amongst African American women has focused on advertisements. In a 1996 study, which explored the concept of colorism of Blacks in advertisements and editorial photographs from 1989 to 1994, the researcher discovered that African Americans in advertisements had lighter skin and more Eurocentric features in ads compared to editorial photographs (Keenan 1996). Furthermore, African American women had lighter skin than African American men (Keenan 1996). Even in African American centered magazines such as *Ebony*, images of African American women continue to glorify and value light skin and White features over more Afrocentric features (Leslie 1995).

Although images of Black women have become more diverse over the years (e.g., Tomiko, Naomi Campbell, Alek Wek, Tyra Banks among others), "bias[es]" against Black women based on their physical appearance [still] persist" (Shorter-Gooden & Jones 2003, p. 178). For instance, in *People* magazine's "50 Most Beautiful People" list from 2005, only four African American women made the list, and, out of the four, all of the women possessed light skin tones and were from mixed Black/White heritages (i.e., Halle Berry, Alicia Keys, and Sophie Okonedo) with the exception of Oprah Winfrey, who has medium skin tone. Thus, this popular magazine list suggests that, even in today's diverse society, light skin is still viewed as being more attractive than darker skin.

Furthermore, even when looking at Black women in films, the first African American woman to be nominated for the Oscar for Best Actress award was Dorothy Dandridge, in 1954, and the first African American woman to win the award for Best Actress was Halle Berry, in 2001; both women have light complexions and Eurocentric features. Although both of these women are very much worthy of their nominations and accolades, one cannot ignore the fact that, maybe, their appearance, which is closer to America's definition of beauty, along with their talent, played a part in their success and acceptance as Hollywood film actors.

Black women are consistently being compared to a White definition of beauty that is virtually unrealistic, and the media tends to perpetuate this plastic and limited definition of beauty. Besides creating a major destructive divide within the Black community, specifically amongst African American women, colorism and media's portrayal of African American women may also affect how other group members evaluate African American women in regard to abilities, likeability, and attractiveness, among other characteristics. As stated by Shorter-Gooden and Jones in their book, which highlights the experiences of African American women, "If movies tend to depict less desirable women as darker skinned or fuller figured, those are the images that the public internalizes and believes" (2003, 198). Therefore, individuals (especially Whites) may view lighter-skin Black women as having more admirable and positive attributes than women of a darker skin tone.

Media's Representation and Colorism for African American Men

With regard to African American men, colorism may not directly relate to attractiveness in the media, but it definitely is associated with perceptions of violence and criminality. Historically, images of African American males during the Emancipation and Reconstruction Era were extremely negative and violent. Images such as the Brute and Buck portrayed African American men as violent, menacing, and dangerous, oftentimes having very dark skin and overly exaggerated, Afrocentric features. Although these images are somewhat a "thing of the past," new images such as Black men being portrayed as thugs, hoodlums, gangsters, and criminals have replaced these more overtly historic, racist images. Thus, the relationship between dark-skinned Black men and violence can still be seen today. For instance, in the case of O. J. Simpson, the infamous mug-shot picture of Simpson, which graced the cover of *Time* magazine, was actually darkened making Simpson appear more sinister, menacing, and violent. As suggested by Harper (1996), the darkening of Simpson's face equated dark skin to criminality—essentially reflecting back to the image of the Black Buck and Brute.

The color of African American males' skin, in addition to their negative portrayal in the media, only enhances negative evaluations toward all African American males, especially those who are darker-skinned. The result of these negative evaluations of darker-skinned males can be seen in several areas beyond criminality, such as socioeconomic status. In a study, which looked at colorism in regard to socioeconomic status of African American males, the investigator found that lighter-skinned African American males had a higher socioeconomic status than men with darker skin (Hill 2000). Furthermore, in other studies (discussed earlier), researchers have found that lighter-skinned African Americans tended to have more schooling, more prestigious jobs, and earn more than African Americans with darker skin tones (Hughes & Hertel 1990; Keith & Herring 1991). These discrepancies in attainment amongst African Americans may be a reflection of the privileges and advantages lighter-skin tone Blacks receive over darker-skin tone Blacks.

Effects of Media's Portrayals

Considering the fact that as Americans we are constantly in contact with images from the media, we cannot help but to subconsciously impose our stereotypical thoughts and ideas on members from other groups. Therefore, the way the media glorifies the White standard of beauty for women, and demonizes dark skin for men, may essentially affect how not just Blacks view themselves but how other group members, specifically Whites, view African Americans based on their skin color. In regard to Whites' judgments of African Americans, Whites may feel more comfortable with lighter-skinned African Americans because they look more like themselves and are often portrayed in a more positive manner versus darker-skinned Blacks who appear physically more distant to Whites and are portrayed more negatively in the media. Furthermore, lighter-skinned Blacks are viewed as being more intelligent, more capable, and essentially "more White" than darker-skinned Blacks, which may be a significant factor in why lighter-skinned individuals are more privileged in our society. Since these media portrayals affect how we feel and judge others, it only makes sense that these negative portrayals of darker-skinned African Americans would affect judgment in regards to other important arenas such as employment opportunities in the workplace.

Racial Discrimination in Employment Selection

Despite the probable treatment differences within the Black race due to issues of colorism, it is important to acknowledge the presence of general racial discrimination in employment, regardless of one's skin color. According to statistics from the U.S. Department of Labor, in America, Blacks are twice as likely to be unemployed than their White counterparts (Brief et al. 2005). While these variations in unemployment may not necessarily be linked to overt forms of discrimination, most often recruitment techniques of organizations are somewhat covertly prejudiced. When certain neighborhoods are targeted with information regarding job openings, or when employers choose to hire from within (Brief et al. 2005), Blacks (and other racial minorities) are automatically put at a disadvantage.

For those Blacks who may be called for an interview, or even ultimately hired for the job, the discrimination they will encounter is typically just beginning. The Fair Employment Council (FEC) has conducted a number of recent studies that illustrate this victimizing treatment. One such study involved the FEC matching Blacks and Whites on their credentials (e.g., qualifications, interviewing skills, and so forth). They found, however, that although candidates were equally-matched, over 20% of employers treated the White applicants more favorably than the Black applicants (Brief et al. 2005).

Further evidence of continuing discrimination between Blacks and Whites is confirmed by the increasing number of disparate treatment and adverse impact cases that continue to be filed under Title VII of the Civil Rights Act of 1964. One of the most well-known cases filed is *Watson v. Fort Worth*. In this particular case, Clara Watson, a Black employee at Fort Worth Bank & Trust, applied four separate times for a promotion to a management position within the bank, where she was rejected each of the four times while a White applicant was given the position for which she applied. Watson was able to provide evidence illustrating that the Fort Worth Bank had never hired a Black employee as an officer or director (only one Black held a managerial position), and gave lower wages to Blacks who had comparable jobs to White employees (Bersoff et al. 1988).

Situations similar to Ms. Watson's are all too common in the American workforce. Many companies "unknowingly" implement selection tools that are used during the application process that ultimately lead to disparate treatment toward Blacks—where a disproportionate number of Whites are hired over Blacks. Most companies claim that the utility of the selection tool was not at all rooted in an attempt to hire more White workers than Blacks, but was merely used to acquire the most qualified candidates for the job, who just happened to be White (Terpstra & Kethley 2002). Thus, companies can now hide behind, or camouflage, discrimination in the selection process by placing the blame on certain selection instruments.

Regardless of whether selection tools play a role in the hiring process or not, one's skin color is ultimately inescapable, especially given that most selection processes involve an interview. Thus, the longstanding history of racial discrimination in our country seems unavoidable in the job selection process. We are not at all proposing that every White individual who is hired over a Black is hired solely because of their being White; however, given the history of favoritism toward Whites and injustice toward racial minorities, especially Blacks in our society, it would be naïve to think that it is never a factor—as previous research has illustrated (Gaertner & Dovidio 2005; Dovidio et al. 2005; Dovidio & Gaertner 2004). We propose, however, that preferential selection extends further in America. Thereby implying that, while Blacks may often be at a disadvantage in the application process, not all Blacks are disadvantaged equally, and that the magnitude of the burden they may face depends heavily on whether or not they have light or dark skin.

Employment Discriminatory Treatment Based on Skin Tone

While the phenomenon of colorism is not a novel topic in America (or western culture, in general) by any means, skin color bias is an issue that is very rarely discussed in regard to its possible implications in the workplace. Due to our country's history and the majority of discrimination cases being gender or racially based, it is uncommon for one to think that discrimination can have different repercussions for individuals of the same race. We argue that this could very well be the case. Given that "we have been conditioned to believe that lighter skin equals success" (Williams 2002, p. 8), it could be assumed that lighter-skinned workers would have an advantage over darker-skinned workers in regard to being hired and selected for promotions.

The presence of a system of skin tone privilege would also support, and possibly help explain, the findings of Hughes & Hertel's 1999 study. Perhaps lighter-skinned Blacks have substantially higher incomes and attain greater education, because our society is structured in such a way that obtainment of schooling and competitively paying jobs is not as difficult a feat for them as it is for darker-skinned Blacks. We are not at all suggesting or proclaiming that light-skinned Blacks do not also receive their fair share of discrimination in the workplace (as the previous section detailed), or in society in general for that matter. Research and media representations, however, do seem to support the notion that the severity of the discrimination received by a Black individual may very well be dependent on whether or not they are light-or dark-skinned.

Given that light skin is associated with white skin, and white skin is associated with competence, lighter-skinned Blacks are more appealing to White employers (Hunter 2002). It was even once considered to be "better business" for a White employer to hire Black workers who had a light complexion (Ross 1997). Therefore, Whites (particularly White males) are commonly perceived as being "gatekeepers" who have permitted disproportionately more light-skinned Blacks into high-status jobs than dark-skinned Blacks (Ransford 1970).

Preferential treatment toward lighter-skinned Blacks extends beyond the common notions surrounding colorism (discussed earlier), but also takes into account the fact that dark-skinned Black men and women are commonly regarded differently from their lighter-skinned cohorts due to common differences in their self-identification. Because darker-skinned Blacks have tended to experience greater levels of discrimination and unfair treatment, they often have a greater awareness of racial discrimination, and, therefore, have an enhanced affection toward their racial identification (Edwards 1973; Hughes & Hertel 1990). In other words, they are more likely to have been forced to realize that their color matters. Furthermore, because dark-skinned Blacks' entrance into general (or White) society is met with such resistance, they sometimes have enhanced frustration and hostility toward Whites (Ransford 1970). Thus, because darker-skinned Blacks tend to have greater racial pride (Edwards 1973), Whites who are not highly developed in their own racial identity [i.e., extent to which one has come to accept their race as well as individuals from other races/ethnicities (Helms 1990)], may perceive this trait as yet another damaging characteristic associated with dark skin; thereby, reinforcing the stereotypes and prejudices that surround the very notion of colorism.

It is important to note, however, that while colorism is present in the work-force for both Black males and females, it is present for very different reasons. Colorism plays a role in the work environment for Black females because of beliefs surrounding attractiveness. Even as children, we are conveyed the message through fairy-tales that it is "fortunate to be beautiful and unfortunate to be ugly" (Webster & Driskell 1983, p. 140). Additionally, "real world" research has shown that there is a positive correlation between attractiveness and perceptions of ability and success (Umberson & Hughes 1987). As stated previously, ideologies surrounding the phenomenon of colorism suggest that

Blacks are perceived as being more attractive when their phenotypic character-istics (e.g., nose shape, lip size, hair texture, and so forth) are more closely aligned with those commonly associated with Eurocentric features (Fears 1998). Thus, because competency is linked with beauty and beauty is linked with lighter skin, it is common for lighter-skinned Black women to have higher salaries than Black women with darker skin who have very similar résumés (Hunter 2002). It was even found in a 2001 study that light-skinned Black women, who are deemed "less ethnic," were more likely to be satisfied with their pay and opportunities for advancement than darker-skinned ("more ethnic") Black females (Catalyst 2001). Thompson and Keith (2001), therefore, describe a dark-skinned Black woman as being in a "triple jeopardy situation" due to her race, gender, and skin tone, all of which have great potential of having negative and damaging effects on her self-esteem and feelings of capability.

Similarly, dark-skinned Black males can consider themselves being in a "*double* jeopardy situation" because of their race and skin tone. Unlike Black women, these men are not necessarily viewed as being less desirable because of their looks in regard to attractiveness but, rather, they are often perceived as being more violent and threatening by the general population (Hall 1995). Because darker-skinned Black males are commonly associated with crime and general civil misconduct, many people have preconceived notions about Black men who have dark skin (Hall 1995). Thus, in the interview portion of the job selection process, these individuals are possibly at an automatic disadvantage as soon as they walk into the interview. Harrison and Thomas found compelling results that support this argument. In their 2006 study, they found that a light-skinned Black male with only a bachelor's degree and minimal managerial work experience received significantly higher ratings for job recommendation than a dark-skinned Black male with an MBA and substantial managerial experience (Harrison & Thomas 2006). Therefore, this study suggests that in the job selection process skin tone is more salient than educational background and/or past work experience—at least, for Black males.

Colorism Among and Within Blacks Themselves

While the majority of this chapter has focused on the ways in which colorism affects the way others view Blacks, it is important to emphasize that Blacks themselves fall prey to this system of stereotyping and categorizing. There have been a number of research studies that have illustrated that Blacks themselves adhere to common negative stereotypes surrounding Blacks with dark skin. Bill Maxwell (2003) even stated: "More than any other minority group in the United States, Blacks discriminate against one another" (p. 7D). And this discrimina-tion is something that actually begins its perpetuation when one is a child. The well-known Clark Study found that young Black schoolchildren often prefer

White dolls and playmates, and actually deny their own skin color because of the early socialization to the negative associations surrounding dark skin (Freeman et al. 1966).

While this study was done over 40 years ago, these findings all seem to persist, and even more surprisingly, these sentiments seem to have persevered into adulthood. This endurance is evidenced by the increasing number of colorism cases being reported by the Equal Employment Opportunity Commission (EEOC), where most cases of skin-tone discrimination involve a Black discriminating against another Black. In 2002, there were 1,382 such cases, and this number rose to 1,555 in 2003—these cases are filed under Title VII of the 1964 Civil Rights Act (Maxwell 2003; Arnn 2004). These rising numbers are illustrative of the fact that Whites are not solitary mediators of color bias in America's workplace, and that research should be done and dialogue should begin, so we can start to investigate the prevalence of colorism values within the Black community itself (Hill 2000).

Conclusion

This chapter has intended to shed light on the need for research and discussion that juxtapose within race preferences based on skin tone in our workforce. Past research has neglected to look at discrimination outside of the normal dichotomous comparisons of Blacks and Whites as groups consisting of homogenous individuals. Given the increasing number of biracial and multiracial Americans, more research in this area should be performed so that Americans can become more aware of the prevalence of color bias in our society. Studies of this nature will perhaps not only enhance their awareness, but also challenge their acceptance of the common belief that whiteness signifies graciousness and beauty (Hill 2000).

Additionally, research and discussions of this nature will help to substantiate, and in some ways expand, current theories regarding privilege and similarity attraction. It is no secret that we live in a society where being White affords many privileges that are not equally awarded to those who are not White (McIntosh 1993). Possibly, however, the privilege one receives extends beyond their race, and is deeply rooted in skin color—where darker skin equates to fewer privileges. Similarly, ideologies surrounding colorism seem to further confirm Byrne's Similarity Attraction Theory, which states people tend to be more attracted to and have a greater comfort level around individuals who are similar to themselves (1971). It is therefore not surprising that lighter-skinned Blacks would be advantaged in the workplace.

Further, research of this nature could also help combat some of the irony that has long existed in social science research of race and race relations. While most social scientists who perform research of this nature make claim that the purpose of their research is to address, and hopefully falsify negative

perceptions and stereotypes surrounding various races, their grouping of individuals into homogenous groups, and assuming life experiences must all be the same for all Blacks or all Whites, does nothing more than perpetuate those very stereotypes they are attempting to falsify. When people are forced to look at races and ethnicities through a heterogeneous lens, it causes them to look at a racial or ethnic group in a way where longstanding stereotypes no longer seem accurate or appropriate.

Moreover, given the increasing number of companies and organizations that are employing affirmative action policies in their selection processes, determining the possible presence of skin tone preference is paramount. Organizations must be more cognizant of the colorism issue in many of their human resource-related procedures. Further, training (within an emphasis on skin tone preference) should be done with diversity recruitment, selection, career development, and wage/salary allotments. While statistics may continue to show that the number of minorities in corporate America is continuing to rise, they are not reporting the possibility that there is a disproportionate number of lighter-complected minorities getting these jobs. Additionally, these lighter-toned minority employees may have more vertical mobility in organizations because of their enhanced, perceived competence. Not tomention, they are possibly compensated more in terms of their salary and/or benefits because of their lighter pigmentation.

The only way we are going to begin to combat some of the inequities that result due to common beliefs and ideologies associated with colorism is by becoming more aware of the prejudices we have regarding skin tone, due to the images we are exposed to on a regular basis. Society and the media paint for us a picture of lighter skin equating to intelligence, likeability, competency, attractiveness, etc., and a much more dismal and bleak picture is given for those who have darker skin. These images are extremely powerful, in that they alter our immediate perceptions of individuals who must then "fit" into the pictures to which we have been exposed. For instance, if one was to imagine a Black physician, attorney, politician, or philanthropist, more than likely most of these images would be of a light-skinned Black. Whereas, if images of a Black factory worker, garbage collector, janitor, or prisoner were conjured up, more than likely they would be of darker pigmentation than those previously listed.

We must begin to combat these negative associations of dark skin and lower expectations, incited fear, and basic incivility. There was a brief period of time during the Black Power Movement where the Black community began to contest these notions that have damaging effects to the self-esteem of Blacks. This period, however, was short-lived, and chants of "Black is beautiful" are not too often still heard. Mantras of this nature must be recited once more if society and the media's representation of Blackness and dark skin are to change. The more we challenge these images, and our own belief systems, the greater is the likelihood we *will* begin to judge someone by the "content of their character," as Dr. King so dreamed.

References

Arnn, B. (2004). A matter of tone. *Operations & fulfillment*, 12 (7), 8.

Bersoff, D. N., Malson, L. P., & Verrilli, D. B. (1988). In the *Supreme Court of the United States: Clara Watson v. Fort Worth Bank & Trust. American Psychologist*, 43 (12), 1019–1028.

Bogle, D. (2001). *Toms, coons, mulattoes, mammies & bucks: An interpretative history of Blacks in American films* (4th ed.). New York: Continuum.

Brief, A. P., Butz, R. M., & Deitch, E. A. (2005). Organizations as reflections of their environments: The case of race composition. In R. Dipboye & A. Colella (Eds.), *Discrimination at work: The psychological & organizational bases*. Mahwah, NJ: Lawrence Erlbaum Associates, Inc.

Byrne, D. (1997). *The attraction paradigm*. New York: Academic Press.

Catalyst. (2001). *Women of color in corporate management: Three years later*. http://www. catalyst.org. Accessed 20 December 2006.

Celious, A., & Oyserman, D. (2001). Race from the inside: An emerging heterogeneous race model. *Journal of Social Issues*, 57 (1), 149–165.

Dixon, T. L. (2005). Schemas as average conceptions: Skin tone, television news exposure, and culpability judgments. Conference Papers: International Communication Association Annual Meeting, New York, New York, (pp. 1–26).

Dixon, T. L., & Linz, D. (2000a). Overrepresentation and underrepresentation of African Americans and Latinos as lawbreakers on television news. *Journal of Communication*, 50 (2), 131–154.

Dixon, T. L., & Linz, D. (2000b). Race and the misrepresentation of victimization on local television news. *Communication Research*, 27, 547–573.

Dovidio, J. F., & Gaertner, S. L. (2004). Aversive racism. In M. Zanna (Ed.), *Advances in experimental social psychology*, 36 (pp. 1–52). San Diego, CA: Elsevier Academic Press.

Dovidio, J. F., Gaertner, S. L., & Pearson, A. R. (2005). On the nature of prejudice: The psychological foundations of hate. In R. Sternberg (Ed.), *The psychology of hate*. Washington, DC: American Psychological Association.

Edwards, O. L. (1973). Skin color as a variable in racial attitudes of Black urbanites. *Journal of Black Studies*, 3 (4), 473–483.

Entman, R. M. (1992). Blacks in the news: Television, modern racism, and cultural change. *Journalism Quarterly*, 69, 341–361.

———. (1994). Representation and reality in the portrayal of Blacks on network television news. *Journalism Quarterly*, 71, 509–520.

Entman, R. M., & Rojecki, A. (2000). *The Black image in the White mind: Media and race in America*. Chicago, IL: University of Chicago Press.

Fears, L. M. (1998). Colorism of Black women in news editorial photos. *The Western Journal of Black Studies*, 22 (1), 30–36.

Freeman, H. E., Armor, D., Ross, J. M., & Pettigrew, T. F. (1966). Color gradation and attitudes among middle-income Negroes. *American Sociological Review*, 31 (3), 365–374.

Fujioka, Y. (1999). Television portrayals and African American stereotypes: Examination of television effects when direct contact is lacking. *Journal & Mass Communication Quarterly*, 76 (1), 52–75.

Gaertner, S. L., & Dovidio, J. F. (2005). Understanding and addressing contemporary racism: From aversive racism to the common ingroup identity model. *Journal of Social Issues*, 61 (3), 615–639.

Givens, S. M. B., & Monahan, J. L. (2005). Priming mammies, jezebels, and other controlling images: An examination of the influence of mediated stereotypes on perceptions of an African American woman. *Media Psychology*, 7 (1), 87–106.

Hall, R. (1995). The bleaching syndrome: African Americans' response to cultural domination vis-à-vis skin color. *Journal of Black Studies*, 26 (2), 172–184.

Harper, P. (1996). *Are we not men? Masculine anxiety and the problem of African American identity.* New York: Oxford University Press.

Harrison, M. S., & Thomas, K. M. (2006). *Colorism in the job selection process: Are there preferential differences within the Black race?* Presented as a paper at the 68th Annual Meeting of the Academy of Management, Atlanta, Georgia.

Helms, J. (1990). *Black and White racial identity: Theory, research, and practice.* New York: Greenwood Press.

Hill, M. E. (2000). Color differences in the socioeconomic status of African American men: Results of a longitudinal study. *Social Forces,* 78 (4), 1437–1460.

Hughes, M., & Hertel, B. R. (1990). The significance of color remains: A study of life chances, mate selection, and ethnic consciousness among Black Americans. *Social Forces,* 68 (4), 1105–1120.

Hunter, M. L. (2002). "If you're light you're alright"—Light skin color as social capital for women of color. *Gender & Society,* 16 (2), 1750193.

Keenan, K. L. (1996). Skin tones and physical features of Blacks in magazines advertisements. *Journalism Quarterly,* 73, 905–912.

Keith, V. M., & Herring, C. (1991). Skin tone and stratification in the Black community. *The American Journal of Sociology,* 97 (3), 760–778.

King Jr., Martin Luther. (1963). I Have a Dream, an address at the March on Washington, DC, August 28, 1963. http://www.mlkonline.net/dream.html. Accessed 30 January 2008.

Leslie, M. (1995). Slow fade to ?: Advertising in Ebony magazine 1957–1989. *Journalism Quarterly,* 72, 426.

Maddox, K. B., & Gray, S. A. (2002). Cognitive representations of Black Americans: Reexploring the role of skin tone. *Personality and Social Psychology Bulletin,* 28 (2), 250–259.

Maxwell, B. (2003). The paper bag test. *St. Petersburg Times,* 31 August 2003, 7D.

McAney, L. (1993). The gallop poll on crime: Racial overtones evident in Americans' attitudes about crime. *Gallop Opinion Poll Monthly,* 37–42.

McIntosh, P. (1993). White male privilege: A personal account of coming to see correspondence through work in women's studies. In A. Minas (Ed.), *Gender basics* (pp. 30–38). Belmont, CA: Wadsworth.

Oliver, M. B., Jackson, R. L., Moses, N. N., & Dangerfield, C. L. (2004). The face of crime: Viewers' memory of race-related facial features of individuals pictured in the news. *Journal of Communications,* 54 (1), 88–104.

Potter, W. J. (1999). *Media violence.* Thousand Oaks, CA: Sage Publishing.

Rada, J. A. (2000). A new piece to the puzzle: Examining effects of television portrayals of African Americans. *Journals of Broadcasting & Electronic Media,* 44 (4), 704–715.

Ransford, H. E. (1970). Skin color, life chances, and anti-White attitudes. *Social Problems,* 18 (2), 164–179.

Ross, L. E. (1997). Mate selection preferences among African American college students. *Journal of Black Studies,* 27 (4), 554–569.

Seltzer, R., & Smith, R. C. (1991). Color differences in the Afro-American community and the differences they make. *Journal of Black Studies,* 21 (3), 279–286.

Shorter-Gooden, K., & Jones, C. (2003). *Shifting: The double lives of Black women in America.* New York: Harper Collins.

Smith, T. (1991). Ethnic images in the United States. *The Polling Report,* 7, 1–5.

Terpstra, D. E., & Kethley, R. B. (2002). Organizations' relative degree of exposure to selection discrimination litigation. *Public Personnel Management,* 31 (3), 277–292.

Thompson, M. S., & Keith, V. M. (2001). The blacker the berry—gender, skin tone, self-esteem, and self-efficacy. *Gender & Society,* 15 (3), 336–357.

Udry, J. R., Bauman, K. E., & Chase, C. (1971). Skin color, status, and mate selection. *The American Journal of Sociology,* 76 (4), 722–733.

Umberson, D., & Hughes, M. (1987). The impact of physical attractiveness on achievement and psychological well-being. *Social Psychology Quarterly*, 50 (3), 227–236.

Webster Jr., M., & Driskel Jr., J. E. (1983). Beauty as status. *The American Journal of Sociology,* 89 (1), 140–165.

Williams, A. (2002). Colorism. *New York Amsterdam News*, 31 January-6 February 2002.

Chapter 4
The Cost of Color: What We Pay for Being Black and Brown

Margaret Hunter

Abstract Most White Americans believe that racism is on the wane, and that any talk about racial discrimination does more harm than good. This phenomenon is referred to by many social scientists as colorblind racism. Among people of color, colorism, like racism, consists of both overt and covert actions, outright acts of discrimination and subtle cues of disfavor. Darker skin color is associated with more race-conscious views and higher levels of perceived discrimination. A rising number of discrimination cases based on skin tone have found their way to the courts. It is tempting to characterize the problem of colorism as equally difficult for both light-skinned people and dark. Dark-skinned people lack the social and economic capital that light skin provides, and are therefore disadvantaged in education, employment, and housing. Additionally, dark skin is generally not regarded as beautiful, so dark-skinned women often lose out in the dating and marriage markets. On the other side, light-skinned men and women are typically not regarded as legitimate members of the African American or Mexican American communities. Only a slow dismantling of the larger system of White racism, in the U.S. and around the globe, will initiate a change in the color hierarchy it has created.

Introduction

There are many reasons not to talk about colorism. Most White Americans believe that racism is on the wane, and that any talk about racial discrimination does more harm than good (Bonilla-Silva 1999). This phenomenon is referred to by many social scientists as colorblind racism. Colorblind racism makes racism invisible while actively perpetuating it. But White Americans aren't the only ones who don't want to talk about colorism. Many African Americans feel that discussions of colorism "air our dirty laundry" for all to see and judge. Or even worse, talking about colorism distracts from the larger and more

M. Hunter
Department of Sociology, Mills College, Oakland, CA, USA
e-mail: mhunter@mills.edu

R.E. Hall (ed.), *Racism in the 21st Century*, DOI: 10.1007/978-0-387-79097-8_4,
© Springer Science+Business Media, LLC 2008

significant problem of racism in the U.S. Many Latinos resist discussions of colorism because they argue that racial discrimination is an American problem, not a Mexican/Puerto Rican/Cuban problem. Latinos come in all colors, they argue. Most people of color agree that colorism is an "in house" issue, a personal one that is a tragedy within communities of color. It is at minimum, embarrassing, and, at its worst, a sign of racial self-hatred.

Despite the many reasons for remaining silent on this topic, this chapter, like the others in this volume, will pull back the curtains on the "hidden" issue of skin-color bias and let the light shine in. The national discourse of colorblindness is strangling our collective voice on racism. We need to challenge the colorblind discourse that obfuscates the pervasiveness of racial inequality and revive a race-conscious, change-oriented national discussion. When acclaimed filmmaker Spike Lee (1988) wrote and directed *School Daze*, which dealt with issues of skin color and Black identity on a historically Black college campus, he was met with both praise and contempt. Many thanked him for exposing the issue of colorism and sparking a larger public discussion of its divisiveness in the Black community. Others openly criticized him for "putting our business out on the street." Some people were ashamed to admit that internalized racism remains a problem for Black America. Does colorism distract the public from the more important issue of racial discrimination? Absolutely not. Colorism is yet one more manifestation of a larger "racial project" that communicates meaning and status about race in the United States (Omi & Winant 1994). Studies on skin color stratification support the contention that racial discrimination is alive and well, and so insidious that communities of color themselves are divided into quasi-racial hierarchies. Without a larger system of institutional racism, colorism based on skin tone would not exist. Hopefully, by pulling on the thread of colorism, we will begin to unravel the heavy cloak of racism.

Even the federal government is becoming increasingly concerned with color-based discrimination. Discrimination complaints based on skin tone are on the rise, according to the Equal Employment Opportunity Commission (EEOC). In the early 1990 s, the EEOC typically received less than 500 complaints of color-bias per year. By 2002, the number had nearly tripled to 1,400 complaints of color-bias (Valbrun 2003). This explosion may be related to increasing cases of discrimination, and it may also be evidence of increasing awareness that color-based discrimination is legally actionable.

A rising number of discrimination cases based on skin tone have found their way to the courts. In 2002, the EEOC sued the owners of a Mexican restaurant in San Antonio, Texas, for color-based discrimination. A White manager at the restaurant claimed that the owners directed him to hire only light-skinned staff to work in the dining room. The EEOC won the case and the restaurant was forced to pay $100,000 in fines (Valbrun 2003). In 2003, a dark-skinned African American won $40,000 from a national restaurant chain for color-based discrimination from a fellow Black employee. The plaintiff argued that he suffered constant taunting and color-based epithets about his dark skin from lighter-skinned African American co-workers (Valbrun 2003). These are just two examples of how colorism affects people of color on a daily basis. Most people of color will not end up in court over color bias, but nearly all people of color have experienced or witnessed unfair treatment or verbal denigration of people because of their skin tone. Although both of these cases highlight co-ethnic perpetrators of skin tone bias, Whites are also engaged in discrimination by skin tone. Sociologists Verna Keith and Cedric Herring, in their path-breaking work on colorism, suggest that, "differential treatment (i.e. greater discrimination against darker Blacks) by Whites as well as by other Blacks continues to occur within this era" (1991, p. 775).

Critics have asked, But what about the Black is Beautiful movement and the Brown Pride movement of the 1960 s and 1970 s? The protest movements of that time created important cultural revolutions that inverted the racist norms of White beauty and celebrated brown skin, African and Indian features, and natural hair. African Americans and Mexican Americans created new language, ("Black" and "Chicano"), new organizations (Black Panthers and Brown Berets), and new aesthetics (black and brown skin) as they imagined a new racial reality in the United States. These movements were significant and were part of the larger struggle for political and economic rights of the times. It was common to hear young Chicanos referring to "Aztec Goddesses" and young Blacks to "Nubian Princesses." But this burgeoning aesthetic, though influential, did not create a substantial, permanent change in American culture. Blacks and Chicanos will forever be imprinted with the proud messages of those days, but many of those values have become more talk than reality as skin-bleaching creams continue to be used and facial cosmetic surgery is on the rise in many communities of color.

Colorism is more than a series of anecdotes in a community's collective memory. And it is more than feeling "less pretty" than the parade of light-skinned models gracing magazine covers and television shows. Although most people of color, dark or light, can think of a time when they felt excluded in a social situation because of their skin color, skin color is not an equal opportunity discriminator. In fact, on all major socioeconomic indicators, such as income, occupation, education, and housing, dark-skinned Blacks and Latinos (and increasingly Asians) pay a steep price for their skin tone. When measuring money and resources, light-skinned people of color are consistently advantaged.

How does skin tone discrimination operate? Systems of racial discrimination operate on at least two levels: race and color. The first system of discrimination is the level of racial category, (i.e. Black, Asian, Latino, etc.). Regardless pf physical appearance, African Americans of all skin tones are subject to certain kinds of discrimination, denigration, and second-class citizenship. The second system of discrimination is at the level of skin tone, darker skin or lighter skin. Although all Blacks experience discrimination as Blacks, the intensity of that discrimination, the frequency, and the outcomes of that discrimination will differ dramatically by skin tone. These two systems of discrimination (by race and by color) work in concert. These two systems are distinct, but inextricably connected. A light-skinned Mexican American may still experience racism, despite the light skin, and a dark-skinned Mexican American may experience racism and colorism simultaneously.

Employment

The vast majority of social science research on skin tone discrimination focuses on the employment experiences of African Americans and Latinos. Latinos are a particularly interesting case to study because social scientists typically treat "Latino" or "Hispanic" as a separate category from race. Consequently, there are Latinos who identify as White, Black, Indian, and" other." There are strong variations by national group as to which of those options Latinos choose (Mexicans are most likely to choose "other race" and Cubans are most likely to choose "White," for instance). Some researchers use the racial self-designations of Latinos as proxies for skin color when an actual skin tone variable is not available.

In 2003, the Lewis Mumford Center for Comparative Urban and Regional Research studied the effects of "race" in the lives of Latinos in the United States. They found that Latinos who identified as White earned about $5000 more per year than Latinos who identified as Black, and about $2500 more per year than Latinos who identified as "some other race." A clear hierarchy is evident among Latinos with Whites at the top, "others" in the middle, and Black Latinos at the bottom. White Latinos also had lower unemployment rates and lower poverty rates than Black Latinos (Fears 2003). Racial designation is not a perfect measure of skin tone, but, in the absence of other data, these researchers suggest that we can use racial label as a proxy for skin tone. Their findings are consistent with other work in this area. Dark skin costs for Latinos, in terms of income, employment, and poverty status.

Other social scientists found that lighter-skinned Mexican Americans and African Americans earn more money than their darker-skinned counterparts (Arce et al. 1987, Allen et al. 2000). Even when researchers account for differences in family background, occupation, and education levels, skin color differences persist. This shows that skin-color stratification cannot be explained away with other variables such as class or family history. In addition to being a historical system, color bias is also a contemporary system that can result in differences of thousands of dollars in yearly income for darker and lighter people who are otherwise similar. Most darker-skinned people would not willingly give up thousands of dollars in income every year, and most light-skinned people would not want to admit that a part of their income may be attributed to skin-color status and not merit. V. Keith and C. Herring (1991) suggest that color discrimination operates after the Civil Rights movement much the way it did before the movement. "Virtually all of our findings parallel those that occurred before the civil rights movement. These facts suggest that the effects of skin tone are not only historical curiosities from a legacy of slavery and racism, but present-day mechanisms that influence who gets what in America" (p. 777).

It can be difficult to imagine how colorism operates on a day-to-day basis. Colorism, like racism, consists of both overt and covert actions, outright acts of discrimination and subtle cues of disfavor. In employment, negotiations over salary and benefits may be tainted by colorism. How much a new employee is "worth" and the assessed value of skills may be affected by appearance. We know from research on physical attractiveness that people who are considered more attractive are also viewed as smarter and friendlier. "Attractiveness" is a cultural construct influenced by racial aesthetics among other things, so lighter-skinned job applicants will likely benefit from the halo effect of physical attractiveness.

The relationship between skin color and perceptions of attractiveness may be particularly important for women of the job. Many feminist scholars have argued that "beauty" matters for women in much the same way that "brains" matter for men. Of course, women's job-related skills are crucial for a successful career, but cultural critic Naomi Wolf (1991) has suggested that "beauty" has become an additional, unspoken job requirement for women in many profes-sions, even when physical attractiveness is irrelevant for job performance. If this is the case, then in "front-office appearance jobs," like restaurant hostess or office receptionist, beauty, and therefore skin color must matter even more. This helps explain why one of the few cases of color-based discrimination fought and won by the EEOC, as discussed in the beginning of this chapter, were based on a restaurant's policy of hiring only light-skinned waitstaff.

There are many facets to fair employment, from hiring, to wages, and even the status of the job itself, often referred to as occupational prestige. Long a favorite variable of sociologists, occupational prestige measures the status or esteem of an occupation. This paints a fuller picture of inequality because there are many jobs that don't have very high salaries, but have high levels of prestige, like clergy or college professors. In 2002, Rodolfo Espino and Michael Franz compared the employment experiences of Mexicans, Puerto Ricans, and Cubans in the United States. They found, "that darker-skinned Mexicans and Cubans face significantly lower occupational prestige scores than their lighter-skinned counterparts even when controlling for factors that influence performance in the labor market," (2002, p. 612). Dark-skinned Puerto Ricans did not face this disadvantage in the labor market. This means that lighter-skinned Mexicans and Cubans have a better chance at attaining a high status occupation than their darker counterparts who are similar in other ways. Skin tone, yet again, provides the light-skinned with advantages and the dark-skinned with penalties.

In this same vein, Mark Hill (2000), in his study of African American men, found that light-skinned Black men retained a significant advantage in the labor market and that skin tone accounted for more differences in social status than did family background. Hill developed a very creative methodology of linking death certificates in the 1980 s to childhood Census forms in the 1920 s. This allowed him to examine parent's race and color as uniquely measured by the "mulatto" category in the 1920 Census. His longitudinal approach clarified the ongoing nature of skin-color bias and challenged the oft-made assertion that light-skin benefits are remnants of an old color-caste system. Research definitely shows that skin tone matters in employment. It stratifies the labor force in all major areas of work: income, unemployment rate, poverty status, and occupational prestige.

Education

It is clear how skin tone matters in the work world, but how about in schools? Do teachers respond more favorably to light-skinned students or do schools operate in a meritocratic fashion with regard to color? Unfortunately, our schools are not immune to the status differences of skin tone. Education levels across the United States also reflect significant differences according to skin color for African Americans and Latinos. In fact, in their groundbreaking study, B. Hughes and M. Hertel (1990) found that the difference in education between Whites and Blacks was nearly identical to the differences in education between light-skinned Blacks and dark-skinned Blacks. From this finding they suggest that colorism plays as significant a role in the lives of African Americans as race does. This finding has been replicated in several different studies with the same and different data sets.

The skin color effect on education has also been shown for Mexican Americans. Murguia and Telles (1996) demonstrated that lighter-skinned Mexican Americans complete more years of schooling than darker-skinned Mexican Americans, even when their family backgrounds are similar. This is a particularly important finding in relation to the steady stream of immigration from Mexico. New immigrants who come here face not only racial/ethnic discrimination but also discrimination by phenotype or skin color. Arce et al. (1987) even included a variable on facial features in their analysis of skin color and education. They found that dark skin color coupled with Indian facial features (as opposed to Anglo) produced a significant depression of educational attainment.

How does skin-color stratification operate in schools? Skin-color hierarchies reflect deeply held cultural beliefs about civility, modernity, sophistication, backwardness, beauty, and virtue. In Western culture, light skin and European facial features have been equated with the positive characteristics mentioned above. In English and in Spanish, the term "fair" or "la güera" means both "light" and "pretty." The conflation of these meanings is just one example of a deeply held cultural value that European or White bodies are superior to others. This gets translated in the classroom in particular ways. Teachers may expect light-skinned students of color to be prettier, smarter, and better-behaved than their darker classmates. Teachers and principals may respond more positively to light-skinned or White parents of children in their classrooms. School counselors may encourage light-skinned students of color to go to college more often than they encourage darker-skinned students of similar academic record. Students in the classroom also express these cultural values. Students of color often valorize their lighter-skinned peers in terms of beauty, brains, and social status, even if they also shun them in terms of ethnic authenticity. There are many ways that skin-color bias may operate in schools, but the bottomline is that light kids benefit and dark kids pay the price.

Housing

In their groundbreaking book, *Black Wealth White Wealth*, Melvin Oliver and Thomas Shapiro argue that home ownership is the major source of wealth for most Americans. The historical, racial gap in home ownership accounts for a significant difference in accumulated wealth between Blacks and Whites. The income gap between Blacks and Whites remains large, but the wealth gap is enormous. As is true with other indicators of socioeconomic status like occupation and education, a color gap persists in housing as well.

Darker-skinned African Americans are more likely to live in racially segregated neighborhoods than light-skinned African Americans. This is a real disadvantage in terms of wealth because racially segregated neighborhoods tend to have depressed home values and therefore do not generate as large a source of wealth as a similar house in a racially mixed or predominantly White neighborhood. Light-skinned or White Latinos have clear and significant advantages in income and wealth relative to their darker or Black-identified counterparts. Richard Alba, John Logan, and Brian Stults, reported, "Hispanics who describe themselves as Black are in substantially poorer and less White neighborhoods than their compatriots who describe themselves as White. The penalty they absorb in neighborhood affluence varies between $3500 and $6000 and thus places them in neighborhoods comparable to those occupied by African Americans (2000). Alba, Logan, and Stults' study of immigrant adaptation and spatial-assimilation theory reveals that despite their immigrant status and identity as Latinos, Black Latinos' housing experience more closely resembles that of native-born African Americans than that of other Latinos. That is, Black Latinos live in more racially segregated neighborhoods with less exposure to non-Hispanic Whites and lower property values. This not only socially isolates but also stunts the opportunity for accumulation of wealth through home ownership.

Spousal Status

It is clear that employment, education, and housing all provide material resources that constitute some form of economic capital. Social ties can also lead to capital, and one of the most important is one's spouse. We know that light-skinned African Americans and Mexican Americans are not more likely to be married than their darker-skinned counterparts. But when we ask the question, "Do light-skinned people marry higher status spouses?, the answer is yes. Study after study has shown that light skin, particularly for African Americans, provides an advantage in the marriage market that results in spouses with higher levels of education and higher incomes than the spouses of darker-skinned African Americans. This finding holds especially true for women.

Udry, Baumann, and Chase (1971) found that light-skinned African American women were more likely to marry high status men than darker-skinned women. Skin tone had a much more muted effect on men's marriage market success than women's. In later work, researchers used "family income" as a proxy for spousal status (Keith & Herring 1991). They found that light-skinned people had higher family incomes than darker-skinned people. Others found that lighter-skinned people married spouses with higher occupational status than did darker-skinned people (Hughes & Hertel 1990). Measured in a variety of ways, the marriage market clearly favors light-skinned African Americans, rewarding them with higher status spouses.

This phenomenon allows light-skinned people to "marry up" and essentially exchange the high status of their skin tone for the high status of education, income, or occupation in their spouse. In fact, this effect was so strong among African American women, that when a very dark-brown woman and a very light-brown woman who are similar in background characteristics choose their marital partners, the very light-brown woman will likely marry a man with an entire year of more education than the very dark-brown woman. This finding suggests that light skin is a valuable commodity for women, allowing them greater access to high status, well-educated spouses (Hunter 2002).

Identity

The economic and social advantages of light skin are clear. In societies where resources are divided by race and color, light-skinned people get a disproportionate amount of the benefits. However, there is a notable cost to light skin, and that is ethnic authenticity. The task of "proving" oneself to be a legitimate or authentic member of an ethnic community is a significant burden for the light-skinned in Latino, African American, and Asian American communities. For many people of color, authenticity is the vehicle through which darker-skinned people take back their power from lighter-skinned people. Darker-skinned people, especially women, often feel put down by the light-skinned. One common way they regain their sense of power and pride is to accuse light-skinned Blacks of not being "Black enough" or light-skinned Chicanos as not being "Chicano enough." This tactic has particular power against those lighter-skinned people who are from racially mixed backgrounds. Not being Black enough, or authentically ethnic enough, in any ethnic community, is a serious insult to many. It implies that they do not identify with their fellow co-ethnics, that they do not care about them, that they think they are better than their co-ethnics, or in extreme cases, that they wish they were White.

Darker skin color is also associated with more race-conscious views and higher levels of perceived discrimination. Among Latinos, skin color is also closely associated with language, where dark skin and Spanish language ability are key identifiers of Chicano identity. Conversely, light skin and "English only" skills are typically identified with Anglo assimilation and thus devalued in many Mexican American communities. Herein lies the contradiction: on one hand, dark skin is associated with being Indian or African and therefore backward and ugly, low status. On the other hand, dark skin is evidence of being Indian or African and therefore, of being truly or authentically Mexican or Black (Hunter 2005). The contradiction between dark skin color as low status and dark skin color as authentically ethnic is true in many communities and is an ongoing source of tension.

The complex relationship between skin color and race consciousness is not a new phenomenon. Although it is true that survey research reveals weaker ethnic identities and weaker group ties among light-skinned and upper-class Black people, it is also true that many influential African American leaders have been light-skinned (Bowman et al. 2004). Two of the most influential and long-standing presidents of the NAACP were extremely light-skinned: W.E.B. Du Bois and Walter White. Julian Bond, Adam Clayton Powell, Malcolm X, and other leaders have also been light-skinned. In fact, it was so common for Black leaders to be light-skinned, that Marcus Garvey's popularity was believed to be due, in part, to his dark skin color. Garvey (1887–1940) was a powerful orator and organizer of Black economic self-sufficiency. His message of Black pride resonated deeply with people of African descent around the globe.

One of the reasons that so many African American civil rights leaders have been light-skinned is because of the history of colorism in Black organizations. Many elite Black organizations have had color tests that potential members had to pass for membership. The most infamous of these tests was the brown bag test. This test required that a person's skin color be lighter than a brown paper bag for entrance. Many Black fraternities and sororities were notorious for admitting only light-skinned people; this is still true for some today. Even some Black churches that had upper-class congregants would discourage dark-skinned worshippers from attending services there. This kind of color-based gatekeeping in elite organizations gave light-skinned people a distinct advantage in terms of education and social networks (Graham 2000). Despite larger trends of dark-skinned people with higher levels of commitment to their communities, the history of Black civil rights leaders includes a disproportionate number of light-skinned men and women.

It is tempting to characterize the problem of colorism as equally difficult for both light-skinned people and dark. Dark-skinned people lack the social and economic capital that light skin provides, and are therefore disadvantaged in education, employment, and housing. Additionally, dark skin is generally not regarded as beautiful, so dark-skinned women often lose out in the dating and marriage markets. On the other side, light-skinned men and women are typically not regarded as legitimate members of the African American or Mexican American communities. They may be excluded from or made to feel unwelcome in community events and organizations. At first glance, it may seem that there are equal advantages and disadvantages to both sides of the color line. Upon closer examination, this proves to be untrue. Although exclusion from some community organizations may be uncomfortable psychologically or emotionally for light-skinned people of color, it rarely has significant material effects. More specifically, emotional turmoil about ethnic identity does not have significant economic consequences. However, the systematic discrimination against dark-skinned people of color in the labor market, educational institutions, and marriage market create marked economic disadvantages. Without minimizing the psychological trauma of exclusion from ethnic communities, it is important to clarify that the disadvantages of dark skin still far outweigh the disadvantages of light.

When compared in this way, it is not simply a case of "the grass is always greener on the other side." Although there are downsides to both ends of the color spectrum, the penalties are more common and more severe for dark skin than for light. This is evidenced by the following observation from interviews with Mexican American and African American women. Nearly all of the dark-skinned women wanted to be lighter at some time in their lives in order to accrue some of the privileges of light skin. In contrast, despite the painful stories of exclusion from many light-skinned women, none reported ever wanting to be darker-skinned (Hunter 2005). This significant difference points to the enduring and substantial privilege of light skin.

Exporting the Color Complex

Globalization, multinational media conglomerates, and the new restructured world economy all work together to export U.S. cultural products and cultural imperialism. Part of this structure of domination is the exportation of cultural images, including images of race. The United States exports images of the good life of White beauty, White affluence, White heroes, and brown and Black entertainers and criminals. As many people in other countries yearn for the "good life" offered in the United States, they also yearn for the aesthetics of the United States: light skin, blonde hair, and Anglo facial features. American cultural imperialism explains why women in Korea, surrounded by other Koreans, pay high sums of money to have eyelid surgery that Westernizes their eyes. American cultural imperialism explains why women in Saudi Arabia, Tanzania, and Brazil are using toxic, skin-bleaching creams to try and achieve a lighter complexion. American cultural imperialism explains why one of the most common high school graduation presents among the elite in Mexico

City is a nose job with the plastic surgeon. And, though all of these choices sound extreme or even crazy at first glance, they all actually are quite rational in the context of global racism and U.S. domination. Unfortunately, new eyelids, lighter skin, and new noses are likely to offer their owners better opportunities in a global marketplace.

The new global racism transcends national borders and infiltrates cultures and families all over the world. It draws on historic ideologies of colonialism and internalized racism buttressed with visions of a new world order. Critical pedagogist, Zeus Leonardo argues that under global racism, "Whiteness stamps its claims to superiority, both morally and aesthetically speaking, on its infan-tilized Other...." (2002). Images associated with White America are highly valued and emulated in the global marketplace. This is part of what makes colorism and racism so hard to battle: the images supporting these systems are everywhere and the rewards for Whiteness are real. Ronald Hall (1994, 1995) suggests that the "Bleaching Syndrome," the internalization of a White aes-thetic ideal, is the result of this barrage of racial images and a historic backdrop of slavery and colonialism. Many people of color, like Whites, come to believe that European features and light or White skin is most beautiful.

Women and men of color have ever increasing opportunities to alter their bodies toward Whiteness. They can purchase lighter-colored contact lenses for their eyes; they can straighten kinky or curly hair; they can have cosmetic surgeries on their lips, noses, or eyes. But one of the oldest traditions of this sort is skin bleaching. There are lots of "old wives tales" recipes for skin bleaching, including baking soda, bleach, toothpaste, or even lye. In the United States, overt skin bleaching with the stated intention of whitening one's skin fell out of favor in many communities after the Civil Rights movements and cultural pride movements of the 1960 s and 1970 s. However, outside of the United States and in many post-colonial nations of the Global South, skin bleaching is reaching new heights.

Skin bleaching creams go by many names: skin lighteners, skin whiteners, skin toning creams, skin evening creams, skin fading gels, and so forth. Essen-tially, they are creams regularly applied to the face or body that purport to lighten or "brighten" the skin. They are marketed as simply another beauty product available to women to increase their beauty, their Whiteness, and therefore, their status. The skin bleaching industry is thriving around the globe, particularly in Third World, post-colonial countries. Skin lighteners are commonly used in places including Mexico, Pakistan, Saudi Arabia, Jamaica, Philippines, Japan, India, Tanzania, Nigeria, Uganda, Kenya, Ghana, and less so but also the United States. These products are everywhere and easy to get. A cursory glance on the website Amazon.com shows that when a consumer searches for "skin lighteners," a list will appear, showing "The most popular items in Skin Lighteners. Updated hourly." The average 40-gram item costs $40.

In many countries previously colonized by Europe, there is still an overt legacy of Eurocentrism and White racism in the culture. Whites or a light-skinned elite typically hold powerful positions in the economy, government, and educational sectors. Embedded in the leftover colonial structure is a strong value of White aesthetics (light hair, straight hair, light eyes, narrow noses, light skin, etc.) This is evident in Latin American popular culture for instance by looking at the stars of the *telenovelas* (soap operas in a miniseries format), almost all of whom look extremely White, unless they are the maids and are then light brown. Movie stars and popular singers in the Philippines are often mestizos, half White, or extremely light-skinned with round eyes. Africans in Ghana still define light-skinned women as more beautiful than dark.

In addition to wrestling with the values of their colonial pasts, many Third World nations are also contending with the onslaught of U.S. produced cultural images valorizing Whiteness and especially White femininity (and the occasional version of light-brown femininity). Television, film, Internet, and print ads all feature White women with blonde hair as not only the cultural ideal but the cultural imperative. White and light-skinned people are rewarded accordingly.

The brown-skinned people of these post-colonial nations are responding to this reality. Skin bleaching seems like one of the few ways to get a piece of the pie in a highly racialized society. This is a multi-billion dollar-a-year industry. Many skin-bleaching products are made outside of North America and Europe, in Mexico and Nigeria, but often under the auspices of larger U.S. and European cosmetics firms. The products may not be made here, but women in the U.S. still use them.

In fact, the pursuit of light skin color can be so important, it can prove fatal. A Harvard medical school researcher found outbreaks of mercury poisoning in countries such as Saudi Arabia, Pakistan, and Tanzania. He came to learn that the mercury poisoning, found almost exclusively in women, was caused by the widespread use of skinbleaching creams containing toxic levels of mercury (Counter 2003). Even children were suffering the effects of mercury poisoning, either from in-utero absorption during pregnancy, or from mothers who put the bleaching cream on their children, eager for them to have the benefits of light skin. These stories may seem to be only far away, but they also happen in the United States. The same team of Harvard researchers found outbreaks of mercury poisoning in the Southwestern U.S., where thousands of Mexican American women use skin bleaching creams to try to achieve a lighter and more valued complexion.

Skin bleaching products usually contain one of three harmful ingredients: mercury, hydroquinone, or cortico-steroids (sometimes used in combination). Some women also use these "beauty creams" on their children or on themselves while they are pregnant or breastfeeding. This causes significant harm to the children because their neurological systems are still developing. I say this not to demonize the women, because many are not aware of the extreme risks involved in these products, but to show how strong the imperative for Whiteness is, particularly in the Global South. In Latin America, Africa, and many parts of Asia, Whiteness is such an important commodity that many women overlook what they perceive to be minor risks in order to attain for themselves or their children the benefits of light skin.

People in the United States have a dual culpability with regard to colorism. As producers of powerful and denigrating images of race, we have a responsibility to change the kinds of images we export. We cannot continue to blindly endorse a "White is right" cultural agenda around the globe and then sit idly, while, people desperate for a piece of the global economic pie, poison themselves trying to attain it. In addition, we are also consumers of these images and they are hurting our communities here in the United States, too. Consumers can use their purchasing power to demonstrate approval or disapproval of various products and ad campaigns that communicate enduring messages about race and human worth.

Skin color continues to shape our lives in powerful ways in the United States and around the globe. The cultural messages that give meaning and value to different skin tones are both deeply historical and actively contemporary. People of color with dark skin tones continue to pay a price for their color, and the light-skinned continue to benefit from their association with a White aesthetic. Only a slow dismantling of the larger system of White racism, in the U.S. and around the globe, will initiate a change in the color hierarchy it has created.

References

Alba, R., Logan, J., & Stults, B. (2000). The changing neighborhood contexts of the immigrant metropolis. *Social Forces*, 79(2), 587–621.

Allen, W., Telles, E., & Hunter, M. (2000). Skin color, income, and education: A comparison of African Americans and Mexican Americans. *National Journal of Sociology*, 12(1), 129–180.

Arce, C., Murguia, E., & Frisbie, P. (1987). Phenotype and life chances among Chicanos. *Hispanic Journal of Behavioral Sciences*, 9, 19–32.

Bonilla-Silva, E. (1999). *Racism and White supremacy in the post-civil rights era*. New York: Lynne Reiner Publishers.

Bowman, P., Muhammad, R., & Ifatunji, M. (2004). Skin tone, class, and racial attitudes among African Americans. In C. Herring, V.M. Keith, and H. D. Horton (Eds.), *Skin deep: How race and complexion matter in the "color-blind" era*. Urbana, IL: University of Illinois Press.

Counter, S. A. (2003). Whitening skin can be deadly. *Boston Globe*, 16 December 2003.

Espino, R., and Franz, M. Latino phenotypic discrimination revisited: The impact of skin color on occupational status. *Social Science Quarterly*, 83(2).

Fears, D. (2003). Race divides Hispanics, report says; Integration and income vary with skin color. *Washington Post*, 14 July 2003.

Graham, L. (2000). *Our kind of people: Inside America's Black upper class*. New York: Perennial.

Hall, R. (1994). The bleaching syndrome: Implications of light skin for Hispanic American assimilation. *Hispanic Journal of Behavioral Sciences*, 16(3), 307–314.

———. (1995). The bleaching syndrome: African Americans' response to cultural domination vis-à-vis skin color. *Journal of Black Studies*, 26(2), 172–184.

Hill, M. (2000). Color differences in the socioeconomic status of African American men: Results of a longitudinal study. *Social Forces*, 78(4), 1437–1460.

Hughes, B., & Hertel, M. (1990). The significance of color remains: A study of life chances, mate selection, and ethnic consciousness among Black Americans. *Social Forces*, 68(4), 1105–20.

Hunter, M. (2002). "If you're light, you're alright": Light skin color as social capital for women of color. *Gender & Society*, 16(2), 175–193.

———. (2005). *Race, gender, and the politics of skin tone*. New York: Routledge.

Keith, V., & Herring, C. (1991). Skin tone and stratification in the Black community. *American Journal of Sociology*, 97(3), 760–778.

Lee, S. (1988) *School daze* [film]. 40 Acres & A Mule Filmworks.

Leonardo, Z. (2002). The souls of White folk: Critical pedagogy, Whiteness studies, and globalization discourse. *Race Ethnicity, and Education*, 5(1), 29–50.

Murguia, E., & Telles, E. (1996). Phenotype and schooling among Mexican Americans. *Sociology of Education*, 69, 276–289.

Oliver, M., & Shapiro, T. (1995). *Black wealth, White wealth*. New York: Russell Sage.

Omi, M., & Winant, H. (1994). *Racial formation in the United States*. New York: Routledge.

Udry, R., Baumann, K., & Chase, C. (1971). Skin color, status, and mate selection. *American Journal of Sociology*, 76(4), 722–33.

Valbrun, M. (2003). EEOC sees rise in intrarace complaints of color bias. *Wall Street Journal*. 7 August 2003.

Wolf, N. (1991). *The beauty myth: How images of beauty are used against women*. New York: Doubleday Books.

Chapter 5
Skin Color, Immigrant Wages, and Discrimination

Joni Hersch

Abstract Immigrant workers with darker skin color have lower pay than their counterparts with lighter skin color. Whether this pay penalty is due to labor market discrimination is explored using data from the New Immigrant Survey 2003 to estimate wage equations that control for skin color, sequentially taking into account a series of individual characteristics related to labor market productivity and personal background. These characteristics include Hispanic ethnicity, race, country of birth, education, family background, occupation in source country, English language proficiency, visa status, employer characteristics, and current occupation. The analysis finds that the labor market penalty to darker skin color cannot be attributed to differences in productivity and is evidence of labor market discrimination that arises within the U.S. labor market. The largest groups of post-1965 immigrants – those from Asia and Latin America – are penalized in the U.S. labor market for their darker skin color.

Introduction

Hispanics and African Americans in the U.S. earn less than whites with comparable observable characteristics. There is also evidence that the effects of Hispanic ethnicity and African American race differ by skin color, with darker skin tone associated with inferior economic outcomes. My earlier work (Hersch 2008) presents strong evidence that immigrants with darker skin color earn less than their counterparts with lighter skin color, controlling for extensive individual and labor market characteristics, as well as for Hispanic ethnicity, race, and country of birth. The findings indicate that discrimination on the basis of skin color is the most likely cause of the wage penalty experienced by immigrants with darker skin color.

In this chapter, I expand on my earlier analysis by considering the contribution of specific individual and labor market characteristics to the observed

J. Hersch
Law School, Vanderbilt University, Nashville, TN, USA
e-mail: joni.hersch@vanderbilt.edu

R.E. Hall (ed.), *Racism in the 21st Century*, DOI: 10.1007/978-0-387-79097-8_5, 77
© Springer Science+Business Media, LLC 2008

penalty to darker skin color among immigrants. As in Hersch (2008), I use data
from the New Immigrant Survey 2003, or NIS-2003 ([NIS]). This survey reports
skin color on a uniquely detailed scale for a large sample of new lawful
immigrants to the U.S. The NIS-2003 is described in the following section,
and the results from alternative specifications of wage regressions are presented
in "Wage Equation Estimates".

Drawing on the findings presented in "Wage Equation Estimates" that are
consistent with the presence of skin color discrimination among immigrants, in
"What Skin Color Can Tell Us About Discrimination" I discuss how we can use
this evidence to understand the importance of discrimination in explaining the
persistent ethnic and racial gap in pay in the United States. The usual method
for identifying discrimination in employment against groups of workers is to
estimate wage regression equations, controlling for productivity-related characteristics. But because inferring discrimination from wage regressions leaves
open the possibility that any estimated pay disparity between groups is actually
caused by omitted productivity characteristics, evidence on the existence of
discrimination derived from wage regressions is not conclusive. The analysis
below controls for an extensive set of explanatory variables that will account for
most of the productivity-related factors that determine wages. As I discuss in
"What Skin Color Can Tell Us About Discrimination", the negative effect on
wages of darker skin color is highly unlikely to be due to productivity differences. Thus, evidence of a negative effect of gradations of skin color on wages
among immigrants provides strong evidence of discrimination.

I conclude with a discussion of the prospects for assimilation of immigrants
into the U.S. labor market.

The New Immigrant Survey 2003

The New Immigrant Survey 2003 is a nationally representative sample of 8,573
immigrants admitted to lawful permanent residence status in the U.S. during
the period May to November 2003.[1] The sample is drawn from the electronic
records compiled by the U.S. government. The sampling design comprised four
strata: spouses of U.S. citizens, employment-visa principals, diversity-visa
principals, and all other visa types. Those with other visa types include non-
spousal family members of U.S. citizens, accompanying spouses of those with
employment or diversity visas, refugees or asylees and accompanying spouses,
and those who achieve lawful permanent residence status through legalization.
The NIS sampling frame undersamples spouses of U.S. citizens and oversam-
ples employment-visa principals and diversity-visa principals. In all statistical

---

[1] For more information, see Jasso, Massey, Rosenzweig, and Smith (forthcoming) and the
survey overview available at http://nis.princeton.edu/overview.html. The data and documentation are available at http://nis.princeton.edu.

analyses, I use sample weights adjusted for the sample design as well as for differences in response by strata. Respondents and spouses provide information on a wide range of topics, including health measures, pre-immigration history, family members, income, assets, transfer payments, insurance, religion, language skills, and labor market information.

Respondents report whether they are Hispanic or Latino and are also asked to report race, choosing from the categories American Indian or Alaskan Native, Asian, Black, Native Hawaiian or Other Pacific Islander, and White. Respondents are not required to select a racial category and have the option of selecting multiple racial categories, although few do so. The majority of those who do not report a racial category report that they are Hispanic or Latino.

Skin color is measured in the NIS using a scale designed by Massey and Martin (2003), which is provided in Fig. 5.1. The color scale shows a series of otherwise identical hands with skin tones that increase in darkness. Interviewers reported the number that most closely matched the respondent's skin color using an 11-point scale, where 0 represents the lightest possible skin color and 10 represents the darkest possible skin color. This scale provides a far greater level of detail than is available in other surveys, which report skin color as one of three to five categories (e.g., very light, light, medium, dark, very dark in the National Survey of Black Americans (NSBA) 1979–1980 and the 1990 Latino National Political Survey; light, medium, dark in the Multi-City Study of Urban Inequality 1992–1994.) In the NIS-2003 data set, skin color is recorded for 4,652 respondents. Those without reported skin color were interviewed entirely by telephone and so were not observed by the interviewer.

The NIS skin color measure is based on interviewer observation, which may be subject to measurement error. Interviewers may differ in how they match up individual skin color with the scale. If there is random measurement error, the estimated effect of skin color on wages will be biased toward zero and will be estimated as smaller than true. Hersch (2008) shows that the skin color values reported in the NIS-2003 for a given country closely track measures of skin color derived by reflectance spectrophotometer reported in Jablonski and Chaplin (2000) for the same country, so any measurement error is likely to be random rather than systematic. In addition, Hersch (2008) shows that the NIS scale can appropriately be treated as an interval scale. This means that the value for skin color can be entered into the regression equation in the same way we

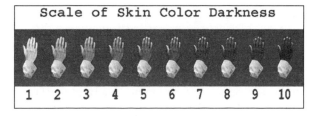

Fig. 5.1 Skin color scale (*See* Color Insert) *Source*: Douglas S. Massey and Jennifer A. Martin, (2003), The NIS Skin Color Scale.

enter years of education or age, rather than as a series of indicator variables denoting the ordinal skin color category.

Figure 5.2 presents histograms of skin color by sex and Hispanic ethnicity or race for the largest groups of immigrants represented in the sample: Hispanic, Asian, non-Hispanic black, and non-Hispanic white. The histograms show considerable variation in skin color ratings both within Hispanic or racial group as well as between groups. Women have lighter skin color on average than men. This difference by sex is consistent with objective skin color measures derived using reflectance spectrophotometer, which show that women have lighter skin than men in all indigenous populations (Jablonski 2006). As the histograms in Fig. 5.2 indicate, skin color is highly correlated with race for those who are black or white. Those who self-report their race as white tend to have the lightest skin color within the sample, while those who self-report their race as black tend to have the darkest skin color within the sample. Hispanic and Asian respondents have skin color between white and black respondents, with the reported skin color of Asians somewhat lighter than the skin color of Hispanics. Although not shown in the histograms, skin color is often correlated with country of birth because country of birth is frequently determinate of race.

The wage regressions reported in the next section are based on the same sample analyzed in Hersch (2008). Because the question of interest is the effect

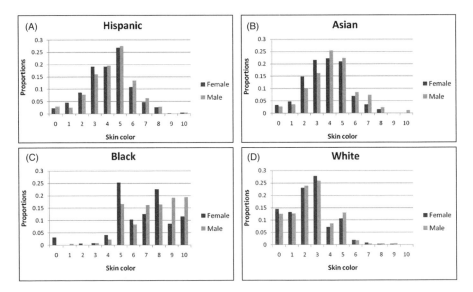

Fig. 5.2 Distribution of skin color by sex and ethnicity or race
Source: Author's calculations from the New Immigrant Survey 2003. All values weighted to account for sample design and response rates. Categories are mutually exclusive. The distribution of skin color for respondents in categories with too few respondents is not presented. These are: non-Hispanic American Indian, Non-Hispanic Hawaiian/Other Pacific Islander, non-Hispanic reporting mixed race, and those reporting neither whether Hispanic nor race.

of skin color on wages controlling for other characteristics that affect wages, the sample is restricted to those who are employed in the U.S. for pay and for whom skin color is reported. Hersch (2008) analyzes two samples: those in which individual country of birth is reported, and those in which either individual country of birth or broad country group is reported. The results presented here are based on the sample of 1,536 observations in which individual country is reported.

Table 5.1 reports sample means and standard deviations for the variables used in the wage equations, as well as the simple correlations between skin color and these variables. Most variables are typically included in wage equation

Table 5.1 Descriptive statistics and correlations with skin color[a]

	Mean (Standard Deviation) or percent	Correlation with skin color[b]
	(1)	(2)
Wage and demographic characteristics		
Skin color	4.26 (2.03)	
Hourly wage	11.83 (8.57)	−0.12**
Male	56.94	0.06*
Age	36.15 (10.13)	0.02
Inches below U.S. gender average height	3.39 (2.73)	0.14**
Inches above U.S. gender average height	2.11 (1.63)	−0.08**
Body mass index	26.13 (5.40)	0.06*
Family background and education		
Father's years of education	7.72 (5.97)	−0.15**
Childhood family income far below average	13.93	0.06*
Childhood family income below average	19.90	0.03
Childhood family income average	49.77	−0.05*
Childhood family income above average	12.37	−0.05
Childhood family income far above average	3.28	0.06*
Education in USA	1.11 (2.67)	−0.02
Education outside USA	10.63 (4.94)	−0.07**
Occupation in last job abroad		
Professional, managerial	15.81	−0.06*
Health	3.36	−0.03
Services	5.33	0.04
Sales and administrative	13.55	−0.03
Production occupation	18.60	0.03
U.S. labor market characteristics and region		
Understand English very well/well	59.47	0.03
New arrival	24.51	−0.04
Potential U.S. work experience	6.33 (6.75)	0.06*
Northeast	24.55	−0.05*
Midwest	16.65	−0.01
West	45.60	0.01
South	13.20	0.07*

Table 5.1 (continued)

	Mean (Standard Deviation) or percent	Correlation with skin color[b]
	(1)	(2)
Visa type		
Spouse of U.S. citizen	34.25	0.03
Employment visa	6.84	−0.08*
Diversity visa	3.30	−0.02
Other visa	55.60	0.02
Current job characteristics		
Tenure	2.80 (4.17)	0.09*
Government employer	3.91	0.02
Union contract	14.49	0.05
Outdoor work highly probable	3.41	0.03
Paid hourly rate	72.17	0.08*
Full-time	82.13	−0.03
Self-employed	4.94	−0.02
Current occupation		
Professional, managerial	11.28	−0.09*
Health	7.42	−0.01
Services	26.25	0.05*
Sales and administrative	17.43	−0.02
Production	37.34	0.04
Ethnicity and race		
Hispanic/Latino	60.54	0.02
American Indian/Alaska Native	3.86	0.03
Asian	18.53	−0.05
Black	7.58	0.42*
Native Hawaiian/Other Pacific Islander	0.59	−0.01
White	58.49	−0.27*
Multiple races	1.05	0.06*
Race not reported	9.90	0.10*

[a]*Source*: Author's calculations from the New Immigrant Survey 2003. All values weighted to account for sample design and response rates. Number of observations = 1536.
[b]** significant at 1%; * significant at 5% (two-sided tests).

analyses and are defined in the customary fashion (see Hersch 2008 for specific definitions). The definitions of the less common variables are as follows. New arrival immigrants acquired their immigrant documents abroad. Those who are not new arrivals are referred to as adjustee immigrants and were already in the U.S. when they reached lawful permanent residence status. Potential U.S. work experience is calculated as the difference between the date of the first job in the U.S. and the interview date. The indicator variable for whether outdoor work is highly probable is included to account for the possibility that outdoor work may both pay lower wages and cause skin color to darken. Failure to account for this possibility may spuriously indicate a negative effect on wages of darker skin color.

As indicated in Table 5.1, the average value of skin color on the 0–11 scale is 4.26. For comparison, the average values of skin color in this sample are 4.29 for Hispanic workers, 4.07 for Asian workers, 7.29 for non-Hispanic black workers, and 2.59 for non-Hispanic white workers.

Of particular interest in Table 5.1 are the simple correlations between skin color and the variables reported in column 2. Although the correlations of skin color with several of the variables are statistically significant, most of the correlations are small in magnitude. The largest simple correlations are with race, either black or white, and with father's years of education. Father's education is lower for those with darker skin color. Similarly, education before the U.S. is negatively correlated with darker skin color, although education in the U.S. is not correlated with skin color. Skin color is correlated with visa type, with those with darker skin color less likely to have an employment visa. Skin color also is correlated with height. Those who are shorter than the U.S. average height for their gender tend to have darker skin color, while those who are taller than the U.S. average height for their gender tend to have lighter skin color. This relation between skin color and height largely reflects the fact that the largest group of immigrants, those from Asia and Latin America, who are on average darker than the U.S. white population, are also on average shorter than the U.S. white population.

Wage Equation Estimates

In Hersch (2008), I show that immigrants with darker skin color earn less than their counterparts with lighter skin color, controlling for extensive individual and market characteristics, as well as controlling for Hispanic ethnicity, race, and country of birth. In this current chapter, I analyze the same sample as in Hersch (2008), expanding the analysis to investigate the contribution of individual variables or groups of variables to the estimated skin color penalty. I start with a basic specification controlling only for skin color and then sequentially add to the wage equation individual and productivity-related control variables. We expect the magnitude of the skin color coefficient to change as we add control variables that are correlated with skin color. The order in which the variables are added is intended to demonstrate the effect on the skin color coefficient as we include variables that themselves have an increasing chance of being affected by potential skin color discrimination.

To help motivate the results that follow, consider for demonstration the relation between wages, education, occupation, and skin color. It is widely established that education has a positive effect on wages and that those in professional and managerial occupations have higher earnings than those in service or production occupations. In addition, a number of studies have shown that among African Americans, darker skin color is associated with lower education (e.g., Hughes and Hertel 1990, Keith and Herring 1991, Hersch

2006), as well as with lower occupational attainment (e.g., Hughes and Hertel 1990, Keith and Herring 1991). If controls for education and occupation are omitted from the wage equation for a sample of African Americans, the coefficient on skin color will pick up the direct effect of skin color as well as the indirect effects of skin color on education and on occupation. The estimated penalty to darker skin color will be larger in wage equations that exclude education and occupation than in equations that include these variables. In general, as we add variables that are negatively correlated with darker skin color and positively correlated with wages, the magnitude of the coefficient on skin color will decline, as part of the skin color effect is explained by these additional control variables.

So, if we are interested in isolating the role of skin color discrimination in employment, should we include or exclude education and occupation in our wage regressions? Generally, wage equations intended to estimate the effect of discrimination should only include as control variables those productivity characteristics that are exogenous to the process of discrimination under study. In the current example, consider the difference between education and occupation. Since education is largely chosen or completed before an individual enters the labor market, education is a pre-market characteristic. Educational attainment may be affected by societal discrimination, but it is not under the control of employers.[2] On the other hand, employers decide whether to hire individuals for specific jobs, and this decision may indeed be affected by discrimination on the basis of skin color. Thus, education is appropriately included in the wage equation, but occupation should only be included if it can be determined that occupation is not influenced by discrimination.

By examining how the inclusion of additional variables affects the coefficient on skin color, we help identify those variables that may themselves be influenced by skin color and can isolate whether the source is pre-market or arises in the labor market. Referring to the simple correlations reported in Table 5.1, we expect that the largest impact on the skin color coefficient will come from adding those variables with the highest correlation with skin color.

Table 5.2 summarizes the coefficient on skin color and the associated adjusted R-squared from a series of wage equations. The dependent variable in all equations is the log of hourly wage. The skin color coefficients and adjusted R-squared values reported in columns 1 and 2 are based on wage regressions that do not control for Hispanic ethnicity, race, or country of birth. All of the skin color coefficients and adjusted R-squared values reported in columns 3 and 4 are based on wage regressions that control for Hispanic ethnicity, race, and country of birth.

---

[2] Note that although I discuss employer discrimination for purposes of this example, other sources of discriminatory treatment include coworkers and customers.

Table 5.2 Coefficients on skin color in log wage equations[a]

Control variables[b]		No controls for Hispanic, race, country of birth		Controls for Hispanic, race, country of birth	
		Skin color coefficient	Adjusted R^2	Skin color coefficient	Adjusted R^2
		(1)	(2)	(3)	(4)
1	Skin color	−0.033**	0.01	−0.017*	0.15
		(0.007)		(0.007)	
2	1 + male, age, height, weight, time period	−0.036**	0.11	−0.021**	0.24
		(0.006)		(0.007)	
3	2 + family background, education	−0.030**	0.21	−0.018**	0.29
		(0.006)		(0.007)	
4	3 + occupation in last job abroad	−0.028**	0.23	−0.018**	0.30
		(0.006)		(0.007)	
5	4 + English language, new arrival, potential U.S. work experience, U.S. region	−0.031**	0.33	−0.017**	0.38
		(0.006)		(0.006)	
6	5 + visa type	−0.027**	0.40	−0.013*	0.43
		(0.005)		(0.006)	
7	6 + tenure, employer characteristics, job characteristics	−0.027**	0.42	−0.014*	0.45
		(0.005)		(0.006)	
8	7 + occupation in USA	−0.024**	0.47	−0.011+	0.49
		(0.005)		(0.006)	

[a]*Source*: Author's calculations from the New Immigrant Survey 2003. Number of observations = 1536. ** significant at 1%; * significant at 5%; + significant at 5.5% (two-sided tests). Table reports coefficients on skin color, with standard errors in parentheses, controlling for the indicated variables. All values are weighted to account for sample design and response weights. See Hersch (2008) for additional information.

[b]Complete list of control variables: skin color (0–11 scale); male; age; age squared; inches below U.S. gender average height; inches above U.S. gender average height; body mass index; indicators for time period; father's education; indicators for relative family income at age 16; years of education before USA; years of education in USA; indicators for occupation in last job abroad; indicators for whether the respondent understands English very well or well and for whether the respondent is a new arrival; potential U.S. work experience; potential U.S. work experience squared; indicators for region of USA; indicators for visa type; tenure with current employer; tenure squared; indicators for government employer, union contract, outdoor work probable, paid hourly rate, full-time employment, self-employed; indicators for occupation in USA. Columns 3 and 4 include indicators for Hispanic ethnicity, race, and country of birth.

Each row in the table reports the coefficient on skin color and the adjusted R-squared for the equation after adding the indicated additional variables to the variables included in the regressions reported in the preceding row. For example, the first row of Table 5.2 reports the coefficient on skin color without controlling for any other variables in the first two columns and reports the coefficient on skin color controlling only for skin color, Hispanic ethnicity, race, and country of birth in the final two columns. The second row of Table 5.2

reports the coefficient on skin color controlling for the demographic characteristics of sex, age, height, and weight, in addition to controlling for skin color.
Similarly, each row adds the variables listed in the row to all of the variables
indicated in the preceding rows. The entire list of variables is reported in the
table note.

Because the dependent variable is the log of hourly wage, the magnitude of
the coefficient on skin color is interpreted as the percent change in wages
associated with a one-unit change in the skin color measure. This means that
the coefficient of -0.033 in row 1, column 1 indicates that without controlling
for any other variables, the effect of a one-unit increase in the skin color rating
lowers wages by 3.3 percent on average. Another way to interpret the magnitude of the skin color effect is to consider the difference between those with the
lightest skin color and those with the darkest. Because the skin color scale goes
from 0 to 10, the coefficient of -0.033 indicates that without controlling for any
other variables, those with the darkest skin color earn on average 33 percent less
than those with the lightest skin color.

First, note the influence of controlling for Hispanic ethnicity, race, and
country of birth on the estimated effect of skin color on wages. A comparison
of columns 1 and 3 shows that inclusion of Hispanic ethnicity, race, and country
of birth accounts for approximately half of the skin color effect on wages. This
large reduction in the skin color coefficient is what we expect to find based on
the correlations reported in Table 5.1, showing that white and black race have
the largest correlations with skin color.

By controlling for Hispanic ethnicity, race, and country of birth, the independent influence of skin color is isolated. Because of the correlation between
race and skin color for whites and blacks, and because it is widely established
that blacks earn less than comparable whites, if race is excluded from the wage
regressions, we may be estimating the effect of race on wages rather than the
independent effect of skin color on wages net of the race effect. It is also
reasonable to control for country of birth, as countries differ in factors such
as quality of education or use of English language and thereby may lead to
genuine differences in market productivity. But we also raise the possibility that
the skin color effect is underestimated because of multicollinearity. Multicollinearity tends to present more problems of interpretation with small sample sizes
such as this, in which there are relatively few observations from most countries
of birth. Presenting both sets of results provides a sense of the range of the effect
of skin color on wages.

Next, consider the effect on the skin color coefficient as we add additional
explanatory variables. Row 2 includes the demographic variables of sex, age,
height, and weight (as well as time period of interview to account for price
changes). The penalty to darker skin color is slightly higher in row 2 because
although women have lighter skin color than men, they also have lower wages.
Row 3 adds variables on family background (relative family income at age 16
and father's education) as well as own education. Row 4 adds indicator variables for occupation in the worker's last job abroad. Those with more education

and higher-status jobs in their last job abroad are expected to earn more in the U.S. To the extent that workers in the sample experience skin color discrimination in their country of birth, those with darker skin color may end up with less education or in worse occupations that result in lower wages in the U.S. In addition, inclusion of family background and father's education will help control for unobserved productivity characteristics that may result from differential treatment in the country of birth on the basis of skin color. While we might have expected that the skin color coefficients would be greatly reduced by controlling for these variables, notably, the magnitudes are almost unchanged relative to the skin color coefficients reported in row 1.

Row 5 adds variables for English language proficiency, whether the worker is a new arrival, potential work experience, and U.S. region. These are characteristics that are unlikely to be affected by any potential skin color discrimination experienced before migrating to the U.S., and they are also characteristics that will have more value in the U.S. labor market than in the source country. Once again, the skin color coefficient changes very little with inclusion of these variables.

The skin color coefficients reported in rows 1–5 are derived from wage regressions that include only variables that are most likely to be exogenous to any possible discrimination in the U.S. labor market. The results reported in row 5, column 3 show that immigrants with the lightest skin color earn on average 17 percent more than comparable immigrants with the darkest skin color, even taking into account Hispanic ethnicity, race, and country of birth.

Rows 6, 7, and 8 add variables that may themselves be affected by skin color discrimination in the U.S. Row 6 adds visa type. As the simple correlations in Table 5.1 indicate, those with darker skin color are less likely to have an employment visa. Those with employment visas are in considerably higher-paying jobs. Eligibility for an employment visa generally requires employer sponsorship, and such sponsorship decisions may be influenced by skin color discrimination in the U.S. The coefficient in column 1 drops from -0.031 in row 5 to -0.027 in row 6, and the coefficient in column 3 drops from -0.017 in row 5 to -0.013 in row 6. Finally, inclusion of other work-related characteristics such as years of experience with current employer (e.g., tenure), type of employer, and occupation results in a slightly lower effect of skin color on wages. The fullest specification reported in row 8, column 3 shows an 11 percent disparity in pay between those with the lightest skin color and their counterparts with the darkest skin color.

What is notable in the current context is that even with very extensive controls, the effect of skin color on wages remains surprisingly close to the estimated effect without controls reported in row 1. The coefficient reported in row 8, which includes the fullest set of controls, is about one-third smaller than the coefficient reported in row 1. The main interpretation of the relatively small reduction in the skin color coefficient as we add controls is that skin color largely does not affect the control variables. This is consistent with the simple correlations between skin color and the variables reported in Table 5.1. Note that this small reduction in the skin color coefficient is not the result of adding worthless variables to the wage regressions; in fact, the explanatory power of the wage regressions increases substantially as we add additional control variables, as demonstrated by the adjusted R-squared values in columns 2 and 4. The adjusted R-squared values in row 8 are 0.47 and 0.49; these values indicate that the explanatory power is quite high relative to wage regressions reported throughout the economics literature. Thus, these results indicate that skin color has an independent and direct effect on wages of new legal immigrants in the U.S.

What Skin Color Can Tell Us About Discrimination

By investigating the role of skin color and earnings among immigrants, this analysis contributes to understanding the persistent ethnic and racial gap in pay observed in the U.S. Wage regressions are typically used to identify whether comparable workers are discriminated against on the basis of their race or sex. Pay disparities on the basis of race or sex that remain after taking into account differences in productivity-related characteristics, such as work experience and education, are often interpreted as arising from discrimination. But, whether any measured pay disparity between groups is due to discrimination remains a topic of debate, as any observed disparity is potentially attributable to omitted productivity variables. For example, neighborhood effects associated with race may indeed lead to differences in realized education quality. If, say, African American students are concentrated in lower-quality schools relative to white students, then the pay gap between African American and white workers with the same years of measured education may arise from difference in actual skills.

Examining whether skin color has an independent effect on wages, net of any ethnic or racial effect, provides a way to isolate whether discrimination plays a role in any observed pay disparity. In contrast to ethnicity and race, differences in skin color do not lead to extreme differences in neighborhood or school quality. Skin color varies considerably within ethnicity and race, and varies even within families. While estimated disparities between minority workers and whites possibly may be accounted for by omitted productivity characteristics rather than discrimination, there is no evidence that skin color could affect pay via omitted productivity characteristics correlated with skin color. Specifically, there is no evidence that the relation between skin color and wages can be due to genetic factors. While there is evidence both that attractiveness is associated with higher wages, and that that those with lighter skin color are rated as more attractive, Hersch (2006) shows that the attractiveness link is not likely to be large enough to explain skin color effects of the magnitude reported here.

However, due to historic differential treatment of African Americans on the basis of skin color in the U.S., we may still be concerned that any estimated skin color effect among African Americans is due to omitted productivity characteristics associated with skin color. In contrast to African Americans, new lawful immigrants to the U.S. will not have experienced any historic differential treatment within the U.S. on the basis of skin color. Furthermore, the effect of skin color persists even with controls for Hispanic ethnicity, race, and country of birth, which take into account the role of ethnic or racial discrimination in the U.S. and differences by country in productivity factors by country, such as quality of education and use of English language.

Skin color discrimination has been reported in a number of countries, and this too may affect actual productivity characteristics. For instance, someone with relatively light skin color in Guatemala may experience better treatment in Guatemala relative to those in their country with darker skin color. However, even if someone has light skin relative to others in their country of birth and correspondingly receive better treatment there, nonetheless, being darker relative to other immigrants in the U.S. lowers his or her wages. Finding that darker skin color adversely affects immigrant earnings after controlling for extensive individual characteristics as well as Hispanic ethnicity, race, and country of birth provides strong evidence of discrimination on the basis of skin color that is not attributable to productivity factors.

Concluding Remarks

This chapter documents a pay disparity of 17 percent between new legal immigrants to the U.S. with the lightest skin color and their counterparts with the darkest skin color. In addition to providing evidence on the presence of discrimination, finding a penalty to darker skin color among immigrants provides information on the potential for assimilation of immigrants into the U.S. labor market. Whether and how rapidly immigrants assimilate into the U.S. labor market are issues of great policy importance and controversy.[3] Early work by Chiswick (1978) using 1970 Census data demonstrates that the earnings of white male immigrants rose rapidly with U.S. labor market experience and eventually exceeded the earnings of native-born workers. But studies analyzing cohorts after the 1970s find a substantial wage gap (e.g., Borjas 1995). In part the wage gap arises from differences in skill levels, particularly education and English language proficiency.[4] The penalty to darker skin color indicates that the largest groups of post-1965 immigrants—those from Asia and Latin America—may have an additional source of disadvantage: darker skin

---

[3] For recent summaries and evidence on assimilation, see Card (2005) and Borjas (2006). Card's analysis shows that U.S. born children of immigrants have successfully assimilated, with education and wages higher than children of natives, while Borjas's analysis shows considerably slower assimilation.

[4] Also of debate is whether the gap in skill levels between immigrants and native born is increasing (e.g., Borjas 1995) or decreasing (e.g., Jasso, Rosenzweig, and Smith 2000). Different conclusions can result from inclusion or exclusion of undocumented immigrants and differences in the definition of a recent immigrant.

color relative to the majority U.S. population that seems to be penalized in the U.S. labor market. The results suggest that observed opposition to immigrants arises in part from discrimination as characterized by outward appearance, with immigrants who have lighter skin faring better than their counterparts who are darker.

References

Borjas, George J. (1995). Assimilation and changes in cohort quality revisited: What happened to immigrant earnings in the 1980 s? *Journal of Labor Economics,* 13(2), 201–245.
———. (2006). Making it in America: Social mobility in the immigrant population. *The Future of Children: Opportunity in America,* 16(2), 55–71.
Card, David. (2005). Is the new immigration really so bad? *Economic Journal,* 115(507), F300–F323.
Chiswick, Barry R. (1978). The effect of Americanization on the earnings of foreign-born men. *Journal of Political Economy,* 86(5), 897–921.
Hersch, Joni. (2006). Skin tone effects among African Americans: Perceptions and reality. *American Economic Review,* 96(2), 251–255.
———. (2008). Profiling the new immigrant worker: The effects of skin color and height. *Journal of Labor Economics,* 26(2), 345–386.
Hughes, Michael, & Hertel, Bradley R. (1990). The significance of color remains: A study of life chances, mate selection, and ethnic consciousness among Black Americans. *Social Forces,* 68(4), 1105–1120.
Jablonski, Nina G. (2006). *Skin: A natural history.* Berkeley & Los Angeles, CA: University of California Press.
Jablonski, Nina G., & Chaplin, George. (2000). The evolution of human skin coloration. *Journal of Human Evolution,* 39(1), 57–106.
Jasso, Guillermina, Massey, Douglas S., Rosenzweig, Mark R., & Smith, James P. (Forthcoming). The U.S. new immigrant survey: Overview and preliminary results based on the new-immigrant cohorts of 1996 and 2003. In Beverley Morgan & Ben Nicholson (Eds.), *Longitudinal surveys and cross-cultural survey design.* London (UK): Crown Publishing, UK Immigration Research and Statistics Service.
Jasso, Guillermina, Rosenzweig, Mark R., & Smith, James P. (2000). The changing skills of new immigrants to the United States: Recent trends and their determinants. In George Borjas (Ed.), *Issues in the economics of immigration* (pp. 185–225). Chicago, IL: University of Chicago Press & NBER.
Keith, Verna M. & Herring, Cedric. (1991). Skin tone and stratification in the Black community. *American Journal of Sociology,* 97(3), 760–778.
Massey, Douglas S. & Martin, Jennifer A. (2003). The NIS Skin Color Scale.
[NIS] New Immigrant Survey. (2003). http://nis.princeton.edu/overview.html. The data and documentation are available at http://nis.princeton.edu.

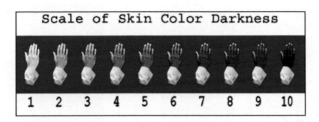

Fig. 5.1 Skin color scale
Source: Douglas S. Massey and Jennifer A. Martin, (2003), The NIS Skin Color Scale.

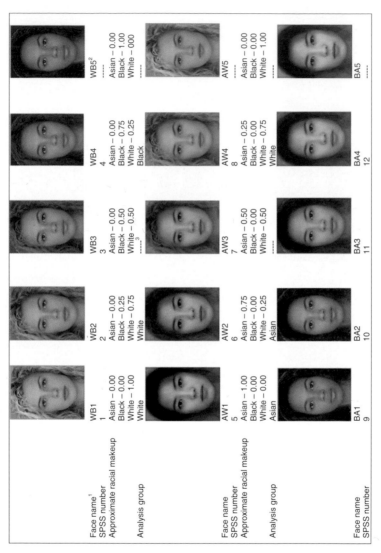

Fig. 6.3 Facial information

[1] Face name refers to the code names given to each face and used throughout the body of this paper with the exception of the Results section for functional purposes. The number assigned to each face for use in the Results section is provided in SPSS number.

[2] Faces WB5, AW5, and BA5 are identical to faces BA1, WB1, and AW1, respectively, and, thus, were not used in data analyses. Therefore, they were assigned neither an SPSS number nor an analysis group.

[3] Faces WB3, AW3, and BA3 were not assigned an analysis group to avoid having the same face in two different groups.

Part III
The Pervasiveness of Racism

Chapter 6
Racial Characteristics and Female Facial Attractiveness Perception Among United States University Students

Nicole E. Belletti and T. Joel Wade

Abstract Research in the area of facial attractiveness has examined the role of race in the perception of beauty, revealing that regardless of our own skin color, we tend to prefer light skin to dark skin in most matters of choice. Subsequently, the current research, utilizing morphed faces combined in varying degrees Black, White, and Asian facial characteristics, was expected to corroborate with past research by showing that participants found the "pure" White face the most attractive and the "pure" Black face the least attractive. Instead, participants found least attractive the "pure" Asian face. The results are discussed in terms of prior research with a focus on the concept of familiarity. Also discussed are possible limitations and opportunities for future research to further examine and clarify the difference between the present data and the existing literature.

Introduction

In recent years, it seems that our global society has placed increasing value on physical appearance. Quick and easy access to myriad forms of mass media, including the Internet, television, and music, facilitates the dissemination of information at mind-blowing speeds, bringing us appearance-obsessed, pop media culture hits such as *America's Next Top Model*, *Extreme Makeover*, *The Swan*, and *My Humps*. Embedded in this media frenzy is an abundance of information instructing us on who and what we ought to look like, how to avoid getting a bikini line when tanning, what clothes to wear, how to achieve the ideal body in under ten days and still manage to have time to shape your eyebrows and curl your eyelashes every day, and what fad diet to try next. In our great individualistic nation, we have become obsessed with the quest to realize our beauty potential, but this value system also leads to harsh, negative representations and interpretations of the body (Poran 1991). This conflict

N.E. Belletti
Department of Psychology, Bucknell University, Walnut port, PA, USA
e-mail: nicole.belletti@gmail.com

R.E. Hall (ed.), *Racism in the 21st Century*, DOI: 10.1007/978-0-387-79097-8_6,   93
© Springer Science+Business Media, LLC 2008

between what one wants to look like and what one actually looks like can make life difficult, particularly for women, for whom the manic pursuit of physical perfection can lead all too often to chronically low self-esteem and eating disorders (Poran 1991).

And yet, this emphasis on physical attractiveness is not wholly unwarranted. Among many things, attractiveness substantially influences mate choice. Men are more likely to consider attractive women as suitable sexual and marital partners, to attribute them with positive personality traits, and to behave altruistically towards them (Badcock 1920, Cunningham 1986, Zebrowitz et al. 2002, Dion et al.1972, Rhodes et al. 1998, Chen et al. 1997). Perhaps it is not, then, that we should not, as individuals and as a society, be concerned about our appearance, but that fixating on it too much can lead to an unhealthy lifestyle, which explains why beauty research is more prevalent today in Psychology than it has been in the past.

Being attractive has more benefits than just snagging a great mate. Attractive job applicants are more likely to be hired than are unattractive applicants, and in court, attractive defendants receive more lenient sentences than do non-attractive ones (Stewart 1980, Mack & Rainey 1990). Moreover, attractive faces are judged to be indicative of positive personality traits, despite the fact that there is little to no existing evidence for any sort of relationship between attractiveness and actual personality (Alley 1988, Dion et al. 1972, Badcock 1920, Chen et al. 1997, Cunningham 1986, Zebrowitz et al. 2002). On the other hand, there is some evidence that attractive women in particular often are viewed as materialistic, vain, and unfaithful (Cunningham 1986). Nevertheless, when all is said and done, we must conclude not only that "What is Beautiful is Good" (Dion 1972), but that it is good to be beautiful.

And it is especially good to have a beautiful face. Studies indicate that one of the reasons that facial attractiveness may be such an outstanding factor in mate selection lies in its power to predict mental and physical health and developmental stability. Attractive faces are perceived as being indicative of intelligence, and facial beauty does, in fact, correlate with actual intelligence (Zebrowitz et al. 2002). Attractiveness is significantly positively correlated with perceived intelligence at all ages, and with actual intelligence at all ages except late adulthood. Even brief exposure to a face affords the observer the ability to judge with significant accuracy the intelligence level of the individual to whom the face belongs, particularly when it belongs to a child or an adolescent. Zebrowitz and her colleagues (2002) suggest that this relationship between beauty and intellect may result from a number of factors, including intelligent individuals' superior grooming skills, exposure to a healthier environment during prenatal growth and after birth, and higher levels of facial symmetry due to healthier development and better genes. Aside from indicating intelligence, attractive faces also reliably denote health. For example, unhealthy skin and asymmetry—both reliable prophets of unattractiveness—also predict poor overall health (Livshits & Kobylianski 1991, Deutsch 1987, as cited in Jones et al. 2004a, 2004b, Fink et al. 2001).

In keeping with the notion that facial beauty indicates physical and mental health, the Sexual Selection Hypothesis (SSH) purports that the specific set of features that come together to make a face extremely attractive and appealing to possible mates is meant to accomplish one simple function: to advertise its owner's good health, superior genome, and high quality as a potential mate (Johnston 2000). According to the laws of natural selection, our proclivity for certain facial features over others stems from evolutionary processes favoring the most adaptive physical features, leading to faces that reflect these adaptive features. Characteristics that are attractive to potential mates and thus are reproductively beneficial, can be expected to spread throughout the gene pool, even if the specific trait actually poses a survival threat to the individual (Johnston 2000). The most noted example of this, and the one offered by Johnston, is that of the male peacock's magnificent tail, the beauty of which elevates his sexual status. Only healthy peacocks can properly care for a full, luxurious tail, so they must be healthy to produce such a gorgeous tail in the first place, and then healthy enough to maintain it. Thus, peacocks with especially magnificent tails are advertising themselves as healthy and viable potential mates. In humans, this phenomenon is evidenced by the fact that, for men, high levels of testosterone lead to the development of facial features that are linked with male attractiveness. Unfortunately, high levels of testosterone also lead to lowered immune system functioning, so males who possess testosterone-mediated facial traits must be extremely healthy in order to cope with the accompanying immune system handicap (as cited in Mealey et al. 1999). Women are lucky not to face this difficulty; for them, the increased levels of female hormones and low levels of male hormones that control the development of such desired feminine features as full lips and a small chin do nothing more than advertise their heightened femininity and fertility (Johnston 2000).

Much of the theory surrounding beauty research is based upon the concept of averageness. If the SSH is correct, most faces should over time come to exhibit at least some of the traits of an attractive face, making these traits normal—average. The existing body of research on the contribution of averageness to facial beauty is somewhat ambivalent. Proponents of the averageness theory point to research showing that averaged faces—faces that actually are composites of several different faces—are more attractive than are the individual component faces used to make the composite (Langlois & Roggman 1990). The concept of combining or morphing faces is not a new one. Sir Francis Galton first thought in 1878, "to superimpose optically the various drawings [or photographs of several persons alike in most respects, but differing in minor details] and to accept the aggregate result" (see Fig. 6.1 Galton 1878). Since then, the technique has flourished, but there has been some concern that averaging or morphing faces might cause alterations such as blurring, increased symmetry, and reduction of blemishes that make them more attractive than so-called normal faces (Johnston 2000, Rubenstien et al. 2002). If this is the case, then it is these averaging artifacts and not the actual averageness of the composite faces that increases their perceived attractiveness. However, the

Fig. 6.1 Example of
composite face from
Galton's 1887 study

The accompanying woodcut is as fair a representation of one of the
composites as is practicable in ordinary printing. It was photographi-
cally transferred to the wood, and the engraver has used his best
endeavour to translate the shades into line engraving. This composite
is made out of only three components, and its three-fold origin is to be
traced in the ears, and in the buttons to the vest. To the best of my
judgment the original photograph is a very exact average of its components; not one feature in it appears identical with that of any one of
them, but it contains a resemblance to all, and is not more like to one of
them than to another. However the judgment of the wood engraver is
different. His rendering of the composite has made it exactly like one
of its components, which it must be borne in mind he had never seen.
It is just as though an artist drawing a child had produced a portrait
closely resembling its deceased father, having overlooked an equally
strong likeness to its deceased mother, which was apparent to its relatives. This is to me a most striking proof that the composite is a true
combination. [I trust that the beauty of the woodcut will not be much
diminished by the necessarily coarse process of newspaper printing.]

increased attractiveness of line-drawn averaged faces over "normal" faces
refutes these fears since the line-drawn faces eliminate possible averaging artifacts (Rhodes et al. 2002, Rhodes & Tremewan 1996). In addition, line-drawn
faces whose facial features have been exaggerated to make them less average
had decreased attractiveness (Rhodes & Tremewan 1996). There do seem to be
limits to the effects of averaging faces since composite faces do not necessarily
become increasingly attractive in direct proportion to the number of component faces used to create them, and since some "normal" faces are more
attractive than averaged ones (Rhodes & Tremewan 1996, Langlois &
Roggman 1990). In general, average faces are considered to be more beautiful
than are "normal" faces, but cross-culturally, the most beautiful faces are
distinctive, exhibiting features that vary methodically from the norm (Perrett
et al. 1999, Rhodes et al. 2002, Jones & Hill 1993, Bauduoin & Tiberghien 2004).
The distinctive and extraordinarily beautiful female faces often have significantly smaller mouth-chin and eye-chin distances, as well as significantly
plumper lips than do "averagely" attractive faces; conflicting evidence
surrounds the possibility of larger-than-average eyes contributing to

greater-than-average beauty (Johnston 2000). This preference for distinctive faces over average ones may result from their recognizability and memorability.

Symmetry is another key element of facial attractiveness, and one that is particularly embraced by the Sexual Selection Hypothesis. Lateral facial symmetry is a robust predictor of attractiveness and is a sign of stable pre- and post-natal development, superior mating quality, and overall good health (Alley & Hildebrandt 1988, Langlois & Roggman 1990, Perrett et al. 1999, Rhodes et al. 1998, Bauduoin & Tiberghien 2004). Facial asymmetry is associated with inbreeding, mental retardation and disorders—including psychosis, and premature birth (Livshits & Kobylianski 1991, Deutsch 1987). Symmetry in the rest of the body also is linked to attractiveness. A study on human fluctuating asymmetry—asymmetries of, for example, the hands and feet that are found in most of the population—found that low attractiveness ratings were predictive of high fluctuating asymmetry[1] (Gangestad et al. 1994). Rhodes and her colleagues (1998) found a direct relationship between both natural and manipulated symmetry and attractiveness ratings, even for otherwise unattractive faces, implicating symmetry as a primal aspect of facial attractiveness. Research using monozygotic twins as stimuli reveals that the more symmetric twin is more attractive than is his or her sibling, and that the difference in their degrees of attractiveness is directly proportional to the difference in their degrees of symmetry (Mealey et al. 1999). Some research with human infants suggests that symmetry may not be as important as is overall facial attractiveness (as cited in Zaidel et al. 2005). Babies prefer "beautiful" faces to faces that are nearly perfectly symmetrical. Furthermore, when presented with faces that have been manipulated to be perfectly symmetrical and with the original, non-symmetric faces, they prefer the asymmetric to the perfectly symmetric faces. Another study—this time with adults—demonstrated that, when forced to choose between two images of two different shots of the same face blended together, participants were no more likely to prefer symmetric faces over the asymmetric ones (Langlois et al. 1995). However, a later study contested this finding when its results showed a significant preference for the symmetric faces (Rhodes et al. 1998). It may be that perfectly symmetric faces are too unusual to be preferred over attractive but asymmetric ones. Certainly, though, investigations in the area of symmetry have proven it to be an important factor in beauty.

Two recent studies add a new twist to the roles of averageness and symmetry in determining attractiveness. Based on findings that the average of any group of objects typically is viewed as familiar even though it actually is completely alien (i.e., the participant has never before seen it), Peskin and Newell (2004) correctly hypothesized that faces manipulated to be familiar would be judged as more attractive than "unfamiliar" faces, regardless of the averageness or distinctness of the faces. The primary explanation for this finding is that, since we

---

[1] An example of "normal" fluctuating asymmetry is having one foot that is slightly larger than the other. High fluctuating asymmetry, which is less common, might manifest itself in feet that are grossly different in size, so much so that one cannot wear the same size shoe on both feet.

like and are more comfortable with familiar objects, averaged faces are preferred because they are more familiar than are the component faces. This explanation works well with the corollary of the Sexual Selection Hypothesis stated earlier: preferred facial features will spread throughout a population until they become the norm. We become accustomed to these features and come to prefer faces that exhibit them because they are familiar to us. The second twist is the discovery is a significant positive relationship between averageness and symmetry (Bauduoin & Tiberghien 2004). This relationship remained stable when averageness was held constant, but not when symmetry was held constant, suggesting that symmetry is important only insomuch as it relates to averageness. The researchers posit that this is because noticeably asymmetric faces tend to move away from the average. For instance, while most people's eyes are not set an equal distance away from the middle of their face, it would be rare for someone to have one eye set noticeably further from the middle of his or her face than the other eye. Such a face would be asymmetric and unique; it also would be unfamiliar. Bauduoin and Tiberghien (2004) also found that the only face traits, when asymmetric, which bore any significant impact on attractiveness were the eyes—their height on the face and their distance from the center of the face, and overall face shape—both sides of the face must be roughly the same size.

The Multiple Fitness Model (MFM) offers an alternative attractiveness theory from the Sexual Selection Hypothesis. This model proposes that female facial attractiveness is based on a combination of three types of features: neonate features of large, wide-set eyes, a small nose, and a small chin; mature features of prominent cheekbones and narrow cheeks; expressive features of high eyebrows, large pupils, and a large smile. The presence of these features accurately predicts high attractiveness ratings and is an extremely important contributor to facial beauty (Cunningham 1986, Wade et al. 2004, Bauduoin & Tiberghien 2004). Faces possessing these features are preferred cross-culturally by both men and women (Cunningham et al. 1995, Dion 2002). Additionally, particular combinations of the three attribute groups are positively correlated with judgments of personal attributes (Cunningham 1986). For instance, women with large eyes and pupils, high eyebrows, small noses, wide cheekbones, and wide smiles are identified as sociable, while women with large eyes, small noses, and wide smiles are perceived to be assertive (Cunningham 1986). Unlike the Sexual Selection Hypothesis, the Multiple Fitness Model addresses the function of personal preference in mate selection (*as proposed by* Cunningham et al. 2002). Cunningham and his colleagues (2002) contend that individual inclinations for particular features enter into the picture only when an "ideal target," i.e., a potential mate who meets completely the Model's attractiveness standards, is unavailable.

Within the three criterion groups of the Multiple Fitness Model, some evidence indicates that certain facial features are more important than others. The eyes—specifically pupil and eye size—and mouth have been implicated as two of the most important features (Alley & Hildebrandt 1988, Terry & Davis

1976, Terry 1977). These features may be of particular importance because they are intricately connected to the expression of emotion (Tipples et al. 2002, Lundqvist et al. 2004, Eyetsemitan 2004). The position of the mouth, for example, can greatly impact attractiveness ratings (Alley & Hildebrandt 1988), which is why most current research opts to use faces with neutral expressions, or, at the very least, faces whose expressions are all positive—smiling—or all negative—frowning. The eyebrows, which are of importance in attraction because they are linked with the eyes, are of special significance for emotion perception (Alley & Hildebrand 1988, Tipples et al. 2002). Although they are most revealing in combination with other facial features—namely the eyes and the mouth—the eyebrows can reliably convey anger even when isolated from the rest of the face (Tipples et al. 2002).

The entire subset of neonate characteristics also has been heavily researched due to its noteworthy contribution to beauty (Jones & Hill 1993, Terry & Davis 1976). Early research revealed a complicated interconnected relationship between juvenilization and attractiveness and this relationship was confirmed by subsequent research (Berry 1991). In a study comparing the effects of youthfulness and femininity on attractiveness Ishi et al. (2004) manipulated male and female faces to make them appear more youthful or more feminine. A strong preference emerged for youthful faces over feminine ones, especially for female faces. In a second experiment, Ishi and colleagues (2004) found that the faces rated as most attractive in their initial experiment were described by participants as "mild," "elegant" and "youthful," words that the participants also associated with femininity. Thus, the attractive juvenilized faces may have been attractive because the juvenilizing process somehow made them more feminine as well. Investigations of neonate characteristics and their impact on beauty continue to be important due to the apparent complexity of their relationship.

Surprisingly, all these findings about beauty do not apply to just one culture or even to only a handful of cultures. Since all cultures and societies place varying degrees of importance on physical attractiveness, and since members of different societies may use differing criteria to judge other-group or same-group attractiveness, it seems natural to assume that beauty is a very culturally-bound concept (Dion 2002). On the contrary, it appears that the cross-cultural similarities between beauty standards far outnumber the differences, that "people's views of facial attractiveness are remarkably consistent, regardless of race, nationality, or age" (Fink et al. 2001a). Agreement exists between attractiveness ratings across societies and cultures, from White and Black American students, to Koreans, to secluded societies and cultures that have very limited, if any, access to Western media and ideals, such as the Ache Indians of Eastern Paraguay and the Hiwi Indians of Southern Venezuala, to name just a few examples (Jones & Hill 1993, de Casanova 2004, Zebrowitz et al. 1993). Some of this homogeneity may be accounted for by the effects of American and European colonialism, which created a strong partiality toward Whiteness and White characteristics (de Casanova 2004, Hall 1998). Members of high socioeconomic classes in societies that were colonized by Whites have more access to Western media and culture than do their lower-class compatriots, thus one might expect them to subscribe to White beauty standards to a more severe degree. Conversely, since individuals in such nations already have a strong predilection for Whiteness, it is thought that increased exposure to Western media might be beneficial because it exposes them to body types and beauty standards other than the White and Latina types with which they are familiar, making socioeconomically elevated individuals more likely to call into question their own beauty ideals (de Casanova 2004). This also can be explained by beauty's biological significance. As suggested by the Sexual Selection Hypothesis, facial features that indicate health and reproductive quality will become widespread throughout a population, seemingly regardless of race or culture.

Some surprising and interesting research supporting the idea of a largely cross-cultural beauty standard examined attractiveness stereotyping, which occurs in a similar manner across several cultures (Dion 2002, Hall 1998, de Casanova 2004, Chen et al. 1997, Zebrowitz et al. 1993). Korean, White American, and Black American students all share analogous cross-race stereotypes, which they use to judge the attractiveness and personality of both in- and out-group members (Zebrowitz et al. 1993). Members of the three groups were able to differentiate between different out-group members, refuting the adage, "They all look alike"; they also all found the same faces attractive. Research with babies provides the last bit of evidence that beauty standards are largely universal, perhaps because they are genetically predetermined. "Attractive" infants who possess exaggerated neonate qualities are perceived by adults as cuter than are babies whose neonate features are less inflated. Finally, infants demonstrate a significant preference for faces rated by adults as attractive, indicating that this is a biologically hardwired preference as opposed to a learned one (Langlois et al. 1987).

With the key components of facial attractiveness and their universality largely established, recent research on facial beauty has begun to explore the effects of skin quality on the attractiveness of women's faces. The skin is the largest human organ, and healthy-looking skin has been hailed as the most unanimously coveted human feature (Morris 1967). Healthy skin indicates overall physical health and outstanding grooming qualities and has revealed itself to be a strong indicator of perceived attractiveness (Jones et al. 2004a, 2004b, Morris 1967, Fink et al. 2001). Studies looking specifically at the impact of skin color on perceived attractiveness have yielded mixed results. Some research finds little to no influence of skin color—that of the stimuli and that of the participants—on attractiveness ratings (de Casanova 2004, Cunningham et al. 1995), while other research finds at least moderate differences (Fink et al. 2001, Wade et al. 2004, Hall 1998). A very limited amount of research serves as evidence for a widespread penchant for dark skin, but it is conjectured that this is a simple reflection of its indication of more leisure time to spend outside or to go tanning (Fink et al. 2001). Typically, the research points toward a unanimous preference for light skin, regardless of the rater's skin color (Wade et al.

2004, Hall 1998). When it occurs among people with dark skin, this phenomenon sometimes is referred to as "brown racism," the result of high exposure to White beauty ideals and White media (Hall 1998). Other explanations that are not related specifically to the race of the participant point toward the link between Whiteness and femininity, as well as that between whiteness and youth and fertility (Hill 2002, Cunningham et al. 1995, Fink et al. 2001).

While the aforementioned findings are informative, the existing body of research on skin-color preferences and its effects on attractiveness is limited in its external validity and ultimately is incomplete. Since facial attractiveness carries so much weight in the perception of women, investigating the effects of racial characteristics—including skin tone, facial shape, and specific facial features—may help fill the void in the current research on beauty and women's facial attractiveness. The current study attempted to do just that by utilizing morphed faces that combine varying degrees of Black, White and Asian facial characteristics. The faces were developed in the research lab of Bernhard Fink, Karl Grammer, and Randy Thornhill (2001) and are designed for use in quasi-experimental research that examines the effects of racial characteristics on perceived facial attractiveness. As reparation for the lack of real-world applicability of past research, these faces are designed to be as realistic as possible; therefore, an entire set of features (i.e., racially linked features such as skin color, hair type, and nose width) as opposed to just skin-tone changes for each face. The symmetry, averageness, and skin quality, however, do not vary across the faces. Although work using these morphed faces has never before looked comparatively at the entire set of fifteen faces, prior research has proved their reliability and validity—as well as that of others like them—for use in examining the effects of race on perceived beauty (Wade & Dautrich 2005, Wade et al. 2004). The three races included in this research do differ importantly in some of their typical facial characteristics. Previous investigations have demonstrated that, in comparison with White faces, Black and Asian faces tend to have significantly greater eye height and wider set eyes, higher eyebrows, wider nostrils and longer noses, larger lips, smaller chins, and wider cheekbones with narrower cheeks when compared with White faces (see Table 6.1). Prior research also has established that the appropriate racially linked features of each face do change as they morph from one race to another (Wade & Dautrich 2005).

Hypotheses

Consistent with the bulk of preceding research, it was expected that the face with the lightest skin tone would be considered the most attractive and receive the most positive personality evaluation of all the faces while the face with the darkest skin tone would be considered the least attractive and would receive the most negative personality evaluation of all the faces.

Table 6.1 Facial dimensions for each face[1]

Face[2]	Length of face	Fore-head height	Cheek-bone prominence	Width of face at Cheek-bone	Eye width	Eye height	Separation of eyes	Eye-brow height	Chin length	Nostril width	Nose Tip width	Nose length	Upper lip length	Lower lip height
1	3	0.8	0.3	2.1	0.5	0.2	1	0.2	0.45	0.6	0.2	0.8	0.1	0.2
2	3	0.8	0.3	2.1	0.5	0.2	1.05	0.25	0.4	0.6	0.2	0.7	0.1	0.2
3	3	0.8	0.3	2.1	0.5	0.2	1.05	0.3	0.4	0.6	0.2	0.7	0.15	0.2
4	3	0.8	0.3	2.1	0.5	0.2	1.05	0.3	0.4	0.65	0.2	0.7	0.2	0.2
5	3	0.8	0.3	2.1	0.5	0.2	1.05	0.25	0.45	0.6	0.2	0.8	0.2	0.2
6	3	0.8	0.3	2.1	0.5	0.2	1.05	0.25	0.45	0.6	0.2	0.8	0.1	0.2
7	3	0.8	0.3	2.15	0.5	0.2	1.05	0.2	0.4	0.6	0.2	0.8	0.1	0.2
8	3	0.8	0.25	2.15	0.5	0.2	1	0.3	0.4	0.6	0.2	0.8	0.1	0.2
9	3	0.8	0.3	2.1	0.5	0.2	1.05	0.3	0.4	0.6	0.2	0.7	0.2	0.2
10	3	0.8	0.3	2.1	0.5	0.2	1.05	0.3	0.45	0.65	0.2	0.7	0.2	0.2
11	3	0.8	0.3	2.15	0.5	0.2	1.05	0.3	0.45	0.65	0.2	0.8	0.2	0.2
12	3	0.8	0.3	2.1	0.5	0.2	1.05	0.3	0.45	0.6	0.2	0.8	0.2	0.2

[1]Measurements are in centimeters.
[2]For face number codes, see Table 6.2.

Method

Participants

Seventy-two participants from a private university in Northeastern United States took part in this study. The participants ranged in age from 18 to 22, $M = 19.4$, $SD = 1.28$. Twenty-seven participants were men; forty-five were women. Fifty-five of the participants self-identified as White, while the other 17 self-identified as Asian/Pacific Islander (10), African American (2), Hispanic (2), Other (2), or Middle Eastern (1). They were from predominately upper-middle class and upper class families, and were recruited from the university's General Psychology course (40) and by e-mail from the general university population (32). Participants enrolled in the General Psychology course received course credit for their time; volunteers from the general population were entered in a drawing to win one of two gift certificates to a local restaurant.

Stimulus Material

Fifteen faces, presented in three groups of five faces were used as stimuli (see Appendix 3). Each set of five faces morphed from one race to another (Black to White, White to Asian, Asian to Black, and the reverse of each of these three possibilities). A single face measured 2.86 centimeters in width by 4.28 centimeters in height and was separated from other faces in its set by a solid grey strip measuring 0.16 centimeters in width. Consistent with prior research, (Cunningham 1986) facial metrics accurate to one millimeter were taken of each individual face (See Fig. 6.2 and Table 6.1). The specific facial features measured and the subsequent calculations were based on the neonate, mature, and expressive determinants of facial attractiveness.

Measures

Participants received one of each set of five faces. The order in which the sets were presented and the direction of the morphing were counterbalanced, creating six different possibilities (White to Black, Asian to White, Black to Asian (WBAWBA); Black to Asian, White to Black, Asian to White (BAWBAW); Asian to White, Black to Asian, White to Black (AWBAWB); Black to White, White to Asian, Asian to Black (BWWAAB); Asian to Black, Black to White, White to Asian (ABBWWA); White to Asian, Asian to Black, Black to White (WAABBW)). Using a 5-point Likert scale, participants were asked to indicate in the space provided under each face their perception of its attractiveness (1 = not at all attractive, 5 = very attractive). Participants again used a 5-point Likert scale to indicate their perception of the women's personality as either highly desirable (=1)—kind, responsible, generous, wise, mentally

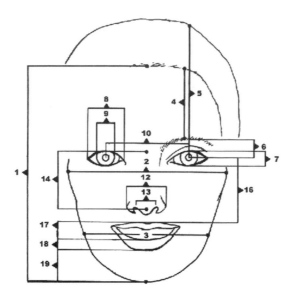

Fig. 6.2 1 = Length of face, distance from hairline to base of chin; **2** = Width of face at cheekbones; **3** = Width of face at mouth, distance between outer edges of cheeks at the level of the middle of the mouth, where the lips meet; **4** = Height of forehead, distance from eyebrow to hairline—length of the face; **5** = Height of upper head, measured from eye center to top of head estimated without hair—length of face; **6** = Height of eyebrows, measured from eye center to lower edge of eyebrow—ratio to length of face; **7** = Height of eyes, distance from upper to lower edge of visible eye within eyelids at eye center—length of face; **8** = Width of eyes, inner corner to outer corner of eye—width of face at cheekbones; **9** = Width of iris, measured diameter—width of face at cheekbones; **10** = Separation of eyes, distance between eye centers—width of face at cheekbones; **11** = Cheekbone width, an assessment of relative cheekbone prominence calculated as the difference between the width of the face at the cheekbones and the width of the face at the mouth; **12** = Nostril width, width of nose at outer edges of nostrils at widest point—width of face at mouth; **13** = Nose tip with, width of protrusion at tip of nose, usually associated with crease from nostril—width of face at mouth; **14** = Length of nose, measured from forehead bridge at level of upper edge of visible eye to nose tip—length of face; **15** = Nose , calculated as the product of the length of the nose and width of nose at the tip—length of face (not shown); **16** = Midface length, distance from eye center to upper edge of upper lip, calculated by subtracting from the length of the face height of the forehead, height of eyebrows, width of upper lip, width of lower lip, and length of chin—length of face; **17** = Thickness of upper lip, measured vertically at center—length of face; **18** = Thickness of lower lip, measured vertically at center—length of face; **19** = Length of chin, distance from lower edge of lower lip to base of chin—length of face. This figure is a modified version of the one created by Michael R. Cunningham (1985, 1986)

sound—or highly undesirable (=5)—greedy, miserly, self-conscious, deceitful, mentally unstable. In addition, participants were asked to indicate their perception of the skin tone of each face using the words "lightest", "light", "medium", "dark", and "darkest; they were able to use each term as many times as they felt necessary. Finally, participants also chose from the entire group of fifteen faces the face that they found most attractive overall and the face that they found least attractive overall.

After evaluating the fifteen faces, participants were next presented with either a 10-item version of the Marlowe-Crowne Social Desirability Scale (SD) or the Cutaneo-Chroma Correlate (CCC) (Hall[2] 1998). These two items were counterbalanced. Thus, there was a total of twelve possible questionnaires participants could receive: SD-CCC-ABBWWA, SD-CCC-AWBAWB, SD-CCC-BAWBAW, SD-CCC-WBAWBA, SD-CCC-BWWAAB, CCC-SD-WAABBW, CCC-SD-ABBWWA, CCC-SD-AWBAWB, CCC-SD-BAWBAW, CCC-SD-WBAWBA, CCC-SD-BWWAAB,

CCC-SD-WAABBW. The CCC is a validated inventory designed to examine participants' beliefs and opinions regarding skin color and its influences on a variety of life situations. Section B of the CCC was used in the current research and focuses on one's personal values regarding skin color.

Lastly, participants completed a 13-item demographics survey that included questions relating to the racial/ethnic and educational background of both themselves and their parents. Participants also ranked in order of personal importance eight physical features known to play important roles in determining facial attractiveness. These features were large eyes, full lips, small nose, high cheekbones, smooth skin, symmetric, familiarity of face, hair.[3] Participants then provided their perception of what "beauty" means to society and of what it means to them personally. The definitions were later coded as (1) purely physical, (2) purely personality, (3) both physical and personality, or (4) other (see Poran 1991). Other items included in this survey addressed participants' age and year in college (Freshman, Sophomore, Junior, Senior, SuperSenior[4]) gender, high school location, and the approximate combined yearly income of their parents.

In this study, the faces were always presented first to ensure that participants' responses to them were not tainted by items in the other parts of the questionnaire. Once participants finished evaluating the faces, they were asked to set them aside and were not permitted to alter their responses to them. They also were prohibited from returning to the other three sections of the questionnaire after completing them. The demographics survey was always the last in the packet.

Procedure

For all participants, the oral instructions given and the general atmosphere and sequence of administration were identical. Upon entering the room, participants

---

[2] The CCC was used in the current research with the express permission of its creator.

[3] Hair is unique among these features in that its texture (i.e., straight or curly) has been shown to have little to no impact on perceived facial attractiveness (Hinsz et al. 2001, Mescko & Bereczkei 2004). This feature was included to address a possible criticism of the research.

[4] The term "SuperSenior" is a term used in particular to this institution. It refers to students who choose to spend a fifth year at the university in order to earn a dual AB-BS degree in engineering. None participated in the study.

were issued an informed consent form and a pencil if needed. They were asked to read over the form, to ask the researcher any questions that arose while reviewing the terms of consent, and to sign where indicated. Once all participants had given consent, each one was handed a questionnaire packet, facedown. They were instructed as follows: "Please do not talk while completing the questionnaire. Once you have finished a section, please set it aside and do not return to it. You may ask me questions, but I may not be able to answer them. The questionnaire should take you between 15 and 20 minutes to complete. You may start."

During the period when the participants were completing the questionnaires, the researcher was present to answer questions and to ensure that participants were neither talking nor returning to already-completed sections of the questionnaire.

After completing the entire questionnaire, participants handed it to the researcher and received their debriefing document. They were urged to contact the researcher with any questions or concerns about the study.

Results

Each face was assigned a number in SPSS (see Fig. 6.3). Because three of the faces were duplicates they were not included in the analyses; these faces were Faces WB5, AW5, and BA5, which are identical to Faces BA1, WB1, and AW1, respectively. Participant race also was manipulated for analysis because of the disproportionate numbers of White and non-White participants. Thus, only three racial groups were used in analyses: (1) White, (2) Asian/Pacific Islander, (3) Other—Black, American Indian, Hispanic, Middle Eastern, "Other".

A series of repeated measures—analysis of variance (ANOVA)—were then computed. First, the data were analyzed to check for order effects. Order did not prove to significantly influence the face ratings. Subsequent analyses were then computed to test the hypotheses.

Attractiveness

There was a significant effect for face, multivariate $F(2, 12) = 7.602, p < 0.0001$ (see Table 6.2). The faces rated as most attractive were faces 1–4 (Faces WB1, WB2, WB3, and WB4) and 8–10 (Faces AW4, BA1, and BA2).

No significant effects were obtained for participant gender ($F(2, 12) = .998$, $p = .46$), Social Desirability score ($F(3, 12) = 1.371$, $p = .212$), race ($F(3, 12) = .878$, $p = .623$), personal definition of beauty ($F(4, 12) = 39.005$, $p = .269$), societal definition of beauty ($F(4, 12) = 24.952$, $p = .788$), class year ($F(4,12) = 1.2338, p = 0.533$), or household income ($F(6,12) = 1.260, p = 0.982$).

Skin Tone

There was a significant effect for face, multivariate $F(2, 12) = 111.419, p < 0.0001$ (see Table 6.2). The faces rated as having the darkest skin tone were faces 3 and 4 (Faces WB3 and WB4) and 9–11 (Faces BA1, BA2, and BA3).

No significant effects were obtained for participant gender ($F(2,12) = .780$, $p = .658$), Social Desirability score ($F(3,12) = .437$, $p = .933$), race ($F(3, 12) = .855, p = .652$), personal definition of beauty ($F(4, 12) = 1.266, p = .173$), societal definition of beauty ($F(4,12) = 1.055$, $p = .408$), class year ($F(4,12) = 0.789, p = 0.694$), or household income ($F(6,12) = .910, p = 0.899$).

The face previously identified by the researcher as Whitest (Face WB1, or, Face 1) was rated most often as the face with the lightest skin-tone, but the face previously identified as darkest face (Face BA1, or, Face 9) never received a rating of "darkest". Instead, Face 10, or BA2, was most often rated as "darkest".

Personality

There was no significant effect for face, multivariate $F(2, 12) = 1.086, p = .390$ (see Table 6.2). Thus, no further analyses were conducted to determine if the lightest face received the most positive personality rating and the darkest face the most negative.

In addition, no significant effects were obtained for participant gender ($F(2, 12) = 1.012, p = .448$), Social Desirability score ($F(3, 12) = 1.487, p = .164$), race ($F(3, 12) = .585, p = .926$), personal definition of beauty ($F(4, 12) = .882$, $p = .654$), societal definition of beauty ($F(4, 12) = .897, p = .599$), class year ($F(4,12) = 1.415 = 0.951$ or household income ($F(6,12) = 1.547, p = 0.996$).

Racial Identification

Since the Cutaneo-Chroma Correlate measures attitudes about skin color, it was used in the current research as an indicator of racial identity. For this population, the CCC was most reliable when item number six was not used in computing participants' scores, $a = .782$.

There was a significant race interaction: the CCC scores of participants in the group "Other" differed significantly from those of White participants, $F(2, 68) = 4.662, p = .013$. This did not, however, have any effect on face ratings and probably was a product of the third group's mixed racial makeup. No significant effects were found for attractiveness ($F(3, 12) = .737, p = .698$), skin tone ($F(3, 12) = 1.803$, $p = .076$), or personality ($F(3, 12) = .840$, $p = .602$), regardless of participant ethnicity. No significant effects were obtained for gender, $F(1,67) = 237, p = .628$.

The face chosen most often as most attractive was Face 2 (Face WB2). This choice differed significantly by race, $X^2 = 34.162$, $p = .047$ (see Table 6.3). Face 9 (Face BA1) was expected to receive the most votes for the least attractive face, but it was beaten by Face 5 (Face AW1). This choice did not differ significantly by race, $X^2 = 11.5379$, $p = .643$ (see Table 6.4).

Table 6.2 Perceived attractiveness, skin tone, and personality as a function of face being rated[1]

Face	Attractiveness	Skin Tone	Personality
1	*4.201 abcdefghijkl*	1.215 abcdefghijkl	2.897 aij
2	*3.858 abcdefgjkl*	1.126 abcdhijkl	2.830 bj
3	*3.492 abcefgkl*	2.837 abcdefghijkl	*2.702*
4	*3.456 abdeefghkl*	3.674 abcdefghijkl	*2.595 dfjl*
5	3.077 abcdefhij	2.256 acdehijk	2.849 ej
6	2.878 abcdfhij	2.293 acdfhijk	2.885 df
7	2.883 abcdghij	2.263 acdghijk	*2.741*
8	*3.745 adefghkl*	1.911 abcdefghijkl	*2.702*
9	*3.729 aefgijkl*	4.515 abcdefghijkl	2.590 ail
10	3.539 abcdefgijkl	3.830 abcdefghijkl	2.487 abefjkl
11	3.047 abcdhijk	*3.063 abcdefghijkl*	2.758 jk
12	3.044 abcdhijkl	2.337 abcdhijkl	2.905 dijl

[1]For attractiveness and skin tone, higher ratings indicate greater attractiveness or darker skin tone. For personality, lower ratings indicate a more desirable personality. Italicized means in each column differ significantly at the .05 level from the non-italicized means with the same letter in each column.

Table 6.3 Counts for the most attractive face broken down by race

		Face												
		1	2	3	4	5	6	7	8	9	10	11	12	Total
Race	White	8	9	1	3	2	1	1	2	3	2	1	0	33
	Asian/ Pacific islander	0	0	0	0	0	1	0	0	0	1	1	1	4
	Other	0	0	0	0	1	0	0	0	2	0	0	0	3
Total		8	9	1	3	3	2	1	2	5	3	2	1	40

Table 6.4 Counts for the least attractive face broken down by race

		Face								
		2	3	4	5	6	7	9	12	Total
Race	White	1	2	1	10	5	6	2	4	31
	Asian/ Pacific islander	0	0	1	0	3	1	0	0	5
	Other	0	0	0	1	0	1	0	0	2
Total		1	2	2	11	8	8	2	4	38

Table 6.5 Mean rankings for specific facial features[1]

Feature	Mean
Smooth skin	2.51
Symmetry	3.17
Hair	3.81
Large eyes	4.51
Familiarity	4.84
Small nose	5.31
Full lips	5.62
High cheekbones	6.22

[1]Lower rankings indicate greater desirability of trait.

Facial Features

The main purpose of the facial features measure was to confirm previous research findings on the salience of several important facial features in determining attractiveness. A Friedman's test was run to determine the significance of the feature rankings, $X^2 = 125.018$, $p < 0.0001$ (see Table 6.5).

Facial feature rankings did not have any significant effect on ratings of attractiveness, skin tone, or personality.

The rankings show the relative importance of each feature in determining facial attractiveness. Interestingly, the rankings from this study represent an upset of the norm. As expected based on prior research, smooth skin was rated as the most important facial feature. However, large eyes and full lips are usually among the most important features, but only large eyes made it into the top of the rankings for the current study, while full lips were rated the second least important feature.

Discussion

Attractiveness

Among Black, White, and Asian faces comprised of varying degrees of features from each race, White faces were perceived as the most attractive. The face chosen most often as the most attractive was Face WB2 one of the Whitest faces. This finding is in line with previous research on race and attractiveness and supports the first part of the hypothesis being tested in this research. The second part of the hypothesis predicted that, as was the case in past research, the face with the darkest skin tone (Face 9, or, Face BA1) would be considered the least attractive, but this was not supported by the results of the current research. The darkest face was ranked fourth for attractiveness—right after the three White faces. The face rated most often as the least attractive was Face AW1, a face composed of 100% Asian characteristics.

There is little existing research to help explain these unexpected results, which seem particularly surprising considering that even though five times as many Asian/Pacific Islander as Black students participated in the research, their responses and those of their White and other ethnically self-identified peers did not significantly differ. One explanation for these results centers around the concept of familiarity. If we consider the findings of Peskin and Newell (2004), familiar faces are more attractive than are unfamiliar ones, thus we might conjecture that the participants found Asian/Pacific Islander faces unattractive because they were for some reason more unfamiliar with them than they were with Black and White faces.

The vast majority of existing attractiveness research involving race focuses only on White's and Black's faces, a reflection of our society's continuing focus on a Black-White dichotomy. If this is the case, it is reasonable to suppose that despite the reality of a growing Asian population in the United States, Asian faces may remain alien on a day-to-day basis to a significant portion of the American population. This alienation might be furthered by our society's dichotomous view of itself. Turning to popular American media, a limited number of Asian celebrities are forward in our minds. Lucy Liu probably is the most famous Asian celebrity of our current time, followed by stars such as Jet Li, Jackie Chan, and Connie Chung. Hollywood's Black celebrity list is much longer and more easily conjured: Oprah Winfrey, Denzel Washington, Halle Berry, Will Smith, Whoopi Goldberg, Eddie Murphy, and nearly any popular rapper spring to mind almost instantly. In the political realm, the National Association for the Advancement of Colored People (NAACP 2008)—an organization that welcomes all colored people and minorities—still is thought of as an African American organization. It is no wonder, then, that Americans have a black-and-white view of their nation and are less familiar with Asian faces than one might wish or expect them to be.

Regarding the specific student population studied in this research, despite the fact that the campus population as a whole is predominantly White, it would be difficult to claim that participants were relatively more familiar with Black faces than they were with Asian ones. For the past five years, self-identified Asian/Pacific Islander students have outnumbered self-identified Black students by approximately two to one (see Table 6.6). Furthermore, over the

Table 6.6 Undergraduate population by race[1]

	NRA[2]	Native American	Hispanic	Black	Asian/ Pacific Islander	White	Total
Fall 2005	100	13	86	89	236	3024	3548
Fall 2004	94	17	80	95	208	3051	3545
Fall 2003	81	15	78	95	208	3081	3558
Fall 2002	68	17	80	102	198	3071	3536
Fall 2001	60	6	93	100	188	3118	3565
Total	403	68	417	481	1038	15345	17752

[1]Special thanks to the Department of Planning and Institutional Research for providing this information at the researcher's request.

[2]NRA (non-resident aliens) refers to students who do not have American citizenship.

same time frame, the number of Black students on campus has been steadily decreasing at the same time as the number of Asian/Pacific Islander students on campus has been steadily increasing. Both Black and Asian/Pacific Islander students have the opportunity to participate on campus in ethnic groups related to their culture, and in fact, there are more clubs devoted to Asian/Pacific Island culture than there are devoted to Black culture. All of the groups for both ethnicities are active on campus, hosting food fairs and other cultural events to spread awareness of and increase exposure to their cultures. Considering these campus demographics, it does not necessarily make sense to suggest that participants saw Asian/Pacific Islander faces on campus less often than they saw Black faces, although it certainly might be the case that a significant number of the participants encountered significantly fewer Asian/Pacific Islanders than Blacks before arriving at college. If this is the case, then Asian faces *would* be relatively unfamiliar to participants when compared with faces from the other two groups, leading to lowered attractive ratings for Asian faces.

Another explanation for the results addresses specifically the racial breakdown of population sample. The sample is relatively small and predominantly White, with a handful of Asian/Pacific Islanders and just a few students of other ethnic backgrounds. It is possible that the somewhat homogeneous characteristics of the campus population and of the sample population confounded the results.

The standard Asian/Pacific Islander ethnic grouping used in the research might be problematic in that it may represent an inaccurate population categorization. Zebrowitz, Montepare, and Lee (1993), found that Black American, White American, and Korean students gave comparable attractiveness ratings to men of all three ethnic groups, and they all found the same faces attractive. But the researchers also found that Korean participants gave in-group faces lower attractiveness ratings than did members of the other two groups. Cunningham et al. (1995) found a similar phenomenon in their study with Whites, Asians, and Hispanics, but this time it was it was the Hispanic participants who harshly rated in-group members. The contradictory findings of these two studies may stem from the fact that the Asian participants in Cunningham's research were Asian American, while those in Zebrowitz's study were Asians living in their country of origin. Certainly, there must be large cultural differences between Asian Americans and native Asians. Furthermore, Cunningham et al. used a general group of Asian Americans of unspecified Asian ancestry, while the Zebrowitz et al. study very specifically included only students of Korean decent. It is highly possible that there are different dynamics between specific groups of Asians of one or another particular ancestry. Asia is the largest continent on the planet, and when grouped together with the Pacific Islands—as it was, for example, in the current research, the "Asian/Pacific Islander" category encompasses individuals from 75 nations,[5] many of which

---

[5] This number includes French, U.S., and Chilean territories.

are incredibly far removed from mainland Asia. This might serve to create strong ethnic ties within each country or between groups of countries while simultaneously estranging Asians/Pacific Islanders from each other as a whole, creating a group of people with very different values and preferences.

Still on the theme of race, in the current research, there was a significant disconnect between participants' skin tone ratings of each face and the actual skin tone of the faces. The actual Whitest face, Face WB1, was rated most often as the lightest-skinned face, but the actual darkest face, Face BA1, never even received a rating of "darkest". The face most often rated as "darkest" was Face WBA2, a face comprised of 75% Black facial features and 25% Asian facial features. This does not seem to have had any significant effects on the facial ratings, though, since both Face WB1 and Face WB2 received significantly high attractiveness and personality ratings. Still, this disagreement between the perceived and actual skin tones of the faces may indicate a larger problem with them. It has been suggested that a potential problem with the study is that neither the "pure" Asian nor the "pure" Black face have dark enough skin tones and, therefore, the faces do not accurately represent the entire gamut of skin tones between the three races. Another possible criticism is that the "pure" Asian face is not very "Asiany", that is, it is not very representative of a typical Asian or Pacific Islander face (of course, as previously discussed, it might be very difficult to accomplish a "typical" face for this racial/ethnic group). It has been further suggested that this face is problematic because it is representative only of Northeast-Asian faces, which, as is clear from the earlier discussion, excludes large sections of Asia and the Pacific Islands. These possible problems may help explain the unexpected results of the study. If both the "pure Black" face and the face perceived by most participants as darkest actually were not very dark, this unrealistically light skin tone may have caused participants to find them more attractive than one would typically expect, "bumping down" the relative attractiveness of the Asian faces. Moreover, if the Asian faces truly are not accurate representations of Asian faces, they may have seemed particularly unfamiliar to the participants. Thus, the low attractiveness ratings given to the Asian faces may have resulted not from a dislike or lack of attraction toward Asians or Asian facial features, but, again, due to unfamiliarity with the Asian faces and inaccurate representations of Black and Asian faces.

Facial Features

Although the facial feature rankings did not have any significant effect on ratings of attractiveness, skin tone, or personality, they did represent a ranking different from that found in previous research. Past research, however, was not quite as forward as was the current research in investigating this question. Instead of running analyses to explore how changes in specific facial features affect attractiveness ratings, participants in this study were asked to assign a rank to each of eight facial features to indicate how important they considered each feature to be in determining facial beauty. It is possible, then, that the results represent a more conscious ranking of the features, as opposed to past results, which one might consider representative of a most subconscious preference. Another possibility is that the relative uniformity of some facial features in the images rated by participants somehow affected the rankings by making certain features more or less salient than others. Skin quality was among the constant features, but because skin tone also was the most perceptible change from one face to another, skin remained salient, which might explain its retention of its normal position as the most important facial feature contributing to attractiveness.

Limitations and Future Research

It was hoped that this research would shed some light onto the epidemic of eating disorders and low self-esteem problems that are rampant in today's society.[6] However, it may have created more questions than answers. A self-esteem scale was not included in the current research, so it impossible to determine any link between participants' self-esteem and their ratings of the faces; this is something future research might examine. Much of the existing body of knowledge in this area demonstrates that, for women, Whites and Latinas tend to have lower self-esteem and greater desire to lose weight than do Blacks (Wade & DiMaria 2003, Parker et al. 1995, Poran 2004). One study, though, found no differences between Hispanic, Black, and White participants' discontent with their bodies (McKnight Investigators 2003). The McKnight group's findings (2003) suggest that factors such as a preoccupation with thinness and social pressure may have more direct impacts on the development of disordered eating and that race may simply mediate these relationships. Race does appear to play an important role in the treatment offered to individuals with disordered eating patterns. White adolescent girls are more likely to be recognized as having disturbed eating patterns than are their African American or Latina peers (Gordon et al. 2001). The researchers hypothesize that this is due to a strong mental association between Whites and slenderness. On the opposite weight extreme, obesity is considered by many people to be a character flaw, but obese women are not all treated equally (Wade & DiMaria 2003). In this study, the researchers confirmed their hypothesis that thin White women and heavy Black women would receive more positive personality and life success ratings than would heavy White women and thin Black women. Clearly, more research is needed in this area, particularly research inclusive of Asian/Pacific Islanders. As a minority group, Asian/Pacific Islanders might be less likely to be diagnosed with an eating disorder, but it seems as though

---

[6] At the time of this research, approximately 0.5–1% of United States adolescents present with diagnosable anorexia nervosa, and 2–3% of adolescents with bulimia nervosa (Eating Disorders Coalition 2006). Many more adolescents and adults suffer from other clinical and sub-clinical disordered eating behaviors.

they should be an at-risk group since the current research demonstrates they are perceived by themselves and by others as unattractive in comparison with White and Black faces.

Several limitations of this study already have been discussed, but there are other possible limitations that future research should address. Although the CCC has proven itself a reliable measure as used by Dr. Ronald Hall (1998), it was reliable for the current population only when one of the items was removed, which may be a product of the small sample population. The CCC also is not truly a measure of racial identification. Future studies should incorporate a measure specifically designed to examine racial-identity attitudes, such as the Multigroup Ethnic Identity Measure (Phinney 1992), the Black Racial Identity Attitude Scale-B Long Form (Parham & Helms 1985), The People of Color Racial Identity Attitude Scale (Helms 1995), or the Cultural Identification Scale (Oetting & Beauvais 1991).

It might also be prudent to include a measurement of demand characteristics since it is difficult to mask the nature of research involving race. It is unlikely that this was a factor in the current research since Social Desirability scores did not have a significant impact on face ratings, but it is possible that this could help elucidate the findings.

Finally, future research should consider seriously the faces it uses as stimuli. It is essential that the facial stimuli represent accurately the racial groups for which they act as archetypes. While the faces used in this study have been used widely in the past and have been shown to be both valid and reliable in past research, concerns about the accuracy of the skin tones represented could be addressed by including more faces or by darkening the skin tone of the pure Asian and pure Black faces.

Appendix 1

Does the thought of a delicious free meal make your mouth water?
Are you interested in beauty and attraction?
Are you worried by the rising incidence of self-esteem and eating disorders in America?

If so, then please volunteer to participate in a psychological study on face perception and beauty among United States university students. *Anyone who participates will be entered into a drawing to win one of two $25 gift certificates to Damon's Grill!*

Remaining dates to participate are **Wednesday, March 8 at 10am**, and **Friday, March 10 at 1 pm or 3 pm**.

Please respond to this email for more information.

Thank you,
Nicole Belletti
nbellett@

Appendix 2

Informed Consent

1. Project Name: Face perception among United States university students
2. Purpose of the research: The purpose of this research is to examine the beauty preferences of the typical American university student.
3. General plan of the research: You will be asked to complete several short questionnaires and to rate the attractiveness of a series of faces.
4. Estimated duration of the research: one (1) hour
5. Estimated total number of participants: 50–100
6. You are encouraged to ask any questions at any time about the study and its procedures, or your rights as a participant.

The investigator's name, address, telephone number, and e-mail address are included below so that you may ask questions and report any study-related problems. We will do everything possible to prevent or reduce discomfort and risk, but it is not possible to predict everything that might occur. If you have unexpected discomfort or think something unusual or unexpected is occurring you should contact Nicole Belletti (nbellett@bucknell.edu; 484-515-7122) or Professor Wade in the Psychology Department (jwade@bucknell.edu).

Your participation is voluntary. Anyone who agrees to participate in this research may change his/her mind at any time. You may refuse to answer any questions and/or withdraw from the study at any time without penalty or loss of benefits to which you are otherwise entitled.

You will receive compensation in the form of credit hours toward your PSYC100 research participation requirement for your participation in this research. This credit will be awarded in accord with the Psychology Department's regulations.

Participation in this research may result in the following benefits either to the subject, others, or the body of knowledge:

- The most important outcome of this study will be the addition of new knowledge to the information that is already in existence on beauty and attraction.
- The applied repercussions of this study could be far-reaching. Results will have implications for the comprehension, diagnosis, and treatment of self-esteem problems and eating disorders since these all-too-common problems typically are rooted in appearance.
- As a participant, you will benefit from the experience of participating in psychological research and will play an important role in bringing about the above-mentioned profits of this study.

All records from this study will be kept confidential. Data will be stored securely and will be made available only to persons conducting the study unless you specifically give permission in writing to do otherwise. No reference will be made in oral or written reports to link you to this study.

In the unlikely event of physical injury resulting from your participation in this research, emergency medical treatment will be provided at no cost to you. You should immediately notify the investigator if you are injured. If you require additional medical treatment, you will be responsible for the cost. No other compensation will be provided if you sustain an injury resulting from this research.

The details of this research cannot be fully described at this time, but at the conclusion of participation, a complete explanation will be provided and you will be permitted to ask questions of the researcher.

I have read the above description of the research. Anything I did not understand was explained to me by Nicole Belletti and I had all of my questions answered to my satisfaction. I agree to participate in this research, and I acknowledge that I have received a personal copy of this signed consent form.

By signing below, I affirm that I am at least 18 years of age or older.

> Signature of Subject:_____(Date)
> Signature of witness:_____(Date)
> Witness address: 207 Swartz
> Witness Telephone Number: 484-515-7122

Appendix 3

Section 1

Instructions: On the next page, you will see three sets of five faces. Please read carefully the following instructions about what to do with these faces and be sure to ask the researcher if you have any questions. You may refer to these instructions while you evaluate the faces.

For each face, please indicate on the designated line beneath it how attractive you find it. If you find the face *not at all attractive*, rate it as **1**. If you find it *somewhat unattractive*, rate it as **2**. If you find it *neither attractive nor unattractive*, rate it as **3**. If you find it *somewhat attractive*, rate it as **4**. If you find the face *very attractive*, rate it as **5**. Please provide only one rating per face.

For each face, indicate on the designated line beneath it your perception of its skin tone using the following terms: **lightest**, **light**, **medium**, **dark**, **darkest**. You may use each term as many times as you wish. Please provide only one response for each face.

For each face, please indicate on the designated line beneath it the type of personality you attribute to the woman possessing it. If you attribute to it a *highly undesirable* personality, rate it as **5**. If you attribute to it an *undesirable* personality, rate it as **4**. If you attribute to it a personality that is *neither*

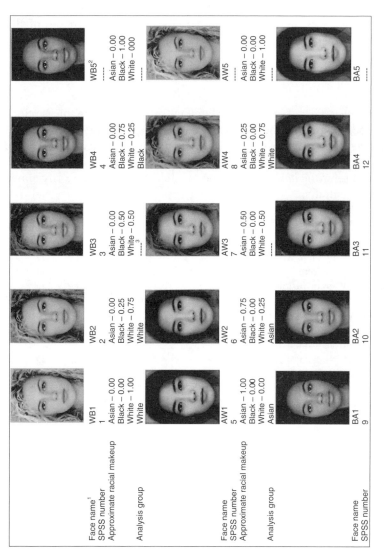

Fig. 6.3 Facial information (*See* Color Insert)

[1] Face name refers to the code names given to each face and used throughout the body of this paper with the exception of the Results section for functional purposes. The number assigned to each face for use in the Results section is provided in SPSS number.

[2] Faces WB5, AW5, and BA5 are identical to faces BA1, WB1, and AW1, respectively, and, thus, were not used in data analyses. Therefore, they were assigned neither an SPSS number nor an analysis group.

[3] Faces WB3, AW3, and BA3 were not assigned an analysis group to avoid having the same face in two different groups.

desirable nor undesirable, rate it as **3**. If you attribute to it a *desirable* personality, rate it as **2**. If you attribute to it a *highly desirable* personality, rate it as **1**. A highly desirable personality possesses the following traits: kind, responsible, generous, wise, mentally sound. A highly undesirable personality possesses the opposite traits: greedy, miserly, self-conscious, deceitful, mentally unstable.

Please **circle** the face that you find *most attractive* out of all fifteen faces. Please draw a **square** around the face that you find *least attractive* out of all fifteen faces.

Section 2

Instructions: Below is a list of incomplete statements. For each item, please circle the letter that best completes the sentence according to your personal values. If you prefer the *lightest* skin tone possible, circle **A**. If you prefer a *light* skin tone, circle **B**. If you prefer a *medium* skin tone, circle **C**. If you prefer a *dark* skin tone, circle **D**. If you prefer the *darkest* skin tone possible, circle **E**.Please circle only **one response** for each item.

1.	Pretty skin is	A	B	C	D	E
2.	The skin color of pretty women is	A	B	C	D	E
3.	The skin color of the man women like is	A	B	C	D	E
4.	I wish my skin color were	A	B	C	D	E
5.	The skin color of smart people is	A	B	C	D	E
6.	The skin color of people who are snobs is	A	B	C	D	E
7.	The skin color of people who are kind is	A	B	C	D	E
8.	The skin color of my best friend is	A	B	C	D	E
9.	I want my child(ren)'s skin color to be	A	B	C	D	E
10.	My ideal spouse's skin color is	A	B	C	D	E
11.	The skin color of my family should be	A	B	C	D	E
12.	The skin color of my race should be	A	B	C	D	E
13.	The skin color of people who are physically strong is	A	B	C	D	E
14.	The skin color of people who are dumb is	A	B	C	D	E
15.	The ideal skin color of my child(ren)'s spouse is	A	B	C	D	E

Section 3

Instructions: Listed below are a number of statements concerning personal attitudes and traits.

Read each item and decide whether the statement is true or false as it pertains to you personally.

Please circle only one response for each item.

1.	I never hesitate to go out of my way to help someone in trouble.	T	F
2.	I have never intensely disliked anyone.	T	F

3. There have been times when I was quite jealous of the good fortune of others.   T   F
4. I would never think of letting someone else be punished for my wrong doings.   T   F
5. I sometimes feel resentful when I don't get my way.   T   F
6. There have been times when I felt like rebelling against people in authority even   T   F
   though I knew they were right.
7. I am always courteous, even to people who are disagreeable.   T   F
8. When I don't know something, I don't at all mind admitting it.   T   F
9. I can remember "playing sick" to get out of something.   T   F
10. I am sometimes irritated by people who ask favors of me.   T   F

Section 4

Instructions: Please answer each question to the best of your ability.

What is your gender? (Please circle only one.)   M   F

What is your age? _____

What year are you? (Please circle only one.) Fr   So   Jr   Sr   SuperSr

What is the name and location of your high school?

Name: _____

Location: _____
City   State

What is your race? (Please choose only one.)

____ African-American

____ American Indian

____ Asian/Pacific Islander

____ Hispanic

____ Middle Eastern

____ White

____ Other (please specify): _____

Please rank the following facial features from 1 to 8 in accordance with how important you find each feature in determining the attractiveness of a woman's face.

One is most important, eight is least important.

___ Large eyes	___ Smooth skin
___ Full lips	___ Symmetric
___ Small nose	___ Familiarity of face
___ High cheekbones	___ Hair

Please give a short definition of what the word "beauty" means **to you**:

_____

_____

_____

Please give a short definition of what you think the word "beauty" means **to society**:

_____

_____

_____

What is the highest level of education completed by your mother? (Please choose only one.)

_____ Less than high school

_____ High school/GED

_____ 2-year college degree (Associates)

_____ 4-year college degree (BA, BS)

_____ Master's degree

_____ Doctoral degree

_____ Professional degree (MD, JD)

_____ Don't know

What is your mother's race? (Please choose only one.)

_____ African-American

_____ American Indian

_____ Asian/Pacific Islander

_____ Hispanic

_____ Middle Eastern

_____ White

_____ Other (please specify): _____

What is the highest level of education completed by your father? (Please choose only one.)

_____ Less than high school

_____ High school/GED

_____ 2-year college degree (Associates)

_____ 4-year college degree (BA, BS)

_____ Master's degree

_____ Doctoral degree

_____ Professional degree (MD, JD)

_____ Don't know

What is your father's race? (Please choose only one.)

_____ African-American

_____ American Indian

_____ Asian/Pacific Islander

_____ Hispanic

_____ Middle Eastern

_____ White

_____ Other (please specify): _____

What is the approximate combined yearly income of your parents? (Please choose only one.)

_____ < $10,000
_____ $10,000 – $40,000
_____ $40,000 – $80,000
_____ $80,000 – $100,000
_____ $100,000 – $150,000
_____ $150,000 – $200,000
_____ >$200,000

Appendix 4

Debriefing

In this study, you were asked to rate the attractiveness of fifteen faces and to choose out of those fifteen faces the single most attractive and the single least attractive faces. The purpose of this study is to investigate the attractiveness perceptions of United States university students. More specifically, however, this study examines the effects of race—that of the participant and that of the woman pictured—on ratings of attractiveness. We hope the results will be applicable to the comprehension, diagnosis and treatment of self-esteem problems and eating disorders since these all-too-common problems typically are rooted in appearance.

If you have any questions or concerns about your participation in this study, or if you are interested in its outcome, please feel free to contact Nicole Belletti (nbellett@bucknell.edu; 484-515-7122) or Professor Wade of the Psychology Department (jwade@bucknell.edu).

References

Alley, T. R. (1988). Physiognomy and social perception. In T. R. Alley (Ed.) *Social and applied aspects of perceiving faces* (pp. 167–190). Hillsdale, NJ: Erlbaum.

Alley, T. R., & Hilebrandt, K.A. (1988). Determinants and consequences of facial aesthetics. In T. R. Alley (Ed.) *Social and applied aspects of perceiving faces* (pp. 101–140). Hillsdale, NJ: Erlbaum.

Badcock, C. F. (1920). The significance of facial beauty. *Scientific Progress*, 15: 70–73.

Bauduoin, J. Y., & Tiberghien, G. (2004). Symmetry, averageness, and feature size in the facial attractiveness of women. *Acta Psychologica*, 117(3): 313–332.

Berry, D. S. (1991). Attractive faces are not all created equal: Joint effects of facial babyishness and attractiveness on social perception. *Personality and Social Psychology Bulletin*, 17(5): 523–231.

Bradshaw, C. K. (1992). Beauty and the beast: On racial ambiguity. In M. P. P. Root (Ed.), *Racially mixed people in America* (pp. 77–90). London: Sage.

Chen, N. Y., Shaffer, D. R., & Wu, C., (1997). On physical attractiveness stereotyping in Taiwan: A revised sociocultural perspective. *Journal of Social Psychology*, 137(1): 117–124.

Cunningham, M. R. (1986). Measuring the physical in physical attractiveness: Quasi-experiments on the sociobiology of female facial beauty. *Journal of Personality and Social Psychology*, 50(5): 925–935.

Cunningham, M. R., Roberts, A. R., Barbee, A. P., Druen, P. B. et al. (1995). 'Their ideas of beauty are, on the whole, the same as ours': Consistency and variability in the cross-cultural perception of female physical attractiveness. *Journal of Personality and Social Psychology*, 68(2): 261–279.

Cunningham, M. R., Barbee, A.P., & Philhower, C. L. (2002). Dimensions of facial physical attractiveness: The intersection of biology and culture. In G. Rhodes & L. A. Zebrowitz, (Eds.). *Facial attractiveness: Evolutionary, cognitive, and social perspectives* (pp. 193–238). Westport, CT: Ablex.

de Casanova, E. M. (2004). 'No ugly woman': concepts of race and beauty among adolescent women in Ecuador. *Gender and Society*, 18(3): 287–308.

Deutsch, C. K. (1987). Disproportion in psychiatric syndromes. In L. G. Farkas & I. R. Munro (Eds.), *Anthropometric facial proportions in medicine* (pp. 131–141). Springfield, IL: Thomas.

Dion, K. K. (2002). Cultural perspectives on facial attractiveness. In G. Rhodes, and L. A. Zebrowitz (Eds.), *Facial attractiveness: Evolutionary, cognitive, and social perspectives* (pp. 239–260). Westport, CT: Ablex.

Dion, K. K., Berscheid, E., & Walster, E. (1972). What is beautiful is good. *Journal of Personality and Social Psychology*, 24, 285–290.

Eating disorders coalition [for research, policy, & action]. (2006). http://www.eatingdisorderscoalition.org/reports/statistics.html. Accessed 16 April 2006.

Eyetsemitan, F. (2004). An exploratory study of the emotion-expressive behaviors of "peace," "contentment," and "annoyed/irritated": Implications for dead and living faces. *Omega: Journal of Death and Dying*, 48(1): 88–99.

Fink, B., Grammer, K., & Thornhill, R. (2001). Human (homo sapiens) facial attractiveness in relation to skin texture and color. *Journal of Comparative Psychology*, 115(1): 92–99.

Galton, F. (1878). Composite portraits. *Nature*, 18: 97–100.

Gangestad, S. W., Thornhill, R., & Yeo, R. A. (1994). Facial attractiveness, developmental stability, and fluctuating asymmetry. *Ethology and Sociobiology*, 15(2): 73–85.

Gordon, K. H., Perez, M., & Joiner Jr., T. E. (2002). The impact of racial stereotypes on eating disorder recognition. *International Journal of Eating Disorders*, 32(2):219–224.

Hall, R. E. (1998). Skin color bias: A new perspective on an old problem. *Journal of Psychology*, 132(2): 238–240.

Helms, J. E. (1995). The people of color (POC) racial identity attitude scale. Unpublished manuscript.

Hill, M. E. (2002). Skin color and the perception of attractiveness among African Americans: Does gender make a difference? *Social Psychology Quarterly*, 65(1): 77–91.

Hinsz, V. B., Matz, D. C., & Patience, R. A. (2001). Does women's hair signal reproductive potential? *Journal of Experimental Social Psychology*, 31(2): 166–172.

Ishi, H., Gyoba, J., Kamahi, M., Mukaida, S., & Akamatsu, S. (2004). Analysis of facial attractiveness on feminised and juvenilised faces. *Perception*, 33(2): 135–145.

Johnston, V. S. (2000). Female facial beauty: The fertility hypothesis. *Pragmatics and Cognition* 8,(1): 107–122.

Jones, B. C., Anthony, A. C., Burt, D. M., & Perrett, D. I. (2004a). When facial attractiveness is only skin deep. *Perception*, 33(5): 569–576.

Jones, B. C., Little, A C., Feinberg, D. R., Penton-Voak, I. S., Tiddeman, B. P., & Perrett, D. I. (2004b). The relationship between shape symmetry and perceived skin condition in male facial attractiveness. *Evolution and Human Behavior*, 25(1): 24–30.

Jones, D., & Hill, K. (1993). Criteria of facial attractiveness in five populations. *Human Nature*, 4(3), 271–296.

Langlois, J. H., & Roggman, L. A. (1990). Attractive faces are only average. *Psychological Science*, 1(2): 115–121.

Langlois, J., Roggman, L. A., & Ritter, J. M. (1987). Infant preferences for attractive faces: rudiments or a stereotype? *Developmental Psychology*, 86: 415–427.

Langlois, J. H., Roggman, L. A., & Musselman, L. (1995). What is average and what is not average about attractive faces? *Psychological Science*, 5(4): 214–220.

Livshits, G., & Kobylianski, E. (1991). Fluctuating asymmetry as a possible measure of developmental homeostasis in humans: A review. *Human Biology*, 63:441–266.

Lundqvist, D., Esteves, R., & Ohman, A. (2004). The face of wrath: The role of features and configurations in conveying social threat. *Cognition and Emotion*, 18(2): 161–182.

Mack, D., & Rainey, D. (1990). Female applicant's personal grooming and personnel selection. *Journal of Social Behavior and Personality*, 5(5): 399–407.

[The] McKnight Investigators. (2003). Risk factors for the onset of eating disorders in adolescent girls: Results of the McKnight longitudinal risk factor. *American Journal of Psychiatry*, 160: 248–254.

Mealey, L., Bridgstock, R., & Townsend, G. C. (1999). Symmetry and perceived facial attractiveness: A monozygotic co-twin comparison. *Journal of Personality and Social Psychology*, 76(1): 151–158.

Mescko, N., & Bereczkei, T. (2004). Hairstyle as an adaptive means of displayed phenotypic quality. *Human nature: An interdisciplinary bisocial perspective*, 15(3): 251–270.

Morris, D. (1967). *The naked ape: A zoologist's study of the human animal.* New York: McGraw-Hill.

NAACP. (2008). http://www.naacp.org/home/index.htm. Accessed 27 January 2008.

Oetting, E. R., & Beauvais, F. (1991). Orthogonal cultural orientation theory: The cultural identification of minority adolescents. *International Journal of the Addictions,* 25: 655–685.

Parham, T. A., & Helms, J. E. (1985). Attitudes of racial identity and self-esteem of Black students: An exploratory investigation. *Journal of College Student Personnel,* 26(2): 143–147.

Parker, S., Nichter, M., Vuckovic, N., Sims, C., & Ritenbaugh, C. (1995). Body image and weight concerns among African American and White adolescent females: Differences that make a difference. *Human Organization*, 54(2): 103–114.

Perrett, D. I., Burt, D. M., Penton-Voak, I. S., Lee, K. J., Rowland, D. A., & Edwards, R. (1999). Symmetry and human facial attractiveness. *Evolution and Human Behavior*, 20(5): 295–307.

Peskin, M., & Newell, F. N. (2004). Familiarity breeds attraction: Effects of exposure on the attractiveness of typical and distinctive faces. *Perception*, 33(2): 147–157.

Phinney, J. S. (1992). The multigroup ethnic identity measure: A new scale for use with diverse groups. *Journal of Adolescent Research*, 7: 156–176.

Poran, M. A. (1991). Denying diversity: Perceptions of beauty and social comparison processes among Latina, Black, and White women. *Sex Roles*, 47(1): 65–82.

Rhodes, G. & Tremewan, T. (1996). Averageness, exaggeration, and facial attractiveness. *Psychological Science*, 7(2): 105–110.

Rhodes, G., Proffitt, F., Grady, J. M., & Sumich, A. (1998). Facial symmetry and the perception of beauty. *Psychonomic Bulletin and Review*, 5(4): 659–669.

Rhodes, G., Harwood, K., Yoshikawa, S., Nishitani, M., & McLean, I. (2002).The attractiveness of average faces: Cross-cultural evidence and possible biological basis. In G. Rhodes & L. A. Zebrowitz (Eds.), *Facial attractiveness: Evolutionary, cognitive, and social perspectives* (pp. 35–58). Westport, CT: Ablex.

Rubenstein, A. J., Langlois, J. H., & Roggman, L. A. (2002). What makes a face attractive and why: The role of averageness in defining facial beauty. In G. Rhodes & L. A. Zebrowitz

(Eds.), *Facial attractiveness: Evolutionary, cognitive, and social perspectives* (pp. 1–34). Westport, CT: Ablex.

Stewart, J. E. (1980). Defendant's attractiveness as a factor in the outcome of criminal trials: An observational study. *Journal of Applied Social Psychology*, 10(4), 348–361.

Terry, R. L. (1977). Further evidence on components of facial attractiveness. *Perceptual and Motor Skills*, 45(1): 130.

Terry, R. L., & Davis, J. S. (1976). Components of facial attractiveness. *Perceptual and Motor Skills*, 42(3): 918.

Tipples, J., Atkinson, A. P., & Andrew, W. (2002). The eyebrow frown: A salient social signal. *Emotion*, 2(3): 288–296.

Wade, T. J., & Dautrich, L. (2005). Racial characteristics and individual differences in men's evaluations of women's facial attractiveness and personality. Unpublished manuscript.

Wade, T. J., & DiMaria, C. (2003). Weight halo effects: Individual differences in perceived life success as a function of women's race and weight. *Sex Roles*, 48(9–10): 461–465.

Wade, T. J., Dyckman, K. A., & Cooper, M. (2004). Invisible men: Evolutionary theory and attractiveness and personality evaluations of 10 African American male facial shapes. *Journal of Black Psychology*, 30(4): 477–488.

Wade, T. J., Irvine, K., & Cooper, M. (2004). Racial characteristics and individual differences in women's evaluations of men's facial attractiveness and personality. *Personality and Individual Differences*, 36(5): 1083–1092.

Zaidel, D. W., Aarde, S. M., & Baig, K. (2005). Appearance of symmetry, beauty, and health in human faces. *Brain and Cognition*, 57(3): 561–263.

Zebrowitz, L.A., Montepare, J. M., & Lee, H. (1993). They don't all look alike: Individual impressions of other racial groups. *Journal of Personality and Social Psychology*, 65(1): 85–101.

Zebrowitz, L. A., Hall, J. A., Murphy, N. A., & Rhodes, G. (2002). Looking smart and looking good: Facial cues to intelligence and their origins. *Personality and Social Psychology Bulletin*, 28(2): 238–249

Chapter 7
Lifetime Prevalence and Quality of Interracial Interactions on Color Consciousness Among White Young Adults

Alfiee M. Breland-Noble, Joy King, Stacy Young, Brea Eaton, Melissa Willis, Keri Hurst, and Chastity Simmons

Abstract Color consciousness occurs when individuals identify and respond to the varied skin tones of others. Specifically, African American issues of color consciousness are rooted in the oppression and enslavement of the first Africans forcibly transported to America. As African Americans moved from the plantations to cities and towns, a color-based caste system followed. This caste system assisted in the establishment of an African American middle class with a disproportionate number of lighter-skinned African Americans. The findings regarding the salience of socioeconomic factors, though not conclusive, point to the continued significance of avoiding the trivialization of skin tone as a stimulus characteristic in Black-White interactions.

Introduction

Color consciousness occurs when individuals identify and respond to the varied skin tones of others. Initial empirical research on the topic was primarily limited to the analysis of census-type data and demonstrated the existence and manifestations of this phenomenon among African Americans (Keith & Herring 1991a). Later research confirmed the presence of color consciousness among African Americans and verified its existence within other ethnic groups including Latinos, East Asian Indians, and Asians (Peggy 2006, Rodolfo & Michael 2002, Sarita & Niva 1997). Outcomes related to color consciousness include socioeconomic disparities, disparities in perceived/experienced racism (Hughes & Hertel 1990) as well as differences in physiological markers like blood pressure, hypertension, and overall health status (Clark 1996, Hill 2000). More recent research has improved upon the works of pioneering scholars in the area and generally upheld earlier findings regarding outcomes (Goldsmith et al. 2006, Hersch 2006, 2007, Maddox 2004).

A.M. Breland-Noble
Department of Psychiatry and Behavioral Sciences, Duke University Medical Center, Durham, NC, USA
e-mail: abreland@psych.duhs.duke.edu

R.E. Hall (ed.), *Racism in the 21st Century*, DOI: 10.1007/978-0-387-79097-8_7,
© Springer Science+Business Media, LLC 2008

Since color consciousness has been well established as an existing phenomenon in communities of color, many researchers have attempted to quantify its causal variables. In this regard, varied precursors to color consciousness have been cited with internalized racism ranking high on the list (Breland 1998, Coard et al. 2001). Other predictive variables have included racial identity (Breland 1998), self-esteem, family socialization (Boyd-Franklin 1991), and media portrayals of people of color (i.e. stereotyping) (Fears 2004, Hall 2005).

Manifestations of Color Consciousness

In the 1999 book *Our Kind of People*, Lawrence Otis Graham, an African American man, describes his childhood as one where he clearly understood, at a very early age, the importance of skin tone and socioeconomic status. He writes, "At age six, I already understood the importance of achieving a better shade of black." (p. 1). He then describes the great distinctions that existed in the 1950 s and 1960 s, and that persist today, regarding African Americans of differing skin tones and the associated stratification with regard to class.

Although early research focused on within-group bias, more recent researchers explore across-group bias; specifically Whites' perceptions of Blacks and other persons of color based on skin tone. A seminal publication by R. L. Zweigenhaft and G. W. Domhoff suggested that one reason for lighter-skinned, African American domination of the upper rungs of job prestige and power in the U.S. is White control of access to higher status occupations, which they reserve for lighter-skinned African Americans and other persons of color with light skin tones (Zweigenhaft & Domhoff 1998). As an example, the authors quote a prominent African American military officer as stating that a primary reason for his acceptance among Whites is that he is not "that Black" because he speaks well and is comfortable in White situations (p. 112). A. H. Goldsmith, D. Hamilton, and W. Darity, Jr. (2006) extend this research and suggest that African Americans of lighter skin tones earn on average higher wages and have higher prestige jobs than darker-skinned African Americans. Generally speaking, most researchers agree that color consciousness exists both within and between racial/ethnic groups and that it is manifested in multiple ways. Few researchers thus far, however, have attempted to quantify the manners in which skin color bias operates across racial groups, with a few notable exceptions (Maddox & Gray 2002). The following study addresses this gap in the research literature:

There are historical antecedents that support the existence of color consciousness among Whites. Specifically, African American issues of color consciousness are rooted in the oppression and enslavement of the first Africans forcibly transported to America. It is a widely held belief that, during slavery, White enslavers afforded privileges to lighter-skinned African descendants (who were often a product of their forced, coerced, and/or consensual "unions" with African women) that were not offered to the darker skinned "full" Africans (Keith & Herring 1991b, Maddox 2004, Sandler 1994). These lighter-skinned African Americans were occasionally freed from slavery, provided with formal and informal education, and allowed to acquire the training necessary to become skilled artisans. With the eradication of slavery in 1865, lighter-skinned African Americans who had disproportionately been established in what were then considered high status occupations were placed in the position of an interracial liaison class. In addition, due to a stratification process that provided Blacks of mixed parentage with opportunities for acquiring property and socialization into the dominant White culture, lighter-skinned African Americans emerged in the upper stratum of the social hierarchy in African American communities (Breland 1998, Hall 1998, Maddox & Gray 2002).

As African Americans moved from the plantations to cities and towns, the color-based caste system followed (Breland 1998, Zweigenhaft & Domhoff 1998). This caste system assisted in the establishment of an African American middle class with a disproportionate number of lighter-skinned African Americans (Graham 1999). Further research has determined that even though darker-skinned African Americans have increasingly moved into the middle class, lighter-skinned African Americans still comprise the largest sub-population of this cultural socioeconomic group. In addition, based on the use of statistical procedures in which generational variables were controlled for, research has demonstrated that their continued presence in this group is not due to the generational benefits of being the offspring of the older lighter-skinned, middle-class members (i.e. descendants of Whites), but may be a function purely of their light skin (Goldsmith et al. 2006, Hersch 2007).

Given the presence of skin-tone bias in White and Black adults, it seems important to ascertain the presence of this bias in youth. Recall that color consciousness has been hypothesized as and demonstrated to be an important phenomenon that exists among African Americans. In addition, it has been suggested that color consciousness operates in interracial interactions between Whites and African Americans to determine psychological and socioeconomic outcomes for African Americans. Finally, recall that limited, though important, empirical evidence exists to support these claims. As such, the significance of this study is as follows: First, concepts regarding color consciousness in the field of African American psychology can be advanced as the researchers provide an empirically tested operational mechanism for the existence of the phenomenon among Whites. Specifically, future research might be developed to ascertain how the effect of color consciousness on Whites' perceptions of African Americans in adolescence "lays the groundwork" for later life-stage interactions between the two groups. For, if it is indeed true that Whites control access to higher status occupations and educational opportunities, then understanding how Whites perceive African Americans based on skin tone in early life stages may provide insight into how they function as the "gatekeepers" into high socioeconomic levels for African Americans in adulthood. Further, understanding these ideas can assist in the development and testing of interventions for use in curbing some of the more deleterious consequences of the practice of color consciousness within both racial groups.

The specific research questions for this study include:

- Do White young adults "differentially attend and respond to shades of Black skin" (i.e. are they color conscious)?
- Do differences exist in the frequency of interactions with African Americans between color conscious White young adults and non-color conscious White young adults?
- Do color conscious White young adults differ from non-color conscious White young adults in SES (proxy: family of origin household income)?
- Does proximity to African Americans differ in color conscious versus non-color conscious Whites?

The authors hypothesized that (a) Whites are color conscious; (b) frequency of interactions with African Americans differ between color conscious and non-color conscious Whites; (c) SES differs between color conscious and non-color conscious Whites; and (d) color conscious Whites' proximity to African Americans differs from that of non-color conscious Whites.

Methods

Subjects

The setting for this study was a large university in the Midwest. The researchers employed a convenience sample that included 74 White college-aged and enrolled undergraduates ranging in age from 18 to 24 (M = 19.35, SD = 1.17) with household incomes falling into four categories: lower income (family of origin household incomes ranging from $10,000 to $40,000; N = 4; 6% of sample); moderate income (family of origin household income ranging from $40,000 to $70,000; N = 21; 30%); high income (family of origin household income ranging from $70,000 to $100,000; N = 26; 37%); and wealthy (family of origin household income $100,000 +; N = 20, 28%). The study sample was comprised mostly of females (82% vs. 18% male). Subjects were categorized as having been reared in urban (N = 49; 69% of sample) or rural (N = 22; 31% of sample) environments. Subjects were recruited from classes in a College of Education via their professors and received course credit for their participation. The final analysis included 71 young adults as three participants were dropped due to excessive missing data. All participants receive $5.00 in compensation.

Measures: The IRF and the MEI

The Impression Rating Form (IRF) was used to assess the presence of color consciousness. It was developed by Dr. Midge Wilson at DePaul University.

The lead author spoke with Dr. Wilson (2000) to obtain permission for use of the measure along with a copy of the form. Participants are required to look at pictures of African Americans who vary in skin tone and complete a checklist assigning attributes to them. Higher scores indicate more favorable impressions and lower scores less favorable impressions.

There are two essential parts of this measure. First, the pictures used as stimulus objects are pictures of the same African Americans, shaded in different colors. For the purpose of this study, two pictures of African Americans (representing both genders) and two pictures of Whites (representing both genders) were taken from a freeware website and judged to be of average attractiveness by independent evaluators. Next, the photos were taken to a graphic design lab where the designers shaded the African American pictures with very light and very dark shades of African American skin tones. The pictures of the White stimulus objects were unaltered. The approach to altering the African American pictures replicated that of Dr. Wilson in prior administrations of the measure. The researchers added the pictures of a White male and White female to create a single blind study (i.e. mask the true nature of the study, which was Whites' impression formation of African Americans).

The Multicultural/Multiracial Experience Inventory (MEI-R) (Ramirez 1998) was developed to assess individual historical patterns and contemporary identities regarding issues of diversity. Although it was originally designed for people of color, it has been modified for use with White subjects. Both versions include an introductory demographic assessment (Part I) followed by a two subscale assessments encompassing Type A and Type B items (Part II). Demographic items include gender, race, race of parents, family of origin household income, parental occupations, and geographic location of residence. The Part II items address the Historical Development Pattern Subscale and the Contemporary Multicultural Identity Subscale. Type A items are scored so that a response of "almost entirely my ethnic group" or "almost entirely people of color" (alternatives 1 and 5, respectively) receives 1 point; responses of either "mostly my ethnic group with a few people of color" or "mostly people of color with a few people of my ethnic group" (alternatives 2 and 4) receive 2 points; responses of "mixed" (my ethnic group and people of color about equally) receive 3 points.

A total score is derived from the addition of the two subscale scores with higher scores indicating more interaction in and comfort with experiences in diversity. The maximum score for each of the subscales and the overall measure is HDP = 33; CMI = 45 and Total = 78.

Procedures

As stated earlier, the sample was a convenience sample of students matriculating at a large Midwestern university. The classes were identified by the first author who solicited the assistance of university professors willing to help with the study. After classrooms of students were identified for participation, two White graduate students administered and collected the measures during one class session. The measurement packet included the IRF and the MEI along with three photographs, including either a White male or female; one light or dark African American male; and one light or dark African American female so that each completed packet included three IRFs. The use of White data collectors was deemed essential to circumvent the potential confound of receiving socially desirable responses from the subjects.

Data Analysis

Analysis Plan

The initial step in the analysis plan included creating the dichotomous variable that would represent color consciousness in White young adults. To do so, we used the 10th and 90th percentiles on the IRFs as an indicator of color consciousness. The total scores and percentile rankings on the IRFs for the African American male were M = 42, 10th percentile score = 34, 90th percentile = 48; and African American female M = 40, 10th percentile score = 31, 90th percentile = 49. Given the nature of the research the investigators believe that this criterion is appropriate for the current design as past research has reported that color conscious individuals are the ones who most likely use visible race as a stimulus variable (Breland 1998, Maddox 2004). Analyses were conducted using the Statistical Package for Social Sciences, SPSS 14.0 (SPSS Inc).

Results

In order to predict color consciousness among White young adults from frequency of interactions with persons of color, community geographic location, and family of origin's annual income the researchers employed logistic regression. The results indicate that the proposed model represented the data marginally well: 2 (5) = 11.27, p = .046. The frequencies of interactions with persons of color and community geographic location for the young adults were not related to color consciousness and the sample reported that, overall, they had had limited opportunities for meeting and interacting with diverse populations (M = 46.55; SD = 9.67) Differences, however, were found in terms of reported annual income for family of origin. The young adults who reported a family income in excess of $100,000 per year were less likely to be color conscious than participants reporting an annual family income ranging from $10,000 to $40,000 (B = . −1.89, p = .01). Specifically, their odds of being color conscious

Table 7.1 Logistic regression analysis predicting color consciousness among white young adults from frequency of interactions with persons of color, and family of origin's annual income (n = 71)

Predictor	Mother		
	B	SE B	e^B
Community Geographic			
Rural (reference)		.	
Urban	−.69	.62	.50
Interaction with People of Color	.01	.08	1.01
Annual Family Income			
$10,000 – $40,000 (reference)			
$40,000 – $70,000	−21.63	19846.63	.00
$70,000 – $100,000	−1.05	.67	.35
Over $100,000	−1.89*	.72	.152
Constant	.21		
χ^2		11.27	
df		5	
% of Color Conscious European Young Adults		32.4	

*$p < .05$. **$p < .01$. ***$p < .001$.

were .89 lower than participants who reported an annual family income ranging from $10,000 to $40,000 (Table 7.1).

Summary and Conclusions

The researchers conducted this study to (a) assess the presence or absence of color consciousness among White young adults and (b) detect any differences in color conscious White adolescents versus. non-color conscious White adolescents on the variables of overall perceptions, frequency of interaction with African Americans and proximity to African Americans. The final two questions were included as a means of determining the possible mechanisms that may influence White young adults' color conscious perceptions. Following, we address each of our original research questions as they relate to the results:

• Do White young adults "differentially attend and respond to shades of Black skin" (i.e. are they color conscious)?

The findings from this study appear to indicate that White young adults do indeed respond differently to shades of African American skin. We base this conclusion on the fact that there were a significant number of extreme scores on the IRF, which point to either highly favorable or highly unfavorable judgments about African Americans formed in response to the skin tone stimulus variable. K. B. Maddox (2004) refers to this as the Racial Phenotypicality Bias and states that, in essence, skin tone is as a proxy for a composite of African American phenotypes that are associated with certain characteristics (Maddox

2004). For example, portrayals of beautiful African American women in popular White cinema have almost always included light-skinned women as the feminine ideal (Breland-Noble 2002) and notably the first African American woman to win the Miss America pageant was very light-skinned with green eyes. These examples speak to the manners in which, when given a choice, many Whites will respond favorably to a lighter-skinned Black person because lighter African American skin tone conveys socially meaningful information or as Maddox describes, "... acts as a proxy for a configuration of phenotypic features relevant to racial subcategorization," (p. 534) and we would add stereotyping (Maddox & Chase 2004).

- Do differences exist in the frequency of interactions with African Americans between color conscious White young adults and non-color conscious White young adults?

Recall that the mean score on the MEI reflected our subjects' limited experiences with non-White persons. Recall also that this factor was not predictive of color consciousness. These findings seem to support the assertion that for most Whites shades of African American skin are not as salient to impression-formation as having Black skin in and of itself. Maddox addresses this phenomenon by suggesting that in situations in which Whites interact with other Whites and limited numbers of Blacks and/or other persons of color, skin tone loses its power as a sole stimulus variable. This would certainly apply to the sample referenced in this study.

- Do color conscious White young adults differ from non-color conscious White young adults in SES (proxy: family of origin household income)?
- Does proximity to African Americans differ in color consciousness versus non-color conscious Whites?

Although frequency of and potential for cross cultural interactions with African Americans may not account for color consciousness, income appears to be a modest marker for skin tone bias. This finding supports research in the area of social psychology, which suggests that with increased income and education (i.e. higher social position) come more sophisticated and ubiquitous means of censoring oneself with regard to controversial issues (i.e. social desirability). Other possible reasons for this finding include the idea that Whites with lower social position may come into more frequent and negative contact with African Americans in the same strata, with whom they are often vying for social and financial capital. Further, it has been demonstrated that darker-skinned Blacks perceive and report more experiences with discrimination than their light counterparts. It is therefore possible that for the segment of the sample reporting lower incomes, they are locked in a more intense struggle for resources with African Americans, hence they are more likely to make negative associations with African Americans. Finally, researchers have reported that youth from lower social position families spend considerably more time watching (and being influenced by) television. This would, of course, lead to more negative associations with African Americans, as generally media portrayals of young African Americans are negative (Breland 2000).

Limitations and Future Directions

One of the most salient limitations to this study is the volunteer, convenience sampling procedure employed. Such a procedure limits the generalizability of the findings, as subject opinions may not be reflective of the general population, but more so of those educated college-aged youth who are well versed and educated in racial bias in general. An additional concern is to be taken in to consideration for the study is the relatively small sample size (N<100). However, given the preliminary exploratory nature of the study a smaller sample size was to be expected. Furthermore, the results from the analyses were consistent with extant literature in regard to color consciousness and SES. Future research will include both larger and representative samples.

Nancy Krieger (2001) defines socioeconomic position (SEP) as, "An aggregate concept that includes both resource-based and prestige-based measures, as linked to both childhood and adult social class position." Our measure of socioeconomic status included only family of origin parental household income. Although such an approach is often used to place individuals into socioeconomic strata, future research might include more comprehensive data collection of socioeconomic variables so that a composite score for SEP might be developed and tested against color consciousness.

Overall, it is clear that Whites use skin tone as a marker for differential treatment and perceptions of African Americans. This finding has grave implications for African American persons across fields including education, employment, and health. Our goal was to open a line of questioning that might lead to answers regarding the root causes of color consciousness among Whites. The findings regarding the salience of socioeconomic factors, though not conclusive, point to the continued significance of avoiding the trivialization of skin tone as a stimulus characteristic in Black-White interactions.

References

Boyd-Franklin, N. (1991). Recurrent themes in the treatment of African American women in-group psychotherapy. *Women and Therapy*, 11(22), 25–40.

Breland, A. M. (1998). A model for differential perceptions of competence based on skin tone among African Americans. *Journal of Multicultural Counseling & Development*, 26(4), 294–311.

———. (2000). *The "true" perpetrators of violence: The effects of the media on public perceptions of youthful violent offenders*. Alexandria, VA: American Counseling Association.

Breland-Noble, A. M. (2002). An exploration of the effects of skin tone on African American life experiences. Paper presented at the 2002 Great Lakes Regional Counseling Psychology Conference.

Clark, R. (1996). Skin tone, coping, and cardiovascular responses to ethnically relevant stimuli. Unpublished Ph.D. thesis, Duke University, Durham, NC.

Coard, S. I., Breland, A. M., & Raskin, P. (2001). Perceptions of and preferences for skin color, Black racial identity, and self-esteem among African Americans. *Journal of Applied Social Psychology*, 31(11), 2256–2274.

Fears, L. M. (2004). Differing reactions to female role portrayals in news editorial photographs. *Race, Gender & Class*, 11(2), 59.

Goldsmith, A. H., Hamilton, D., & Darity Jr., W. (2006). Shades of discrimination: Skin tone and wages. *The American Economic Review*, 96(2), 242.

Graham, L. (1999). Our kind of people: Inside America's Black upper class (1st ed.). New York: Harper Collins.

Hall, R. E. (1998). Skin color bias: A new perspective on an old social problem. *The Journal of Psychology*, 132(2), 238.

———. (2005). The Euro-Americanization of race: Alien perspective of African Americans vis-a-vis trivialization of skin color. *Journal of Black Studies*, 36(1), 116.

Hersch, J. (2006). Skin-tone effects among African Americans: Perceptions and reality. *The American Economic Review*, 96(2), 251.

———. (2007). Profiling the new immigrant worker: The effects of skin color and height [Electronic Version]. Retrieved 29 January 2007. http://www.ssrn.com/abstract = 927038.

Hill, M. E. (2000). Color differences in the socioeconomic status of African American men: Results of a longitudinal study. *Social Forces*, 78(4), 1437.

Hughes, M., & Hertel, B. R. (1990). The significance of color remains: A study of life chances, mate selection, and ethnic consciousness among Black Americans. *Social Forces*, 68(4), 1105.

Keith, V. M., & Herring, C. (1991a). Skin tone and stratification in the Black community. *The American Journal of Sociology*, 97(3), 760.

———. (1991b). Skin tone and stratification in the Black community. *American Journal of Sociology*, 97(3), 760–778.

Krieger N. (2001). A glossary for social epidemiology. *Journal of Epidemiology and Community Health*, 55: 693–700.

Maddox, K. B. (2004). Perspectives on racial phenotypicality bias. *Personality & Social Psychology Review*, 8(4), 383–401.

Maddox, K. B., & Chase, S. G. (2004). Manipulating subcategory salience: Exploring the link between skin tone and social perception of Blacks. *European Journal of Social Psychology*, 34(5), 533–546.

Maddox, K. B., & Gray, S. A. (2002). Cognitive representations of Black Americans: Reexploring the role of skin tone. *Personality & Social Psychology Bulletin*, 28(2), 250–259.

Peggy, A. L. (2006). Race, gender, and work in São Paulo, Brazil, 1960–2000. *Latin American Research Review*, 41(3), 63.

Ramirez, M. (1998). *Multicultural/multiracial psychology: Mestizo perspectives in personality and mental health*. Northvale, NJ: Jason Aronson Inc.

Rodolfo, E., & Michael, M. F. (2002). Latino phenotypic discrimination revisited: The impact of skin color on occupational status. *Social Science Quarterly*, 83(2), 612.

Sandler, K. (1994). Essay: Finding a space for myself in a question of color. *Washington Informer* (p. 20). 19 January 1994.

Sarita, S., & Niva, P. (1997). Skin-color preferences and body satisfaction among South Asian-Canadian and European-Canadian female university students. *The Journal of Social Psychology*, 137(2), 161.

SPSS Inc. [software vendor and product of the same name]. Available at http://www.www.spss.com.

Wilson, M. (2000). Personal communication.

Zweigenhaft, R. L., & Domhoff, G. W. (1998). *Diversity in the power elite: have women and minorities reached the top?* New Haven, CT: Yale University Press.

Chapter 8
Skin Color Biases: Attractiveness and Halo Effects in the Evaluation of African Americans

T. Joel Wade

Abstract Since the early days of slavery a bias favoring fair skin has been a significant and discriminatory distinction made by both White and Black Americans. Recent research indicates that African Americans are considered more attractive by others if they have fair skin. Clearly, skin color exerts strong effects on many aspects of African Americans' lives. Skin color may also affect the beauty and life chances of other non-African American groups since skin color affects perceptions in India, Israel, Korea, Japan, the West Indies, South Africa, Britain, and South America. But, until additional research examining this issue is conducted one cannot be certain that it is true. Hopefully, now that more work is being done examining skin color the public will be made aware of this and additional research examining the impact of skin color in the afore-mentioned cultures will also be conducted.

Introduction

Since the early days of slavery a bias favoring fair skin has been a significant and discriminatory distinction made by both White and Black Americans (Lincoln 1968). Lighter-complected Blacks and mulattos were considered genetically superior to dark-skinned or Negroid-featured Blacks because light skin and Caucasoid features were seen by Whites as a sign of White ancestry (Lincoln 1968, Myrdal 1944, Parrish 1944, Reuter 1918). Therefore, during slavery, mulattos were generally assigned coveted positions such as house servant, artisan, craftsman, and skilled laborer. Consequently, fair skinned slaves commanded a higher price on the auction block (Drake & Cayton 1962, Myrdal 1944, Parrish 1944). Also, African Americans were said to long for fair skin and strive to approximate Whites in facial features and hair type (cf. Johnson 1941, Gray 1944). Not surprisingly, as C. E. Lincoln (1968) points out, skin color became the most important index for the evaluation of African Americans by

T.J. Wade
Department of Psychology, Bucknell University, Walnut Port, PA, USA
e-mail: jwade@bucknell.edu

R.E. Hall (ed.), *Racism in the 21st Century*, DOI: 10.1007/978-0-387-79097-8_8,
© Springer Science+Business Media, LLC 2008

Whites and African Americans and it played a fundamental role in African Americans' search for identity (Lincoln 1968). African Americans identified with Whites due to the positions of power and status that Whites occupied and as a result skin color became the basis for most if not all evaluations (Lincoln 1968).

The civil rights and Black pride movements, coining the phrase "Black is beautiful," claimed to have pulled away from White superiority notions such as this, instilling an appreciation for dark skin and Negroid features. However, Lincoln (1968) reports that the bias continued despite the civil rights movement. Whites and African Americans continued to evaluate African Americans based on their skin color. More recently, K.B. Maddox (2004), M. Hughes and B. R. Hertel (1990), and V.M. Keith and C. Herring (1991) report that the skin color bias still plagues this country with fair-skinned African Americans faring better than dark-skinned African Americans. In fact, skin color accounts for the same degree of disadvantage within the African American community as race does between African Americans and Whites (Hughes & Hertel 1990). With such powerful effects, one would expect this bias to have a psychological impact on African Americans. One would expect the attractiveness and the self-concept of African Americans to be affected. Basically, fair-skinned individuals would be expected to experience psychological as well other types of benefits because skin color affects conceptions of beauty. Some may feel that this is trivial because beauty is often thought of as a trivial factor. However, this is not a trivial issue. Beauty exerts a strong impact in many areas of society, such as hiring (Dipboye et al. 1977, Cash & Kilcullen 1985, Gilmore et al. 1986), judicial/legal decisions (Mazella & Feingold 1994), personality evaluations (Dion et al. 1972, Eagly et al. 1991, Feingold 1990), mate selection criteria (Buss 1989, Buss & Schmitt 1993, Wade 2000, 2003), and mental health decisions (Allen & Wroble 1975, Mathes & Kahn 1975, Wade et al. 2003).

Beauty

Consistent with Lincoln (1968), recent research indicates that African Americans are still considered more attractive by others if they have fair skin (Russell et al. 1993, Sandler 1992). Additionally, M. R. Cunningham, A. R. Roberts, A. P. Barbee, P. B. Druen, and C.-H. Wu (1995) report that both Black and White men judge fair-skinned African American women as more attractive than darker-skinned women since fair skin is equated with neoteny (youth), consistent with Charles Darwin (1874). Youth is related to greater health and reproductive fitness (Kenrick & Keefe 1992) and P. L. van den Berghe and P. Frost (1986) report that fair-skinned women in the U.S. as well as countries where slavery was not a factor are more fertile with greater reproductive health. Consequently, fair-skinned women are considered more attractive and are preferred as mates due to their heightened fertility and fecundity (van den

Berghe & Frost 1986). A. M. Neal and M. L. Wilson (1989) suggest that females are affected more because attractiveness is associated with fair skin and is more important for women in our society (Buss 1989, Buss & Schmitt 1993). Other research also reports sex differences are associated with skin-color biases. Fair-skinned women are considered more attractive and are preferred by dark-skinned men and dark-skinned men may augment perceivers' opinions of themselves by marrying a fair-skinned woman. These men receive "better" evaluations from social perceivers (cf. Clark & Clark 1980, Drake & Cayton 1945, 1962, Parrish 1944, Udry et al. 1971). However, as women are not judged based on their spouses' physical characteristics (cf. Bar-Tal & Saxe 1976, Sigall & Landy 1973), dark-skinned women cannot augment perceptions of themselves by marrying a fair-skinned man.

Skin color can also affect more specific forms of attractiveness. Physical attractiveness deals with general handsomeness while sexual attractiveness is based on the possession of sexual maturity characteristics (Udry & Billy 1987, Wade 2000, 2003, 1996). Global attractiveness includes a degree of each of these characteristics (Wade et al. 1989, Wade 1996). Consequently, each can have a different relationship with skin color. Prior research has not examined how skin color affects observers' perceptions of African Americans' sexual attractiveness. But, research has examined how skin color affects self-perceived global, physical, and sexual attractiveness. Wade (1996) reports that at the global as well as the more general physical levels of self-perceived attractiveness' skin color is not a factor.

However, skin color affects self-perceived sexual attractiveness more than self-perceived physical attractiveness and it only affects men's self-perceptions of their sexual attractiveness. T. J. Wade (1996) reports that dark-skinned men's self ratings of sexual attractiveness are higher than those of fair-skinned men, but women's self ratings do not differ. This rating is a product of marketplace theory where skin color is viewed as an asset (Wade & Bielitz 2005).

Marketplace theory (Elder 1969), which derives from exchange theory (Blau 1964, Edwards 1969, Merton 1941, Murstein 1976) and comes directly out of social learning theory (Homans 1961, Thibaut & Kelley 1959), has been used in the attractiveness realm primarily to explain mate selection. From this perspective, attractiveness is considered an asset in our society. Individuals learn that certain physical characteristics are more positively evaluated than others due to the positive sentiments they evoke, their associated aesthetic pleasures, or the benefits they ensure. These physical characteristics then become more valued in society and may serve as the standard upon which to judge others and one's self. Basically, as J. N. Edwards (1969) suggests, individuals are rated in terms of how their attractiveness compares to other most attractive individuals and/or an attractiveness standard (the attractiveness marketplace). If they compare favorably they are rated highly, possessing an asset. If they do not compare favorably they are rated lowly, devoid of that asset. These individuals can exchange that asset for something of value from another individual. Wade (1991) and B. I. Murstein, J. R. Merighi, and T. E. Malloy (1989) have shown that this theory applies to the perception of individuals. Individuals who are most attractive have a most valuable asset and are evaluated as such. Attractiveness main effects occur.

Applying this theory to skin-color perception and personality evaluation of African Americans, skin color can be considered a commodity. This is consistent with Murstein et al. (1989), who report that African American skin color can be used as an exchange variable by Whites. Similarly, L. Ross (1997) reports that skin color is used for mate selection and the general evaluation of African Americans by African Americans. Accordingly, skin color perception can be characterized as an economic function that may work differently for African American men and women such that attractiveness and social desirability are a function of skin color (attractiveness and social desirability = f(skin color)).

This theory applies to Wade's (1996) findings regarding self-perceived sexual attractiveness in the following manner: African American men, in general, are stereotyped as sexual animals (Kovel 1971, Schulman 1974) and or physically fit noble savages, especially dark-skinned African American males (Riggs 1986). Sexual attractiveness is influenced by biological pressures such that the most physically fit (dominant) males are the best choices to ensure reproductive fitness (Buss & Schmitt 1993, Singh 1993) and are considered most sexually attractive (Wade 2000, 2003). Therefore, as a result of the stereotype, dark-skinned men feel that dark-skinned African American males are more physically fit, or dominant. Consequently, their self ratings of sexual attractiveness are higher than those of fair-skinned men. Due to the stereotype, dark-skinned males feel they have a valuable asset in the sexual attractiveness marketplace.

Alternatively, the idea of dark skin as an asset for African American men is further supported by the fact that many of the prominent African American entertainers and athletes are dark skinned. For example, some of the most prominent and highest paid African American male entertainers, Eddie Murphy (the highest paid African American actor of all time), Denzel Washington, Louis Gossett, Jr., Danny Glover, Wesley Snipes, and many of the best and highest- paid professional African American athletes including Michael Jordan, Dwayne Wade, LeBron James, Shaquille O'Neal, Barry Bonds, and Ken Griffey, Jr. all have dark skin (Wade 1996). Since these individuals are very prominent and also earn very high, if not the highest, salaries, they are considered to be of high status due to their socioeconomic class. Reproductive fitness for males is based on dominance-related characteristics such as status, and males of high status are also assumed to be the most reproductively fit males (Wade 2003). Dark-skinned males, by virtue of their skin color, identify with the aforementioned dark-skinned individuals and as such rate their sexual attractiveness higher than fair-skinned individuals rate themselves. Due to their perception of enhanced reproductive fitness, based on their identification with prominent high status, dark-skinned African Americans, African American men feel their dark skin is an asset in the sexual attractiveness marketplace. This does not, however, mean that fair-skinned males do not identify with the aforementioned individuals. They may also identify with these individuals, but for this group the identification is based more on sex rather than on sex and skin tone. As a result, the identification may not be as strong. Thus, fair-skinned men's self ratings of sexual attractiveness are high, but not as high as those of dark-skinned.

Skin color does not affect women's ratings of their self-perceived attractiveness. The lack of a difference for women is surprising. But, it can also be explained in marketplace terms. However, the same evolutionary theory argument does not apply for African American women since women's reproductive fitness is based more on internal characteristics such as fecundity (Singh 1993). Rather, in the sexual attractiveness marketplace dark skin may no longer be of little market value for women. Most of the changes and programs to deal with the skin color bias have targeted women, i.e., dolls, cosmetics, and so forth. Consequently, African American women may feel skin color is no longer an exchange variable or the exchange value of dark skin for African American women is now equal to the exchange value of fair skin. As a result, dark- and fair-skinned women's self ratings of attractiveness do not differ, both rate their attractiveness equally highly.

Alternatively, a possible explanation for the sex difference is that skin color may be more important for male attractiveness because African American men are subject to more pressures to assimilate and also have an easier time assimilating. African American women, however, find it harder to assimilate and are less likely to assimilate (Fine & Bowers 1984). Since fair skin leads to easier acculturation with Whites (Myrdal 1944), dark-skinned men would have a harder time assimilating. Perhaps only fair-skinned men are pressured to assimilate, or are more strongly pressured to assimilate. As a result, dark-skinned men's desires to assimilate may be heightened by this rejection. To deal with or compensate for this rejection they may rate their sexual attractiveness higher than fair-skinned men rate themselves. While others may feel dark-skinned men do not have an asset in the sexual attractiveness marketplace by virtue of their dark skin, these men more strongly feel that they do have an asset in the sexual attractiveness marketplace. This is a self-corrective response to a societal bias for fair skin. To feel they have valuable assets in the sexual attractiveness marketplace, dark-skinned men's self ratings are higher.

Researchers have not directly examined how male and female perceivers respond to skin color. One might expect women to place more emphasis on fair skin color since women are better judges of attractiveness than men (Rand & Hall 1983). However, women are more aware of skin color issues than men (Sandler 1992, Wade 1996). Furthermore, research shows that women are less racially biased than men (Ekehammar & Sidanius 1982, Nosek et al. 2002, Schuman et al. 1997) and are more egalitarian than men (Sidanius et al. 2000). Additionally, men may place more emphasis on skin color due to its relation to women's attractiveness and fertility. Research shows that men place more emphasis on women's attractiveness due to its relationship with reproductive fitness (Buss & Schmitt 1993).

Since attractiveness is more important for African American women (Neal & Wilson 1989) and self concept and attractiveness are linked for African American women, but not for African American men (Wade et al. 1989); does this mean that skin color plays a role in the self-esteem of African American men and women?

Self-esteem

Research on racial self-esteem has advanced conclusions regarding skin color and African Americans' self-esteem or has been used to talk about skin color and African Americans' self-esteem (cf. Clark & Clark 1939a, 1939b, 1947, Goodman 1952, Morland 1962, Powell-Hopson & Hopson 1988). But, the conclusions from this research do not support a bias among African Americans in terms of racial self-esteem and should not be used to do so (cf. Banks 1976, Banks et al. 1979, Rosenberg 1989). This research focused on intergroup attitudes, not intragroup attitudes (Wade 1996). Additionally, this research has been questioned on methodological grounds and has not actually included empirically validated and reliable measures of self-esteem (cf. Banks 1976, Banks et al. 1979, Rosenberg 1989). Thus, as Rosenberg (1989) states, it should not be used to and cannot adequately answer questions regarding actual intragroup self-esteem and skin color. In methodologically sound research examining skin color in relation to self-esteem, Wade (1996) found that self-esteem ratings do not differ across skin color. This is because attractiveness for African Americans is not very strongly related to self-esteem (Wade et al. 1989). This is a very positive finding. Even though others evaluate African Americans dependent on their skin color, and African American men with dark skin view their beauty in terms of their skin color, African Americans are able to resist having skin color become a part of their self-concept.

While self-esteem is not affected by skin color the relationship between Black consciousness, skin color, and self-esteem is less clear. M. Hughes and B. R. Hertel (1990) report that skin color effects are not related to Black consciousness or Black identity measures. However, other research investigating the relationships between skin color and self-esteem and skin color and self-perceived physical attractiveness incorporating Black consciousness measures finds that self-perceived physical attractiveness and self-esteem are mediated by Black consciousness levels (cf. Azibo 1983, Chambers et al. 1994, Smith et al. 1991). African Americans with higher Black consciousness tend to value and appreciate dark skin more than those with lower Black consciousness levels. While skin color does not affect self-esteem, and since it does affect perceived attractiveness, there are also halo effects, where fair-skinned individuals are assumed to be "better," associated with it. The majority of this research has focused on how Whites perceive African Americans rather than on how African Americans perceive other African Americans. However, according to prior research this is not a problem. Cunningham et al. (1995) and K. Sandler (1992) report that Blacks and Whites respond similarly to African American's skin color with respect to attractiveness. Additionally, K. J. Gergen (1968) reports that the meaning of skin color in the Black community can be passed on to Whites as a result of cross cultural interaction. More recently, K. B. Maddox (2004) and Maddox and S. A. Gray (2002) report that both Whites and Blacks are aware of the stereotypes associated with African American skin color. Thus, with respect to skin color, the manner in which Whites perceive African Americans should parallel the way African Americans perceive themselves.

Skin Color Halo Effects

Since skin color affects perceived attractiveness and attractiveness leads to "halo" effects, where attractive individuals receive the "best" personality evaluations (perceived as possessing the socially desirable personality traits), one would expect skin color also to be related to personality evaluations for African Americans. However, prior research shows that skin color does not influence observers' evaluations of African Americans' personality traits related to social desirability (Wade & Bielitz 2005). From a marketplace theory perspective, Wade and S. Bielitz (2005) conclude that skin color has no effect on personality/social desirability evaluations because society has taken a step toward eliminating the skin color bias. They argue that there is more programming directed at eliminating the skin color bias evident in society today than in the past. So, Whites are unwilling to use stereotypical notions of skin color when judging African American's social desirability. But, research has not yet investigated how skin color affects more meaningful aspects of personality, such as the Big-5 dimensions, so it is not known whether the effects associated with personality/social desirability apply to more meaningful aspects of personality. It is conceivable that skin color biases may indeed apply to more meaningful personality evaluations. While skin color does not affect the less important personality evaluations of African Americans it does affect other beauty-related evaluations such as intelligence, parenting skill, enthusiasm, and friendliness.

Intelligence Perception

Wade and Bielitz (2005) report that fair-skinned, African American women are perceived as more intelligent than fair-skinned, African American men. This difference is also explained in terms of marketplace theory where fair skin is a greater asset for the perception of African American women's intelligence. The halo effect that occurs here is also due to the differential effect of skin color on the educational success of men and women. Fair-skinned individuals receive more education than dark-skinned individuals (Hughes & Hertel 1990, Keith &

Herring 1991). Additionally, fair-skinned African Americans are perceived as smarter than dark-skinned African Americans (Herskovits 1934, Maddox & Gray 2002, Wade 1996). Thus, since African American women receive more education than African American men (Chideya 1995) participants feel fair-skinned, African American women are more intelligent than fair-skinned, African American men.

Dark-skinned, African American men and women are rated equivalently in terms of perceived intelligence because dark skin is not considered an asset for intelligence perception. Social perceivers equate dark skin with high income and physical dominance for African American men since some of the most prominent and highest paid African American entertainers regularly presented by the media and many of the best and highest- paid all have dark skin (Wade 1996). However, since athletes and entertainers are often stereotyped as less intelligent they are not perceived as being highly intelligent and individuals who are similar in color to them are also not perceived as highly intelligent. But, the sex of the perceiver can be a factor in evaluations of the intelligence of African Americans. White women rate dark-skinned African Americans as more intelligent than men do while fair-skinned individuals are rated equivalently by men and women. This is due to educational and vocational differences and the media. Since fair skin is equated with educational attainment (Hughes & Hertel 1990, Keith & Herring 1991) men and women feel fair skin is an asset for intelligence. In addition, women rate the dark-skinned person higher than men do because women are less racist than men (Ekehammar & Sidanius 1982, Nosek et al. 2002, Schuman et al. 1997). White women are stating that dark skin is also an asset. But, do these assets also apply to mate selection criteria such as perceived parenting skill?

Parenting Skill

For perceived parenting skill, African American women with fair skin are rated as having better parenting skills than African American men with fair skin. However, perceptions of dark-skinned, African American men and women did not differ. From a marketplace theory perspective, fair skin is an asset for African American women due to perceived parental investment potential. Fair skin is related to neoteny, and neoteny is related to perceived healthiness and reproductive fitness assessments for women (Cunningham et al. 1995). Evaluations of women's parental investment potential can be a product of whether the women appear to be healthy, reproductively fit, and consequently better able to produce and take care of offspring (Trivers 1972). Therefore, fair skinned women are perceived as having better parenting skills. Men's parental investment potential can be based on status or physical dominance (Buss & Schmitt 1993, Cunningham 1986, Cunningham et al. 1990, Cunningham et al. 1995, Kenrick et al. 1994, Sadalla et al. 1987, Singh 1995, Wade 2000). Since fair skin is equated with better social relations (Neal & Wilson 1989, Sandler 1992), fair-skinned men are perceived as having higher status. Individuals of high financial status are assumed to have better social relations (Wade 1991). Since dark-skinned, African American men are perceived as physically and financially dominant (Wade 1996), evaluations of fair- and dark-skinned men do not differ. Both fair- and dark-skinned men are perceived as being able to invest parentally.

Enthusiasm

Skin color biases consistent with marketplace theory concepts also operate for evaluations of African American's enthusiasm. Wade and Bielitz (2005) report that White women rate dark-skinned African Americans as more enthusiastic than fair-skinned African Americans while White men rate fair-skinned and dark-skinned African Americans similarly. The halo effect occurs here because women are, in general, less racist than men (Ekehammar & Sidanius 1982, Nosek et al. 2002, Schuman et al. 1997). Consequently, women see dark skin as an asset here and rate dark-skinned African Americans as more extroverted.

Skin color biases consistent with marketplace concepts do not operate for White men's ratings due to stereotypes associated with skin color. As mentioned previously, fair-skinned African Americans are thought to have better social relations (Neal & Wilson 1989, Sandler 1992) while dark skinned individuals are stereotyped as loud and expressive (Zebrowitz et al. 1993). Therefore, White men feel that both fair- and dark-skinned African Americans would be enthusiastic about life. While there are skin color halo effects associated with some aspects of personality, does skin color affect employment opportunities of African Americans?

Employment

Historically, fair skin has increased African Americans' chances for acculturation with Whites (Hughes & Hertel 1990) such that skin color became a criterion for the attainment of prestige in the African American community (cf. Davis et al. 1941, Dollard 1957, Drake & Cayton 1945, Hughes & Hertel 1990, Myrdal 1944). This effect has not changed appreciably. Hughes and Hertel (1990) report that a comparison of the main effects for skin color from 1950 to 1980 shows that fair-skinned African Americans still fare better economically, vocationally, and educationally (Hughes & Hertel 1990, Keith & Herring 1991). Their family income is more than 50% greater than dark-skinned African Americans and their personal income is 65% greater than that of dark-skinned African Americans (Keith & Herring 1991). Fair-skinned African Americans are also more likely to be employed in professional/technical positions (Keith &

Herring 1991) and their spouses tend to have more education and obtain higher occupational prestige (Hughes & Hertel 1990). Moreover, fair-skinned African Americans obtain more than 2 + years of education over dark-skinned African Americans (Keith & Herring 1991). In fact, according to Keith and Herring (1991) skin color predicts educational attainment, occupation, and personal and family incomes over and above sociodemographic variables like age, socio-economic status, and parental background. Also, fair-skinned African Americans have higher financial status (Hughes & Hertel 1990) Since in the eyes of observers fair skin is still considered more beautiful than dark skin for African Americans, and fair-skinned African Americans have higher financial status, one would expect them to fare better in an employment context. Prior to the civil rights movement this was indeed the case.

Gunnar Myrdal (1944) reports that historically the White aristocracy preferred fair-skinned African Americans for personal service. In addition, fair-skinned African Americans, who were the offspring of slave masters and slaves, were given household duties rather than fieldwork (Franklin 1980, Frazier 1957b, Keith & Herring 1991, Landry 1987, Myrdal 1944). Recent research shows that this pattern still occurs and it differs depending on the sex of the person being evaluated. Wade, M. J. Romano, and L. Blue (2004) report that fair-skinned African Americans receive "better" treatment in employment contexts. Specifically, they find that fair-skinned African Americans are more likely to be hired and that men equate fair skin with "good" characteristics for both men and women applicants. This difference has been explained in terms of unconscious biological concerns where men rate fair-skinned women higher, due to mate selection concerns. Specifically, since fair skin is an index of women's fertility, men feel fair-skinned women are "better." They rate fair-skinned men higher since fair skin is equated with high status. Male perceivers feel a fair-skinned man is more likely to be a high status man and would have better administrative skills due to this high status. Women do not respond this way due to heightened societal skin color and beauty programming directed at women, as Wade (1996) reports. Having been exposed to a great deal of programming, women compensate for the fair-skin bias by evaluating a dark-skinned person more favorably negating any differences between fair- and dark-skinned individuals. Does skin color affect other life chances?

Judicial System

Very few studies have examined how skin color affects judicial decisions that involve African Americans. However, I. V. Blair, C. M. Judd, and K. M. Chapleau (2004) in archival research report that African Americans with dark skin receive harsher criminal sentences than African Americans with fair skin. Additionally, J. L. Eberhardt, P. G. Davies, V. J. Purdie-Vaughans, and S. L. Johnson (2006) report that African Americans with darker skin tones are more likely to receive the death penalty. While upsetting, these findings are not surprising. Blair, C. M. Judd, M. S. Sadler, and C. Jenkins (2002) report that stereotypic attributes of African Americans are more strongly applied to dark-skinned African Americans. Additionally, as mentioned previously, fair skin color is related to attractiveness and attractive individuals are less likely to be found guilty and receive less severe sentences when they are found guilty (Mazella & Feingold 1994). Therefore, dark-skinned African Americans who are considered unattractive and more strongly stereotyped are treated more negatively in the U.S. judicial system. Since skin color and beauty are related and beauty affects mental health (Allen & Wroble 1975, Mathes & Kahn 1975) and perceived mental health (Wade et al. 2003) does skin color also lead to biases in the mental health arena for African Americans?

Mental Health

Surprisingly, little if any research has been directed at the issue of skin color biases and mental health issues. However, researchers have documented that African American racial heritage leads to negative treatment in psychiatric facilities (Bond et al. 1988) and Neal and Wilson (1989) report that dark-skinned women's mental health can be adversely affected due to ideas they have internalized regarding beauty and dark skin. African American women begin to internalize negative conceptions of themselves if they have dark skin, and their lives may become more stressful due to having to ardently avoid letting their skin color and features negatively impact their lives. Additionally, fair-skinned women have to deal with stress related to questions regarding their heritage and Black consciousness.

Conclusion and Future Directions

Clearly, skin color exerts strong effects on many aspects of African Americans' lives. With such strong impacts, the public needs to be educated regarding the dangers of judging African Americans based on their skin color to help eradicate the biases associated with skin color.

Skin color may also affect the beauty and life chances of other non-African American groups, and skin color affects perceptions in India, Israel, Korea, Japan, the West Indies, South Africa, Britain, and South America (Franklin 1968, Hall 1992, Henik et al. 1985, Wade 1996). But, until additional research examining this issue is conducted one cannot be certain that it is true. Hopefully, now that more work is being done examining skin color the public will be made aware of this and additional research examining the impact of skin color in the aforementioned cultures will also be conducted.

References

Allen, B. P., & Wroble, S. (1975). Attractive people like themselves better than unattractive people-most of the time: Self-descriptions employing the AGT. Paper presented as the Midwestern Psychological Association Convention, Chicago, IL.

Azibo, D. (1983). Perceived attractiveness and the Black personality. *Western Journal of Black Studies*, 7(4), 229–238.

Banks, W. C. (1976). White preference in Blacks: A paradigm in search of a phenomenon. *Psychological Bulletin*, 83(6), 1179–1186.

Banks, W. C., McQuater, G. V., & Ross, J. A. (1979). On the importance of White preference and the comparative difference of Blacks and others: Reply to Williams and Morland. *Psychological Bulletin*, 86(1), 33–36.

Bar-Tal, D., & Saxe, L. (1976). Perceptions of similarly and dissimilarly attractive couples and individuals. *Journal of Personality and Social Psychology*, 33, 772–781.

Blair, I. V., Judd, C. M., & Chapleau, K. M. (2004). The influence of Afrocentric facial features in criminal sentencing. *Psychological Science*, 15(10), 674–679.

Blair, I. V., Judd, C. M., Sadler, M.S., & Jenkins, C. (2002). The role of Afrocentric features in person perception: Judging by features and categories. *Journal of Personality and Social Psychology*, 83, 5–25.

Blau, P. M. (1964). *Exchange and power in social life*. New York, Wiley.

Bond, C., Di Canada, C., & McKinnon, J. R. (1988). Response to violence in a psychiatric setting. *Personality and Social Psychology Bulletin*, 14, 448–458.

Buss, D. M. (1989). Sex differences in human mate preferences: Evolutionary hypotheses tested in 37 cultures. *Behavioral and Brain Sciences*, 12, 1–49.

Buss, D. M., & Schmitt, D. P. (1993). Sexual strategies theory: Evolutionary hypotheses tested in 37 cultures. *Behavioral and Brain Sciences*, 12, 1–49.

Cash, T. F., & Kilcullen, R. N. (1985). The eye of the beholder: Susceptibility to sexism and "beautyism" in the evaluation of managerial applicants. *Journal of Applied Social Psychology*, 15, 591–605.

Chambers, J., Clark, T., Dantzler, L., & Baldwin, J. (1994). Perceived attractiveness, facial features and African self-consciousness. *Journal of Black Psychology*, 20(3), 305–324.

Chideya, F. (1995). *Don't believe the hype: Fighting cultural misinformation about African Americans*. New York: Penguin Books, Inc.

Clark, K., & Clark, M. (1939a). The development of consciousness of self and the emergence of racial identification in negro preschool children. *Journal of Social Psychology*, 10, 591.

———. (1939b). Segregation as a factor in the racial identification of Negro preschool children: A preliminary report. *Journal of Experimental Education*, 8, 161.

———. (1947). Racial identification and preference in Negro children. In T. Newcombe & E. C. Hartley (Eds.), *Readings in social psychology* (pp. 159–169). New York: Holt.

Clark., K. B., & Clark, M. P. (1980). What do Blacks think of themselves? *Ebony*, 11, 176–182.

Cunningham, M. R. (1986). Measuring the physical in physical attractiveness: Quasi-experiments on the sociobiology of female facial beauty. *Journal of Personality and Social Psychology*, 50, 925–935.

Cunningham, M. R., Barbee, A., & Pike, C. (1990). What do women want? Facialmetric assessments of multiple motives in the perception of male facial physical attractiveness. *Journal of Personality and Social Psychology*, 59, 61–72.

Cunningham, M. R., Roberts, A. R., Barbee, A. P., Druen, P. B., & Wu, C.-H. (1995). "Their ideas of beauty are, on the whole the same as ours": Consistency and variability in the cross cultural perception of female physical attractiveness. *Journal of Personality and Social Psychology*, 68, 261–279.

Darwin, C. (1874). *The descent of man and selection in relation to sex*. New York: Hurst.

Davis, A., Gardner, B. R., & Gardner, M. R. (1941). *Deep South*. Chicago, IL: University of Chicago Press.

Dion, K., Berscheid, E., & Walster, E. (1972). What is beautiful is good. *Journal of Personality and Social Psychology*, 24, 285–290.

Dipboye, R. L., Arvey, R. D., & Terpstra, D. E. (1977). Sex and physical attractiveness of raters and applicants as determinants of resume evaluation. *Journal of Applied Psychology*, 62, 288–294.

Dollard, J. (1957). *Caste and class in southern town*. Garden City, NY: Doubleday.

Drake, S. C., & Cayton, H. (1945). *Black metropolis*. New York: Harcourt Brace.

———. (1962). The measure of a man. In S. C. Drake and H. Cayton, (Eds.), *Black metropolis: A study of Negro life in a northern city* (vol. 2, pp. 495–525), New York: Harper.

Eagly, A., Ashmore, R. D., Makhijani, M. G., & Longo, L. C. (1991). What is beautiful is good, but: A meta-analytic review of research on the physical attractiveness stereotype. *Psychological Bulletin*, 110, 109–128.

Eberhardt, J. L., Davies, P. G., Purdie-Vaughans, V. J., & Johnson, S. L. (2006). Looking deathworthy: Perceived stereotypicality of Black defendants predicts capital-sentencing outcomes. *Psychological Science*, 15(5), 383–386.

Edwards, J. N. (1969). Familial behavior as social exchange. *Journal of Marriage and The Family*, 31, 518–526.

Ekehammar, B., & Sidanius, J. (1982). Sex differences in socio-political ideology: a replication and extension. *British Journal of Social Psychology*, 21, 249–257.

Elder, G. (1969). Appearance and education in marriage mobility. *American Sociological Review*, 34, 519–533.

Feingold, A. (1990). Gender Differences in effects of physical attractiveness on romantic attraction: A comparison across five research paradigms. *Journal of Personality and Social Psychology*, 59, 981–993.

Fine, M., & Bowers, C. (1984). Racial self-identification: The effects of social history and gender. *Journal of Applied Social Psychology*, 14(2), 136–146.

Franklin, J. H. (1968). Introduction: Color and race in the modern world. In J. H. Franklin (Ed.), *Color and race*. Boston, MA: Houghton Mifflin.

———. (1980). *From slavery to freedom*, 5th edition. New York: Knopf.

———. (1957b). *The Negro in the United States*. New York: McMillan.

Gergen , K. J. (1968). The significance of skin color in human relations. In J. H. Franklin (Ed.), *Color and race*. Boston, MA: Houghton Mifflin.

Gilmore, D. C., Beehr, T. A., & Love, K. G. (1986). Effects of applicant sex, applicant physical attractiveness, type of rater and type of job on interview decisions. *Journal of Occupational Psychology*, 59, 103–109.

Goodman, M. E. (1952). *Race awareness in young children*. Cambridge, MA: Addison-Wesley.

Gray, S. (1944). The wishes of Negro school children. *Journal of Genetic Psychology*, 64, 225–237.

Hall, R. E. (1992). Bias among African Americans regarding skin color: Implications for social work practice. *Research on Social Work Practice*, 2(4), 479–486.

Henik, A., Munitz, S., & Priel, B. (1985). Color, skin color preferences and self color identification among Ethiopian- and Israeli-born children. *Israeli Social Science Research*, 3, 74–84.

Herskovits, M. J. (1934). A critical discussion of the "mulatto hypothesis." *Journal of Negro Education*, 3(3), 389–402.

Homans, G. C. (1961). *Social behavior: Its elementary forms*. New York: Harcourt, Brace & World.

Hughes, M., & Hertel, B. R. (1990). The significance of color remains: A study of life chances, mate selection, and ethnic consciousness among Black Americans. *Social Forces*, 68(4), 1105–1120.

Johnson, C. S. (1941). *Growing up in the Black belt: Negro youth in the rural south*. Washington, DC: American Council on Education.

Keith, V. M., & Herring, C. (1991). Skin tone and stratification in the Black community. *American Journal of Sociology*, 97(3), 760–778.

Kenrick, D. T., & Keefe, R. C. (1992). Age preferences in mates reflect sex differences in human reproductive strategies. *Behavioral and Brain Sciences*, 15, 75–133.

Kenrick, D. T., Neuberg, S. L., Zierk, K. L., & Krones, J. M. (1994). Evolution and social cognition: Contrast effects as a function of sex, dominance, and physical attractiveness. *Personality and Social Psychology Bulletin*, 20(2), 210–217.

Kovel, J. (1971). *White racism: A psychohistory*. New York: Random House.

Landry, B. (1987). *The new Black middle class*. Berkeley and Los Angeles: University of California Press.

Lincoln, C. E. (1968). Color and group identity in the United States. In J. H. Franklin (Ed.), *Color and race*. Boston, MA: Houghton Mifflin.

Maddox, K. B. (2004). Perspectives on racial phenotypicality bias. *Personality and Social Psychology Review*, 8(4), 383–401.

Maddox, K. B., & Gray, S. A. (2002). Cognitive representations of Black Americans: Reexploring the role of skin tone. *Personality and Social Psychology Bulletin*, 28(2), 250–259.

Mathes, E., & Kahn, A. (1975). Physical attractiveness, happiness, neuroticism, and self-esteem. *The Journal of Psychology*, 90, 27–30.

Mazella, R., & Feingold, A. (1994). The effects of physical attractiveness, race, socioeconomic status, and gender of defendants and victims on judgments of mock jurors: A meta-analysis. *Journal of Applied Social Psychology*, 24(15), 1315–1338.

Merton, R. K. (1941). Intermarriage and the social structure: fact and theory. *Psychiatry: Journal for the Study of Interpersonal Processes*, 4, 361–374.

Morland, J. K. (1962). Racial acceptance and preference of nursery school children in a southern city. *Merrill Palmer Quarterly of Behavior and Development*, 8, 271–280.

Murstein, B. I. (1976). *Who will marry whom?: Theories and research in marital choice*. New York: Springer.

Murstein, B. I., Merighi, J. R., & Malloy, T. E. (1989). Physical attractiveness and exchange theory in interracial dating. *Journal of Social Psychology*, 129(3), 325–334.

Myrdal, G. (1944). *An American dilemma*. New York: Harper & Row.

Neal, A. M., & Wilson, M. L. (1989). The role of skin color and features in the Black community: Implications for Black women and therapy. *Clinical Psychology Review*, 9, 323–333.

Nosek, B. A., Banaji, M. R., & Greenwald, A. G. (2002). Harvesting implicit group attitudes and beliefs from a demonstration website. *Group Dynamics*, 6(1), 101–115.

Parrish, C. (1944). The significance of color in the Negro community. Unpublished Doctoral Dissertation: University of Chicago.

Powell-Hopson, D., & Hopson, D. (1988). Implications of doll color preferences among Black preschool children and White preschool children. *Journal of Black Psychology*, 14(2), 57–63.

Rand, C. S., & Hall, J. A. (1983). Sex differences in the accuracy of self-perceived attractiveness. *Social Psychology Quarterly*, 46, 359–363.

Reuter, E. B. (1918). *The mulatto in the United States*. (1969 reprint). New York: Negro Universities Press.

Riggs, M. (Producer/Director) (1986). *Ethnic notions* [Film]. San Francisco, CA: California Newsreel.

————. (1989). Old myths die hard: The case of Black self-esteem. *Revue Internationale de Psychologie Sociale*, 2(3), 355–365.

Ross, L. (1997). Mate selection preference among African American college students. *Journal of Black Studies*, 27, 554–580.

Russell, K., Wilson, M., & Hall, R. (1993). *The color complex: The politics of skin color among African Americans*. New York: Harcourt Brace Janovich.

Sadalla, E. K., Kenrick, D. T., & Vershure, B. (1987). Dominance and heterosexual attraction. *Journal of Personality and Social Psychology*, 52(4), 730–738.

Sandler, K. (Producer/Director) (1992). *A question of color* [Film] San Francisco, CA: California Newsreel.

Schulman, G. I. (1974). Race, sex and violence? A laboratory test of the sexual threat of the Black male hypothesis. *American Journal of Sociology*, 79, 1260–1277.

Schuman, H., Steeh, C., Bobo, L., & Krysan, M. (1997). *Racial attitudes in America: Trends and interpretations.* Cambridge, MA: Harvard University Press.

Sidanius, J., Levin, S., Liu, J.H., & Pratto, F. (2000). Social dominance orientation and the political psychology of gender: An extension and cross cultural replication. *European Journal of Social Psychology*, 30, 41–67.

Sigall, H., & Landy, D. (1973). Radiating beauty: Effects of having a physically attractive partner on person perception. *Journal of Personality and Social Psychology*, 65(2), 293–307.

Singh, D. (1993). Adaptive significance of female physical attractiveness: Role of waist- to-hip ratio. *Journal of Personality and Social Psychology*, 65(2), 293–307.

———. (1995). Female judgment of male attractiveness and desirability for relationships: Role of waist-to-hip ratio and financial status. *Journal of Personality and Social Psychology*, 69(6), 1089–1101.

Smith, L., Burlew, A., & Lundgren, D. (1991). Black consciousness, self-esteem, and satisfaction with physical appearance among African American female college students. *Journal of Black Studies*, 20(1), 62–74.

Thibaut, J. W., & Kelley, H. H. (1959). *The social psychology of groups.* New York: Wiley.

Trivers, R. (1972). Parental investment and sexual selection. In B. Campbell, (Ed.), *Sexual selection and the descent of man: 1871–1971* (pp. 136–179). Chicago, IL: Aldine.

Udry, J. R., & Billy, J. O. G. (1987). Initiation of coitus in early adolescence. *American Sociological Review*, 52, 841–855.

Udry, J. R., Bauman, K. E., & Chase, C. (1971). Skin color, status, and mate selection. *American Journal of Sociology*, 76, 722–733.

van den Berghe, P. L., & Frost, P. (1986). Skin color preference, sexual dimorphism and sexual selection: A case of gene culture co-evolution? *Ethnic and Racial Studies*, 9(1), 87–113.

Wade, T. J. (1991). Marketplace economy: The evaluation of interracial couples. *Basic and Applied Social Psychology*, 12(4), 405–422.

———. (1996). The relationships between skin color and self-perceived global, physical, and sexual attractiveness, and self-esteem for African Americans. *Journal of Black Psychology*, 22(3) 358–373.

———. (2000). Evolutionary theory and self-perception: Sex differences in body esteem predictors of physical and sexual attractiveness and self-esteem. *International Journal of Psychology*, 35(1), 36–46.

———. (2003). Evolutionary theory and African American self-perception: Sex differences in body esteem predictors of physical and sexual attractiveness, and self-esteem. *Journal of Black Psychology*, 29(2), 123–141.

Wade, T. J., & Bielitz, S. (2005). The differential effect of skin color on attractiveness, personality evaluations, and perceived life success of African Americans. *Journal of Black Psychology*, 31(3), 215–236.

Wade, T. J., Thompson, V., Tashakkori, A., & Valente, E. (1989). A longitudinal analysis of sex by race differences in predictors of adolescent self-esteem. *Personality and Individual Differences*, 10(7), 717–729.

Wade, T. J., Milanak, M. A., Minaya, E. F., Schnure, K., & Shanley, A. (2003). Attractiveness and individual differences in men's perceived mental health. Presented at the American Psychological Association Convention, Toronto, Canada, August 2003.

Wade, T. J., Romano, M. J., & Blue, L. (2004). The influence of African American skin color on hiring decisions. *Journal of Applied Social Psychology*, 34(12), 2550–2558.

Zebrowitz, L. A., Montepare, J. M., & Lee, H. K. (1993). They don't all look alike: Individuated impressions of other racial groups. *Journal of Personality and Social Psychology*, 65(1), 85–101.

Chapter 9
The Latin Americanization of Racial Stratification in the U.S.

Eduardo Bonilla-Silva and David R. Dietrich

Abstract Aside from what exists in the U.S. there is another layer of complexity in Latin American racial stratification systems. They include three racial strata, which are internally designated by "color." In addition to skin tone, phenotype, hair texture, eye color, culture, education, and class matter is the phenomenon known as pigmentocracy, or colorism. Pigmentocracy has been central to the maintenance of White power in Latin America because it has fostered: (a) divisions among all those in secondary racial strata; (b) divisions within racial strata limiting the likelihood of within-strata unity; (c) mobility viewed as individual and conditional upon "whitening;" and (d) white elites being regarded as legitimate representatives of the "nation" even though they do not look like the average member of the "nation." A related dynamic in Latin American stratification is the social practice of "Blanqueamiento," or whitening, not a neutral mixture but a hierarchical movement wherein valuable movement is upward. Racial mixing oriented by the goal of whitening shows the effectiveness of the logic of White supremacy. As a Latin America-like society, the United States will become a society with more, rather than less, racial inequality but with a reduced forum for racial contestation. The apparent blessing of "not seeing race" will become a curse for those struggling for racial justice in years to come. We may become "All Americans," as commercials in recent times suggest, but paraphrasing George Orwell: "some will be more American than others."

Introduction

"We are all Americans!" This, we contend, will be the racial mantra of the United States in the years to come, as nationalist statements denying the salience of race are the norm all over the world. Countries such as Malaysia or Indonesia, Trinidad or Belize, or, more significantly for our discussion,

E. Bonilla-Silva
Department of Sociology, Duke University, Durham, NC, USA
e-mail: ebs@soc.duke.edu

R.E. Hall (ed.), *Racism in the 21st Century*, DOI: 10.1007/978-0-387-79097-8_9,
© Springer Science+Business Media, LLC 2008

Iberian countries such as Puerto Rico, Cuba, Brazil, or Mexico, all exhibit this ostrich-approach to racial matters. That is, they all stick their heads deep into the social ground and say, "We don't have races here. We don't have racism here. We are all Mexicans, Cubans, Brazilians, or Puerto Rican!" However, we argue in this chapter that race and racial stratification in Latin America exists as a three-tiered racial hierarchy and racial stratification in the United States is evolving into a similar tri-racial system.

How Race Works in Latin America?

Bonilla-Silva and Lewis (1999) has argued that racial stratification systems operate in most societies without races being officially acknowledged. For example, racial data in Latin America is gathered inconsistently or not at all, and most Latin Americans, including those most affected by racial stratification, do not recognize inequality between "whites" and "non-whites" in their countries as racial. "Prejudice"—Latin Americans do not talk about "racism"— is viewed as a legacy from slavery and colonialism, and inequality is regarded as the product of class dynamics (Wagley 1952). Racial hierarchies in many Latin American countries are less obvious because they are more complex. In contrast to the historically biracial system of the United States, Latin America has a historically ensconced and pronounced tri-level racial stratification system which includes an intermediary mixed racial category. The latter is a product of historical miscegenation that led to the development of a socially and, sometimes, legally recognized intermediate racial strata of *mestizos*, browns, or "*trigueños*." Even though this group did not achieve the status of "white" anywhere, it nonetheless had a better status than the Indian or Black masses and, therefore, developed its own distinct interest and buffered sociopolitical conflicts.

Moreover, there is another layer of complexity in Latin American racial stratification systems. The three racial strata are also internally stratified by "color" (in quotation marks because, in addition to skin tone, phenotype, hair texture, eye color, culture and education, and class matter in the racial classification of individuals in Latin America), the phenomenon known as pigmentocracy, or colorism (Kinsbrunner 1996). Pigmentocracy has been central to the maintenance of White power in Latin America because it has fostered: (a) divisions among all those in secondary racial strata; (b) divisions within racial strata limiting the likelihood of within-strata unity; (c) mobility viewed as individual and conditional upon "whitening;" and (d) White elites being regarded as legitimate representatives of the "nation" even though they do not look like the average member of the "nation."[1] A related dynamic in

---

[1] Few Latin Americans object to the fact that most politicians in their societies are "white" (by Latin American standards). Yet, it is interesting to point out that Latin American elites always

Latin American stratification is the social practice of "Blanqueamiento," or whitening. Whitening "is just not neutral mixture but hierarchical movement...and the most valuable movement is upward" (Wade 1997, p. 342). Racial mixing oriented by the goal of whitening shows the effectiveness of the logic of white supremacy.

Despite these indicators of racial awareness, most Latin Americans, even those obviously "black" or "Indian," refuse to identify themselves in racial terms. Instead, they prefer to use national (or cultural) descriptors such as "I am Puerto Rican or Brazilian."[2] This behavior has been the subject of much confusion and described as an example of the fluidity of race and racism in Latin America (Rodríguez 2000). However, defining the nation and the "people" as the "fusion of cultures" (even though the fusion is viewed in a Eurocentric manner) is the logical outcome of all of the factors mentioned above. Nationalist statements such as "We are all Puerto Ricans" are the direct manifestation of the racial stratification peculiar to Latin America rather than evidence of non-racialism. Although these statements also represent nonwhites' agency to carve a space in the nation, these statements, which are taught to *Latinomericanos* in schools and at home as historical truths, also help maintain the traditional racial hierarchy by hiding the fact of racial division and racial rule (Goldberg 2002).

Racial Stratification in the United States

In this chapter, we contend that racial stratification and the rules of racial (re)cognition in the United States are becoming Latin America-like. We suggest that the bi-racial system typical of the United States, which was the exception in the world-racial system (Goldberg 2002; Mills 1997; Winant 2002), is becoming like the "norm," that is, it is evolving into a complex racial stratification system.[3] Specifically, we argue the United States is developing a tri-racial system with

---

object to the few "minority" politicians on *racial* grounds. Two recent cases are the racist opposition in the Dominican Republic to the election of black candidate José Peña Gómez (Howard 2001) and the opposition to mulatto President Hugo Cesar Chavez in Venezuela by the business elite.

[2] When pushed to choose a racial descriptor, many Latin Americans self-describe as White or highlight their white heritage no matter how remote or minimal it might be. For example, according to a recent study in a community in Brazil, a third of the Afro-Brazilians there were registered as Whites and a large proportion of the remainder were registered as *pardos* (Twine 1998, p. 114). For a similar discussion on Puerto Ricans, see Arlene Torres (1998).

[3] To be clear, our contention is not that the black-white dynamic ordained race relations throughout the United States. Instead, our argument is that at the national macro level, race relations have been organized in the United States along a white-nonwhite divide. This large divide, depending on contexts, included various racial groups (Whites, Blacks, and Indians or Whites, Mexicans, Indians, and Blacks or other iterations), but under the white-nonwhite racial order, "whites" were often treated as superior and "nonwhites" as inferiors.

"whites" at the top, and intermediary group of "honorary whites"—similar to the coloreds in South Africa during formal apartheid, and a non-white group or the "collective black"[4] at the bottom. We suggest the "white" group will include "traditional" whites, new "white" immigrants and, in the near future, assimilated Latinos, some multiracials (light-skinned ones), and other subgroups. We predict the intermediate racial group or "honorary whites" will comprise most light-skinned Latinos (e.g., most Cubans and segments of the Mexican and Puerto-Rican communities) (Rodríguez 1999), Japanese Americans, Korean Americans, Asian Indians, Chinese Americans, the bulk of multiracials (Rockquemore and Arend 2002),[5] and most Middle Eastern Americans. Finally, the "collective black" will include blacks, dark-skinned Latinos, Vietnamese, Cambodians, Laotians, and maybe Filipinos.

This map is heuristic rather than definitive and, thus, is a guide of how we think the various ethnic groups will line up in the new emerging racial order. We acknowledge that the position of some groups may change (e.g., Chinese Americans, Asian Indians, and Arab Americans), that the map is not inclusive of all the groups in the United States (for instance, Samoans, Micronesians, and so forth are not in the map), and that, at this early stage of this project and given some serious data limitations, some groups may end up in a different racial strata altogether (e.g., Filipinos may become "honorary whites" rather than another group in the "collective black" strata). More significantly, if our Latin Americanization thesis is accurate, there will be categorical porosity as well as pigmentocracy, making the map useful for group- rather than individual-level predictions. Porosity refers to individual members of a racial strata moving up (or down) the stratification system (e.g., a light-skin middle class black person marrying a White woman and moving to the "honorary white" strata). Pigmentocracy, as noted above, refers to the rank ordering of groups and members of groups according to phenotype and cultural characteristics (e.g., Filipinos being at the top of the "collective black" given their high level of education and income as well as high rate of interracial marriage with whites). This strategy for determining racial and ethnic stratification views groups as soft-, not hard-bounded or having the definitive closure of traditional ethnic groups. Instead, these groups occupy spaces in the field of race that are not cleanly delineated; thus, they have an element of pluralism. Research suggests that there is a world tradition of preference for lightness (Bashi 2004; see also Weiner 1997 and Ashikari 2005) and that phenotype may be a better predictor of stratification outcomes in the U.S. than the three major racial-ethnic categorizations of

---

[4] We are adapting Antonio Negri's idea of the "collective worker" to the situation of all those at the bottom of the racial stratification system. See 1984, *Marx beyond Marx: Lessons on the Grundrisse*, edited by Jim Fleming. South Hadley, MA: Bergin and Garvey.

[5] Rockquemore and Arend (2002) have predicted, based on data from a mixed-race student sample (one Black and one White parent), that most mixed-race people will be honorary whites, a significant component will belong to the collective black, and a few will move all the way into the White strata.

White, Hispanic, and African American (Hunter 2005). We predict that phenotype will become an even greater element of stratification in America's racially mixed future. However, we cannot make a stronger empirical case for the importance of pigmentocracy because there is neither census data on phenotype nor a single data set that includes systematic data on the skin tone of all Americans.

We recognize that our thesis is broad (attempting to classify where everyone will fit in the racial order) and hard to verify empirically with the available data. Nevertheless, we believe it is paramount to begin pushing for a paradigm shift in the field of race relations, and we consider our efforts here as a preliminary effort in that direction.

Why Latin Americanization Now?

Why are race relations in the United States becoming Latin America-like at this point in our history? The reasons are multiple. First, the demography of the nation is changing. Racial minorities are up to 30 percent of the population today and, as population projections suggest, may become a numeric majority in the year 2050 (U.S. Bureau of the Census 2001). This rapid darkening of America is creating a situation similar to that of Puerto Rico, Cuba, or Venezuela in the 16th and 17th centuries, or Argentina, Chile, and Uruguay in the late 18th and early 19th centuries. In both historical periods, the elites realized their countries were becoming "black" (or "non-white") and devised a number of strategies (unsuccessful in the former and successful in the latter) to whiten their population (Helg 1990). Although whitening the population through immigration or by classifying many newcomers as White (Gans 1999) is a possible solution to the new American demography, for reasons discussed below, we do not think this is likely. Neither do we believe that development of a mestizo "we" is likely in the U.S. because the U.S. "we" is rooted in the Judeo-Christian Anglo tradition. Moreover, the emphasis on the white element in the so-called *mestizo* "we" of Latin America suggests that, even if the U.S. developed a *mestizo* situation, it would give privilege to the white component culturally. Hence, a more plausible accommodation to the new racial reality in the U.S. is to (a) create an intermediate racial group to buffer racial conflict; (b) allow some newcomers into the white racial strata; and (c) incorporate most immigrants into the collective black strata.

Second, as part of the tremendous reorganization that transpired in America in the post-civil rights era, a new kinder and gentler white supremacy emerged, which Bonilla-Silva has labeled the "new racism" (Bonilla-Silva and Lewis 1999; Bonilla-Silva 2001). In post-civil rights America, the maintenance of systemic white privilege is accomplished socially, economically, and politically through institutional, covert, and apparently non-racial practices. Whether in banks or universities, in stores or housing markets, "smiling discrimination"

(Brooks 1990) tends to be the order of the day. This new white supremacy has produced an accompanying ideology that rings Latin America all over: the ideology of color-blind racism. This ideology, as is the norm in Latin America, denies the salience of race, scorns those who talk about race and increasingly proclaims "We are all Americans" (For a detailed analysis of color-blind racism, see Chapter 5 in Bonilla-Silva 2001).

Third, race relations have become globalized (Lusane 1997). The once almost all-white Western nations have now "interiorized the other" (Miles 1993). The new world-systemic need for capital accumulation has led to the incorporation of "dark" foreigners as "guest workers" and even as permanent workers (Schoenbaum and Pond 1996). Thus, today European nations have racial minorities in their midst who are progressively becoming an underclass (Cohen 1997), have developed an internal "racial structure" (Bonilla-Silva 1997) to maintain white power, and have a curious racial ideology that combines ethnonationalism with a race-blind ideology similar to the colorblind racism of the U.S. today (Bonilla-Silva 2000). This new global racial reality, we believe, will reinforce the Latin Americanization trend in the United States as versions of color-blind racism will become prevalent in most Western nations.

Fourth, the convergence of the political and ideological actions of the Republican Party, conservative commentators and activists, and the so-called "multi-racial" movement (Rockquemore and Brunsma 2002) has created the space for the radical transformation of the way we gather racial data in America. One possible outcome of the Census Bureau categorical back-and-forth on racial and ethnic classifications is either the dilution of racial data or the elimination of race as an official category.

Lastly, the attack on affirmative action, which is part of what Stephen Steinberg (1995) has labeled as the "racial retreat," is the clarion call signaling the end of race-based social policy in the U.S. The recent Supreme Court *Grutter v. Bollinger et al.* decision, hailed by some observers as a victory, is at best a weak victory because it allows for a "narrowly tailored" employment of race in college admissions, imposes an artificial 25-year deadline for the program, and encourages a monumental case by case analysis for admitting students that is likely to create chaos and push institutions into making admissions decision based on test scores. Again, this trend reinforces our Latin Americanization thesis because the elimination of race-based social policy is, among other things, predicated on the notion that race no longer affects minorities' status. Nevertheless, as in Latin America, we may eliminate race by decree and maintain—or even increase—the level of racial inequality.[6]

---

[6] We acknowledge that the United States has never had a monolithic racial order. Historically, areas that had "Latin American-like" racial situations, like South Carolina, Los Angeles, and other parts of the west coast, have more pluralistic racial orders. However, varieties of racial orders and exceptions to the national trend do not mean they replace the larger macro dynamics. We claim that the more plural racial orders in the U.S., which are due

A Look at the Data

Objective Standing of "Whites," "Honorary Whites," and "Blacks"

If Latin Americanization is happening in the United States, gaps in income, poverty rates, education, and occupational standing between whites, honorary whites, and the collective black should be developing. The available data suggests this is the case. In terms of income, as Table 9.1 shows, "white" Latinos (Argentines, Chileans, Costa Ricans, and Cubans) are doing much better than dark-skinned Latinos (Mexicans, Puerto Ricans, etc.).[7] Table 7.1 also shows that Asians exhibit a pattern similar to that of Latinos. Hence, a severe income gap is emerging between honorary white Asians (Japanese, Koreans, Filipinos, and Chinese) and those Asians we contend belong to the collective black (Vietnamese, Cambodian, Hmong, and Laotians).

Table 9.1 Mean per capita income[1] ($) of selected Asian and Latino Ethnic Groups, 2000

Latinos	Mean income	Asian Americans	Mean income
Mexicans	9,467.30	Chinese	20,728.54
Puerto Ricans	11,314.95	Japanese	23,786.13
Cubans	16,741.89	Koreans	16,976.19
Guatemalans	11,178.60	Asian Indians	25,682.15
Salvadorans	11,371.92	Filipinos	19,051.53
Costa Rican	14,226.92	Taiwanese	22,998.05
Panamanians	16,181.20	Hmong	5,175.34
Argentines	23,589.99	Vietnamese	14,306.74
Chileans	18,272.04	Cambodian	8,680.48
Bolivians	16,322.53	Laotians	10,375.57
Whites	17,968.87	Whites	17,968.87
Blacks	11,366.74	Blacks	11,366.74

Source: 2000 PUMS 5% Sample.
[1] We use per capita income as family income distorts the status of some groups (particularly Asians and Whites) as some groups have more people than others contributing toward the family income.

---

to five or six different demographic and political elements, are not becoming part of the national macro level trend.

[7] The apparent exceptions in Table 1 (Bolivians and Panamanians) are examples of self-selection among these immigrant groups. For example, four of the largest ten concentrations of Bolivians in the U.S. are in Virginia, a state with just 7.2 percent Latinos (U.S. Bureau of the Census 2005). Whereas the Bolivian Census of 2001 reports that 71 percent of the Bolivians self-identify as Indian, less than 20 percent have more than a high school diploma, and 58.6 percent live below the poverty line, 66 percent of Bolivians in the United States self-identify as white, 64 percent have 12 or more years of education, and have a per capita income comparable to that of whites (Censo Nacional de Población y Vivienda 2002). Thus, this seems like a case of self-selection because Bolivians in the United States do not represent Bolivians in Bolivia.

Table 9.2 Educational attainment of selected Asian and Latino Ethnic Groups, 2000

Latinos	Median years	Percent college*	Asian Americans	Median years	Percent college*
Mexicans	9.00	14.85	Chinese	12.00	49.65
Puerto Ricans	11.00	23.54	Japanese	14.00	59.44
Cubans	12.00	35.02	Koreans	12.00	48.97
Guatemalans	7.50	15.36	Asian Indians	14.00	55.95
Salvadorans	9.00	14.13	Filipinos	14.00	54.14
Costa Ricans	12.00	36.94	Taiwanese	14.00	65.22
Panamanians	12.00	46.11	Hmong	5.50	11.51
Argentines	12.00	48.11	Vietnamese	11.00	32.19
Chileans	12.00	44.44	Cambodians	9.00	17.87
Bolivians	12.00	44.08	Laotians	10.00	17.45
Whites	12.00	39.12			
Blacks	12.00	27.10			

Source: 2000 PUMS 5% Sample.
*Includes "some college," "college graduate," and "advanced degree".

Table 9.2 exhibits similar patterns in terms of education. Light-skinned Latinos have between three and four years of educational advantage over dark-skinned Latinos, and elite Asians have up to eight years of educational advantage over most of the Asian groups we classify as belonging to the collective black. A more significant fact, given that the American job market is becoming bifurcated (good jobs for the educated and bad jobs for the under-educated), is that the proportion of white Latinos with "some college" is equal or higher than the White population. Hence, as Table 7.2 shows, 35 percent of Cubans, 37 percent of Costa Ricans, 48 percent of Argentines, and 44 percent of Chileans have attained "some college" or higher levels of education, propor-tions that compare very favorably with the 39 percent of Whites. In contrast, the bulk of Mexican Americans, Salvadorans, Puerto Ricans, and Guatemalans (74–86%) have just attained 12 or less years of education. Likewise, the educa-tional attainment of Asians reveals a similar pattern between elite and collective black Asians, that is, elite Asians substantially outperform their brethren (and even Whites) in having at least some college. It is worth pointing out that the distance in educational attainment between elite and collective black Asians is larger than that between White and a dark-skinned Latinos (e.g., whereas about 50 percent of Chinese, Japanese, and Koreans have "some college" or higher level of educational attainment, more than 80 percent of Hmong, Laotians, and Cambodians have attained a "high school diploma" or less).

Substantial group differences are also evident in the occupational status of the groups. The light-skinned Latino groups have achieved parity with Whites in their proportional representation in the top jobs in the economy. Thus, the share of Argentines, Chileans, and Cubans in the two top occupational cate-gories ("Manager and Professionals" and "Sales and Office") is 55 percent or higher, which is close to Whites' 59 percent share (see Table 9.3). In contrast, the

Table 9.3 Occupational status of selected Latino Groups, 2000

Ethnic Groups	Occupational status (%)					
	Managr. & Prof. Related Occup.	Sales & Office	Services	Construction, Extraction, & Maintenance	Production, Transport. & Material Moving	Farming, Forestry, & Fishing
Mexicans	13.18	20.62	22.49	14.41	23.76	5.54
Puerto Ricans	21.14	29.46	21.40	8.34	19.01	0.66
Cubans	27.84	28.65	16.09	10.21	16.68	0.53
Guatemalans	9.49	16.13	29.73	14.59	27.55	2.51
Salvadorans	8.96	17.29	32.11	15.44	24.84	1.37
Costa Ricans	23.35	22.76	25.46	11.61	16.27	0.55
Panamanians	31.07	32.82	20.27	5.61	9.94	0.29
Argentines	39.77	24.68	14.84	9.24	10.96	0.51
Chileans	32.12	23.92	20.05	10.32	13.13	0.46
Bolivians	27.20	25.80	23.85	11.19	11.73	0.23
Whites	32.07	27.03	15.02	10.12	14.77	1.00
Blacks	21.48	26.48	23.96	7.57	19.84	0.65

Source: 2000 PUMS 5% Sample.

bulk of the dark-skinned Latino groups such as Mexicans, Puerto Ricans,[8] and Central Americans are concentrated in the four lower occupational categories. Along the same lines, the Asian groups we classify as honorary whites are even more likely to be well represented in the top occupational categories than those we classify in the collective black. For instance, whereas 61 percent of Taiwanese and 56 percent of Asian Indians are in the top occupational category, only 15 percent of Hmong, 13 percent of Laotians, 17 percent of Cambodians, and 25 percent of Vietnamese are in that category (see Table 9.4).

Subjective Standing of Racial Strata

Social psychologists have amply demonstrated that it takes very little for groups to form, to develop a common view, and to adjudicate status positions to nominal characteristics (Ridgeway 1991). Thus, it should not be surprising if gaps in income, occupational status, and education among these various strata are contributing to group formation and consciousness. That is, honorary whites may be classifying themselves as "white" and believing they are different (better) than those in the collective black category. If this is happening, this group should also be in the process of developing white-like racial

---

[8] The concentration of Puerto Ricans in the lower occupational categories is slightly below 50 percent. However, when one subdivides the category "Sales and Office," where 20.46 percent of Puerto-Ricans are located, one finds that Puerto-Ricans are more likely to be represented in the low-paying jobs.

Table 9.4 Occupational status of selected Asian Ethnic Groups, 2000

Ethnic Groups	Managr. & Prof. Related Occup.	Sales & Office	Services	Construction, Extraction, & Maintenance	Production, Transport. & Material Moving	Farming, Forestry, & Fishing
Chinese	47.79	22.83	15.04	2.77	11.42	0.15
Japanese	46.90	28.05	13.24	4.50	6.70	0.60
Koreans	36.51	31.26	15.65	3.97	12.38	0.23
Asian Indians	55.89	23.39	8.07	2.25	10.03	0.37
Filipinos	34.87	28.70	18.49	4.62	12.35	0.98
Taiwanese	60.95	24.78	8.44	1.34	4.43	0.06
Hmong	14.67	24.14	17.33	4.51	38.57	0.77
Vietnamese	25.21	19.92	19.64	6.02	28.50	0.71
Cambodians	16.66	25.37	17.26	5.45	34.67	0.59
Laotians	12.55	20.60	15.02	6.07	44.96	0.81
Whites	32.07	27.03	15.02	10.12	14.77	1.00
Blacks	21.48	26.48	23.96	7.57	19.84	0.65

Source: 2000 PUMS 5% Sample.

attitudes befitting of their new social position and differentiating (distancing) themselves from the collective black. In line with our thesis, we expect Whites to be making distinctions between honorary whites and the collective black, specifically exhibiting a more positive outlook toward honorary whites than toward members of the collective black. Finally, if Latin Americanization is happening, we speculate that the collective black should exhibit a diffused and contradictory racial consciousness as blacks and Indians do throughout Latin America and the Caribbean (Hanchard 1994). We examine some of these matters in the subsections that follow.

Latino Self-reports

Historically, most Latinos have classified themselves as "white," but the proportion of Latinos who self-classify as such varies tremendously by group. Hence, as Table 9.5 shows, whereas 60 percent or more of the members of the Latino groups we regard as honorary white self-classify as white, about 50 percent or fewer of the members of the groups we regard as belonging to the collective black do so. As a case in point, whereas Mexicans, Dominicans, and Central Americans are very likely to report "Other" as their preferred "racial" classification, most Costa Ricans, Cubans, Chileans, and Argentines choose the "white" descriptor. This Census 1990 data mirrors the results of the 1988 Latino National Political Survey (de la Garza, DeSipio, Garcia, and Falcon 1992).

Table 9.5 Racial self-classification by selected Latin America Origin Latino Ethnic Groups, 2000

	White	Black	Other	Native American	Asian
Dominicans	28.21	10.93	59.21	1.07	0.57
Salvadorans	41.01	0.82	56.95	0.81	0.41
Guatemalans	42.95	1.24	53.43	2.09	0.28
Hondurans	48.51	6.56	43.41	1.24	0.29
Mexicans	50.47	0.92	46.73	1.42	0.45
Puerto Ricans	52.42	7.32	38.85	0.64	0.77
Costa Ricans	64.83	5.91	28.18	0.56	0.53
Bolivians	65.52	0.32	32.79	1.32	0.05
Colombians	69.01	1.53	28.54	0.49	0.44
Venezuelans	75.89	2.58	20.56	0.36	0.60
Chileans	77.04	0.68	21.27	0.44	0.56
Cubans	88.26	4.02	7.26	0.17	0.29
Argentines	88.70	0.33	10.54	0.08	0.35

Source: 2000 PUMS 5% Sample.

"Racial" Distinctions Among Asians

Although for political matters, Asians tend to vote panethnically (Espiritu 1992), distinctions between native-born and foreign-born (e.g., American-born Chinese and foreign-born Chinese) and between economically successful and unsuccessful Asians are developing. In fact, according to various analysts, given the tremendous diversity of experiences among Asian Americans, "all talk of Asian panethnicity should now be abandoned as useless speculation" (San Juan 2000, p. 10). Leland Saito (1998), in his *Race and Politics*, points out that many Asians have reacted to the "Asian flack" they are experiencing with the rise in Asian immigration by fleeing the cities of immigration, disidentifying from new Asians, and invoking the image of the "good immigrant." In some communities, this has led to older, assimilated segments of a community to dissociate from recent migrants. For example, a Nisei returning to his community after years of overseas military service told his dad the following about the city's new demography: "Goddamn dad, where the hell did all these Chinese came from? Shit, this isn't even our town anymore" (Saito 1998, p. 59).

Latinos' Racial Attitudes

Although researchers have shown that Latinos tend to hold negative views of blacks and positive views of whites (Mindiola et al. 1996; Yoon 1995), the picture is more complex. Immigrant Latinos tend to have more negative views about blacks than native-born Latinos. For instance, a study of Latinos in Houston, Texas, found that 38 percent of native-born Latinos compared to

47 percent of foreign-born held negative stereotypes of blacks (Mindiola et al. 1996). This may explain why 63 percent of native-born Latinos versus 34 percent of foreign-born report frequent contact with blacks.

But the incorporation of the majority of Latinos as "colonial subjects" (Puerto Ricans), refugees from wars (Central Americans), or illegal migrant workers (Mexicans) has foreshadowed subsequent patterns of integration into the racial order. In a similar vein, the incorporation of a minority of Latinos as "political refugees" (Cubans, Chileans, and Argentines) or as "neutral" immigrants trying to better their economic situation (Costa Rica, Colombia) has allowed them a more comfortable ride in America's racial boat (Pedraza 1985). Therefore, whereas the incorporation of most Latinos in the U.S. has meant becoming "nonwhite," for a few it has meant becoming almost White.

Nevertheless, given that most Latinos experience discrimination in labor and housing markets as well as in schools, they quickly realize their "nonwhite" status. This leads them to adopt a plurality of identities that signify "otherness" (Flores-Gonzales 1999). Thus, dark-skinned Latinos are even calling themselves "black" or "Afro-Dominicans" or "Afro-Puerto Rican" (Howard 2001). For example, José Ali, a Latino interviewed by Clara Rodríguez (2000) stated, "By inheritance I am Hispanic. However, I identify more with blacks because to white America, if you are my color, you are a nigger. I can't change my color, and I do not wish to." When asked, "Why do you see yourself as Black?" he said, "Because when I was jumped by Whites, I was not called 'spic,' but I was called a 'nigger'."

Asian's Racial Attitudes

Various studies have documented that Asians tend to hold anti-black and anti-Latino attitudes. For instance, L. Bobo, C. Zubrinsky, J. Johnson, and M. Oliver (1995) found that Chinese residents of Los Angeles expressed negative racial attitudes toward Blacks. One Chinese resident stated, "Blacks in general seem to be overly lazy," and another asserted, "Blacks have a definite attitude problem" (Bobo et al. 1995, p. 78). Studies on Korean shopkeepers in various locales have found that over 70 percent of them hold anti-black attitudes (Weitzer 1997; Yoon 1997; Min 1996).

The Collective Black and Whites' Racial Attitudes

After a protracted conflict over the meaning of Whites' racial attitudes (Bonilla-Silva and Lewis 1999), survey researchers seem to have reached an agreement: "a hierarchical racial order continues to shape all aspects of American life" (Dawson 2000, p. 344). Whites express/defend their social position on issues such as affirmative action and reparations, school integration and busing, neighborhood integration, welfare reform, and even the death penalty (see Sears et al. 2000; Tuch and Martin 1997; Bonilla-Silva 2001). Regarding how Whites think about Latinos and Asians, not many researchers have separated the groups that comprise "Latinos" and "Asians" to assess if Whites are making distinctions. However, the available evidence suggests Whites regard Asians highly and are significantly less likely to hold Latinos in high regard (Bobo and Johnson 2000). Thus, when judged on a host of racial stereotypes, whites rate themselves and Asians almost identically (favorable stereotype rating) and rate negatively (at an almost equal level) both Blacks and Latinos. Bobo and Johnson (2000) also show that Latinos tend to rate Blacks negatively and that Blacks tend to do the same regarding Latinos.

Social Interaction Among Members of the Three Racial Strata

If Latin Americanization is happening, one would expect more social (e.g., friendship, associations as neighbors, etc.) and intimate (e.g., marriage) contact between Whites and honorary whites than between Whites and members of the collective black. A cursory analysis of extant data suggests this is in fact the case.

Interracial Marriage

Although most marriages in America are still intra-racial, the rates vary substantially by group. Whereas 93% of whites and blacks marry within-group, 70% of Latinos and Asians do so and only 33% Native Americans marry Native Americans (Moran 2001, p. 103). More significantly, when one disentangles the generic terms "Asians" and "Latinos," the data fits even more closely the Latin Americanization thesis. For example, among Latinos, Cuban, Mexican, Central American, and South Americans have higher rates of outmarriage than Puerto Ricans and Dominicans (Gilbertson et al. 1996). Although interpreting the Asian American outmarriage patterns is very complex (groups such as Filipinos and Vietnamese have higher than expected rates in part due to the Vietnam War and the military bases in the Philippines), it is worthy to point out that the highest rate belongs to Japanese Americans and Chinese (Kitano and Daniels 1995), and the lowest to Southeast Asians.

Furthermore, racial assimilation through marriage ("whitening") is significantly more likely for the children of Asian-white and Latino-white unions than for those of black-white unions, a fact that bolsters our Latin Americanization thesis. Hence, whereas only 22% of the children of Black fathers and White mothers are classified as White, the children of similar unions among Asians are twice as likely to be classified as white (Waters 1999). For Latinos, the data fits even closer our thesis, as Latinos of Cuban, Mexican, and South American origin have high rates of exogamy compared to Puerto Ricans and Dominicans

(Gilbertson et al. 1996). We concur with Moran's (2001) speculation that this may reflect the fact that, because Puerto Ricans and Dominicans have far more dark-skinned members, they have restricted chances for outmarriage to whites in a highly racialized marriage market.

Residential Segregation Among Racial Strata

An imperfect measure of interracial interaction is the level of neighborhood "integration."[9] Nevertheless, the various indices devised by demographers to assess the level of residential segregation, allow us to gauge in broad strokes the level on interracial contact in various cities. In this section, we focus on the segregation of Latinos and Asians as the high segregation experienced by blacks is well-known and studied (Massey and Denton 1993; Yinger 1995).

Researchers have shown that Latinos are less segregated from and are more exposed to whites than blacks (Charles 2003). Yet, they have also documented that dark-skinned Latinos experience black-like rates of residential segregation from whites. J. R. Logan (2001) reports indices of dissimilarity[10] and exposure[11] for the Hispanic-white dyad in various SMAs for 2000. In SMAs with high concentration of Latinos, such as New York, Long Beach, Fresno, Hartford, or San Antonio, the dissimilarity index is relatively high and the exposure index is very low. Although the latter index is impacted by the relative size of the populations while the former is not, it is worth pointing out that when Latinos have a significant presence in an area (10–40%), the level of exposure does not seem to fit (that is, it is lower than expected). For example, in Fresno, Long Beach, and San Antonio, with Latino populations ranging from forty-four to forty-seven percent, one would expect high levels of exposure to whites. Yet, the index of Hispanic-white exposure Logan reported in these cities was 28, 17, and 22 respectively. In predominantly Latino areas (e.g., Laredo, El Paso, and Brownsville, cities which are 80% or more Latino) or in white dominated areas (e.g., Altoona, Missoula, and Madison, cities which are less than 3.5% Latino), the indices seemed to fit the expected pattern (Logan 2001). Thus, in cities with few whites, the index of dissimilarity is relatively low and the

---

[9] For some of the limitations of this index, see Eduardo Bonilla-Silva and Gianpaolo Baiocchi (2001), "Anything but Racism: How Sociologists Limit the Significance of Racism," *Race and Society*, 4, 117–131.

[10] The dissimilarity index expresses the percentage of a minority population that would have to move to result in a perfectly even distribution of the population across census tracts. This index runs from 0 (no segregation) to 100 (total segregation) and it is symmetrical (not affected by population size).

[11] The exposure index measures the degree of potential contact between two populations (majority and minority) and expresses the probability of a member of a minority group meeting a member of the majority group. Like the dissimilarity index, it runs from 0 to 100, but, unlike it, it is asymmetrical (it is affected by population size).

exposure index is very low—ranges from about fourteen percent in El Paso to five percent in Laredo. Conversely, in cities that are dominated by whites, the index of dissimilarity is also low but the index of exposure is extremely high.

But these indices may misrepresent race relations on the ground in these cities. First, the latter cities are cities that have not yet reached the "racial tipping point" for white flight.[12] Second, in these cities the experiences for white- and dark-skinned Latinos may be totally different. In Madison, Wisconsin, where the first author lived for nine years, white Latinos have a vastly different racial existence than dark-skinned ones. Lastly, in predominantly Latino cities such as Miami, new forms of residential segregation are emerging (e.g., segregation by streets, segregation by not associating with Latinos even if living in "mixed" neighbor-hoods, and so forth), which are not captured by any of these indices.

Of all minority groups, Asian Americans are the least segregated. However, they have experienced an increase in residential segregation in recent years (Frey and Farley 1996). C. Z. Charles (2003) found that from 1980 to 2000, the index of dissimilarity for Asians had increased 3 points (from 37 to 40) while the exposure to whites had declined 16 points (from 88 to 62). Part of the increase in segregation (and the concomitant decrease in exposure) may be the result of the arrival of newer immigrants from Southeast Asia (Vietnam, Cam-bodia, and Laos) over the last two decades (Frey and Farley 1996).

Logan (2001) also reports the dissimilarity and exposure indices for the Asian-white dyad in selected areas of the United States for 2000. The observed patterns fit our thesis. Honolulu, the only Asian-majority area in the United States, has a moderate dissimilarity index of 40.5 and a low exposure index of 15.6 (however, Whites are only 20% of the population). San Francisco, with a relatively large Asian population (about 25%), has a dissimilarity index of 35.2, which is close to the Latino index of 47.9, but less than the 62.5 index for Blacks.[13] These lower dissimilarity indexes and higher exposure indexes vis-à-vis Latinos and particularly Blacks, tend to fit our prediction of the bulk of Asians belonging to the honorary white category.

Conclusion

We have presented a broad and bold thesis about the future of racial stratifica-tion in the United States.[14] However, at this early stage of the analysis and given the serious limitations of the data on "Latinos" and "Asians" (most of the data

[12] Researchers on residential segregation have documented that when neighborhoods reach about 7 percent blacks, a process of "white flight" begins. However, the real big "white flight" accelerates when the proportion black reaches 20 percent (Gladwell 2000).

[13] Data on Latinos and blacks from website of Lewis Mumford Center for Comparative Urban and Regional Research, http://www.albany.edu/mumford/census/index.html.

[14] We are not alone in making this kind of prediction. Arthur K. Spears (1999), Suzanne Oboler (2000), Gary Okihiro (1994), Mari Matsuda (1996) have made similar claims.

is not parceled out by sub-groups and hardly anything is separated by skin tone), it is hard to make a conclusive case. It is plausible that factors such as nativity or other socioeconomic characteristics explain some of the patterns we documented.[15] Nevertheless, almost all the objective, subjective, and social interaction indicators we reviewed suggest a trend toward Latin American-ization. The objective data clearly show substantive gaps between the groups we labeled "white," "honorary whites," and the "collective black," and a variety of subjective indicators signal the emergence of internal stratification among racial minorities. Finally, the objective and subjective indicators have an inter-actional correlate. Data on interracial marriage and residential segregation shows that Whites are significantly more likely to live near honorary whites and intermarry with them than members of the collective black.

If our predictions are right, what will the consequences of Latin American-ization be for race relations in the United States? First, racial politics will change dramatically. The "us" versus "them" racial dynamic will lessen as "honorary whites" grow in size and social importance. They are likely to buffer racial conflict—or derail it—as intermediate groups do in many Latin Amer-ican countries. Second, the ideology of colorblind racism will become even more salient among whites and honorary whites and will also impact members of the collective black. Colorblind racism (Bonilla-Silva 2001), an ideology similar to that prevalent in Latin American societies, will help glue the new social system and further buffer racial conflict. Third, if the state decides to stop gathering racial statistics, the struggle to document the impact of race in a variety of social venues will become monumental. More significantly, because state actions always impact civil society, if the state decides to erase race from above, the social recognition of "races" in the polity may become harder. We may develop a Latin American-like "disgust" for even mentioning anything that is race-related. Nevertheless, the deep history of black-white divisions in the United States has been such that the centrality of the Black identity will not dissipate. The research on even the "black elite" shows that they exhibit racial attitudes in line with their racial group (Dawson 1994). That identity, as we argued in this chapter, may be taken up by dark-skinned Latinos, as it is being rapidly taken

---

[15] A powerful alternative explanation to many of our preliminary findings is that the groups we label "honorary whites" come with high levels of human capital *before* they achieve honorary white status in the United States, that is, they fit this intermediate position not because of their color or race but rather because of their class background. Although this is a independent effect in this process (Kasinitz et al. 2001). It is also important to point out that, even when some of these groups may do "well" objectively, comparison of their returns to their characteristics shows how little they get for what they bring to the fore (Butcher 1994). And, as Waters and Eschbach (1995: 442) stated in a review of the literature on immigration, "the evidence indicates that direct discrimination is still an important factor for all minority subgroups except very highly educated Asians."

up by most West Indians. For example, Al, a 53-year-old Jamaican engineer interviewed by Milton Vickerman (1999), stated:

> I have nothing against Haitians; I have nothing against black Americans... If you're a nigger, you're a nigger, regardless of whether you are from Timbuktu...There isn't the unity that one would like to see...Blacks have to appreciate Blacks, no matter where they are from. Just look at it the way I look at it: That you're the same.

However, even among Blacks, we predict some important changes. Their racial consciousness will become more diffused. For example, Blacks will be more likely to accept many stereotypes about themselves (e.g., "We are more lazy than Whites") and have a "blunted oppositional consciousness" (see Chapter 6 in Bonilla-Silva 2001). Furthermore, the external pressure of "multi-racials" in white contexts (Rockquemore and Brusma 2002) and the internal pressure of "ethnic" blacks may change the notion of "blackness" and even the position of some "blacks" in the system. Colorism may become an even more important factor as a way of making social distinctions among "blacks" (Keith and Herring 1991).

Finally, the new racial stratification system will be more effective in maintaining "white supremacy" (Mills 1997). Whites will still be at the top of the social structure, but will face fewer race-based challenges. The standing and status of "honorary whites" will be dependent upon Whites' wishes and practices. "Honorary" means that they will remain secondary, will still face discrimination, and will not receive equal treatment in society.

Although some analysts and commentators may welcome Latin Americanization as a positive trend in American race relations, those at the bottom of the racial hierarchy will discover that behind the statement "We are all Americans" hides a deeper, hegemonic way of maintaining White supremacy. As a Latin America-like society,[16] the United States will become a society with more, rather than less, racial inequality, but with a reduced forum for racial contestation. The apparent blessing of "not seeing race" will become a curse for those struggling for racial justice in years to come. We may become "All Americans," as commercials in recent times suggest, but, paraphrasing George Orwell, "some will be more American than others."

---

[16] Latin America-like does not mean exactly like Latin America. The 400-year history of the American "racial formation" (Omi and Winant 1994) has stained the racial stratification order forever. Thus, we expect some important differences in this new American racial stratification system compared to that typical of Latin American societies. First, "shade discrimination" (Kinsbrunner 1996) will not work perfectly. Hence, for example, although Asian Indians are dark-skinned, they still will be higher in the stratification system than, for example, Mexican American *mestizos*. Second, Arabs, Asian Indians, and other non-Christian groups will not be allowed complete upward mobility. Third, because of the 300 years of dramatic racialization and group formation, most members of the non-white groups will maintain "ethnic" (Puerto Ricans) or racial claims (e.g., blacks) and demand group-based rights.

References

Ashikari, M. (2005). Cultivating Japanese whiteness: The "whitening" cosmetics boom and the Japanese identity. *Journal of Material Culture*, 10(1), 73–78.

Bashi, V. (2004). Globalized anti-Blackness: Transnationalizing western immigration law, policy, and practice. *Racial and Ethnic Studies*, 27(4), 584–606

Bobo, L., & Johnson, D. (2000). Racial attitudes in a prismatic metropolis: Mapping identity, stereotypes, competition, and views on affirmative action. In L. Bobo, M. Oliver, J. Johnson, & A. Valenzuela (Eds.), *Prismatic Metropolis*. New York: Russell Sage Foundation.

Bobo, L., Zubrinksy, C., Johnson, J., & Oliver, M. (1995). Work orientation, job discrimination, and ethnicity. *Research in the Sociology of Work*, 5, 45–85.

Bonilla-Silva, E. (1997). Rethinking racism: Toward a structural interpretation. *American Sociological Review*, 62(3), 465–480.

———. (2000). This is a White country: The racial ideology of the western nations of the world-system. *Sociological Inquiry*, 70(2), 188–214.

———. (2001). *White supremacy and racism in the post-civil rights era*. Boulder, CO: Lynne Rienner Publishers.

Bonilla-Silva, E., & Baiocchi, G. (2001). Anything but racism: How sociologists limit the significance of racism. *Race and Society*, 4(2), 117–131.

Bonilla-Silva, E., & Lewis, A. (1999). The new racism: Toward an analysis of the U.S. racial structure, 1960 s–1990 s. In P. Wong, (Ed.), *Race, ethnicity, and nationality in the United States*. Boulder, CO: Westview Press.

Brooks, R. L. (1990). *Rethinking the American race problem*. Berkeley, CA: University of California Press.

Butcher, K. F. (1994). Black immigrants in the United States: A comparison with native Blacks and other immigrants. *Industrial and Labor Relations Review*, 47(2), 265–283.

Censo Nacional de Población y Vivienda. (2002). *Bolivia: Caraterísticas de la población, Serie resultados 4*. La Paz: Ministerio de Hacienda.

Charles, C. Z. (2003). The dynamics of racial residential segregation. *Annual Review of Sociology*, 29, 167–207.

Cohen, R. (1997). *Global diasporas: An introduction*. Seattle, WA: University of Washington Press.

Dawson, M. (1994). *Behind the mule: Race and class in African American politics*. Princeton, NJ: Princeton University Press.

———. (2000). Slowly coming to grips with the effects of the American racial order on American policy preferences. In D. Sears, J. Sidanius, & L. Bobo, *Racialized politics: The debate about racism in America*. Chicago, IL: University of Chicago Press.

De la Garza, R. O., DeSipio, L, Garcia, F. C., Garcia, J, & Falcon, A. (1992). *Latino voices: Mexican, Puerto Rican, & Cuban perspectives on American politics*. Boulder, CO: Westview Press.

Espiritu, Y. L. (1992). *Asian American panethnicity: Bridging institutions and identities*. Philadelphia. PA: Temple University Press.

Flores-Gonzales, N. (1999). The racialization of Latinos: The meaning of Latino identity for the second generation. *Latino Studies Journal*, 10(3), 3–31.

Frey, W. H., & Farley, R. (1996). Latino, Asian, and Black segregation in U.S. metropolitan areas: Are multi-ethnic metros different? *Demography*, 33(1), 35–50.

Gans, H. J. (1999). The possibility of a new racial hierarchy in the twenty-first century United States. In M. Lamont (Ed.), *Cultural territories of race: Black and white boundaries*. Chicago, IL: University of Chicago Press.

Gilbertson, G. A., Fitzpatrick, J. P., & Yang, L. (1996). Hispanic intermarriage in New York City: New evidence from 1991. *International Immigration Review*, 30(2), 445–459.

Gladwell, M. (2000). *The tipping point: How little things can make a big difference.* New York: Little, Brown, and Company.

Goldberg, D. T. (2002). *The racial state.* Malden, MA: Blackwell Press.

Grutter v. Bollinger et al. (02-241) 539 U.S. 306 (2003).

Hanchard, M. (1994). *Orpheus and power: The movimiento Negro of Rio de Janeiro and São Paulo, Brazil, 1945–1988.* Princeton, NJ: Princeton University Press.

Helg, A. (1990). Race in Argentina and Cuba, 1880–1930: Theory, policies, and popular reaction. In R. Graham (Ed.), *The idea of race in Latin America, 1870–1940.* Austin, TX: University of Texas Press.

Howard, D. (2001). *Coloring the nation: Race and ethnicity in the Dominican Republic.* Boulder, CO: Lynne Rienner Publishers.

Hunter, M. L. (2005). *Race, gender, and the politics of skin tone.* New York: Routledge.

Kasinitz, P., Battle, J., & Miyares, I. (2001). Fade to black? The children of West Indian immigrants in southern Florida. In R. G. Rumbaut & A. Portes (Eds.), *Ethnicities: Children of immigrants in America.* Berkeley, CA: University of California Press.

Keith, V. M., & Herring, C. (1991). Skin tone and stratification in the Black community. *American Journal of Sociology, 97*(3), 760–778.

Kinsbrunner, J. (1996). *Not of pure blood: The free people of color and racial prejudice in nineteenth-century Puerto Rico.* Durham, NC: Duke University Press.

Kitano, H. H. L., & Daniels, R. (1995). *Asian Americans: Emerging minorities* (2nd ed.). Englewood Cliffs, NJ: Prentice Hall.

Logan, J. R. (2001). *From many shores: Asians in census 2000. Report by the Lewis Mumford Center for Comparative Urban and Regional Research.* Albany, NY: University of Albany.

Lusane, C. (1997). *Race in the global era: African Americans at the millennium.* Boston, MA: South End Press.

Massey, D. S., & Denton, N. A. (1993). *American apartheid: Segregation and the making of the underclass.* Cambridge, MA: Harvard University Press.

Matsuda, Mari J. (1996). *Where is Your Body? And Other Essays on Race, Gender, and the Law.* Boston: Beacon Press.

Miles, R. (1993). *Racism after race relations.* London (UK): Routledge.

Mills, C. W. (1997). *The racial contract.* Ithaca, NY: Cornell University Press.

Min, P. G. (1996). *Caught in the middle: Korean communities in America's multiethnic cities.* Berkeley, CA: University of California Press.

Mindiola, T., Rodríguez, M., & Niemann, Y. F. (1996). *Intergroup relations between Hispanics and Blacks in Harris County.* Houston, TX: University of Houston, Center for Mexican American Studies.

Moran, R. F. (2001). *Interracial intimacy: The regulation of race and romance.* Chicago, IL: The University of Chicago Press.

Negri, A. (1984). *Marx beyond Marx: Lessons on the Grundrisse.* South Hadley, MA: Bergin & Garvey.

———. (2000). It must be a fake! Racial ideologies, identities, and the question of rights in Hispanics/Latinos. In J. J. E. Gracia & P. De Greiff (Eds.), *Hispanics/Latinos in the United States: Ethnicity, race, and rights.* New York: Routledge.

Okihiro, G. (1994). *Margins and mainstreams: Asians in American history and culture.* Seattle, WA: University of Washington Press.

Omi, M., & Winant, H. (1994). *Racial formation in the United States from the 1960s to the 1990s.* New York: Routledge.

Pedraza, S. (1985). *Political and economic migrants in America: Cubans and Mexicans.* Austin, TX: University of Texas Press.

Ridgeway, C. L. (1991). The social construction of status value: Gender and other nominal characteristics. *Social Forces, 70*(2), 367–386.

Rockquemore, K. A., & Arend, P. (2002). Opting for White: Choice, fluidity, and identity construction in post-civil rights America. *Race and Society, 5*(1), 49–64.

Rockquemore, K. A., & Brunsma, D. L. (2002). *Beyond Black: Biracial identity in America.* Thousand Oaks, CA: Sage Publications.

Rodríguez, C. E. (2000). *Changing race: Latinos, the census, and the history of ethnicity in the United States.* New York: New York University Press.

Rodríguez, V. M. (1999). Boricuas, African Americans, and Chicanos in the "far west": Notes on the Puerto Rican pro-independence movement in California, 1960s–1980s. In R. D. Torres & G. Katsiaficas (Eds.), *Latino social movements: Historical and theoretical perspectives.* New York: Routledge.

Saito, L. T. (1998). *Race and politics: Asian Americans, Latinos, and Whites in a Los Angeles suburb.* Urbana, IL: University of Illinois Press.

San Juan, E. (2000). The limits of ethnicity and the horizon of historical materialism. In E. M. Ghymn, *Asian American studies: Identity, images, issues past and present.* New York: Peter Lang.

Schoenbaum, D., & Pond, E. (1996). *The German question and other German questions.* New York: St. Martin's Press.

Spears, A. K. (1999). *Race and ideology: Language, symbolism, and popular culture.* Detroit, MI: Wayne State University Press.

Steinberg, S. (1995). *Turning back: The retreat from racial justice in American thought and policy.* Boston, MA: Beacon Press.

Torres, A. (1998). La gran familia Puertorriqueña "ej prieta de beldá" (the great Puerto Rican family is really really Black). In N. E. Whitten & A. Torres (Eds.), *Blackness in Latin America and the Caribbean: Social dynamics and cultural transformations* (vol. II). Bloomington, IN: Indiana University Press.

Tuch, S. A., & Martin, J. K. (1997). *Racial attitudes in the 1990s.* Westport, CT: Praeger.

Twine, F. W. (1998). *Racism in a racial democracy: The maintenance of White supremacy in Brazil.* New Brunswick, NJ: Rutgers University Press.

U.S. Bureau of the Census. (2001). *Population projections of the United States by age, sex, race, and Hispanic origin: 1995 to 2050.* Washington, DC: U.S. Government Printing Office.

U.S. Bureau of the Census. (2005). *American Community Survey (ACS): Public Use Microdata Sameple (PUMS)* [Computer file]. Washington, D.C.:U.S. Bureau of the Censes.

Vickerman, M. (1999). *Crosscurrents: West Indian immigrants and race.* New York: Oxford University Press.

Wade, P. (1997). *Race and ethnicity in Latin America.* Sterling, VA: Pluto Press.

Wagley, C. (1952). *Race and class in rural Brazil.* Paris: UNESCO.

Waters, M. C. (1999). *Black identities: West Indian immigrant dreams and American reality.* Cambridge, MA: Harvard University Press.

Waters, M. C., and Eschbach, K. (1995). Immigration and ethnic and racial inequality in the United States. *Annual Review of Sociology,* 21, 419.

Weiner, M. (1997). *Japan's minorities: The illusion of homogeneity.* New York: Routledge.

Weitzer, R. (1997). Racial prejudice among Korean merchants in African American neighborhoods. *Sociological Quarterly,* 38(4), 587–606.

Winant, H. (2002). *The world is a ghetto: Race and democracy since World War II.* New York: Basic Books.

Yinger, J. (1995). *Closed doors, opportunities lost: The continuing costs of housing discrimination.* New York: Russell Sage Foundation.

Yoon, I. (1995). Attitudes, social distance, and perceptions of influence and discrimination among minorities. *International Journal of Group Tensions,* 25(1), 35–56.

Yoon, I. (1997). *On My Own: Korean Businesses and Race Relations in America.* Chicago: University of Chicago Press.

Chapter 10
Skin Color and Latinos with Disabilities: Expanding What We Know About Colorism in the United States

Keith B. Wilson and Julissa Senices

Abstract With the influx of Latinos increasing in many of the major and minor cities across the United States, cultural competency is vital. Contrary to other studies looking at Vocational Rehabilitation (VR) acceptance rates, race, and ethnicity, there is evidence that the proportions of White Americans and African Americans found eligible for VR services are significantly different. In summary, Latinos with disabilities who classified as White Latino or non-Latino (Note: most non-Latinos classified themselves as the White American race) are likely to be accepted for VR services when compared to Black Latinos with disabilities in the United States. The Black and White Latino results are similar to VR studies comparing African Americans and White Americans with disabilities. Evidence suggests that there is a high correlation between VR and general outcomes of people with a darker hue. Correlating colorism with people with disabilities (i.e., Black and White Latinos) is a very exciting line of research that we hope will continue to grow as resources become more available to produce more knowledge in this area.

Introduction

With Latinos increasing in many cities across the United States, cultural competency is vital (Quiñones-Mayo et al. 2000). The Census projects that racial and ethnic minorities will become a numerical majority by the year 2050; however, according to some private polls, this demographic shift will occur by the year 2030 (Sue 1996). Therefore, it is likely that future human service workers, counselors, and educators will be serving a much larger number of clients with racial and ethnic minority backgrounds (Sue et al. 1992, Wilson 2002). It has been substantiated for several years that access to

K.B. Wilson
Department of Counselor Education, Counseling Psychology and Rehabilitation Services, The Pennsylvania State University, State College, PA, USA
e-mail: kbw4@psu.edu

R.E. Hall (ed.), *Racism in the 21st Century*, DOI: 10.1007/978-0-387-79097-8_10,   171
© Springer Science+Business Media, LLC 2008

vocational rehabilitation (VR) services is more difficult for people of color (i.e., Black Latinos and African Americans) than for non-minorities (i.e., White Americans) (Wilson, Harley et al. 2001, Wilson & Senices 2005). The difficulties in accessing the VR system are underscored by changing U.S. demographics. For example, between 1980 and 1990 the White American population increased only 7.7%, while the African American population increased by 15.8% (Rogers et al. 1992). While demographic trends are gradually changing to reflect more diversity in the United States, people who work in the human services, for example, must change how they relate to people who do not. This is the challenge of the 21st century.

General Latino Demographics

It is increasingly clear that Latinos are likely to classify as "White American" when selecting a racial group. Census 2000 reports that 50% of the Latino population identified as White American (United States Bureau of the Census 2001, March). In the 1990 U.S. Census a little more than half (52%) of Latinos in the United States identified as White American. Using a national database from the United States Department of Education (Rehabilitation Services Administration), Wilson and Senices (2005) report that approximately 92% of all Latinos tended to select White American as their race. It appears that most Latinos, when given a choice, may select the race that will gain them more benefit in the United States. While there was no way of knowing whether Latinos in the aforementioned references phenotypically looked like they were White American; cursory evidence suggest that most Latinos may look more like majority group members (i.e., White Americans) than members of a racial minority group (e.g., African Americans).

Census 2000 also reported that the Latino population is becoming the largest ethnic minority group in the United States. For example, in 1980, Latinos made up 6.4% of the total population in the United States; and in 2000, the Latino population grew to over 12.5% of the total United States population (United States Census Bureau 2001). Furthermore, "within several short decades, Hispanic/Latino Americans will become the largest ethnic minority group in the United States, surpassing African Americans" (Sue et al. 1998, 24). The burgeoning increase of Latino immigrants is partly to blame for the increase in the Latino population in the United States (Camarillo & Bonilla 2001, Torres 1999). By 2010, Latinos are expected to be the largest of the principal minority groups (i.e., African Americans, Latino Americans, Asian Americans and Native Americans) in the United States (Torres 1999). Therefore, it seems necessary to understand the influence of skin color within the Latino population. Variability of skin color exists within Latin American and Caribbean communities, with those at the lighter end of the continuum having access to more opportunities (Falicov 1998). Yet, the numerous color gradations in Latin America and the Caribbean make it challenging for racially mixed individuals to classify themselves in a color-coded hierarchy. Racially mixed individuals have the opportunity to fall on the lighter end of the color continuum and therefore develop a "White" identity, which is associated with more opportunities and privilege. As we have outlined from Census 2000, 2002, and the Rehabilitation Services Administration reports, most Latinos tend to select White American as their race. Thus, reinforcing that most Latinos may have more privileges than other groups who are considered "minority." As we will see later in this chapter, there is empirical support for the "more privilege" assertion regarding White Latinos.

While being a Latino may be one salient variable of discrimination in the United States, it is really important to understand that being a Latino with a disability is considered a "double whammy," two potentially salient variables of discrimination on one person. Being a White American with a disability will not have the same intensity and will only account for one (disability) significant variable of bias. If one adds gender to the equation, there is potential for a "triple whammy." Thus, people who are Latino and people with disabilities are likely to experience discrimination because of one or both of these salient variables of prejudice. Lastly, because research on colorism in the United States tends to focus on the comparisons of African Americans and White Americans in the general population, the inclusion of research in VR comparing African Americans, other minorities, and White Americans outcomes will be highlighted, followed by VR research on Black and White Latinos with disabilities in the VR system. As stated at the beginning of this chapter, we conceptually view race and colorism in synonymous ways. Theoretically, this view of colorism and race is supported by several authors (e.g., Carter 1995, Wilson & Senices 2005).

A Literature Review on Vocational Rehabilitation Acceptance in the United States General History

Across Groups with Disabilities and VR Acceptance

Atkins and Wright (1980) was the first research team to analyze VR acceptance by race (African Americans in relation to White Americans). They found that African Americans were accepted proportionately less for VR services than their White American counterparts with disabilities. Herbert and Martinez (1992) provided similar findings to those of Atkins and Wright, indicating a higher VR acceptance rate among White Americans than among African Americans and other racial and ethnic minorities with disabilities (e.g., Native Americans). Particularly, Herbert and Martinez reported that persons of color were more likely to be determined ineligible for VR services and less likely to be successfully rehabilitated than White American clients with disabilities. Additionally, using various minority groupings, Herbert and Martinez reported that African Americans and Hispanics were more likely to be found ineligible for VR services than other minority groups in their study. It appears that minority racial and ethnic groups tend to have problems accessing VR services when compared to their White counterparts with disabilities.

As VR discrepancies became apparent in rehabilitation counseling literature, growing evidence indicated that racial minorities with disabilities tended to have different VR experiences than White Americans with disabilities in the United States. One year after the Herbert and Martinez (1992) investigation, Dziekan and Okocha (1993) examined the accessibility of rehabilitation services among racial and ethnic minorities (i.e., African Americans, Latinos, Native Americans, and Asian Americans) and White Americans with disabilities for the years 1985–1989. Dziekan and Okocha's findings were consistent with those reported earlier by Atkins and Wright (1980) and Herbert and Martinez (1992), showing that White Americans were accepted for VR services at a higher rate than racial/ethnic minorities, both individually and collectively, in each of the five years of the study. In addition, in 2000 and 2002, Wilson's results empirically supported the finding that racial minorities (i.e., African Americans) are less likely to be accepted for VR services than White Americans—congruent with other researchers' findings regarding race, ethnicity, and VR acceptance (e.g., Atkins & Wright 1980, Bowe 1992, Feist-Price 1995, Herbert & Martinez 1992). Likewise, Capella (2002) reported, "differences based on race do still exist for some minority groups in terms of acceptance rates and employment outcomes" (150). It is evident that groups with a darker-skin color/hue (i.e., African Americans with disabilities) tended to be accepted less for VR services than clients with a lighter color/hue (e.g., White Americans with disabilities). It is also clear based on the outcomes of the aforementioned studies that preferential treatment of lighter- skinned individuals may be due to skin color at either the conscious or unconscious level. Although most VR investigations looking at outcomes based on skin color have consistent findings, a small sample of other studies did not detect a difference between groups studied.

Contrary to other studies looking at VR acceptance rates and race and ethnicity, Wheaton (1995) concluded, "the proportions of White Americans and African Americans found eligible for VR services are not significantly different statistically" (228). Similar to Wheaton's findings in 1995, Peterson (1996) and Wilson (1999) also found no statistical differences between African American and White American clients in VR acceptance rates. Although several studies did not find a statistical significant difference in VR acceptance based on race, it is clear that racial and ethnic minorities do not achieve acceptance status within the VR system when statistical significant differences were noted.

Latinos with Disabilities and VR Acceptance/Access

One of the first studies to report Latino outcomes in VR was Herbert and Martinez, in 1992. Herbert and Martinez reported that Black Hispanics tended to be accepted less for VR services than White Americans and White Hispanics. Furthermore, Herbert and Martinez also reported that, once accepted for VR services, Black Latinos tended to be less successful in getting a job than White Latinos with disabilities in the VR system. Not only do Black Latinos have problems gaining access to VR services but, once they gain access to VR services, they are less likely to find a job, which is the primary purpose of the VR system when compared to White Latinos. While VR acceptance research is still in its early days, Herbert and Martinez was one of the first research teams to divide people who classified as Latino into two groups, Black and White. The findings reported by the team of Herbert and Martinez also highlighted the positive correlation that people with lighter skin color (White Hispanic and White Americans) are more likely to have more access to VR services than people with a darker skin color (e.g., Black Latinos). Although Latinos are highlighted in this section, the results are very similar to what is reported when other minority groups are compared to White Americans with disabilities in the VR system, based on phenotype (i.e., skin color). While several explanations may exist to explain VR discrepancies among certain groups with disabilities, the consistent results make it difficult to deny that the Herbert and Martinez investigation is another example of lighter-skinned people with disabilities having preferential treatment based on skin color in the VR system.

The following year, Dziekan and Okocha (1993) was the second research team to report findings relative to Latinos with disabilities in the VR system. Dziekan and Okocha explored the accessibility of VR services between various underrepresented groups (i.e., African Americans, Hispanics, Native Americans, and Asian Americans) and White Americans in the VR system as part of their state investigation. They reported that Latinos with disabilities are less likely to get accepted for VR services when compared to White Americans with disabilities in a Midwestern VR agency. White Americans with disabilities in the study tended to be more likely accepted for VR services than any of the racial and/or ethnic groups in the study. However, it was not clear whether the Latinos in the Dziekan and Okocha study were Black, White, or a combination of both Black and White Latinos. Based on the limited literature, Black Latinos with disabilities tend to have limited access to VR services when compared to their White American counterparts. While the first two studies investigating Latinos with disabilities were an excellent start, they were State VR studies that could not be generalized to the United States because of the sampling frame used. The following studies by Wilson and his colleagues employed a sampling frame that allowed for more external validity.

In a national study in 2005 looking at the VR acceptance rates of Latinos and non-Latinos with disabilities, Wilson and Senices reported that Latinos (i.e., White Latinos) tended to be accepted for VR services more than non-Latinos (e.g., African Americans, Native Americans, and so forth). Wilson and Senices also reported that 92% of all identified Latinos with disabilities in the database tended to classify themselves racially as White American. Thus, the term Latino can be synonymous to White Latinos. In another study, Wilson (2005) reported that the majority of Latinos in the VR system tended to classify themselves racially as White Americans with disabilities, as in the prior study with Wilson and Senices. It is apparent that Latinos have the flexibility to classify themselves racially that is not afforded other groups who are marginalized. Again, based on how Latinos are racially classifying them-selves in this particular database, the word Latino can be synonymous to White Latinos. As we will see later in this chapter, there are some noted benefits to being able to classify yourself racially in the United States. While classifying oneself based on phenotype is common, Latinos who classify themselves as Black have similar outcomes as African Americans, not only in the VR system but in the general population empirical studies as well. Thus, the results of the studies by Wilson and his colleagues could be labeled as a microcosm of the general society.

An interesting observation found in the Wilson (2005) examination is worth noting. Mainly, the majority of non-Latinos with disabilities (i.e. Black Latinos) tended to classify racially as African Americans (Black Latino) and not be accepted for VR services. In contrast, non-Latinos who classified as White Latinos tended to be accepted more often for VR services than those non-Latinos who are African Americans (Black Latinos). It appears that it does not matter whether a person classifies as non-Latino or Latino, the outcomes are likely to be positive if they select White Latino compared to Black Latino in either classification. Again, there is a strong correlation in the Wilson (2005) study based on phenotype (i.e., Black skin or White skin). The outcomes regarding Black and White Latinos are similar to the comparison of race (i.e., skin color/colorism) when VR outcomes of other racial minorities (e.g., African American with disabilities) and White Americans with disabil-ities in the United States were observed. The overwhelming outcomes based on the skin color of the participants in the Wilson 2005 investigation leads us to believe that skin color plays an important part in the selection process of the VR system.

In summary, Latinos with disabilities who classified as White Latino or non-Latino (Note: most non-Latinos classified themselves as the White American race) are likely to be accepted for VR services when compared to Black Latinos with disabilities in the United States. The Black and White Latino results are similar to VR studies comparing African Americans and White Americans with disabilities. The consistent theme in these studies is, the darker one's phenotype (i.e., hue/skin color), the more difficult it is to access human services for people with disabilities.

Colorism: A Brief Historical Perspective

Colorism is a form of prejudice that is found in many places, including the United States. The key characteristic of colorism is distinguishing people with lighter-skin hues over darker-skin hue individuals, based on a higher value being placed on lighter-skinned individuals. Colorism is a topic rarely approached in many professions, including VR. It is also important to note that the results of colorism discrimination in the VR system are considered a microcosm of the society in which we live. As a result, colorism is such an unfortunate part of the lives of people of color that it is vital to give a brief historical account of the effects and rise of colorism in the United States.

The influence of skin color on individuals' life chances has been largely ignored by psychologists and researchers (Hall 2002, Montalvo 1987). Yet, the presence of darker hues has indirectly shaped the experiences of many throughout history (Hall). During colonialism (the time period in which Europeans were conquering the Americas), a social hierarchy was established with Europeans designating Whites as superior and people of other races as inferior (Lancaster 1999). Colorism, defined by Lancaster (1999) as preferential treatment due to skin color, was one of the determinants of the social structure, given that skin color is the most notable racial characteristic (Phinney 1996). Furthermore, the influence of skin color became loaded with connotations of conquest, domination, power, morality, wealth, and status, implying a natural phenomenon, that it is appropriate, even "natural" for Whites to be accorded higher status over non-Whites (Lancaster 1999, Loewen 1995). Citizenry privilege, based on skin color, continues to be problematic for people who have darker hues. In the early years of the United States, discrimination based on skin color was a severe problem.

As White colonials established themselves in conquered lands, they also established a system of assigning rights and privileges to those of European ancestry, using skin color as the most salient criterion. European colonists generated multiracially stratified societies to maintain power and control of those who did not have light skin. As a consequence, individuals born in European countries were assigned the highest prestige. In the hierarchal structure of power and privilege that was based on skin color, individuals born in America with European heritage had the next markers of privilege, followed by a large intermediate group, such as individuals with mixed heritage. Finally, those with pure native and/or African lineage were at the bottom of the social order. In time, the two White populations (those born in European countries and those born in America with European heritage) fused, developing a social hierarchy based on skin color (Montalvo 1991). While there are numerous reasons why one's skin color served as either a disadvantage (i.e., people with a darker hue/skin color) or advantage (i.e., people with less hue/skin color) in past and present societies, it is clear from the history in the North American continent that people of color are still at the bottom of the social, political, and economic hierarchy largely because of the color of their skin. Undoubtedly, skin color is not the problem; the problem is what skin color represents in the minds of others.

In the United States, the concept of skin color has spawned a biracial society. Despite the various racial compositions in this country, the United States has historically operated biracially, with light skin color and White American/ Caucasian features deemed more worthy than Asian, Native American, or African racial features (Montalvo 1991). As with the VR literature in the United States, most of the literature on skin color in the U.S. has revolved around the African American community. As a result, prior research has clarified how blackness has become a marker in discrimination, by identifying the lack of material gain and privilege for Blacks in the United States (Hughes & Hertel 1990, Jones 1966, Lee 1999). Therefore, it seems important to highlight the influence of colorism outside the United States as well.

Colorism Influences Outside of the United States: Latinos

As an overview, the term Latino includes individuals of diverse Latino-based national origins including Mexico, the countries of Central America (i.e., Guatemala, Honduras, Costa Rica, El Salvador, Nicaragua, and Panama), the Spanish-speaking countries of South America (i.e., Colombia, Venezuela, Peru, Chile, Ecuador, Uruguay, Paraguay, Argentina), the Spanish-speaking countries of the Caribbean (i.e., Cuba, the Dominican Republic), and the U.S. territorial island of Puerto Rico (Casas & Pytluk 1995). Latinos exemplify a rainbow of skin colors and diverse physical attributes. Few studies in the United States have empirically investigated the influence of skin color within the Latino community. Yet, skin color has had a direct impact on most Latino families due to the variability of skin color within Latin American and Caribbean communities, with those at the lighter end of the continuum having access to more opportunities (Falicov 1998). The numerous color gradations (in Latin America and the Caribbean) make it challenging for racially mixed individuals to classify themselves in a color-coded hierarchy. Racially mixed individuals have the opportunity to fall on the lighter end of the color continuum and therefore develop a "White" identity, which is associated with more opportunities and privilege. However, there is no empirical research investigating how self-perceived "whiteness" influences the opportunities afforded to Latinos.

Several international studies have investigated the influence of skin color within the Latino community. Caribbean societies have been shown to function under a multiracial stratification system that uses color gradations, ranging from White to Brown to Black, in association with class status and nationality, to maintain a social hierarchy. For example, in the Dominican Republic, Haitians are physically indistinguishable from dark-skinned Dominicans, but Dominicans reserve the category of Black solely for Haitians (Duany 1998).

Haitian immigrants work the menial jobs in the Dominican Republic, and, as a result, represent the lowest echelon of the Dominican class system. Although Dominicans are racially mixed, they blur the distinctions between Creoles, Whites, light Coloreds, and Mulattos, thereby creating the impression of and functioning as a predominantly White population. Additionally, most Dominicans have held on to the perspective that they belong to the lighter end of the color continuum in order to maintain status in their country, highlighting the influence of skin color in this society (Itzigsohn & Dore-Cabral 2000). As Dominicans migrate to the United States, they retain their view of color with pride and reject any identification with African ancestry (Duany 1998). Privileges based on skin color certainly have international consequences for people outside of the United States, particularly Dominicans.

Similar to how Dominicans perceive race, Puerto Ricans view race on a continuum ranging from White to Mulatto to Black. Puerto Rican society emphasizes "progressive whitening," which encourages individuals to establish their identity on the basis of color, more specifically, as White (Duany 1998). Puerto Rican society expects Black Puerto Ricans to shed their color by encouraging the assimilation of Afro-American and Indian heritage with White heritage in order to adopt White European norms and values (Duany 1998, Safa 1998). As a result, most Puerto Ricans identify as White and reject those who are Black (Duany). As observed in both Dominican and Puerto Rican societies, within-group colorism results from the need to socially classify as White. One has to wonder about long the term effects on a people when assimilation can be detrimental to one's values and national interests.

Nicaraguan society uses skin color as the determining factor in allocating resources within family structures (Lancaster 1999). Nicaraguan families with children of varying skin tones have an underlying preference for the lighter-skinned children. This preference is characterized by parents rejoicing over having lighter-skinned children, whereas dark-skinned children are associated with shame and conflict. Parents are more likely to encourage lighter-hued children to study at a university and take up a profession than their darker children (Lancaster). In Nicaraguan society, family members use color to determine which child receives the most resources based on skin color. It is apparent that being born with a darker- hue in Nicaraguan society can result in a lifetime of poverty and despair. While children born with white skin receive many benefits from parents and people in the Nicaraguan community, parents may experience mental stress that may add to the internal conflict experienced by their children. It is also apparent that children growing up in a society that values lighter skin over darker skin will eventually, as adults, begin to evaluate and allocate resources (i.e., jobs and opportunities) to people with lighter hues. As we are reminded looking at the VR studies of Black and White Latinos, it is possible that the Black and White Latino outcomes are a prime example of allocating resources to certain people based on skin color within the VR agency.

In summary, Dominican, Puerto Rican, and Nicaraguan societies are examples of how Latino countries use skin color to determine the allocation of rights and privileges (Duany 1998, Lancaster 1999, Safa 1998). The societies described above represent the Caribbean and Latin American countries and capture the influence of skin color in the various Latino countries. These studies have been highlighted to give a perspective on the overall social structures within Latino countries (Falicov 1998, Montalvo 1991). In order to elucidate these and other points central to colorism, a brief review follows of key studies found in Colorism literature for both African Americans and Latinos.

Evidence to Support Colorism in the United States (Able-Bodied Latinos)

While it is very difficult to know unless directly accessed, we assume that the majority of the samples in the following studies are people without disabilities (i.e., able-bodied).

Cota-Robles de Suarez (1971) investigated whether Chicano children were aware of their skin color by interviewing 28 low-income children from Los Angeles, between four and five years of age. The children were in two separate Head Start programs with one group consisting of 12 children (five boys and seven girls) and the other group consisting of 16 children (nine boys and seven girls). The children were individually presented with a Choice test (a modification of R. E. Horowitz' test on African American preschoolers), which consists of two drawings: a Chicano boy or girl (depending on the participants' gender) and a White American boy or girl. Children were then asked by the interviewer to choose from the drawings who they would befriend. The authors tabulated the frequency of responses and found that for the Choice test, over 58% of Chicano children wanted to befriend the Anglo (White) drawing.

The Cota-Robles de Suarez (1971) second test, the Coloring test (a modification of a test devised by the Clarks for African American children), consisted of blank drawings of boys and girls that participants had to color. The blank drawings were again distributed by sex, with boys receiving boy figures and girls receiving the girl figures. The Chicano students were later asked what color they wanted the drawings to be. For the Coloring test, 25% of the Chicano students colored their response brown, about 31% colored the drawings pink, and the 44% of the drawings were irrelevant (i.e., children picked colors that did not relate to human skin tones). As a result, more children in the sample preferred light-skinned playmates and chose pink as an ideal face drawing (Cota-Robles de Suarez). It seems as if Latino children are also affected by the influences of color in many parts of the world. Thus, when they become adults, Latino children may implement similar patterns, observed in their homes, yielding more privileges to lighter- skinned individuals. It is also important to note that kids can receive the preferences for lighter tones explicitly and implicitly. Nonetheless, the message that "lighter skin is right" will continue to impact both lighter- and darker-skinned Latinos internationally and in the United States as well.

Nineteen years later, Codina (1990) investigated the relationship between skin color (measured by interview ratings), low SES (measured by education and family income), and acculturation (measured by language acquisition) and mental health, using a Mexican/Mexican American sample (N = 991). Data were collected from the National Chicano Survey, a national area probability sample of Mexican-origin heads of household. The results indicated that U.S. born participants with darker skin colors (including Indian features) who reported low SES had lower self-esteem, while Mexican born participants with a low SES had higher self-esteem. In addition, Mexican-born participants, choosing the Mexican label had a darker skin color, as well as more Native features and less English proficiency. The Mexican born participants choosing the Mexican American label had lighter complexions, as well as European features and higher levels of English proficiency. Finally, the results indicated that darker Latinos had very little English proficiency. The findings from Codina seem to relate to the stereotypical beliefs that dark Latinos retain their native language because they are unable to assimilate, developing a marginal identity (Montalvo 1991). Individuals with a marginal identity find themselves on the margin of each cultural group but a member of neither (Park 1928, Stonequist 1935). Because skin color is an obvious phenotypical feature, it is very difficult for darker- skinned Latinos to assimilate when compared to their White Latino counterparts.

Six years after the Codina (1990) investigation, Rosenbaum (1996) examined the relationship between racial identity and discrimination in housing patterns in New York City by using a multinomial logit model with a sample of 5,726 households drawn from over 18,000 public-housing apartments. Five mutually exclusive categories of race (using the categories of the U.S. census) and Latino origin were used: Anglo (non-Latino White), African American (non-Latino Black), White Latino, other-race Latino, and Black Latino. Rosenbaum hypothesized that White Latinos had a competitive edge over African Americans, other-race Latinos (since the study hypothesized that People of Latino origin may be of any race), and Black Latinos in obtaining apartments that were vacated by Anglos. The median incomes reported for the five racial categories used in the sample were as follows: Anglos, at $24,621; African Americans, at $14,264; Black Latinos, at $13,503; White Latinos, at $12,311 and Other-Race Latinos median incomes at $10,943. Group differences in household composition related to the differences in economic status. For example, African American and Latino households were more likely than Anglo households to consist of a single- parent home, which contribute to their lower incomes. The five groups differed in their pattern of residential locations: African Americans and Black Latinos were both concentrated in Brooklyn, whereas White Latinos and other-race Latinos were predominantly located in the Bronx and Brooklyn. As a result, people of Color tend to reside close to each other. Compared to the other minority groups, White Latinos were most likely to relocate to Queens, a predominantly Anglo location (Rosenbaum), suggesting that Whites and White Latinos have a higher probability of residing in close proximity to one another. The study indicates how housing allocations were related to individuals' racial identity and skin color.

More specifically, the findings in the Rosenbaum (1996) investigation indicated that racial/ethnic composition of housing areas was related to the odds of the racial groups obtaining housing. For example, the odds of African Americans (6.94 × greater), White Latinos (2.32 × greater), other-race Latinos (2.41 × greater), and Black Latinos (4.87 × greater) moving into a predominantly minority location were greater than Anglo moving into a minority location. The aforementioned odds suggest that the darker the skin color, the more likely one is to move into racial minority neighborhoods. Predominantly minority areas also reduced the odds of White Latino moving into (in-movement) racial minority neighborhoods, compared to the odds of in-movement by African Americans (.34 × greater), other race Latinos (.68 × greater), and Black Latinos (.48 × greater). It seems that White Latinos were less likely to move into neighborhoods consisting predominantly of minority groups, when compared to all other minority groups. Rosenbaum (1996) inferred that the results also indicated the isolation of residential locations of Anglos from those of African Americans and Latinos, which may result in a barrier that deters minority in-movement to predominantly Anglo housing areas. Based on skin color, there is a strong correlation on the likelihood that Black and White Latinos will reside in different neighborhoods. Furthermore, it appears that White Latinos are more likely than other minority groups (e.g., African American and Black Latinos) to reside in neighborhoods where White Americans reside, increasing the supposition that skin color has social, educational, and residential consequences in the United States.

Finally, Rosenbaum (1996) concluded that unlike other minority households, such as African Americans, other-race Latinos, and Black Latinos, White Latinos are better able to gain access to housing in Anglo sub-areas even though they are not economically in the best position. Furthermore, White Latinos have a better opportunity in replacing out-moving Anglo households and in gaining access to units in high quality areas. Rosenbaum suggested that White Latinos are better able than non-White minority members to gain entry into predominantly Anglo sub-areas because of their non-Black status. The findings seem to illustrate color prejudice in the housing market is alive and well in many parts of the world, including the United Sates (also see Hacker 1995, Smith 2006).

Discussion

Based on the information presented in this chapter, it appears that White Latinos with or without a disability may enjoy similar privileges as White Americans in the United States. There is also a high correlation between the skin color and VR access as well. Would the "color" (Black or White) of certain Latinos facilitate VR acceptance in the United States? We think a resounding, yes! The investigations by Wilson and Senices (2005) and Herbert and Martinez (1992) indicate that White Latinos with disabilities are more likely to get accepted for VR services when compared to Black Latinos. It is unmistakable that Black and White Latinos with disabilities have different experiences in the VR system, just as African Americans and White Americans tend to have diverse experiences, not only in the VR system but in the general United States population. To lend further support to the phenotype discrimination assertion, Rosenbaum (1996) compared both White and Black Latinos and controlled for a host of independent variables in his investigation (e.g., socioeconomic status and place of residence). He concluded that White Latinos may have privileges similar to those enjoyed by White Americans in the United States, based on skin color. Based on the VR outcomes, Latinos with disabilities share similar privileges as able-bodied Latinos. Evidence clearly suggests that when several demographic variables are controlled, one's phenotype is a salient feature for being discriminated against in the United States.

Being a Black Latino or White Latino is not the problem in our society. It is the value we attach to being a Black or White Latino that is the problem. Explicitly, it is the worth we as a society attach to the color/hue of being Black Latino and White Latino that has been beneficial for White Latinos/White Americans and a negative for people of color (e.g., Black Latinos and African Americans) for hundreds of years in the United States (Wilson, Edwards et al. 2001). There are many privileges that people enjoy based on their phenotype (i.e., physical characteristics of people. Skin color discrimination is further complicated when other salient variables of discrimination are added to the phenotype equation. For example, it may be very difficult to determine whether a person is gay or lesbian based on our prescribed norms of how a gay person or lesbian person should physically look and behave in our society. Because of the difficulties that people who are gay and lesbian encounter in our society with outward (e.g., physical violence and verbal abuse) discrimination and prejudice, many gays and/or lesbians may look phenotypically opposite than their internalized sexual orientation. Therefore, the amount and intensity of discrimination based on "not appearing to be gay or lesbian," for example (e.g., masculine and/or feminine characteristics) is decreased. Based on the phenotypical markers, or what a person who classifies as gay or lesbian may outwardly look like, many gays and lesbians who are White American can choose to "come out." However, this is not the same for African Americans and Black Latinos. Black Latinos can be immediately distinguished by the pigmentation of their skin color, and thus, more readily targeted for discrimination. The same illustration can be used for females in our society as well. In most cases, because there are certain physical features that "females" share, people in our society who are sexist can readily target women, because of general physical markers of what females look like. The act of targeting females based on their gender is called sexism. The more identifiable a person is, based on their skin color/hue, the more discrimination they are likely to encounter based on how people perceive that particular phenotype characteristic. Although acknowledging that many variables (e.g., race, gender, sexual orientation) cause people to be discriminated against in the United States is painful, unfortunate, and sometimes life threatening, skin color (i.e., race) is the most divisive when it comes to the experiences faced by people of color (i.e., Black Latinos & African Americans, with disabilities and able-bodied).

General Limitations of Research on Colorism Able-Bodied Population

Prior studies focusing on skin color have used subjective measures, which were considered to be a limitation of most studies researching colorism. The literature on skin color has suffered because researchers are skeptical of the validity of studies that only use subjective measures. For example, in certain studies (e.g., Arce et al. 1987), indicators of phenotype were based on the subjective interviewer ratings since the raters had no points of reference. It is unclear whether interviewers systematically assigned participants to a phenotype category, which suggests possible interviewer bias increasing the likelihood that the measure of skin color is unreliable. Objective measures of skin color are costly, limiting the use of objective measures in the skin color literature. In addition, prior studies have neglected to explore the influence of gender differences in the skin color literature. Men and women are socialized differently, which makes the influence of gender identity on skin color significant and worthy of future research consideration.

Vocational Rehabilitation and People with Disabilities

In many of the studies looking at Latinos with disabilities in the VR system, there was no way in which the researcher could validate whether White Latinos were indeed White Latinos (i.e., Latinos with light or white skin tone and/or White European American features). Many of the studies investigating Latinos with disabilities in the VR system used a secondary source to retrieve the data for analysis. When using many secondary data sources, the actual participants in the study are not being observed. More specifically, only the numbers with values associated with the numbers in the database are seen. Although Wilson and Senices (2005) reported they had no way of knowing whether Latinos in the VR system could visibly pass as White American or White Latino, based on their skin color, the results from the Rodriquez and Cordero-Guzman (1992) investigation reports that people who are Latino (Puerto Rican) are prone to identify as White American, if they think people from the United States, for example, would view them as White American. We think that the Rodriquez and Cordero-Guzman study supports the notion that people who classify themselves as White Latino may indeed have European features like White Americans, phenotypically. Nevertheless, the results pertaining to studies of Latinos with disabilities reflect the growing number of Latinos in the United States laced with Latinos' possible identification with White Americans, and the continued racial flexibility within the Latino population in the United States.

As reported, several investigations relied on a secondary data analysis (archival data). Thus, no cause and effect can be assumed. For example, being Latino (Black or White) does not cause one to be accepted into VR. Likewise, being non-Latino (Black or White) does not cause one to be rejected for VR services in the United States. However, may investigations found a significant relationship/correlation (dependence) between race/ethnicity (Latino versus non-Latino and Black Latino and White Latino) and VR acceptance in the United States. It is also important to note that the research findings reported in all of the VR disability studies that highlighted discrepancies were statistically significant.

Lastly, the external validity is also a limitation to the races and ethnicities that were used in the colorism investigations. The VR studies can only be generalized to the populations used in the sampling procedure. While there is a strong case to be made for generalizing the results of the VR studies because the latter studies used a national sampling frame, caution must be stressed when looking beyond the groups used in the study. On the other hand, there is evidence to support that Latinos with disabilities and able-bodied Latinos who are Black are likely to get more overt discrimination as a result of being darker than their White Latino counterparts in the United States and other parts of the world. Thus, the case for being able to reasonably generalize to other populations not used in these investigations is tenable.

Strengths of Research on Colorism

The most obvious strength of conducting research on colorism is to pay attention to the different kinds of phenotype (i.e., hue or skin color) discrimination experienced by different groups in the United States. While people of non-color (e.g., White Americans and White Latinos) have consistently denied the intensity of discrimination based on color/hue in the United States (Smith 2006), this disparity in perceptions is not uncommon among people of color and non-color. However, we view exposure to research on colorism as a way to increase the knowledge base of another variable of discrimination that is experienced by a significant part of the racially marginalized population in the United States. Thus, research on colorism is a way for people to openly communicate and dialogue about the degrees in which perceptions differ among certain groups. The fact of the matter is that people do experience discrimination based on certain phenotype characteristics. Thus, becoming knowledgeable about colorism issues can assist in greater numbers people of non-color facilitating social justice issues for people of color, potentially.

While some studies might have sample size limitations, the sample size given in much of the VR outcome research regarding Black and White Latinos with disabilities is a major plus. For example, the study by Wilson and Senices (2005) used a national database to gather the needed information for their investigations. More specifically, Wilson and Senices used the Rehabilitation Services Administration database from the United States Department of Education. A study regarding able-bodied individuals by and Hughes and Hertel (1990) used the National Survey to gather data for their sampling frame. Both samples in the aforementioned studies represented several hundred cases to use in their respective analysis, increasing the statistical power to make it easier to detect a statistical difference. Although the authors acknowledge the likelihood of finding significance with a greater number of participants, the possibility of creating a Type I error tends to increase with more cases in the sample. Thus, there is a balance between having a large sample and making sure that your findings are likely to represent the trends in your sampling frame.

Research looking at outcome differences for people with disabilities has been around for several decades. In VR, these differences tended to center on race and the kind of disability connected to services received or not received, generally. In the few VR studies that looked at services received, rarely did research teams break down services received and acceptance rates by race and then by ethnicity (i.e., Latino). The results of the more recent studies by Wilson and his colleagues confirm that the experiences of Black and White Latinos with disabilities is a microcosm of what Black and White Latinos experience in the larger context of our society (also see Wilson 2005).

Directions for Future Research

Although there is an obvious lack of research looking at colorism relative to people with disabilities in the United States, future researchers might want to use more objective measures in appraising phenotype (i.e., hue/skin color) discrimination. Using more objective measures will continue to ensure that researchers are measuring what they aim to measure. Additionally, future studies should incorporate multiple measures of skin color as well. This way, it may be possible to cross validate research findings with other assessments that measure the same or similar variables related to skin color. As stated before in this chapter, some prior studies on skin color, using subjective measures of skin color, have been deemed unreliable. For example, if using self-reports it seems important to cross validate self-reports with other criteria, such as an objective measure of skin color. While the results of many studies on colorism are relatively consistent, the use of multiple measures might continue to increase the likelihood of consistency among future outcomes regarding colorism.

Finally, it seems important for future studies to be sensitive to gender differences. Prior studies investigating skin color seemed to neglect the influence of gender differences (Arce et al. 1987, Relethford et al. 1983, Vasquez et al. 1997). Yet, it seems that gender identity allows for variability in the socialization process. Males have more of a tendency to adopt the norms, values, and beliefs of the dominant culture (Massey & Denton 1993), which may possibly be due to their higher level of involvement with the American culture. For example, Latino men are expected to be the primary breadwinner and therefore spend more time away from home. Thus, Latino women place a higher priority on the home, which allows for more involvement with their ethnic culture. Adding gender to the equation on phenotypes will enhance what we know about the relationship between other variables and colorism in the United States. Because gender intersects with so many variables, it would be interesting to weed out the gender effects of colorism in future research.

Implications

Based on prior research (e.g., Massey & Denton 1989, Rodriquez & Cordero-Guzman 1992), it is obvious that people have different experiences based on the color of their skin. Because there is also an obvious lack of research looking at colorism relative to people with disabilities in the United States, more research should focus on this population to: (a) increase the visibility of an often isolated group of individuals and (b) increase discussions about skin color and discrimination relative to people who are Latino with disabilities in the United States.

Since Black Latinos with disabilities tend to experience similar kinds of discrimination as do African Americans with disabilities, the VR systems might want to consider training VR counselors to avoid being discriminatory toward people with disabilities who are Black Latinos. It is hoped that this kind of training would increase the acceptance and success rate of people who classify as Latino in the VR system.

It is clear that White Latinos have better outcomes when they are people with disabilities or able-bodied in the United States. Since many human service workers do not ask how their clients identify racially or ethnically, the VR counselor, for example, should not assume that all people who identify as Latino have similar experiences because they are Latino. As Wilson and Senices reported in 2005, Latinos have the flexibility to "race" select and human services professionals may not want to assume that clients who look like they are Latino will have similar experiences as all Latinos. It is apparent from the research on Latinos with disabilities that White and Black Latinos have different experiences in the United States. Wilson and Senices also reported that human service workers may not want to assume that the ethnicity of that particular individual is more salient than another demographic variable (e.g., gender, sexual orientation, and so forth). If there is any doubt, ask. Opening up the lines of communication is a vital part of being able to accurately reflect the experiences as seen through the eyes of most individuals.

Conclusion

Existing empirical data on skin color has centered on the African American community, with minimum attention to other minority groups. Even more limited in the colorism literature is the focus on people with disabilities and outcomes based on skin color. More importantly, it seems necessary to focus on the influence of skin color of various minority groups, i.e. Latinos—which is the largest growing minority group, to determine if the research on skin color generalizes to other groups. While there seems to be research that supports that colorism affects other racial groups in similar ways, more research on Latinos (Black and White) with disabilities might strengthen, what we think we know about, the broad implications of colorism in the United States.

It is reasonable to conclude that discrepancies among Black and White Latinos with disabilities, for example, are due to other external forces and conditions. On the other hand, evidence suggests that there is a high correlation between the VR and general outcomes of people with a darker hue (e.g., Black Latinos with disabilities) and those without a darker hue (White Latinos with disabilities). Black Latinos are more than likely not to be accepted to VR and, when accepted, Black Latinos are more likely not to be closed successful as well. For Latinos, their increased numbers have augmented the challenge for culturally competent services in many parts of the United States. While there is not a lot of information on colorism and people with disabilities, there is a need for more research with people with disabilities who are not in the VR system. Correlating colorism with people with disabilities (i.e., Black and White Latinos) is a very exciting line of research that we hope will continue to grow as resources become more available to produce more knowledge in this area.

References

Arce, C. H., Murgia, E., & Frisbie, W. P. (1987). Phenotype and life chances among Chicanos. *Hispanic Journal of Behavioral Sciences*, 9, 19–22.

Atkins, B. J., & Wright, G. N. (1980). Three views: Vocational rehabilitation of Blacks: The statement. *Journal of Rehabilitation*, 46(2), 40, 42–46.

Bowe, F. (1992). *Adults with disabilities: A portrait*. Washington, DC: President's Committee on Employment of People with Disabilities, U.S. Department of Labor.

Capella, M. E. (2002). Inequities in the VR system: Do they still exist? *Rehabilitation Counseling Bulletin*, 45, 143–153.

Camarillo, A. M., & Bonilla, F. (2001). Hispanics in a multicultural society: A new American dilemma. In N. J. Smelser, W. J. Wilson, and F. Mitchell (Eds.), *America becoming: Racial trends and their consequences*, vol. 1 (pp. 103–134). Washington, DC: National Academy Press.

Carter, R. T. (1995). *The influence of race and racial identity in psychotherapy: Toward a racially inclusive model.* New York: John Wiley.

Casas, J. M., and Pytluk, S. D. (1995). Hispanic identity development: Implications for research and practice. In J. G. Ponterotto & J. M. Casas (Eds.), *Handbook of multicultural counseling* (pp. 155–180). Thousand Oaks, CA: Sage.

Codina, G. E. (1990). Race, class, ethnicity, and Chicano mental health: A psychosocioeconomic model. Unpublished doctoral dissertation, University of Michigan, Ann, Arbor, Michigan.

Cota-Robles de Suarez, C. (1971). Skin color as a factor in the racial identification and preference of young Chicano children. *Aztlan,* 2, 107–150.

Duany, J. (1998). Reconstructing racial identity. *Latin American Perspectives,* 25(3), 147–172.

Dziekan, K. I., & Okocha, A. G. (1993). Accessibility of rehabilitation services: Comparison by racial-ethnic status. *Rehabilitation Counseling Bulletin,* 36, 183–189.

Falicov, C. J. (1998). *Latino families in therapy.* New York: Guilford Press.

Feist-Price, S. (1995). African Americans with disabilities and equity in vocational rehabilitation services: one state's review. *Rehabilitation Counseling Bulletin,* 39, 19–129.

Hacker, A. (1995). *Two nations: Black and White, separate, hostile, unequal.* New York: Macmillan.

Hall, R. E. (2002). A descriptive methodology of color bias in Puerto Rico: Manifestations of discrimination in the new millennium. *Journal of Applied Social Psychology,* 32(7), 1527–1537.

Herbert, J. T., & Martinez, M. Y. (1992). Client ethnicity and vocational rehabilitation case service outcome. *Journal of Job Placement,* 8, 10–16.

Hughes, M., & Hertel, B. R. (1990). The significance of color remains: A study of life chances, mate selection, and ethnic consciousness among Black Americans. *Social Forces,* 68, 1105–1120.

Itzigsohn, J., & Dore-Cabral, C. (2000). Competing identities? Race, ethnicity, and panethnicity among Dominicans in the United States. *Sociological Forum,* 15(2), 225–247.

Jones, B. F. (1966). James Baldwin: The struggle for identity. *British Journal of Sociology,* 17, 107–121.

Lancaster, R. (1999). Skin color, race, and racism in Nicaragua. *Ethnologies,* 30, 339–353.

Lee, W. (1999). One whiteness veils three uglinesses: From border crossing to a womanist interrogation of gendered colorism. In T. K. Nakayama & J. N. Martin (Eds.), *Whiteness: The communication of social identity,* (pp. 27–41). Thousand Oaks, CA: Sage Publications.

Loewen, J. W. (1995). *Lies my teacher told me.* New York: Touchstone.

Massey, D., & Denton, N. (1993). *American apartheid: Segregation and the making of the underclass.* Cambridge, MA: Harvard University Press.

Massey, D. S., & Denton, N. (1989). Racial identity among Caribbean Hispanics: The effect of double minority status on residential segregation. *American Sociological Review,* 54, 790–808.

Montalvo, F. F. (1987). *Skin color and Latinos: The origins and contemporary patterns of ethnoracial ambiguity among Mexican Americans and Puerto Ricans* (Monograph). San Antonio, TX: Our Lady of the Lake University.

———. (1991). Phenotyping, acculturation, and biracial assimilation of Mexican-Americans. In M. Sotomayor (Ed.), *Empowering Hispanic families* (pp. 97–120). Milwaukee, WI: Family Service America.

Park, R. E. (1928). The bases of race prejudice. *Annals of the American Academy of Political and Social Science,* 11–20.

Peterson, G. E. (1996). An analysis of participation, progress, and outcome of individuals from diverse racial and ethnic backgrounds in the public vocational rehabilitation program in Nevada. Unpublished doctoral dissertation, University of Northern Colorado, Greeley, Colorado.

Phinney, J. S. (1996). When we talk about American ethnic groups, what do we mean? *American Psychologist*, 51, 918–927.

Quiñones-Mayo, Y., Wilson, K. B., & McGuire, M. V. (2000). Vocational rehabilitation and cultural competency for Latino populations: Considerations for rehabilitation counselors. *Journal of Applied Rehabilitation Counseling*, 31, 19–26.

Rehabilitation Services Administration (RSA). (1995). *Reporting manual for the case service report (RSA-911) (RSA-PD-95-04)*. Washington, DC: Rehabilitation Services Administration.

Rehabilitation Services Administration. (2004). *Reporting manual for the RSA 911 case service report*. Washington, DC: Author.

Relethford, J. H., Stern, M. P., Gaskill, S. P., & Hazuda, H. P. (1983). Social class, admixture, and skin color variation in Mexican-Americans and Anglo-Americans in San Antonio, Texas. *American Journal of Physical Anthropology*, 61, 97–102.

Rodriquez, C. E., & Cordero-Guzman, H. (1992). Placing race in context. *Ethnic and Racial Studies*, 15, 523–542.

Rogers, M., Conoley, J., Ponterotto, J., & Wiese, M. (1992). Multicultural training in school psychology: A national survey. *School Psychology Review*, 21, 603–616.

Rosenbaum, E. (1996). The influence of race on Hispanic housing choices: New York City, 1978–1987. *Urban Affairs Review*, 32(2), 217–243.

Safa, H. I. (1998). Introduction. *Latin American Perspectives*, 25, 3–20.

Smith, T. W. (2006). *Taking American's pulse III: Intergroup relations in contemporary America*. National Opinion Research Center. NORC, University of Chicago. The National Conference for Community and Justice.

Stonequist, E. V. (1935). The problem of the marginal man. *American Journal of Sociology*, 41, 1–12.

Sue, D. W. (1996). ACES endorsement of the multicultural counseling competencies: Do we have the courage? *Spectrum*, 57(1), 9–10.

Sue, D. W., Arrendondo, P., & McDavis, R. J. (1992). Multicultural competencies/standards: A pressing need. *Journal of Counseling and Development*, 70, 477–486.

Sue, D. W., Carter, R. T., Casas, J. M., Fouad, N. A., Ivey, A. I., Jensen, M., LaFromboise, T., Manese, J. E., Ponterrotto, J. G., Vazqueq-Nutall, E. (1998). *Multicultural counseling competencies: Individual and organizational development* (v 11). Thousand Oaks, CA: Sage.

Torres, V. (1999). Validation of a bicultural orientation model for Hispanic college students. *Journal of College Student Development*, 40, 285–298.

United States Bureau of the Census (1990). *1990 U.S. Census with race and ethnicity with Hispanic origin*. United States Department of Commerce, Bureau of the Census, Washington, DC.

———. (2001, March). Overview of race and Hispanic origin: Census 2000 brief. http://www. census.gov/prod/2001pubs/cenbr01-1.pdf. Accessed 27 January 2007.

———. (2001). Residential segregation of Hispanics or Latinos: 1980 to 2000. Census 2000 news releases [On-line]. http://www.census.gov/hhes/www/housing/resseg/ch6.html [27 November 2002].

Vasquez, L. A., Garcia-Vasquez, E., Bauman, S. A., & Sierra, A. S. (1997). Skin color, acculturation, and community interest among Mexican American students: A research note. *Hispanic Journal of Behavioral Sciences*, 19, 377–386.

Wheaton, J. E. (1995). Vocational rehabilitation acceptance rate for European Americans and African Americans: Another look. *Rehabilitation Counseling Bulletin*, 38, 224–231.

Wilson, K. B. (1999). Vocational rehabilitation acceptance: A tale of two races in a large Midwestern state. *Journal of Applied Rehabilitation Counseling*, 30, 25–31.

———. (2000). Predicting vocational rehabilitation acceptance based on race, education, work status, and source of support at application. *Rehabilitation Counseling Bulletin*, 43, 97–105.

————. (2002). The Exploration of vocational rehabilitation acceptance and ethnicity: A national investigation. *Rehabilitation Counseling Bulletin*, 45, 168–176.

————. (2005). Vocational rehabilitation closure statues in the United States: Generalizing to the Hispanic ethnicity. *Journal of Applied Rehabilitation Counseling*, 36(2), 4–11.

Wilson, K. B., Edwards, D. W., Alston, R. J., Harley, D. A., & Doughty, J. D. (April 2001). Vocational rehabilitation and the dilemma of race in rural communities: The debate continues [Electronic version]. *Journal of Rural Community Psychology*, 2, 55–81. http://www.events.im.com.au/reviewers/search.asp. Accessed 14 April 2002.

Wilson, K. B., Harley, D. A., McCormick, K., Jolivette, K., & Jackson. R. (2001). A literature review of vocational rehabilitation acceptance and explaining bias in the rehabilitation process. *Journal of Rehabilitation*, 32, 24–35.

Wilson, K. B., & Senices, J. (2005). Exploring the vocational rehabilitation acceptance rates of Hispanics and non-Hispanics in the United States. *Journal of Counseling and Development*, 83(1), 86–96.

Chapter 11
Brown Outs: The Role of Skin Color and Latinas

Christina Gómez

Abstract Skin color has long been a topic of discussion among non-white groups in the United States. How dark- or light-skinned an individual is has been linked to beauty, self-esteem, and life chances. This desire for light skin has become so ubiquitous that a cosmetic product marketed across Mexico called "White Secret" guarantees lighter skin through a process of skin bleaching. These findings suggest that preferences for light-skinned women continue within the Latino community. The issues of skin color and discrimination against dark-skinned women of color have persisted in the Americas, as well as other regions. Latina women are one of the most marginalized groups in the United States; but not all Latina women are the same. This study hopes to begin a discussion that will broaden our understanding of racism and prejudice, how it is practiced, and what some of the consequences might be.

Introduction

Skin color has long been a topic of discussion among non-white groups in the United States. How dark- or light-skinned an individual is has been linked to beauty, self-esteem, and life chances. Research on skin color and the African-American community is plentiful (Franklin 1980, Hughes & Hertel 1990, Keith & Herring 1991, Russell et al. 1992). However, fewer studies exist that examine the effects of skin color on Latinos, now the largest "minority" group in the United States. This is especially the case for Latinas.

Overall, the phenotype studies and personal testimonies I discuss below point to the continual significance of skin color in the Latino/a community. I have delivered this paper in various forms at conferences, and inevitably women have shared with me their personal experiences with skin-color discrimination. "Ya salte del sol, te vas a poner muy negra," ("Get out of the sun, you will get too dark") was a common request many women heard as youngsters.

C. Gómez
Department of Sociology, Northeastern Illinois University, Chicago, IL, USA
e-mail: cgomez@neiu.edu

R. Hall (ed.), *Racism in the 21st Century*, DOI: 10.1007/978-0-387-79097-8_11,   193
© Springer Science+Business Media, LLC 2008

Commentary on the color of newborn babies' skin color and hair texture is general parlance in many Latino homes (Portillo 1993). This aversion to dark skin, as well as Indian or African physical characteristics, is a leftover legacy from colonialism, slavery, and the current racist discourse that still predominates in our society today. This paper is a preliminary investigation of how skin color affects Latinas' lives, specifically its relationship to achievement, life chances, and marriage. My goal is to open a conversation and discuss how skin color continues to limit the Latino community, and, in particular, Latinas. Furthermore, I suggest that we continue to explore the intersections of skin color and Latino/a sub-groups; dark- and light-skin affects various Latinos groups differently.

Skin Color and Literature

Essays, novels, and poems on how "colorism" affects the Latino community have been a theme in Latino literature since its inception. The work of the Recovering the U.S. Literary Heritage Project has shown that literature created by Hispanics, in territory we now know as the United States, has existed from the colonial period (Kanellos 2002). Many novels, personal narratives, and poems have discussed the pain and discrimination faced by dark-skinned Latinos (Acosta 1972, Casal 1978, Colón 1982, Santiago 1995, Villarreal 1959).

In his celebrated novel, *Down These Mean Streets*, Piri Thomas (1967) poignantly portrays the issues of race and racism among Puerto Ricans:

"Hey, you," he said. "What nationality are ya? "
I looked at him and wondered which nationality to pick.
And one of his friends said, "Ah, Rocky, he's black enuff to be a nigger. Ain't that what you is, kid? "
My voice was almost shy in its anger. "I'm Puerto Rican," I said. "I was born here."
I wanted to shout it, but it came out like a whisper (Thomas 1967).

In particular, narratives by Latinas who are "darker" are prominent in literature. For example, Angela Jorge writes: "As the black Puerto Rican woman goes through the various stages of life—childhood, adolescence, and adulthood—the blackness of her skin and the clearly Negroid physical characteristics make her experiences within each stage different from those of her lighter-skinned sister in struggle for emancipation and liberation" (Jorge 1979). In her essay, she describes the triple discrimination she faces in society: as a woman, as a Puerto Rican, and as a person who is black within Puerto Rican community. Her negative experiences are not only from outside groups but from her own community and family that judges her dark skin and African features harshly.

Ana Castillo (1994), in her essay about Chicanas/mestizas, writes: "Some of us 'look' more Amerindian than others of us. In this color-conscious society, shade and hue will obviously cause each of us to experience our indigenous lineage differently. In other words, the more Indian we look the more poor we look (and often are), the more gravely we suffer from the differentiated negative treatment of white dominant culture "(Castillo 1994). Castillo understands the real cost of having dark skin and indigenous features. She echoes the privileges of whiteness of which Latinas everywhere are well aware.

Studies on Phenotype

One of the earliest studies of phenotype among Latinos was accidental. When studying the Amerindian genetic factor in diabetes among Mexican Americans, a research team discovered that their sample became progressively lighter as the researchers moved from low-income barrios to the more affluent San Antonio suburbs (Relenthford et al. 1983). They measured the skin color of their Latino subjects with a spectrophotometer. The results first documented a statistical relationship between skin color and social class in the U.S. (Codina & Montalvo 1994).

Various studies using the 1980 National Chicano Survey (Arce) have found that phenotype matters for Mexican Americans. A study by Carlos Arce, E. Murguia, and W. Frisbie (1987) found that Mexican Americans with a European physical appearance attained higher socioeconomic status than Mexican Americans with an indigenous Native American physical appearance. Their results also evidenced that phenotype differences had affected life chances of Chicanos in past generations, as demonstrated by fathers' and mothers' education and occupational prestige. Another study by E. Telles and E. Murguia (1990) found that Mexican American males with a dark and Native American phenotype received significantly lower wages than those of a lighter and European phenotype. A third study by Murguia and Telles (1996) revealed that light-skinned Mexican Americans had about 1.5 more years of schooling than darker Chicanos. This was especially true among cohorts before World War II and those schooled in Texas. They conclude that:

> [W]e found a system of both categorical racial discrimination (exemplified by the U.S. system) and continuum racial discrimination (characterized by the Mexican system). We believe that this racial system exists even today. Specifically, people have paid a penalty for being Mexican, and some have paid an even greater penalty for being both Mexican and dark and Indian looking (Murguia & Telles 1996).

Research in the health sciences has found that phenotype is related to higher rates of depression (Codina & Montalvo 1994). Because discrimination based on race in the United States is often linked to denigration of ethnicity, self-worth, and ability, the researchers expected that phenotype would have its greatest impact among the U.S.-born Mexicans than among those born in Mexico. In Mexico, the "mestizo prototype" describes 90% of the population, although Indians continue to live in poor conditions. Their study found that those U.S.-born and raised Chicano men with darker and more Indian phenotypes in particular suffered high rates of depression regardless of education, family income, and their proficiency in the Spanish or English language.

The pattern was clear and unmistakable and was believed to be linked to their greater exposure to discrimination and thus to have fewer life chances. Light European-looking males generally fared better, which might be attributed to their having a better life in general and escaping discrimination (Codina & Montalvo 2001).

Paradoxically, their findings showed the opposite result for women. Light-skinned, Mexican-born women living in the U.S. fared worse than dark-skinned Mexican women. One explanation might be that light-skinned Mexican women felt ambivalent about their ethnicity because their group loyalty is questioned by their own group as well as by the majority (Montalvo & Codina 2001).

Using the National Chicano Survey of 1980 and the National Survey of Black Americans, M. L. Hunter (2002) analyzes the effect of skin color on women of color. Her results conclude that light skin functions as a form of social capital. For both groups, light skin predicts higher educational attainment, and predicts higher personal earnings for African American women and indirectly influences personal earnings for Mexican American women. In addition, she finds that light-skinned African American women had an advantage in the marriage market and that they were more likely to marry high-status men than were darker-skinned women. For Mexican American women, this was not the case, but this might have been affected by the lack of variation in educational levels of spouses in the sample.

Skin Color Stratification in the Americas

This form of stratification, which values lighter skin, exists in the United States as well as in Latin American countries and has been so for centuries. In Latin America, phrases like *hay que limpiar la raza* (literally, it means "a need to clean the race") have been echoed throughout history. Research in countries such as Columbia, Venezuela, and Mexico (just to name a few) documents the elite position Whites have historically held and how darker skin and other non-European physical characteristics placed individuals in inferior positions (Carroll 1991, Wright 1990, Wade 1993).

This desiring of light skin has become so ubiquitous that a cosmetic product marketed across Mexico called "White Secret" guarantees lighter skin through a process of skin bleaching. Through infomercials this product reinforces the mantra "light is right" and shows before-and-after shots of women who have obtained whiter skin by using the creams *para aclarar and desmanchar*—to clarify and remove dark spots (Winders et al. 2005).

Latinos in the U.S. are not immune to this and skin color appears to be significant in influencing life chances such as education, occupation, and income, as well as everyday social interactions. Given the importance that phenotype variables have played in previous studies, we, as researchers and as the "documentors" of our communities, must dig deeper in understanding the more subtle differences within the various Latino groups. In addition, we must be honest about our own internal racism in the Latino community. As a community, we have not escaped the legacy of colonization and the devastating effects of racist ideologies that pervade our society. We must also be careful to disaggregate the Latino group. Although many phenotype studies have focused on Mexican Americans, fewer studies exist on other Latino groups such as Puerto Ricans, Dominicans, Cubans, and Central Americans (Montalvo & Codina 2001). The present study was designed to begin to fill the gap in this literature by examining the effects of skin color in the lives of Latinas, specifically Puerto Rican and Dominican women.

Data and Findings

The data for this analysis derives from the Boston Social Survey Data of Urban Inequality, conducted in 1993 and 1994 (Johnson et al. 1994). The sample used for this study consists of respondents who reported themselves as Latina and were part of the labor force, and for whom information was available for all variables. Ultimately, the sample consisted of 199 Latinas, who were Puerto Rican and Dominican. As with the few other surveys that have included the skin color variable, this one was based on interviewer ratings made after the interview was completed. In the Boston Social Survey, the interviewer was asked to code the respondent as dark, medium, or light based on his or her visual estimation. It should also be made clear that only skin color was coded, not physical attributes such as hair texture or facial features (Candelario 2000).

Table 11.1 presents the mean values of skin color by socioeconomic indicators and personal characteristics. This table shows that, for this sample, few differences exist in the means of the various variables concerning skin color. What is clear is that these women have low incomes, little more than a high-school education, and are dominant Spanish speakers regardless of skin color.

The only variable that is statistically significant is marital status. Light-skinned Latinas were twice as likely to be married as dark-skinned Latinas. Because being married is associated with increased wages relative to the wages of single women the effects of skin color on marriage are important with respect to women's financial outcomes (Waldfogel 1994). Also, lighter-skinned women received more education than their darker-skinned counterparts, a variable that is strongly related to income attainment. I will return to a discussion of this result later in the paper.

In this sample, women's (log) wages are lower for dark Latinas, although the difference is minimal. In order to estimate the effects of skin color on earnings, I use a natural log wage regression to measure the differences in earnings. The assumption is that differences in income between phenotype groups that cannot

Table 11.1 Mean values and significance test by skin color: Latina sample

Variables	Skin Color				
	Mean for all	Light	Medium	Dark	FF.
Hourly Wages (log)	2.12	2.03	2.01	1.89	0.97
Income	$13,705	$10,248	$10,409	$10,420	0.01
Education (yrs)	12.01	11.05	11.19	10.91	0.11
Home ownership	0.18	0.19	0.12	0.13	0.72
Marriage	0.26	0.44	0.34	0.22	2.30 **
Spanish usage					
at home	0.95	0.97	0.96	0.91	1.04
U.S. Citizen	0.70	0.69	0.60	0.53	1.31
Age (yrs)	36.50	35.60	34.90	38.30	1.01
(N) unweighted		59	108	32	
		(30%)	(54%)	(16%)	

*$p<.05$, **$p<.10$

Note: Income from all jobs (before taxes) in 1993, for those individuals who worked.
Source: Boston Social Survey Data of Urban Inequality 1993–1994.

be explained by the variables known to relate to human capital variables and thus higher earnings are either a consequence of discrimination or an unmeasured difference in the attributes of members of different groups (Becker 1971, Telles & Murguia 1990). Human capital variables such as educational attainment, work experience, age, industry variables, union membership, and marriage status have been shown to influence wage earnings.

Because this study is about Latinas, other variables need to be considered— presence of children, education outside the U.S. citizenship status, foreign language usage, and contact with other minorities. Concerning women, human capital theory predicts that women's wages will be negatively affected by their time spent outside the labor market, for childbearing and,, that this difference in labor market experience helps explain the wage gap between mothers and women without children. However, other research has established that even after controlling for actual labor market experience, a direct effect of children on women's wages remains (Becker 1971, Fuchs 1988, Waldfogel 1994, 1997). In other words, women suffer a wage penalty when they have children. My model includes the presence of children in the household. This sample also includes some women born outside the U.S. thus, controls also include variables that measure education outside of the U.S. citizenship status, and foreign language usage. The variable "contact with other minorities" measures the composition of the employees in the workplace. Previous research has documented an earnings penalty for Latino workers employed at jobsites where co-ethnics predominate, net of individual, job, and occupational characteristics (Catanzarite & Aguilera 2000). Other studies have found similar pay discrepancies, although some show mixed evidence (England et al. 1988, Sorenson 1989, Tomaskovic-Devey 1993).

Table 11.2 Regression coefficients and betas for models of (LN) Hourly Wages on skin color and selected independent variables

Independent Variables	Latinas	
	b	B
Skin Color		
Medium	0.037	0.039
Dark	−0.098	−0.075
Education	0.016	0.105
Education outside of U.S.	0.019	0.029
Foreign language usage	−0.053	−0.023
Citizen of U.S.	0.083	0.084
Age	0.005	0.108
Marriage	0.087	0.086
Children under 18 yrs.	−0.050	−0.028
Union membership	0.223 ***	0.205
Contact w/ minorities in workforce	−0.036	−0.035
Industry		
Construction	−0.214	−0.031
Manufacturing	−0.556 ***	−0.514
Transportation	−0.280	−0.121
Wholesale	0.219	0.032
Retail Trade	−0.504 ***	−0.328
Finance/Insurance	−0.183	−0.079
Personal Services	−0.426 **	−0.298
Professional Services	−0.327 **	−0.323
Constant	1.957	
R2	0.266	
Adjusted R2	0.189	
(N)	(199)	

$*p<.10, ** p<.05, ***p<.01$
b = unstandardized regression coefficient.
B = standardized regression coefficient.
Source: Boston Social Survey Data of Urban Inequality.

Table 11.2 shows the results of a regression model using a logarithmic earnings function for Latinas. For each equation the unstandardized (b) and standardized regression coefficients (B) are shown. The standardized coefficients explain how many standard deviations the dependent variable changes with an increase of one standard deviation in the independent variable. Union membership and some industry variables are significant (the omitted category is public administration). The lack of significance of educational attainment might be due to the type of jobs they perform, generally low skilled for this sample. As described in Table 11.1, this group of Latinas generally consisted of low-paid workers (earning less than $11,000) with little more than a high-school degree.

Skin color, however, is not itself significant. In contrast to their male counterparts, dark-skin color does not negatively influence earnings in this sample (Gómez 2000). These results accord with other results indicating that within the female labor market there is less variance overall and consequently differences in skin color might not be significant (Rodriguez 1991).

Although skin color does not affect earnings directly for this sample, it might, however, be influencing it indirectly through marriage. Table 11.1 revealed that light-skinned women married at higher rates than their medium- and dark-skinned counterparts. I test this assertion by modeling the effects of skin color and other selected characteristics on the likelihood of marriage. In order to estimate the effects of skin color and marriage, a logistic regression model is used which includes the independent variables skin color, age, income, health, citizenship, education, and Spanish usage—characteristics that might be viewed as attractive to mate selection (Fitzgerald 1999, Nakosteen 1997, Ross 1997, Sprecher 1994, Waldron 1996).

Table 11.3 (below) presents the maximum likelihood estimates of the effects of the independent variables (described above) on whether or not a woman is

Table 11.3 Coefficients from logistic regression on likelihood of marriage on skin color and selected independent variables

	Latinas	
Independent Variables	Bivariate Estimates	Full Model
Skin Color		
Medium	0.069	0.117
	(1.017)	(1.125)
Dark	−0.552*	−0.730
	(0.576)	(0.482)
Education	−0.022	−0.022
	(0.979)	(0.978)
Spanish usage	0.207	0.292
	(1.226)	1.339
Citizen of U.S.	0.151	0.275
	(1.163)	(1.017)
Age	0.025	−0.019
	(1.025)	(1.019)
Income	0.000	0.000
	(1.000)	(1.316)
Health	−0.043	0.265
	(0.958)	(1.000)
Constant	–	−1.105
−2 log likelihood	–	240.951
Chi-Square	–	17.163
N	199	199

Note: Dependent Variable is "married vs. not married."
Numbers in parenthesis are odds ratios.
*p<.10 **p<.05 ***p< .01
Source: Boston Social Survey Data of Urban Inequality.

married. The first and third columns display the bivariate estimates for each independent variable showing its unmediated relationship to the likelihood of marriage. To the right of these columns are the full models, which control for all variables. The logged parameters associated with these models and the more interpretable odds ratios derived from them are presented. The bivariate estimates show that skin color is significant. The coefficients for dark skin color for Latinas are negative and significant. The full model shows that after personal characteristics such as age, education, income earned, and health are taken into account darker skin color decreases the probability of marriage for Latinas as compared to light-skinned Latinas. Odd ratios imply that dark-skinned Latinas were less than half as likely to be married as light-skinned Latinas.

Discussion and Conclusion

This study began with an examination of skin color for Latinas, specifically Puerto Rican and Dominican women in the Boston area. Although Latino men's wages have been negatively impacted by dark skin color, women in this sample did not show negative effects on their wages specifically due to skin color. This result might be explained by the sample of this data set; these Latinas were low-wage earners with generally little more than a high- school education. In other words, these women were poor and their wages low with little variability.

What did prove significant was the role skin color plays in their likelihood of marriage. Latinas who were dark-complexioned were half as likely to be married as their light-skinned counterparts. This finding concurs with previous research and personal testimonials by women of color (Hall 1994, Jorge 1979, Relenthford et al. 1983). The following is in an essay about black Puerto Rican women:

> When she begins attempting to establish meaningful relationships with the opposite sex, her blackness presents other unique problems for her. The Puerto Rican obsession with adelantar la raza make it impossible for her to make a choice independent of the consideration of color. Whether the phrase has been said seriously or en forma de broma the family has reaffirmed the inferiority of her blackness and the need for her to change that situation by marrying someone very light, if not white (Relenthford 1983).

The negative effect, however, that dark or medium skin color has on the likelihood of marriage does come at a cost. Research on the benefits of the institution of marriage has shown that married individuals profit from greater wealth, extended longevity, better health, more happiness, and the beneficial impact of marriage on children (Keith 1997, Lee et al. 1991, Stack 1998, Waite 1996). More recent research by L. J. Waite and M. Gallagher (200) also presents evidence that on average married women have lower mortality, higher wealth and family income, better health, and have more sex than their single counterparts. In other words, marriage still imparts real benefits to women and even more to men. While I am not advocating that all women should marry or that it is the ideal situation for women, women with darker complexions should not be denied this option either.

My findings suggest that preferences for light-skinned women continue within the Latino community. Historically in Latin America, more Europeanized women (i.e. having lighter skin, straight hair, blue or green eye color) have been favored as marriage partners. Research by Suárez-Findlay (1999) on Puerto Rican women finds that during the late 1800 s and early 1900 s whiter females were viewed as being more honorable and respectable than their darker or mixed-race counterparts. This is a global phenomenon. Notions of female desirability and respectability are tainted by historical colonial domination and by current consumer media today. Women of color in particular have been marginalized for not fitting into socially constructed "notions of beauty"—blue eyes, blonde hair, and white skin. This phenomenon has had real costs for women of color through wages, education, occupational attainment, marriage selection, health, and self-esteem.

Finally, I would like to argue that racial and ethnic categories such as "Latina" do not tell enough about how and why we discriminate against each other. The category encompasses far too wide a spectrum of variables—income, education, occupation, language access, citizenship, national origin, and more. Specifically in studying discrimination and inequality, we, as researchers, must be more precise in defining our samples. This is no easy task, and at times an impossible one due to data limitations. Yet, if we are to be honest about our results we need a better understanding of gender, class, and phenotype differences. Latina women are one of the most marginalized groups in the United States; but not all Latina women are the same. This study hopes to begin a discussion that will broaden our understanding of racism and prejudice, how it is practiced, and what some of the consequences might be.

References

Acosta, O. Z. (1972). *The autobiography of Brown Buffalo*. New York: Vintage Books.

Arce, C., Murguia, E., & Frisbie, W. (1987). Phenotype and life chances among Chicanos. *Hispanic Journal of Behavioral Sciences*, 9, 19–32.

Becker, G. (1971). *The Economics of discrimination*. Chicago, IL: University of Chicago Press.

Candelario, G. (2000). Hair race-ing: Dominican beauty culture and identity production. *Meridians*, 1(1), 128–56.

Carroll, J. (1991). *Blacks in colonial Veracruz: Race, ethnicity, and regional development*. Austin, TX: University of Texas Press.

Casal, L. (1978). Images of Cuban society among pre-and post-revolutionary novelists. Ph.D. Dissertation. New York: New School of Social Research.

Castillo, A. (1994). *Massacre of the dreamers: Essays on Xicanisma*. Albuquerque, NM: University of New Mexico Press.

Catanzarite, L., & Aguilera, M. (2000). Working with co-ethnics: Earnings penalties for Latino immigrants at Latino jobsites. Paper presented at the Annual Meeting of the American Sociological Association, Washington, DC.

Codina, G. E., & Montalvo, F. (1994). Chicano phenotype and depression. *Hispanic Journal of Behavioral Sciences*, 16(3), 296–306.

Colón, J. (1982). *A Puerto Rican in New York and other sketches.* New York: International.

England, P., Farkas, G., Kilbourne, B., & Dou, T. (1988). Sex segregation and wages. *American Sociological Review*, 53, 544–58.

Fitzgerald, K. (1999). Who marries whom? Attitudes and behavior in marital partner selection. Ph.D. Dissertation. Boulder, CO: University of Colorado.

Franklin, J. H. (1980). *From slavery to freedom.* New York: Knopf.

Fuchs, V. (1988). *Women's quest for economic equality.* Cambridge, MA: Harvard University Press.

Gómez, C. (2000). The continual significance of skin color: An exploratory study of Latinos in the northeast. *Hispanic Journal of Behavioral Sciences*, 22(1), 94–103.

Hall, R. E. (1994). The "Bleaching Syndrome": Implications of light skin for Hispanic American assimilation. *Hispanic Journal of Behavioral Sciences*, 16(3), 307–14.

Hughes, M., & Hertel, B. (1990). The significance of color remains: A study of life chances, mate selection, and ethnic consciousness among Black Americans. *Social Forces*, 68(4), 1105–20.

Hunter, M. L. (2002). "If you're light you're alright:" Light skin color as social capital for women of color. *Gender and Society*, 16(2), 175–93.

Johnson Jr., J. H., Oliver, M., & Bobo, L. (1994). Understanding the contours of deepening urban inequality: theoretical underpinnings and research design of a multi-city study. *Urban Geography*, 15(1), 77–89.

Jorge, A. (1979). The Black Puerto Rican woman in contemporary American society. In E. Acosta-Belén (Ed.), *The Puerto Rican woman: Perspectives on culture, history, and society* (Pp. 180–87). New York: Praeger Scientific.

Kanellos, N. (2002). *Herencia: The anthology of Hispanic literature of the United States.* New York: Oxford Press.

Keith, V. M. (1997). Life stress and psychological well-being among married and unmarried Blacks. In Taylor, Jackson, & Chatter (Eds.), *Family life in Black America* (pp. 95–116). Thousand Oaks, CA: Sage.

Keith, V. M., & Herring, C. (1991). Skin tone and stratification in the black community. *The American Journal of Sociology*, 97(3), 760–79.

Lee, G. R., Seccombe, K., & Shehan, C. (1991). Marital status and personal happiness: An analysis of trend data. *Journal of Marriage and the Family*, 53(4), 839–44.

Montalvo, F., & Codina, E. (2001). Skin color and Latinos in the United States. *Ethnicities*, 1(3), 321–41.

Murguia, E., & Telles, E. (1996). Phenotype and schooling among Mexican Americans. *Sociology of Education*, 69, 276–89.

Nakosteen, R. A. (1997). Men, money, and marriage: are high earners more prone than low earners to marry? *Social Science Quarterly*, 78, 66–82.

Portillo, Lourdes. (1993). [film] *Mirrors of the heart.* Americas Series. Annenberg/CPB. Boston, MA: WGBH.

Relenthford J. S., Gaskill, M., & Hazuda, H. (1983). Social class, admixture, and skin color variation among Mexican Americans and Anglo Americans living in San Antonio, TX. *Journal of Physical Anthropology*, 62, 97–102.

Rodriguez, C. (1991). The effects of race on Puerto Rican wages. In E. Melendez, C. Rodriguez, & J. B. Figueroa (Eds.), *Hispanics in the labor force.* New York: Plenum Press.

Ross, L. E. (1997). Mate selection preferences among African American college students. *Journal of Black Studies*, 27(4), 554–69.

Russell, K., Wilson, M., & Hall, R. (1992). *The color complex: The politics of skin color among African Americans.* New York: Harcourt Brace Jovanovich.

Santiago, R. (1995). *Boricuas: Influential Puerto Rican writings—an anthology.* New York: One World.

Sorenson, E. (1989). Measuring the effect of occupational sex and race composition on earnings, In R. T. Michael, H. I. Hartmann, & B. O'Farrell (Eds.), *Pay equity: Empirical issues*.Washington, DC: National Academy Press.

Sprecher, S. (1994). Mate selection preferences: Gender differences examined in a national sample. *Journal of Personality and Social Psychology*, 66, 1074–80.

Stack, S. (1998). Marital status and happiness: A 17-nation study. *Journal of Marriage and the Family*, 60(2), 527–36.

Suárez-Findlay, E. (1999). Imposing decency: The politics of sexuality and race in Puerto Rico, 1870–1920. Durham, NC: Duke University Press.

Telles, E., & Murguia, E. (1990). Phenotype discrimination and income differences among Mexican Americans. *Social Science Quarterly*, 71, 682–96.

Thomas, P. (1967). *Down these mean streets*. New York: Knopf.

Tomaskovic-Devey, D. (1993). *Gender and racial inequality at work: The sources and consequences of job segregation*. Ithaca, NY: ILR Press.

Villarreal, J. A. (1959) *Pocho*. New York: Doubleday.

Wade, P. (1993). *Blackness and race mixture: The dynamics of racial identity in Colombia*. Baltimore, MD: Johns Hopkins University Press.

Waite, L. J. (1996). Social science finds: "Marriage matters." *The Responsive Community*, 6(3), 26–35.

Waite, L. J., & Gallagher, M. (2000). *The case for marriage*. New York: Doubleday.

Waldfogel, J. (1994). Women working for less: Family status and women's pay in the U.S. and U.K. Ph.D. dissertation, issued as Working Paper #D-94-1, Malcolm Wiener Center for Social Policy, Kennedy School of Government. Cambridge, MA: Harvard University.

———. (1997). The effect of children on women's wages. *American Sociological Review*, 62(4), 209–17.

Waldron, I. (1996). Marriage protection and marriage selection—prospective evidence for reciprocal effects of marital status and health. *Social Science and Medicine*, 43(1), 113–23.

Winders, J., Jones III, J. P., & Higgins, M. J. (2005). Making güeras: Selling white identities on late-night Mexican television. *Gender, Place and Culture–A Journal of Feminist Geography*, 12(1), 71–93.

Wright, W. R. (1990). *Café con leche: Race, class, and national image in Venezuela*. Austin, TX: University of Texas Press.

Chapter 12
"There Is No Racism Here": Understanding Latinos' Perceptions of Color Discrimination Through Sending-Receiving Society Comparison

Wendy D. Roth

Abstract Studies showing that lighter phenotypes are associated with better socioeconomic outcomes among Latinos attribute this pattern to color discrimination. Yet surveys consistently find low levels of Latinos reporting discrimination experiences. Drawing on 120 qualitative interviews and participant observation in New York, San Juan, and Santo Domingo, I explore this paradox by examining how Dominicans and Puerto Ricans subjectively understand discrimination. Cultural narratives in the sending societies create obstacles to recognizing discrimination by: (a) limiting the definition to its overt, institutional forms; and (b) portraying the victims of discrimination as culpable for their failure to have "improved their race." Although migrants bring these narratives to the U.S., these views are challenged by exposure to American perspectives, both before and after migration. Transnational contact serves a potential means for those in the sending nations to perceive colorism in their own societies.

Introduction

Skin color is especially relevant for the lives and life chances of Latinos. Their significant range of phenotypes, spanning across traditional U.S. racial boundaries, is unparalleled among other ethnic groups. Whether they appear White, Black, Indigenous, or somewhere in between can differentiate the experiences of Latinos even within the same ethnic group.

A considerable body of research shows that lighter or more European phenotypes are associated with better socioeconomic outcomes within many Latino groups in the U.S., a pattern usually attributed to discrimination based on color (Arce et al. 1987, Espino & Franz 2002, Gómez 2000, Hochschild & Weaver 2003, Murguia & Telles 1996, South et al. 2005, Telles & Murguia 1990). In these studies, discrimination is measured indirectly, a statistical residual after other relevant explanations are accounted for. But how do Latinos

W.D. Roth
Department of Sociology, University of British Columbia, Vancouver, BC, Canada
e-mail: wroth@interchange.ubc.ca

R.E. Hall (ed.), *Racism in the 21st Century*, DOI: 10.1007/978-0-387-79097-8_12,   205
© Springer Science+Business Media, LLC 2008

subjectively experience and understand discrimination? Focusing on this question, as I do in this chapter, reveals a great deal about their belief systems and what influences can cause those systems to change.

Many Latinos, in fact, tend to deny the existence of color discrimination. In the U.S., studies of working class and less educated samples consistently find lower reported levels of discrimination for Latinos than for African Americans, with Latinos in some cases reporting lower levels of discrimination than Whites (see Krieger et al. 2005). In many Latin American countries as well, many maintain they have never experienced discrimination and that racism on the basis of skin color does not exist in their society (Jimenez Román 1996, Menéndez Alarcón 1994, Wade 1997). While sociologists often show that people are not always aware of the structural forces that affect them, it is also valuable to understand how their views are formed, why they are maintained, and when they are challenged. An interpretive understanding of Latinos' beliefs about color discrimination also helps to contextualize survey findings suggesting lower levels of color discrimination than might be expected from statistical analyses of outcomes.

I maintain that perceptions of color discrimination stem from the cultural constructs that Latino migrants bring with them from their countries of origin. Most Latino ethnic groups in the U.S. are not far removed from their immigrant roots; approximately 40% of all Latinos were foreign-born in 2005.[1] To understand Latinos' interpretations of interactions in the U.S. it is necessary to comprehend how color discrimination is interpreted in their societies of origin, by examining the beliefs of those who stay in the countries of origin as well as those who migrate.

The cultural attitudes toward discrimination that Latino migrants bring with them from their home societies are not completely unmediated in the receiving society, however. Interactions in a multiethnic context, where Latinos find themselves a racialized minority rather than the majority, can challenge migrants' beliefs about discrimination and the importance of skin color. Latino migrants' perceptions of color discrimination are thereby shaped by their structural position and opportunities for meaningful interethnic interaction within the racial landscape of the U.S. as well as by the cultural background they bring with them to their new society.

I address these issues by focusing on Dominicans and Puerto Ricans—two groups with considerable color diversity that incorporates European, African, and Indigenous phenotypes. Drawing upon participant observation and 120 qualitative interviews with Dominican and Puerto Rican migrants to New York and non-migrants (those who have never lived outside their home country) in San Juan, Puerto Rico, and Santo Domingo, the Dominican Republic,

---

[1] 2005 American Community Survey. This figure does not include Puerto Ricans born on the island of Puerto Rico.

I examine how discrimination is experienced by Dominicans and Puerto Ricans of different skin tones.

Color discrimination exists and shapes the opportunities and daily lives of Dominicans and Puerto Ricans in both their home countries and in the U.S.[2] But in the Dominican Republic and, to a lesser extent, Puerto Rico, cultural narratives around discrimination create obstacles to recognizing it in two ways: (a) by defining discrimination in only its overt, institutional forms; and (b) by portraying the victims of color discrimination as worthy of shame for their inferior ancestry and their failure to have "improved their race." Although many migrants bring these narratives with them to the U.S., these views are also challenged by exposure to American perspectives on discrimination, both before and after migration. I suggest that transnational contact with U.S. ties allows those remaining in the home countries to redefine discrimination and to perceive colorism in their own society. In the U.S. context, what challenges these views most is entering the middle class. While working-class migrants can more easily accept discrimination on the basis of ethnicity, Puerto Rican and Dominican migrants who ascend to professional careers in the U.S. are more likely to experience and to appreciate how color creates additional barriers in their lives beyond their ethnic status.

Colorism at Home and Abroad

If prejudice consists of "irrationally based, negative attitudes" against groups of people and their members (Pettigrew 1982, p. 2) then color prejudice consists of negative attitudes toward people with particular phenotypes. I define color discrimination as unfair treatment on the basis of color prejudice that disadvantages people with certain phenotypes. In the U.S., Latinos are officially classified as an ethnic group who may be of any race, although in practice they are often treated as a racial group. Scholars often speak of "racial" discrimination against Latinos to indicate discrimination on the basis of Latino status rather than phenotype. By contrast, in Puerto Rico and the Dominican Republic, "racial" discrimination refers to that enacted on the basis of color prejudice. The original population groups which comprised these islands—Africans, Indians, and Spanish—intermarried to such an extent, creating a blending of phenotypes, that "race" is much more fluid and in this context refers to phenotype more than membership in any cohesive social group. To acknowledge this contextual distinction, I refer to "color prejudice" and "color discrimination" in my discussion, but, in direct quotes from non-migrant respondents, I maintain their use of the terms "racism" and "racial discrimination" to describe the same phenomena.

---

[2] Although Puerto Rico is part of the U.S., I adopt the terminology used by Puerto Ricans themselves and refer to the mainland U.S. simply as "the U.S."

In the U.S., attention to color has long been obscured by a discourse focusing on racial categories, which sometimes subsume considerable color variation. However, most studies that have examined the impact of phenotype on Latinos' socioeconomic outcomes have found higher outcomes among those with lighter phenotypes that cannot be explained by measured differences in attributes or skills. Several studies show that Latinos with more European phenotypes have advantages in earnings and occupations. Arce et al. (1987) found significant bivariate associations between European phenotypes and higher socioeconomic indicators among Mexican Americans. Mexican Americans of darker, more Indian phenotype also reported significantly more discrimination than their lighter counterparts. In another study, Telles and Murguia (1990) revealed that dark Mexican American men suffered a significant earnings disadvantage that was not explained by personal endowments or human capital. They concluded that most of the earnings difference was due to labor market discrimination. Gómez's (2000) study of Latinos in Boston (most of whom are Puerto Rican and Dominican) showed that light-skinned men earn higher wages than dark men when human capital variables are controlled; however, color has no significant effect on the wages of Latina women. Looking at the impact of skin color on occupational status for Puerto Ricans, Cubans and Mexicans, Espino and Franz (2002) found that darker-skinned Mexicans and Cubans have significantly lower occupational prestige than their lighter co-ethnics, controlling for factors that influence labor market performance, but showed no significant skin color effect for Puerto Ricans.[3]

Research on Mexicans shows that darker phenotype is also associated with lower levels of educational attainment (Arce et al. 1987, Hochschild & Weaver 2003). Murguia and Telles (1996) found that Mexican Americans with light skin and European features had about 1.5 years more schooling than those with dark skin and Indian features, even when other determinants of educational attainment were controlled. Among the primarily Puerto Rican and Dominican Latinos in Boston, Gómez (2000) found that those with lighter skin have more education, although the difference is not statistically significant.

Phenotype is also associated with different residential outcomes among U.S. Latinos. In their study of Mexicans in San Antonio, Texas, Relethford et al. (1983) found that those living in high- and middle-income suburban neighborhoods were lighter than those living in poor, urban areas. In a recent study on Mexicans, Cubans, and Puerto Ricans, South et al. (2005) showed that, compared with their lighter-skinned co-ethnics, darker-skinned Puerto Ricans move into areas with significantly fewer White American residents, net of controls for other predictors of inter-neighborhood migration. They find the same pattern for

---

[3] The authors speculate that Puerto Ricans may benefit from their regional concentration in New York City, an area that a 1990 General Account Office report showed to have lower levels of discrimination against Latinos than regions with large Mexican populations. However, the discrepancy between their findings and those of Gómez may also lie in their failure to test for gender effects.

Cubans although the effect is weaker, yet find no significant effect of skin color on Mexicans' spatial assimilation. Together this research shows that skin color matters for Latinos apart from their ethnic and racial classification.

The traditional discourse in many Latin American countries presents a quite different picture: one where skin color does not matter and racism does not exist. Latin America and the Caribbean have often been described as regions of "racial democracy," where race relations were less harsh and oppressive and where races have mixed together in contrast to the strict segregation of the United States (Blanco 1942, Degler 1971, Hoetink 1967, Tannenbaum 1946). One of the strongest proponents of this view in Puerto Rico, Tomas Blanco begins his treatise on the topic by stating, "In Puerto Rico we still do not know racial prejudice very well [my translation]" (1942, p. 9). He insists that the Jim Crow laws of the United States exemplify true racism. In Puerto Rico, inter-racial marriage and the lack of racial segregation are taken as evidence that race prejudice cannot exist. Any prejudice that is expressed is seen as "social," based upon class status, rather than racial. Tumin and Feldman's (1971) subsequent study of Puerto Rican social stratification supported this commonly held view that skin color does not significantly affect the life chances of Puerto Ricans. Similar views have predominated in the Dominican Republic since the mid-19th century (Torres-Saillant 1998). Mejía-Ricart (1953) wrote about the country in 1953, "there is no violent racial discrimination, and no social color barriers exist outwardly" (cited in Howard 2001, p. 51).

Despite the view that color prejudice does not exist, some evidence shows that light skin is associated with higher incomes and status in Puerto Rico and the Dominican Republic. Rivera-Batiz (2004) showed that, in Puerto Rico, individuals who identified themselves as White on the 2000 Census receive significantly higher wage returns for their education than do those who identi-fied themselves as Black.[4] Sidanius et al. (2001) argue that a pigmentocracy exists in the Dominican Republic whereby *blancos* are perceived to have the highest level of social status and social status ratings decline with progressively darker descriptions of appearance. Many recognize that the social elite tend to include those with the most European phenotypes (Howard 2001). Further-more, in these as in many Latin American nations, light skin is culturally valued, making those who are dark less desirable as employees, marriage partners, and patrons in upscale establishments (Hall 2000, Menéndez Alarcón 1994, Wade 1997, Whitten & Torres 1998).

How is it that in societies where Whiteness is associated with high status people say racial prejudice does not exist? The issue, I maintain, is one of definition. Many Latin Americans—and especially Dominicans in this study—define racial prejudice as the type of overt, state-sanctioned discrimina-tion characterized by the Jim Crow era in the U.S. South. But with the demise of

---

[4] The association between racial self-identification and racial appearance is unreliable in Puerto Rico, however, where 80% of the population identified itself as White in 2000 (Duany 2002).

Jim Crow, U.S. scholars have recognized a shift from overt to more covert forms of racism (Bobo et al. 1997, Kinder & Sears 1981). Instead of formal segregation and violence based on race, modern forms of racism may be hidden or unarticulated, inaction as opposed to action, or acts with a racial impact that are not framed in racial terms.

Definitions of racial prejudice have not similarly shifted in the Dominican Republic, although they have, somewhat, in Puerto Rico. Thus, covert actions—for example, those allowing dress codes which club bouncers can cite as a reason for excluding those with dark skin, or job advertisements citing vague criteria such as "good presence" to offer jobs to lighter candidates—may not be defined as racial discrimination because darker individuals are not formally barred. Nor are individual preferences for lighter skin defined as racism because they are not institutionalized in the state apparatus. But just as it is questionable to impose Americanized perspectives onto another society, sensitivity to local cultures should not lead us to ignore actions with clear discriminatory impact. To understand color discrimination among Puerto Ricans and Dominicans in both their own countries and in the U.S. we need to explore both what happens in people's interactions and how they interpret those events.

Methodology

Between September 2002 and December 2003, I conducted participant observation and 120 in-depth interviews with Puerto Rican and Dominican migrants in New York and non-migrants in San Juan and Santo Domingo. I restricted the migrant sample to those in the New York metropolitan area who were born in Puerto Rico or the Dominican Republic, who came to the U.S. at age 14 or older, and who had lived in the U.S. for at least seven years.[5] The non-migrant sample included those in the San Juan or Santo Domingo metropolitan area who had not lived outside of their home country for more than six months, and who identified both parents as Puerto Rican or Dominican, respectively. Each group was stratified by skin color—classified as light, medium, or dark based on my observation—as well as age, sex, and occupational status[6] (see Table 12.1). For the migrant samples, I also sought variation in respondents'

---

[5] I excluded migrants who had lived anywhere beside the mainland U.S. and their country of origin, as well as those who had returned to their home country for more than six months after migrating.

[6] High occupational status includes managerial and professional specialty occupations. Medium occupational status includes technical, sales, and administrative support occupations. Low occupational status includes service occupations; production, craft, and repair occupations; operators, fabricators and laborers.

Table 12.1 Distribution of sampling characteristics (N)

	Non-Migrant Puerto Ricans	Non-Migrant Dominicans	Migrant Puerto Ricans	Migrant Dominicans
Color				
Light	13	11	14	11
Medium	11	7	10	12
Dark	6	12	4	9
Age				
21–35	11	11	5	16
36–50	11	11	9	10
Above 50	8	8	14	6
Sex				
Male	15	15	14	13
Female	15	15	14	19
Occup. Status				
High	10	11	13	11
Medium	11	8	5	8
Low	9	11	10	13
Age at Migration				
14–18 yrs old			16	22
19–25 yrs old			10	4
Above 25 yrs old			2	6
Time in the U.S.				
7–13 years			4	11
14–20 years			5	10
More than 20 yrs			19	11
Total	30	30	28	32

age at arrival in the mainland U.S. and the amount of time they had spent in the U.S.

I generated quota samples by combining several methods, intended to produce samples of individuals who were unknown to one another. Different strategies proved more successful for recruiting respondents in some sites than others. For the New York samples, some respondents were referred by interviewees in the Longitudinal Study of Second Generation Immigration to New York. The study included random samples of 429 second-generation Puerto Ricans and 427 second-generation Dominicans. Those interviewees were contacted by native Spanish speakers and asked for the names of friends or relatives in the first generation who might be willing to participate in my study.[7]

In all three locations, I found some respondents by canvassing particular neighborhoods and passing out flyers in public locations, including malls,

---

[7] In cases where the named second-generation contact had moved, current residents who were Puerto Rican or Dominican were also allowed to refer first-generation contacts or to participate if they met the study criteria.

shops, and buses. I knocked on doors in some neighborhoods, and recruited people with whom I came into contact over the course of my daily interactions in restaurants, shops, and other public places. Some respondents were referred by personal contacts, often by my Research Assistants or by staff in the research institutes where I was affiliated. In order to find respondents with high occupational status, I contacted some professional organizations, which contacted their membership on my behalf. Others were located through forwarded e-mails. I did not interview more than one respondent referred by any given individual or organization.

Interviews were conducted in Spanish,[8] with both myself and a native Spanish-speaking Research Assistant present. We varied who led the interview, in order to test for American/native interviewer effects. I also discussed the interviews with my Research Assistants to get their perspective on the responses. Some of these discussions were tape-recorded and form part of my data.

A segment of the interview addressed respondents' perceptions of and experiences with discrimination, although the word "discrimination" was not used in interview questions. Non-migrant respondents were asked: "Have you ever suspected you were being treated unfairly because of your race, color or your appearance, even if you didn't know for sure?" For migrant respondents, the question asked about unfair treatment "because of your skin color or because you are Puerto Rican/Dominican."[9] After this general question, respondents were asked follow-up questions about five specific scenarios: (a) experiencing worse service or treatment in a store or restaurant than other customers; (b) having security guards watching them more closely than other people when in a store; (c) feeling they were treated unfairly in getting an apartment; (d) feeling they were treated unfairly in getting a job or a promotion; and (e) being stopped by the police for reasons they felt were related to their appearance or race. A number of other in-depth questions probed all respondents' perceptions of racism and discrimination in their society: for example, if people are treated differently because of their race, color, or appearance; and if the opportunities for economic success were the same for someone (for migrants: Hispanics) with dark skin as for someone with light skin. Migrants were additionally asked how Americans treat Puerto Ricans/Dominicans, if the opportunities are the same for someone from Puerto Rico/the Dominican Republic as for most Americans, and if they feel completely accepted in U.S. society. Other experiences with discrimination arose elsewhere in the interview, which also covered topics such as experiences with/attitudes toward migration, transnational connections, labor market experiences, social networks, racial identity, and racial classification.

---

[8] In two cases, the respondent preferred to conduct the interview in English.

[9] Most migrants identified their race as Puerto Rican, Dominican, or Latino in an open-ended question. For further discussion of the meaning of race for Puerto Ricans and Dominicans, see Roth (2006), Chapters 3–4.

At the beginning of each interview, I mentally rated each respondent's skin color on a scale from 1 (very light) to 10 (very dark).[10] As soon as possible after the interview, I completed a more detailed form describing the respondent's appearance, including hair color and texture, eye color, nose, lips, how I believe Americans might see the person's race, and a detailed prose description of appearance. For the purposes of this paper, I classify respondents' color as light (1–3 on scale), medium (4–6), and dark (7–10) based on my observations.[11] However, recognizing that phenotype and how people are perceived racially is much more complex than skin tone alone, I refer to other aspects of appearance when appropriate.

The interview data only relate to respondents' interpretations of their treatment by others. An individual may say she was watched more closely by security guards than other customers but attribute it to something other than her skin color. Nonetheless, by comparing the experiences respondents relate, we can uncover patterns across respondents of different colors, both in what they experience and how they interpret those interactions.

Perceptions of Color Discrimination in the Sending Societies

Among non-migrant respondents in San Juan and Santo Domingo, those with dark skin have more experiences where they feel they were treated unjustly than people with light skin. Nearly half of non-migrant respondents with dark skin (47%) described such experiences, compared to about one-fifth of those with light skin (23%). In contrast to the traditional view that color prejudice does not exist, most Puerto Ricans and some Dominicans also believe that people are treated differently based on race or color in their society in a way that disadvantages those with darker skin. Yet most respondents are reluctant to see themselves as victims of color discrimination. When asked a general question about whether they had ever suspected they were treated unfairly because of race, color, or appearance, most responded in the negative. However, after probing for the specific forms of discrimination detailed above, many with dark skin revealed they had experienced some of those forms. Individuals do not always attribute those experiences to discrimination or believe they are related to skin color. Nonetheless, respondents with darker skin—even across different class backgrounds—were more likely to experience worse service than other

---

[10] To anchor my observations, I previously applied this rating scale to a set of photographs in an instrument used during the interview to explore the racial schemas respondents use.

[11] Respondents used the same scale during the interview to rate their own color, as well as the color of individuals in the photographs, and their friends and acquaintances mentioned in their social network. Interviewer observations do not always correspond with self-classifications (Rodríguez et al. 1991, Rodríguez & Cordero-Guzman 1992), nor did they always here. For this paper, observed color is a more appropriate measure than self-identified color because it is on the basis of observations that color prejudice is acted out.

Table 12.2 Non-migrants' perceptions of color discrimination, by Nationality and Skin Tone

	Puerto Ricans Light	Medium	Dark	Dominicans Light	Medium	Dark
Are people treated differently based on race or color?	Yes	Yes	Yes	Some yes. Some no.	Some yes. Some no.	Some yes. Some no.
Does color affect one's opportunities for economic success?	Yes	Yes	Yes	Some yes. Some no.	Some yes. Some no.	Some yes Some no.
Have you experienced any unjust treatment?	No, helped by color	No	No	No	No	No
Probes reveal unjust treatment	No, claim this only happens in the U.S.	Yes, but claim not due to color	Yes	No	No, with discomfort	Some yes Some no, with discomfort N = 60

clients in a shop or restaurant, experience being watched by security guards more than other shoppers, being treated unfairly in their search for an apartment, job or promotion, or being targeted by police for reasons they believed related to their color or appearance.

There are clear differences in the responses of Puerto Ricans and Dominicans. Puerto Ricans reveal the strongest differences between those with light and dark skin, while Dominicans of all phenotypes are generally more reluctant to believe in color discrimination or perceive it in their own lives. Yet in both nations, respondents with medium skin tones were the most resistant to the idea of color discrimination, and often the least comfortable with questions about whether they had experienced it themselves. These patterns, which I explore in detail in this section, are summarized in Table 12.2.

Belief in the Existence of Color Discrimination

Academics in the U.S. have identified a shift from overt forms of racial and color discrimination to subtler, covert forms. For many in the Dominican Republic, a similar shift in thought has not taken place. For them, racism (what we might call colorism) continues to refer to the overt, institutionalized forms of racial violence and segregation that characterized the pre-Civil

Rights Era United States. Because such overt forms of racism are seldom found, this definition promotes the view that there is no racism in their country. And yet, while many continue to hold this view, many others have adopted a perspective more similar to that found in the U.S. Approximately half of all Dominican respondents (47%)—and the vast majority of Puerto Rican respondents (87%)—believe that color discrimination exists in their country and adopt a view that preferential treatment for those with lighter skin constitutes color prejudice even if those with dark skin are not formally excluded. I put forward the hypothesis—to be tested through representative research—that increased exposure to the U.S. and its discourse of discrimination is what enables non-migrants to view covert acts as racism and to perceive them in their country. Those with the least contact with people in the U.S. or the greatest political resistance to its culture are most likely to maintain a traditional view of overt racism.

Geraldo represents the traditional Dominican view toward color discrimination. A professional in politics, Geraldo has dark skin and African features. In his view, racial violence, murder, and segregation qualify as racism. But the view held by many Dominicans that they need to marry someone lighter than themselves in order to "improve the race" of their children does not. He explains why there is no racism in the Dominican Republic:

> No, well, because racism kills. At least as far as I know no one has been killed here. Before there were encounters but in today's day and age they have not killed anybody because of racism. It hasn't happened here like in the U.S. in the 1960 s, [like] Martin Luther King. No, that case has not happened here. Here, a *negro* can go to different places.
>
> *Q: In your opinion, what is racism? How would you define it?*
> Racism is the superiority of one race over the other, depending on how you see it. For the *blancos* the *blanca* race is the best, but maybe for an African *negro*, maybe the *negra* race is the best.
>
> *Q: And when people talk here about improving the race or refining the race, that's not racism?*
> No, because that is a term that came with the colony, when for example my ancestors were light, let's say they were *blanco*, a Spaniard married a *negra*. That has been [passed down] here from family to family. If I am like that, they may say, "*Muchacho*, go improve the race." But it's a term, it's not racism.
>
> *Q: And isn't that the idea that a race is better, or superior than the other?*
> No, because if it was superior they wouldn't mix with the other. It's absurd. And in some cases, a *negro* goes to the same school as a *blanco*, for example...There aren't buses for the *blancos* and buses for the *negros*. Everybody goes to the same place, there isn't a cemetery for *blancos* and a cemetery for *negros*. There is no racism here. (Geraldo, Dominican non-migrant, political campaigner)

Geraldo asserts the view, frequently put forth by proponents of the "racial democracy" thesis, that widespread intermarriage and integrated neighborhoods are evidence that the society cannot be racist. This supports the view that formal segregation in marriage, schools, and even cemeteries is what makes a society racist. In his view, racism kills; a society cannot be racist if it does not progress to this level of violence and overt hostility.

At unrelated points in the interview, Geraldo reveals a very negative opinion of the U.S. Unlike many of his fellow nationals, he has no interest in moving there. This is partly because he believes in staying to improve one's own society, but also because he has a firm dislike for U.S. culture. He is particularly worried about the imperialist influence the U.S. has had on the Dominican Republic, both politically and culturally. He feels that too much of Dominican culture is being eaten away by globalization, mainly through the infiltration of American culture. Perhaps to counteract this tendency, he is very involved with a Dominican folklore group which travels throughout the country and overseas to maintain and promote Dominican cultural traditions. It is no coincidence that Geraldo resists an Americanized perspective that perceives racism in Dominican society.

A similar view is expressed by Adelina, a Dominican woman with light skin, who formerly worked as a secretary but has been unemployed for nearly a decade. Clarifying what she considers racism, she explains that only formal race-based state actions qualify by her definition:

> People have their preferences, but I say that [discrimination] doesn't exist officially. There is no racial discrimination here, but there are preferences. For example, it's not that rights are denied to *negros* here, as it happens in some countries. I understand that still in the U.S. there are places for *blancos* and places for *negros*. That doesn't exist here...Now, there are people that have their preferences. Just like they don't want to get married to a *negro*, they don't want to marry a Chinese person (Adelina, Dominican non-migrant, former secretary).

While there may be preferences for light skin, such preferences, and even covert actions based on them, do not merit the label of racism in many Dominicans' eyes. Adelina, too, expresses a negative view of U.S. culture and claims she would not want to live there. She has lost all contact with her family in the U.S. and claims the cultural differences are too great.

In fact, some Dominicans express concern that Americans are not just imposing their culture on the Dominican Republic, but are trying to spread their own culture's racial views, which label Dominican society as racist. Historically, much of the Dominican Republic's rejection of its own African heritage comes from its tense relations with neighboring Haiti (Baud 1996, Howard 2001, Torres-Saillant 1999). But most of my respondents insist that their problems with Haiti are cultural and historical, not racial.

My Research Assistant, Ramona, a Dominican woman of medium-brown color who would herself have qualified for the study, explained Dominicans' concern over the way foreign perspectives on race were being imposed by international agendas:

> There is a tendency that tries to put us as if we discriminate against, to make a racial problem between Haitians and Dominicans. And in reality that does not exist, as they are trying to make it appear. In fact, even by many international organizations. Here, there are NGOs that get paid to plant that in the minds of people and it's working because when you repeat something many times, it becomes a reality. (Ramona, Dominican non-migrant, Research Assistant).

Those who maintain that there is no racism or discrimination in the Dominican Republic are resisting foreign definitions of racism that include its covert forms.

Many Dominican respondents do not focus on what racism means and express no concern with American cultural imperialism. But they see their country as a meritocracy where skin color does not matter.

This view is asserted by Rodolfo, a dark-skinned man with African hair and European facial features, who asserts that color discrimination does not exist:

Q: Do you think that the opportunities for economic success or for jobs here are the same for Dominicans with dark skin as for Dominicans with light skin?

That has nothing to do with it. Here, if you know how to do your job, it doesn't matter if you are Haitian, *blanco*, no. If you know how to do it, there's no problem. It all depends on how much you know, if it's your profession or something. But I don't believe that the color determines someone for a job.

Q: And if there are two candidates, one is light and the other is dark, one is not going to have an advantage over another?

No. That's going to depend on the capacity of each one. (Rodolfo, Dominican non-migrant, part-time social work assistant)

Rodolfo's belief in a Dominican meritocracy is colored by his own biography. Coming from a very poor, rural background, as a young child he cut crops on coffee plantations, shined shoes, and sold coal with his father. After relocating to Santo Domingo to seek a better living, he worked his way up to a semi-professional position. Starting as a school gardener, cutting weeds and planting seeds, he advanced first to an office position, and then after attaining a two-year post-secondary degree, he progressed to working in the school part-time as a social work assistant and part-time as a physical education teacher. My Research Assistant, Ramona, perceived him as someone who was very confident in his abilities and therefore able to see clearly that his color did not hold him back. The flip side of this perspective, however, is that those who believe in color discrimination are usually viewed as seeking excuses for their own failings, as I discuss more below.

Nearly half of the Dominican non-migrants I interviewed rejected this traditional view, however. They maintain that there is racism in the Dominican Republic and color does matter. Those who answer in the affirmative to these questions accept covert or subtle acts as racism.

A teacher with light skin, European hair, and facial features showing only slight evidence of racial mixture, Alicia perceives subtle differences in treatment as evidence of racism. She describes how subtle status markers are used to differentiate *blancos* from *negros*, for example the treatment she receives compared with that directed toward her darker friend, Lena:

Q: Do you think that people here are treated differently according to their race?
   Yes, I believe so...That is, what costs me one [amount], a person of *negra* race of the same sex as me, it costs them three times [as much]...You go to a restaurant for example and to me the waiter, it's likely he'll ask me, "What do you want, *señora*?" I have seen it, I see it every day. But to the person, for example, my friend, [Lena], they say "*Y tú*? What do you want?" You see? There is a very large difference in the treatment.
Q: With the language?
   Yes, yes, yes, the way they are treated. "*Y tú*? What do you want" [versus] *usted*, what do you want?"...Or, look, you go to the supermarket to buy cheese, and there is a line. [The clerk would say:] "Tell me, *señora*, what would you like?"...Even if you go to buy a cheap cheese and the *morenita* [darker woman] goes to buy a more expensive cheese. But I am sure that the clerk pretends he hasn't seen her and leaves her for last. It's not that I am seeing things, nor that I'm becoming partial. It's that I see it like that. (Alicia, Dominican non-migrant, teacher)

Using the informal *tú* is a sign of condescension. Alicia sees this disrespectful voice taken with darker customers, while she and others of light skin tone receive the more respectful formal address of "*señora*" and "*usted*." Alicia also feels a need at the end to justify her view, as if she recognizes that her perspective goes against the norm and is likely to be doubted.

   Mónica, a Dominican woman of medium skin tone and facial features revealing a mixture of African and European origins, is an accountant although she is not currently working. Even though she does not benefit from color preferences, as does Alicia, she also believes that color matters in her society and that even subtle preferences qualify as racism. She says:

   They say here that being *blanco* is a profession...because if you are *blanco* doors open up. If you are *blanco* they hire you even if you don't know [anything]. . ..

Q: Even if you don't have an education?
   Yes, even if you don't have an education, because you are *blanco*, because it looks good and that sells. They use it a lot for sales, beautiful people...Let's say a person that sells door to door, people would open the door much easier to a *blanco* than to a *negro* because you can confuse the *negro* with a thief. Even if the *blanquito* is a thief you think that he is not going to steal. (Mónica, Dominican non-migrant, unemployed accountant)

According to Mónica, lighter skin color results in better treatment and better job opportunities. As far as she is concerned, this is color discrimination.

What distinguishes Dominicans who believe there is racism in the Dominican Republic, and adopt a more lenient definition that includes covert racism, from those who do not? The sample is split between these contrasting views, and people with each perspective are divided fairly evenly across lines of color, class, gender, and most other characteristics. Even whether the individuals believe they have themselves been the target of any color prejudice does not distinguish between those with these different views. In fact, the only measured characteristic where those with opposing views on color discrimination vary is in the extent of contact they have with friends or relatives in the U.S. While all Dominican respondents know someone who has moved to the U.S., three-fifths (62%) of those who maintain there is no color discrimination in the Dominican Republic have effectively no contact with ties in the U.S. (once a year or less). Out of those who do believe there is racism or color discrimination in the Dominican Republic, only one-eighth (12.5%) have almost no contact with ties in the U.S. Half of this group (50%) is in contact with their U.S. ties monthly or more frequently. Both Alicia and Mónica, for example, talk to friends and family in the U.S. every week, while Geraldo talks with his migrant contacts less than once a year and Adelina maintains no contact. Whether this pattern is statistically representative needs to be tested quantitatively, but the association between Dominicans' perspectives on the existence of color prejudice and their contact with people in the U.S. provides reason to hypothesize a causal link.

Evidence from Puerto Rican non-migrants lends support to this hypothesis. In this country where the cultural and social influence of the U.S. is so strong, nearly everyone—regardless of their own skin color—adopts an Americanized view and believes that covert acts are evidence of color discrimination in their society. The majority also maintain that color does affect their opportunities in life. Some people with light skin do say that Puerto Ricans with light and dark skin all have the same opportunities, but the majority of light-skinned respondents take the opposite position. It would seem that Puerto Ricans have come to view the idea of racial democracy as a myth.

Diana, a librarian in San Juan in her mid-40s, has dark skin and mixed facial features, but would appear Black by U.S. standards. While she is careful to insist that she has never been discriminated against, she does believe that racism exists in Puerto Rico:

Q: Do you think that Puerto Ricans with light skin are treated better than those with dark skin?

Sometimes. Sometimes, not all the time, but it happens sometimes. . .Yes, in jobs. Again, I haven't had the experience. . . .I wouldn't say that I've received any discrimination for color, do you understand? At all. But, yes, I know in job areas, here in Puerto Rico there are many companies that do field sales and deal with clients, and it's the image [that matters]. Remember that the street vendor, the street representative is the company's image, and many people, sometimes in the job classifieds, they say "that has experience," and sometimes there is, very delicately they say "of good image." What good image does the company want to represent? Well. . .it's not something that they'll tell you. Almost never have I seen a classified that says "we want a person of *blanca* race, of *negra* race, such and such physical definitions," they don't say that. But they say "good image.". . .But, yes, I know of a lot of people who have been rejected, [who are] very well prepared, with good experience, and maybe, well, they choose someone that doesn't even know, or who isn't prepared, but he represented a good image maybe because he's *blanco*. Maybe because the fear they have is that [the person] who represents the company is a *negro*. (Diana, Puerto Rican non-migrant, librarian).

Almost all Puerto Rican non-migrants believe that subtle acts, including racial slights and preferences for people of light skin, qualify as racism.

A Puerto Rican woman in her mid-20 s, Carmela has light skin but mixed facial features. She views Puerto Rico as a racist society, and as evidence of how people are treated differently based on their color she describes an incident where a dark-skinned friend came to visit her and they both tried to get into a disco:

> Look, I've seen it at discos. It's like for example, this disco has this dress code, that you have to go [dressed] very formal. And it can be that a *blanco*, or someone with *blanco* skin, doesn't go dressed so formally, but the *negro*, if he wants to get in, has to go very well dressed. Because what they can do is use the dress code [as an] excuse to deny you entrance. And I have lived that with friends of mine. I have a friend, the same one who visited me, we were going to celebrate something and my brother was already at the place and some friends and I went with him. I went in sandals and some mid-leg pants and I had something else that they didn't allow in the place, but I don't remember what it was. And he had some jeans and a shirt, not a T-shirt, a buttoned shirt, and they didn't want to let him in. He didn't have sandals. He didn't have the other things that they didn't allow. He simply had jeans. When we managed to get in, after talking, because we wanted to see the people inside, there were people wearing polo shirts, with *blanca* skin, with polos and jeans. And they were allowed to enter. (Carmela, Puerto Rican non-migrant, former customer service representative)

As Carmela notes, color discrimination has here become covert. People with dark skin are not formally excluded from the club, but other criteria such as a dress code, are used to pick and choose customers who are racially desirable.

Puerto Rican respondents have much more contact with U.S. society than do Dominicans. Although both groups had equal levels of contact with their friends and relatives in the mainland U.S., all but one Puerto Rican (97%) had been to visit the mainland and two-thirds (67%) had been to visit three or more times, while less than a third of Dominicans (30%) had ever visited the U.S. Furthermore, through their nation's political status, Puerto Ricans are exposed to U.S. institutional structures, including its legal system and federal discrimination laws. One Puerto Rican respondent, a regional manager for a retail outlet with responsibility for some stores on the mainland U.S., had even had to deal with racial discrimination cases initiated there. With the strong cultural and institutional influence of the U.S., Puerto Ricans have grown accustomed to a American racial discourse, one that includes covert racism in its definition of racial prejudice.

Whether or not non-migrants believe that color discrimination exists in their society is unrelated to their own skin color or to other characteristics we might suspect of having an influence. I allege that concepts of racial prejudice in Puerto Rico and the Dominican Republic are becoming Americanized. Increased contact with the U.S. exposes non-migrants to a way of thinking about prejudice that extends beyond the formal, institutionalized inequities of eras past.

Experiences with Color Discrimination

Regardless of what they believe about the society overall, the majority of non-migrants, across all skin color groups, say they themselves have not experienced unjust treatment associated with their color or race. And yet, further probes about specific types of experiences reveal that those with darker skin have, in fact, experienced many of the types of interactions in question. Compared to those with light skin, non-migrants with dark skin are particularly likely to have experiences with security guards, with police, or in their search for housing where they felt they were unfairly treated or targeted because of their skin color. Many respondents, particularly those with medium skin tones, seemed uncomfortable with the questions about their own experiences. They quickly denied each form of potential discrimination with a terse "No," almost before hearing the question, and even if they had been extremely loquacious throughout the rest of the interview. Why are these non-migrants reluctant to perceive themselves as the targets of color discrimination or even discuss this?

Examining how color discrimination is interpreted within these societies helps to answer this question. In some societies, those who discriminate are viewed as violating social norms and the victim may direct anger or feelings of violation toward the perpetrator. In many Latin American societies, being the target, rather than the perpetrator, of color discrimination is a sign of a personal failing. It calls forth evidence of an individual's "inferior" roots because of their ties to African slaves. Furthermore, because color in many ways is seen as something that one can control, the failure to lighten oneself and one's descendants may be interpreted as a source of inadequacy and shame.

Rosaria exemplifies the way that many respondents perceive color prejudice in their society, but are initially reluctant to see themselves as its targets. A middle-aged Puerto Rican woman, Rosaria has very dark skin and African features. She lives in public housing in a *barrio*[12] on the outskirts of San Juan.

---

[12] In contrast to an *urbanización*, or planned neighborhood, barrios are neighborhoods that are typically not planned, which developed as people assembled housing structures on land they did not own. These are mostly very poor neighborhoods.

With a 4th-grade education, Rosaria occasionally finds temporary clerical work and supplements her income selling cakes to people in the neighborhood. As the following exchange reveals, Rosaria believes there is subtle racism in Puerto Rico, but initially claims she has not experienced any herself until a relevant experience is revealed with additional probes.

Q: Do you think that people here are treated differently based on their race or their color?

> At least here in Puerto Rico, it's not so openly. If there is, it's like more hidden. More hidden...It's like in the TV commercials. The majority of the TV commercials, they're all *blanquitos*, blondes....

Q: Do you think that the opportunities for economic success are different for someone with dark skin as for someone with light skin?

> It's said that the one with darker skin has to struggle more than the one with lighter skin. For instance, [in] the banks, there are more people who are lighter, *blanca*, than people who are *negra*. And in places like that you have to struggle more, and make a bigger effort. You don't see it a lot, [but] it can't be said that it isn't there....

Q: Have you ever suspected that someone has treated you unfairly due to the color of your skin or because of your race, even if you're not sure?

> ...No ....

Q: And have you had an experience of being treated worse or of receiving worse service than other customers in a store or restaurant?

> No. Thank God, no.

Q: Or when you are in a store, have you been watched more by the security guards than other customers?

> That, yes (laughs). That, yes. For instance, the supermarket over there, the one that is behind here, the man, why is he following me so much? If every day he sees my face, he thinks that I'm going to steal something from here? That, yes, that, yes. That's over there in the stores. Once people who are darker than others, more *negra*, well, they pursue them more. (Rosaria, Puerto Rican non-migrant, temporary clerical worker).

Rosaria does not recall these incidents immediately when asked generally about unjust treatment based on her color. Whether her later recall is a matter of refreshing her memory or explaining what types of experiences might qualify under this category, it suggests that surveys and cursory examinations of discrimination may fail to adequately capture these experiences.

Unlike many respondents, Rosaria quickly attributes her experience in the supermarket to her skin color. Others, after describing a similar experience of being watched more closely than other customers, might speculate that it was because of the way they were dressed or their social class. This is a particularly common explanation among Puerto Ricans with medium skin tones.

For example, Teresita, a college student with light brown skin and moderately African features, explains that any uncomfortable treatment she has received is because of her social class, although in describing her experience, she subtly makes skin color an issue:

Q: Have you ever suspected that you've been treated unfairly due to the color of your skin or because of your race, even if you're not sure?

No, I don't know. If I've thought that they've treated me badly, [it's] because of my social class...When you're poor, you suffer many things...I consider that a lack of respect and I'm treated badly because I'm from the lowest social class, and well, not by my color, but by my social class, due to the economic question.

Q: At any time, because of your color—or because of your social class—have you had an experience of being treated worse or of receiving a worse service in a store or a restaurant than other customers?

Well, yes. I think that when you go to stores where I know I'm never going to buy anything, I can give you an example, a store called Nous, it's French. For clothes. For example, if I go to Nous, but a *blanquita* goes, they're not going to serve me, they're not even going to notice me, they're not going to offer me anything, but they are to her. (Teresita, Puerto Rican non-migrant, college student).

The word *blanquita* refers to someone who is wealthy and light-skinned, two traits which often correspond in Puerto Rico. Thus, Teresita is suggesting that the salespeople will ignore her to help someone who is well dressed, who looks like she might purchase something. But she also notes that this person is often White. Even if Whiteness is not the trait which motivates the salespeople's actions, or it is impossible to separate the impact of wealth and Whiteness in their judgment, people with darker skin are more likely to receive poorer service and to attribute it to something other than their color. A study from the 1960s found that most Puerto Ricans of visible African descent did not think that they had suffered racial prejudice (Kinsbruner 1996). While many of my Puerto Rican respondents eventually described experiences that may be related to their color, their initial response is to deny it or attribute it to something else.

Dominican non-migrants are similarly reluctant to attribute any of their own experiences to color discrimination, and there is evidence that this response is found in many Latin America countries. A 1995 nationwide survey of Brazilians also found that 77% of those who identified themselves as Black or Mulatto said they had never been the subject of discrimination. Wade (1997) found that Blacks in Columbia similarly denied being discriminated against. They believed admitting to discrimination was effectively admitting to being the type of person who might be discriminated against—someone who is untrustworthy or stupid. Thus they imply that any discrimination they suffer would be their own fault. Similarly in Puerto Rico, people who complain of racism are labeled overly sensitive or of having an inferiority complex (Jimenez Román 1996).

To be discriminated against because of color produces feelings of shame and embarrassment. Having African ancestry is stigmatized because of the negative associations of slavery and extreme poverty. Color discrimination reminds the recipient of the negative stigma their African ancestors bore, and their inability to escape it. When one person calls attention to another's dark color or degrades her for it, the act highlights the fact that "inferior" ancestry courses through her veins. The act of color discrimination thus does not produce outrage or anger at the perpetrator, but internalization and feelings of individual unworthiness. A common defense against such disgrace is to deny it ever occurred or make light of it. Explicitly racial comments are merely a "joke" and any unpleasant interaction must have been for some other reason. This also produces a backlash against any who seek to attribute their own experiences to racial discrimination.

One Dominican non-migrant in his early 20s, José Luis, touches on why having African heritage is a source of shame. José Luis has medium skin color and mixed facial features. He works as a machine operator in a factory, but is slowly working toward a Bachelor's degree and hopes to become a lawyer. Early in the interview, when speaking of his own racial identity, he described himself as the mixture of races that form the Dominican history and culture; when I asked which races, though, he mentioned only the Indigenous and Spanish races, leaving out any mention of African roots. Later, I asked him if there are many Dominicans who do talk about having African heritage. He responded:

> Some talk about it, but most don't mention it like that, but it's known that it is that way.
> Q: *But that's something that's not talked about?*
> No, it's not talked about.
> Q: *Why?*
> Maybe, because of the same economic differences that existed in previous times, maybe, we can't talk about that.
> Q: Because the Africans were poorer?
> Poorer, so, maybe, they don't talk about that because it's not a favorable commentary, and nobody talks about what's not in their interest...I think that it was a bad status and that's why they don't comment about that. When it comes to a favorable color, they don't talk about that. "I am *negro*" for example, "I am *negro*." Nobody benefits from saying that, so instead they keep it quiet.
> Q: *But they talk about their Indian or Spanish heritage?*
> Yes. (José Luis, Dominican non-migrant, factory worker)

Because Africans were formerly slaves, and accordingly were poor with low social status, people prefer not to mention this part of their heritage, but instead associate themselves with the group that had more money and power. Most non-migrants, like José Luis, feel some embarrassment about their own African heritage and prefer not to talk about it. Experiences where that heritage was called to mind through mistreatment based on their skin color are equally unsavory recollections.

Another Dominican non-migrant explained why people avoid talking about color discrimination specifically. Pilar is one of the Dominicans who believe that color discrimination exists in her country. A dark-skinned woman with hazel eyes, Pilar had attended an elite college and worked as a nurse before a series of personal tragedies led to a remarkable fall in her social status. She now lives in an impoverished shantytown on the outskirts of Santo Domingo, in some of the worst conditions I observed during my fieldwork. The roads were unpaved and filled with massive holes. Children ran around half-clothed, playing hide-and-seek behind pieces of rusty scrap metal that temporarily patched up several houses. This was the only interview where I was not invited inside, but instead asked to conduct it on the open patio area; my Research Assistant, Ramona, later suggested that Pilar was embarrassed for me to see her home. Even more unusual, Pilar now works part-time as a domestic in the home of her brother. Although she did not say so directly, several comments Pilar made throughout the interview suggested that this is actually her half-brother. This brother, as well as Pilar's cousins, are *blancos*, and belong to a wealthy and prominent family. The family was known to Ramona, who suspected that Pilar may be the child of an extramarital relationship. Although her wealthy relatives paid for her college education and helped her find work, this family dynamic and her high education level help explain why Pilar is able to explain how color discrimination is interpreted.

Pilar explains that Dominicans interpret discrimination as a personal humiliation, not a structural problem:

> There are people that are affected by color because there are people...that, maybe, have not found jobs because of their color. Because if I go and a *blanco* person goes, they'll choose the *blanco* more easily because they think that they'll have a better presence than a dark person. So that affects the person. So, unfortunately, hard jobs have to be done by those with dark skin, that is to say, the jobs that the *blancos* turn down mostly.
>
> *Q: Do you know people that had this problem?*
> I had a friend that, because she was Haitian, they took her out of several jobs. They don't even like to hire her in family homes. So she started to sell candy...on the street and stuff.
>
> *Q: Do you know Dominican people that are dark and have this problem?*
> You see, because these are things that you don't talk about. Things that happen to you and you're not going to say it because you're embarrassed and you're ashamed. For example, if I were turned down because of my color, I would be embarrassed to talk about it with my friends. Well, I'm going to feel bad. (Pilar, Dominican non-migrant, domestic worker).

I was impressed by Pilar's perceptiveness and her openness to discussing such delicate themes. After talking with Pilar, I discussed her interview with

Ramona. To my surprise, Ramona asserted what she assured me was the more customary interpretation: Pilar clearly had a "color complex" if she believed that there is discrimination. She was simply embarrassed for her fallen state and was looking for excuses. Ramona pointed out that Rodolfo, who was slightly darker than Pilar, had worked his way up from cutting crops in the coffee plantations to a semi-professional position and did not believe there is any color discrimination. By this perspective, anyone who admits to feeling discriminated against is doubly victimized by those who view it as evidence of an inferiority complex.

There is a tendency in these and other Latin American countries to think of color as something one can control. One can marry "lighter" and thereby "improve the race" for one's children. Through skin creams and beauty treatments, one can lighten one's own skin. Or, one can simply become wealthy enough to overcome the negative status of having dark skin. Degler (1971) argues that the possibility of becoming Whiter, and the desire of Whitening to achieve higher status, creates "inner burdens of color." Because there is a possibility of escaping Blackness, being Black assumes a connotation of a personal failing. Dark skin and African features suggest an inability to attract a lighter mate or to achieve upward mobility. Being a target of color prejudice is therefore interpreted by many as evidence of personal failure to achieve the ideal of light skin.

This helps explain why people with medium skin tones seem most uncomfortable talking about experiences where they might have been the target of color prejudice. Their color provides them with a certain amount of status compared to those further toward the dark end of the color spectrum (Degler 1971, Torres-Saillant 1998). Those with very dark skin are unlikely to avoid the stigma of Blackness; those of medium skin tone hope to do so and are accordingly more sensitive of reminders of how their appearance or heritage may negatively affect their status. Reflecting on negative interactions that may have been related to their skin color is a reminder of the African part of their roots they often wish to forget. Their attitudes toward the questions, and the fact that no one wants to talk about having been the target of color discrimination, is as revealing as the experiences themselves.

Respondents with light skin rarely reveal the same type of discomfort with questions about color discrimination. Many even admit that they benefit from colorism because they are helped by their light color.

Daniel, an unemployed medical technician from Puerto Rico, who has light skin and more European features, claims: "I think I have received preferences because of my [color]. It's like because of prejudging me, they see me as the profile of a clean-cut [person]. They prejudge me favorably. I believe, maybe, a *negra* person would have fewer advantages." Although he claims the distinction is subtle, noting, "It wasn't like 'You're White, you're in,'" nevertheless he perceives an advantage over others and has never experienced treatment he believed was as discriminatory.

In the case of Inés, a Dominican with European phenotype, Whiteness literally does open doors. She describes an experience where both she and some darker-skinned women were waiting to pick up documents at an embassy:

> There is a strong racism here...I've gone through a door without being asked a question only because I have a certain color. That's clearly racism...That happened to me in the Spanish embassy, when I went there to take care of something, they let me go through a door and didn't ask me anything and when these *morenitas* went they stopped them and didn't let them through, and I felt very bad from seeing how they felt...They always give the preference to the most *blanquito*. (Inés, Dominican non-migrant, beauty salon owner)

Among light-skinned Puerto Ricans, several claim that the only discrimination they have ever experienced is when they have visited the mainland U.S. There, they are targeted for being Latino when people hear them speaking Spanish.

Because of the way color discrimination is defined and interpreted in Puerto Rico and the Dominican Republic, many non-migrants do not perceive it in their society and even more are reluctant to admit having been its target. Nevertheless, more dark-skinned respondents eventually describe discriminatory experiences than light-skinned respondents. Color does affect the opportunities of non-migrant respondents, even though many choose not to believe it.

Experiencing Color Discrimination in the U.S.

Puerto Rican and Dominican migrants bring these cultural constructs with them when they move to the U.S. There, too, we see a denial of the existence of color discrimination among many migrants, especially Dominicans. One might think that if contact with the U.S. is what influences people's concepts of racism in the home countries then migrants who have been in the U.S. longer would be more willing to see themselves as victims of color discrimination. In fact, migrants who have spent more time in the U.S. are more likely to believe that there is discrimination, but on the basis of Hispanic origin rather than skin color. In the multiethnic environment of the U.S. being Latino is a more salient identifier for these migrants, and discrimination on this basis does not evoke the same cultural interpretation of inferiority.

In the receiving society context, however, Puerto Ricans' and Dominicans' experiences are refracted by the prism of social class. The higher they climb up the professional ladder, the more migrants recognize how skin color shapes their opportunities and which doors are closed off to them. While being Latino may matter for all migrants, skin color matters most not at the bottom of the class structure but at the top.

Most of the migrants I interviewed in working-class occupations maintained that Hispanics with light skin do not have advantages in the U.S. over those with dark skin, and assert that their own skin color does not affect their opportunities. Just like non-migrants in the sending countries, many migrants conveyed discomfort with the discrimination questions and several respondents quickly denied each one. Migrants who deny the existence of color discrimination believe that those claiming to be its victims are merely making excuses for individual failings that can be overcome.

Marco, a Dominican migrant with medium skin, was fairly monosyllabic throughout our interview. The only time he became animated and expressed any opinion forcefully was when I asked him whether skin color affects Latinos' opportunities in the U.S.

Q: Some people say that Hispanics with light skin do better here that Hispanics with dark skin—

No, that's a lie.

Q: You don't agree with that?

Of course, not.

Q: Why don't you agree with that?

Well, because sometimes they are justifications...In certain races like the Latinos and others, I see that more in the Blacks and also the Latinos, that they put themselves down: "Well, no, because I can't [do it] if the *blanquito*—" Who knows if this guy, while you...weren't doing anything, [he] was studying, he was doing this. And he's *blanquito* and he's a Hispanic, a White Dominican, for example. The *moreno* [says], "Ah, I'm *moreno*. I'm a tigre."[13] With that in mind, they don't move forward...Here there's opportunity for everybody. In all parts of the world there is opportunity for everybody...What happens is that sometimes people look for justifications. (Marco, Dominican migrant, doorman).

Marco believes that opportunities are available to all, and looks down on those who point to their color as an explanation for their outcomes. Working-class migrants with dark and medium skin, especially Dominicans, are particularly likely to express this view, and thus particularly loath to accept color discrimination as an explanation for any negative incidents they experience themselves.

But unlike their counterparts in the sending societies, migrants live in a multiethnic environment where they are defined as an ethnic minority. Working-class respondents do not uniformly hold fast to the belief that America offers equal opportunities to all. Many believe they do face structural barriers—as Latinos—while firmly denying the existence of color discrimination.

A hotel cleaner from the Dominican Republic, Margarita insists that when Latinos are treated badly in the U.S. it is "not because of skin color. I think it's more because of customs." Americans classify her race from her Spanish language, her Dominican dress and habits, she claims. And when they refuse to let her enter the upscale building where she works as a home aide, this is what they

---

[13] A "tigre" refers to someone who is tough, streetwise, macho. One respondent translates it as "thug." A colloquial English equivalent of how Marco uses the expression here might be a "bad-ass."

notice, not whether she looks White or Black. Marisela, a brown-skinned Dominican, insists that Latinos' skin color does not matter to Americans: "If you are Hispanic, you are Hispanic. You will always be Hispanic for the Whites."

Discrimination on the basis of Hispanic origin is more palatable to migrants than color discrimination. It is less of a reminder of one's African roots per se, something which is stigmatized in their home culture, and more of a reminder of the cultural and racial mixture of Spanish, African, and Indian people in the Latin American identity—something in which migrants take considerable pride. This type of discrimination can therefore be blamed more easily on the injustices of the receiving society and not on migrants' own shortcomings. Regardless of their own skin color, most Puerto Rican and Dominican migrants with working-class occupations say that color discrimination does not exist, even if ethnic discrimination against Latinos is prevalent.

As migrants enter the middle class, however, they become more aware of the way that their skin color matters in mainstream institutions in addition to their ethnicity. In contrast to those with less education, Puerto Rican and Dominican migrants with a college degree almost unanimously assert that skin color affects Latinos' opportunities in the U.S. Professional migrants report the most instances of color discrimination in shops and restaurants, partly because their middle-class status brings them to upmarket establishments where they feel that color is a particular issue. Those with dark skin also report the most workplace discrimination and those with light skin the least. Among college-educated migrants, 75% of those with dark skin reported workplace discrimination, compared with 63% of those with medium skin, and 50% of those with light skin. Although not representative of a larger population, this pattern is noteworthy because it occurs in a context where one's ethnicity is known by colleagues and employers. In the professional world, being Latino may affect your opportunities, but color adds an extra layer of barriers to confront.

Middle-class respondents observe in the social circles around them how dark-skinned Latinos often fare the worst.

With his medium-light skin, Hugo avoids many forms of racial bias. Yet he notices how his wife, whom he describes as *negra*, receives the brunt of it when they enter a high-end establishment. He personally has never received worse service than other clients in a shop, he claims,

> ...but my wife has...We went into a jewelry store and my wife wanted to see a watch and the Indian guy didn't really want to. He thought that if he gave us the watch we were going to run away with the watch. And the guy was real nasty. My wife got very offended and she cursed him out. (Hugo, Puerto Rican migrant, Information Technologies Manager)

Professional migrants also observe the dynamics of the work world around them. For instance, Angela, who works in the financial world and socializes with many other professional Dominicans, suspects that skin color must play some role in who ends up in this high-status group:

> As I see it, by my experience, all of this environment where I function professionally,
> I think that there are a few morenos and everybody is blanco. I don't know, but there
> has to be something there...Of 50 Dominican people that I know, that three are
> moreno. (Angela, Dominican migrant, investment banker)

It may partly be due to their social class backgrounds, Angela posits, but she
also recognizes the advantage of looking White.

As Filomena, a lawyer with light skin, notes, "When you get here, to the
United States, you are Hispanic. But if you are a dark Hispanic, you're doubly
stereotyped."

Light-skinned Latinos are more accepted socially, professional migrants
maintain. Racism is partly visual, and thus even when someone's Latino ethnicity is known, it may not matter as much if she looks White. Rafaela, an
accountant who looks Black by U.S. standards, notes:

> Wanda is my friend that works with the Italians. And she's light-skinned and has
> straight hair. She would easily pass as a White American person. And I don't know,
> I think that at least Italians, they pay attention a lot to the physical appearance and
> those things. Maybe, with them, she'd have more advantage. I've never seen a *negro*
> employed by Italians. (Rafaela, Dominican migrant, accountant)

Latinos who appear White are better able to blend in with the mainstream
population in situations where it is advantageous for them to do so:

Raquel, who has light skin and mixed facial features, believes there is a
difference between how Latinos with light skin and dark skin fare socially and
economically in the U.S.:

> I think that there is a difference because, in this country, even though there
> are a lot of opportunities...I think that if you are Hispanic and you lean
> more towards your European ancestry, you are more accepted, the possibi-
> lities are better, etc. There is a guy who went to college with me. He's a
> reporter on channel 41. I remember when I saw him walking through the
> campus I'd say 'He is so cute!' (laughing) And I never knew he was Hispanic.
> I never heard him speak in Spanish, until a lot later, maybe, in the last year of
> school, [I asked him, 'David,] are you Hispanic?' He said, 'Yes. I'm
> Peruvian.' 'And why don't you ever speak Spanish?' 'Oh, no, because there's
> no necessity. Why?' So if you look more like the mass of Whites, sometimes
> you mix in and shut up and, if you don't have the accent in English, there's no
> necessity to say. Well, I think so.
>
> Q: *But for the people of dark skin it isn't the same?*
>
> No, because if you [look] Hispanic or Black and that's it. And you're in the
> other mass. (Raquel, Dominican migrant, assistant principal)

Others note that those with light skin have more residential options and can
move into White neighborhoods, an observation supported by studies on a
larger scale (Denton & Massey 1989, South et al. 2005).

Respondents who look Caucasian describe less discrimination and feel more
accepted in U.S. society. Even they are not completely free from the burden of

the Latino stereotype, but they have tools to confront it. Signals of their Latino origin may still trigger negative responses from others.

César, who looks European, notes that his infrequent experiences with discrimination or hostile treatment usually revolve around his surname or his accent.

> I've never felt that much prejudice. Of course there is some when I send a resumé and they see my last name. I have many qualifications, and sometimes I feel that just because of my last name there's an issue. It's the name of any Latino and they think it's something bad. It's because of the stereotype. (César, Puerto Rican migrant, film producer)

Normally, security guards pay him no mind when César enters a shop; however, if he enters while speaking Spanish on his cell phone, he notices guards paying him more attention. But where darker migrants evoke the same reactions, César is better able to combat them. If he is applying for a job, he likes to stop in so they can put a face to a name. When employers see that he looks like any other middle-class White person, the stereotypes of Latinos that his surname evokes frequently disappear. His appearance helps him get his foot in the door.

> Sometimes Americans don't know where I'm from and I feel like they're more open to me until I tell them...When the theme comes up of where I come from, I establish a relationship with the person. They say, "Oh wow, that's interesting" and there's no change. But that's once I establish the relationship. (César, Puerto Rican migrant, film producer).

His friends who "have the Hispanic look" have more trouble getting to the point where they can establish a relationship and illustrate what they have to offer as an individual, not a member of an ethnic group.

Those who attend college in the U.S. or who enter the professional workforce are much more likely to have meaningful contact with non-Latinos and mainstream and elite institutions than those at the lower end of the socioeconomic spectrum. In many professional contexts, being Latino can be an advantage, whether employers are motivated by diversity goals or seek to attract a Latino clientele. But the color of one's skin can also limit who gets to be a part of the 'in-crowd' in these institutions.

Conclusion

Perspectives on color discrimination never occur within a social vacuum, but all too often immigrant populations' experiences are examined as if they began on the point of entering a new society. Latino migrants bring with them to the U.S. an incredible wealth of culture and history, and along with it they import a cultural reluctance to interpret situations as motivated by color discrimination. While it is important to understand the cultural context from which migrants arrive, these constructs are also mediated in the receiving society. Migrants' structural position within class hierarchies influences their attitudes toward color discrimination, with those toward the top of the hierarchy becoming most aware of the barriers color creates in the professional world.

An interpretive approach to Puerto Ricans' and Dominicans' subjective experiences with color discrimination helps to illuminate the meaning behind the lower levels of discrimination that Latinos report in national surveys. These Latinos' reluctance to view themselves as targets of colorism offers an explanation to the disparity between socioeconomic analyses that uncover phenotype discrimination against Latinos and their own self-reports of discrimination experiences. At the same time, this investigation reveals how social class influences the likelihood of perceiving color discrimination. Many studies of reported discrimination among African Americans and Latinos focus on working class, less educated, and lower income populations (Krieger et al. 2005, Stuber et al. 2003, Yen et al. 1999). To obtain a more accurate picture of the complexity of Latinos' experiences with discrimination, a wider population with greater class diversity needs to be examined in this literature.

Under conditions of rapid globalization, fostered by heavy migration streams, some cultural perspectives and analytical constructs permeate the traditional fabric of foreign societies. In Puerto Ricans' and Dominicans' concepts of racism and discrimination, we see how cultural exchange works in both directions. Migrants transport their home country's culture to a new receiving society, and non-migrants' views are changed by interpersonal contact with their friends and relatives abroad as well as larger institutional and political structures. Although there are many reasons to protect traditional cultures from the threats of globalization, the capacity of an international exchange of ideas to identify and contest forms of racial injustice wherever they may be is one potential outcome to be valued.

References

Arce, C., Murguia, E., & Frisbie, W. (1987). Phenotype and life chances among Chicanos. *Hispanic Journal of Behavioral Sciences, 9*, 19–32.

Baud, M. (1996). 'Constitutionally White': The forging of a national identity in the Dominican Republic. In G. Oostindie (Ed.), *Ethnicity in the Caribbean: Essays in honor of Harry Hoetink*, (Pp. 121–151). London: Macmillan Education Ltd.

Blanco, T. (1942). *El prejuicio racial en Puerto Rico*. San Juan, PR: Biblioteca de Autores Puertorriqueños.

Bobo, L., Kluegel, J., & Smith, R. (1997). Laissez-faire racism: The crystallization of kinder, gentler, anti-Black ideology. In S. A. Tuch and J. K. Marin (Eds.), *Racial attitudes in the 1990 s: Continuity and change* (Pp. 15–41). Greenwood, CT: Praeger.

Degler, C. (1971). *Neither Black nor White: Slavery and race relations in Brazil and the United States*. New York: Macmillan.

Denton, N., & Massey, D. (1989). Racial identity among Caribbean Hispanics: The effect of double minority status on residential segregation. *American Sociological Review. 54*, 790–808.

Duany, J. (2002). *The Puerto Rican nation on the move: Identities on the island and in the United States*. Chapel Hill, NC: University of North Carolina Press.

Espino, R., & Franz, M. (2002). Latino phenotypic discrimination revisited: The impact of skin color on occupational status. *Social Science Quarterly*, 83, 612–623.

Gómez, C. (2000). The continual significance of skin color: An exploratory study of Latinos in the northeast. *Hispanic Journal of Behavioral Sciences*, 22, 94–103.

Hall, R. (2000). A descriptive analysis of skin color bias in Puerto Rico: Ecological applications to practice. *Journal of Sociology and Social Welfare*, XXVII, 171–183.

Hochschild, J., & Weaver, V. (2003). From race to color: Does skin color hierarchy transform racial classification? Paper presented at The Color Lines Conference, 30 August -1 September 2003, Cambridge, MA.

Hoetink, H. (1967). *The two variants of Caribbean race relations: A contribution to the sociology of segmented societies*. London: Oxford University Press.

Howard, D. (2001). *Coloring the nation: Race and ethnicity in the Dominican Republic*. Oxford, UK: Signal Books.

Jimenez Román, M. (1996). Un hombre (Negro) del pueblo: José Celso Barbosa and the Puerto Rican "race" toward Whiteness. *CENTRO: Journal of the Center for Puerto Rican Studies*, 8, 9–29.

Kinder, D., & Sears, D. (1981). Prejudice and politics: Symbolic racism versus racial threats to the good life. *Journal of Personality and Social Psychology*, 40, 414–431.

Kinsbruner, J. (1996). *Not of pure blood: The free people of color and racial prejudice in nineteenth-century Puerto Rico*. Durham, NC: Duke University Press.

Krieger, N., Smith, K., Naishadham, D., Hartman, C., &. Barbeau, E. M. (2005). Experiences of discrimination: Validity and reliability of a self-report measure for population health research on racism and health. *Social Science & Medicine*, 61, 1576–1596.

Mejía Ricart, M. A. (1953). Las clases sociales en Santo Domingo. Ciudad Trujillo, Dominican Republic: Libreria Dominicana.

Menéndez Alarcón, A. V. (1994). Racial prejudice: A Latin American case. *Research in Race and Ethnic Relations*, 7, 299–319.

Murguia, E., & Telles, E. (1996). Phenotype and schooling among Mexican Americans. *Sociology of Education*, 69, 276–289.

Pettigrew, T. (1982). Prejudice. In S. Thernstrom, A.Orlov, and O. Handlin (Eds.), *Dimensions of ethnicity. A series of selections from the Harvard Encyclopedia of American ethnic groups* (Pp. 1–29). Cambridge, MA: Harvard University Press.

Relethford, J., Stern, M. P., Gaskill, S., & Hazuda, H. (1983). Social class, admixture, and skin color variation in Mexican-Americans and Anglo-Americans living in San Antonio, Texas. *American Journal of Physical Anthropology*, 61, 97–102.

Rivera-Batiz, F. (2004). Color in the tropics: Race and economic outcomes in the island of Puerto Rico. Unpublished paper. New York: Teacher's College, Columbia University.

Rodríguez, C., & Cordero-Guzman, H. (1992). Placing race in context. *Ethnic and Racial Studies*, 15, 523–542.

Rodríguez, C., Castro, A., Garcia, O., & Torres, A. (1991). Latino racial identity: In the eye of the beholder? *Latino Studies Journal*, 2, 33–48.

Roth, W. (2006). Caribbean race and American dreams: How migration shapes Dominicans' and Puerto Ricans' racial identities and its impact on socioeconomic mobility. Ph.D. Dissertation. Cambridge, MA: Harvard University.

Sidanius, J., Peña, Y., & Sawyer, M. (2001). Inclusionary discrimination: Pigmentocracy and patriotism in the Dominican Republic. *Political Psychology*, 22, 827–851.

South, S., Crowder, K., & Chavez, E. (2005). Migration and spatial assimilation among U.S. Latinos: Classical versus segmented trajectories. *Demography*, 42, 497–521.

Stuber, J., Galea, S., Ahern, J., Blaney, S., & Fuller, C. (2003). The association between multiple domains of discrimination and self-assessed health: A multilevel analysis of

Latinos and Blacks in four low-income New York City neighborhoods. *Health Service Research*, 38, 1735–1759.

Tannenbaum, F. (1946). *Slave and citizen: The Negro in the Americas*. New York: Vintage Books.

Telles, E., & Murguia, E. (1990). Phenotypic discrimination and income differences among Mexican Americans. *Social Science Quarterly*, 71, 682–696.

Torres-Saillant, S. (1998). The tribulations of Blackness: Stages in Dominican racial identity. *Latin American Perspectives*, 25, 126–146.

———. (1999). *Introduction to Dominican Blackness*. New York: CUNY Dominican Studies Institute, City College of New York.

Tumin, M., & Feldman, A. (1971). *Social class and social change in Puerto Rico*. Indianapolis, IN: The Bobbs-Merrill Company.

Wade, P. (1997). *Race and ethnicity in Latin America*. Chicago, IL: Pluto Press.

Whitten, N., & Torres, A. (1998). *Blackness in Latin America and the Caribbean: social dynamics and cultural transformations*. Bloomington, IN: Indiana University Press.

Yen, I., Ragland, D., Greiner, B., & Fisher, J. (1999). Racial discrimination and alcohol-related behavior in urban transit operators: Findings from the San Francisco Muni Health and Safety Study. *Public Health Reports*, 114, 448–458.

Chapter 13
Conclusion

Ronald E. Hall

Abstract The historical impact of colonization has predisposed post-colonial people of color to the internalization of Western skin color ideals. Overtly motivated by post-colonials and covertly condoned by people of color, racism via skin color is an unspoken factor in the various confrontations encountered by people of color with social institutions. Their color also correlates with a lack of economic and political power, apparent in post-colonized nations where the West has had considerable impact in establishing the genesis of light skin as the ideal of superiority. The manifestation of racism in the 21st century via the idealization of light skin is relevant to people of color who migrate West, for as members of outgroups they are confronted by the need to assimilate. Motivated by assimilation, some among people of color exhibit a willingness to tolerate the racist denigration of dark skin that has enabled the Bleaching Syndrome (Hall 1995). The Bleaching Syndrome is a complex of behaviors that could ultimately lead to the complete disappearance of all but Western ideals. Science has already seen technology end the tyranny of repetitive labor. The West has led the world in charting the course of mankind in a new direction and along the course of this new direction will come the human effort to reorganize social life, to reinvent the family, and to liberate dark-skinned peoples from the tyranny of their universal denigration. Unfortunately, absent this effort, skin color among people of color will prevail as a manifestation of racism well into the 21st century.

Vision as a Social Sense, and Skin Color Idealization

The ability of man to see his physical environment allowed for the evolution of an acute sense of vision. That sense of vision has also proven socially potent in how we perceive and assess others the basis of skin color. Other means such as touch and sounds that allow mankind to further perceive and assess the

R.E. Hall
School of Social Work, Michigan State University, East Lansing, MI, USA
e-mail: hallr@msu.edu

R.E. Hall (ed.), *Racism in the 21st Century*, DOI: 10.1007/978-0-387-79097-8_13,   235 members of its population merely serve to enhance the breadth and depth of this evolved sense of vision. For lower species of animals, the ability to see enables hunting and survival skills, as the social is less potent. Therefore it is difficult to accurately determine the role of animal-to-animal assessments among such lower species. However, it also is safe to assume that some form of assessment does exist among lower species, geared to the ability of lower animals to reproduce and, in so doing, enable the continuation and betterment of its kind.

For human beings, the ability to see serves more than survival skills and is much more complex because sight serves a social function beyond what might be required for survival. We, as humans, also utilize sight in the perpetuation and acting out of values, norms, ideals, and other phenomena in our social environment. As it pertains to racism in the 21st century, light skin color among all humanity, in particular people of color, has enabled a status hierarchy whereby those who are light-skinned and/or closest in proximity to the Western ideal are perceived as more worthy in the categories of life that matter. Thus, the ability to see, more than any other sense, has allowed for the idealization of light skin in this post-colonial era and is indicative of a new, unprecedented variant of racism. As a result, those humans who are characterized by the alternative dark skin are stigmatized via our sense of vision as inferior and otherwise undesirable. For dark-skinned people of color, the desire to be perceived as worthy or otherwise equal may ultimately become a near impossible aspiration in the aftermath of continued racism. That is because, in the shadows of Western colonization, light skin has replaced the white race category, evolving as the most desirable trait to have in a white Western society. Light skin, being the trait of colonials, consequently defined dark skin as the most undesirable, and thus the trait of the lowly colonized "other." Light skin color served as a vehicle of post-colonization and differentiation between the powerful and the powerless, which in the context of quality of life became significant. Without the necessity for *du jour* applications, light skin connoted the superior and dark skin the inferior. Furthermore, light skin color, being endemic to the more powerful West, evolved as the status ideal and basis of its social hierarchy, not irrelevant between and among people of color. Dark skin, in contrast to light skin, provided the means to extend a continued form of colonization in which the prevailing domination of the West could be maintained by a less violent but equally effective course of action. The difference in the 21st century is that victims may now contribute to the perpetuation of racism in concert with their post-colonial superiors.

The historical impact of racism has predisposed post-colonial, people of color to the internalization of Western skin color ideals. Logically, their common experience with skin color discrimination would have otherwise fostered a sense of solidarity with other oppressed populations, including poor whites and others. However, under the circumstances, for people of color the potential solidarity was disrupted. That interruption is extended from the fact that among all people of color, colonization remains a significant force of their continued oppression. Such tenacious oppression then encouraged their indiscriminate application of Western ideals with little consideration for the personal and societal outcomes. The uppermost in status became those whose color approximated that of the mainstream power structure assuming them to be not only superior but having other quality of life traits, such as attractiveness, intelligence, and moral grounding. In an effort to circumvent humiliation, people of color accommodated this self-denigration by their idealizing light skin. In the aftermath, their own oppression was enabled, which the Western-Eurocentric power structure welcomed enthusiastically. The result, enabled by people of color, is reflected in job discrimination, beauty standards, marital patterns, the Bleaching Syndrome (Hall 1995), and various other forms of societal domination.

Reconceptualizing Racism

People of all colors and racial types have some idea of what racism is and how it is manifested socially, politically, and economically in the world today. They understand that it is both covert and overt, acted out by individuals and within the institutions they control. That thought consistently conjures an image of dark-skinned people being denigrated in various ways due to their lack of idealized skin color traits. As a point of historical fact, such suffering cannot be denied. However, current trends in marriage during an era of increased worldwide migration necessitate a completely different strategy for conceptualizing racism in this the new 21st century. Although Western racism or some other form of colonial oppression will persist in essence into the foreseeable future, the West, by virtue of increasing migration and racial intermarriage, must begin to conceptualize racism in a less overt and less racial context. The objective of such a notion is an attempt to inform the 21st century generation in particular about the implications of skin color as it relates to their current and future quality of life. The aim is to facilitate an active dialogue and enable the ability of humanity in general to incorporate a new perspective that will accommodate recent shifts in the Western population. The subject of the conversation must begin to account for colonial crimes against humanity and not just colonial victims. That is because unlike most of the literature to date, racism in the 21st century will not be as localized—as was true of the antebellum South—but will extend to incorporate a role to be played by people of color. Thus the conversations about racism in the 21st century will address the descendents of Africans, Asians, Native-Americans, and Latinos who have all been enslaved, conquered, colonized, or otherwise dominated by white colonials.

Outdated conversations about the concept of racism more often characterized it as some malicious, intentional overt act by groups or individuals. In fact, as racism occurs in the post-colonial era, this is a half-truth. The more covert and seemingly harmless acts can be the most devastating, in perceptions of superiority or inferiority. For example, a number of countries throughout the world believe that the more European a woman looks the more beautiful and refined she is apt to be; some beauty contest judges, regardless of their race—which would include people of color—believe light skin and femininity go hand-in-hand and should be the sole criterion for determining who is beautiful and who is not. Such judges may not intend to stigmatize dark skin, but, when their beliefs result in the exclusion of certain segments of the worldwide feminine population who are darker-skinned, these beliefs qualify as an act of racism. If there is any doubt about this contention, a quick review of all Miss Universe contestants will dispel any such doubts. Thus, contrary to the belief of many, the racist intent to stigmatize is not always a precondition of overt racist acts. In fact, unintended acts are similar to flooding waters that spill out with unthinking, unfeeling movement. Much like flooding water, those who take part in post-colonial, 21st-century racism cannot easily be held accountable for their actions. Their impersonal objectivity is responsible for our tolerating some of the most generic examples of racism known in recent times. In order to comprehend the extent of the problem, people of color and white Americans—together—must understand that the dynamics of every major institution in the West operate on the basis that some degree of color stigmatization and racism is acceptable. Whether or not it is rhetorically acceptable, it is at least expected and considered unavoidable. For example, the Miss Universe contest outcomes have shown that dark-skinned women of color are less likely to reach the final competition. The norms and ideals of institutions, including those that define feminine beauty are, in effect, standards for all the people. They are the expectations that tell an individual what is required under the appropriate circumstances. When he/she starts challenging norms or aspiring beyond his/her designated role, the person is punished or otherwise denigrated by the appropriate power structure. That power structure has engaged numerous efforts pertaining to the racist stigmatization of dark skin, which explains the circumstances of dark-skinned women of color who are considered to be ugly by all Western standards.

Racism and the Reality of Having Light or Dark Skin

Before Western influence, evidence was lacking that the various groups of color intended to stigmatize and/or colonize one another, on the basis of race category, although there was and continues to be competition and some prior sensitivity to skin color. However, after having migrated West in the current era, there is evidence among some groups of a change in attitude. The most potent problem for people of color in the post-colonization era has perpetuated a status hierarchy that is based on their ability to idealize light skin. The emergence of international commercial interests selling bleaching creams increased their penchant for light skin, as noted by the popularity of mestizo or mestizo-looking children. Had this not occurred, inevitably, a hierarchy might still exist. However, prejudice and color variation, indicative of Western life in general, means that the variation within any other group, given their identity strength, is susceptible to intragroup tension, i.e.: racism in the 21st century. In the midst of tension, light-skinned people of color are no less loyal to their ethnic roots, but are regarded somewhat different at home and abroad. This does not infer that life for them is bliss, but there is some advantage to having light skin in a world where light skin is valued and idealized. Sometimes it may cause difficulty; it may reinforce hierarchies as it has done during both the colonial and the post-colonial era. The results push some to a marginal status that encourages additional problems within the group based on color. Thus, people of color of the various hues may guard feelings toward one another during social activities. Those within their community play a role in this hierarchy, but the lighter-skinned are less stigmatized in society because they are endowed with attributes that are complimentary and less offensive to it. As a result, light-skinned people of color may make their way with relative ease in white social circles, even those of the most conservative and class conscious of the mainstream, while the same ability for their darker-skinned counterparts is all but impossible regardless of their class, education, or social distinction.

Considering the influence of colonization and the implication for racism and to suggest special provisions to alleviate the outcome is ill advised. It is true that colonial conditions are pathological for a disproportionate number of those people of color who are characterized by dark skin, but the situation will not improve by assigning them to some privileged societal status. Dark-skinned people of color are obviously not inferior as would be implied by the idealization of light skin. Thus, it is plausible that much of the problem extends from the fact that the larger society including people of color tolerates its own bias. The larger society has also decided that there is no need to celebrate dark-skinned beauty; it has chosen instead to believe that the predominance of all manner of superiority is grounded among those who have light skin. It matters little in the 21st century whether light skin is by race category or miscegenation. In other words, much of the racism against dark skin is no longer overt and/or overtly racist, since Western colonization ended long ago.

Aside from the racism that has occurred in the U.S. the stigmatization of dark skin has also had a devastating impact worldwide. Directly motivated by post-colonial whites and covertly condoned by people of color, racism via skin color is an unspoken factor in the various confrontations encountered by people of color with societal social institutions. Their color also continues to correlate with a lack of economic and political power, apparent in post-colonized nations where the West has had considerable impact in establishing the genesis of light skin as the ideal of superiority all over the world.

Exclusion and Skin Color

By virtue of actions, the idealization of light skin, like racism, is ultimately intolerable because it facilitates the efforts of a dominant group to exclude a dominated group from sharing in the material and symbolic rewards of status and power. It differs from other forms of exclusion in that qualification is contingent on observable and assumed physiological traits. Such traits imply the inherent superiority hence idealization of power groups, which are then rationalized as a natural order of the ideal human universe. The most zealous proponents for the idealization of light skin contend that lighter-skinned people are preferred by all, being superior to darker-skinned people as a matter of fact. In almost every known region, it has been postulated that humans who are light in color, regardless of race as in years past, have been uniquely endowed with the capacities necessary to reach the zenith of civilization. This so-called trek to the zenith of civilization was initially a thinly veiled form of color bias, devoted to justifying post-colonial influence. By way of racism, the post-colonial era was set in motion and left no domain of the human environment untouched. The result has necessitated a universal, almost mystic, worldwide belief in the superiority of light skin.

Much of the literature now characterizes the institutionalization of light skin in a manner that is construed as beneficial to all light-skinned people, regardless of race or other group membership. Nothing could be further from the truth. Light-skinned people of color are in some ways just as victimized, psychologically, by the post-colonial hierarchy as are those who are dark-skinned. Unfortunately, dark-skinned people of color have always harbored a distrust of others, based on the idealization of light skin. No doubt, they have suffered greater stings of prejudice because their skin happens to be a potent contrast to the assumed superior race ideal. However, what everyone must realize is that light-skinned people of color are merely pawns in the process. To vent frustration on such members of any group encourages group demise. It may manifest as a host of social difficulties whose origins seem so elusive, but yet so very potent.

Assimilation and Idealized Skin Color

The manifestation of racism in the 21st century via the idealization of light skin is continually relevant to people of color who migrate West, for as members of outgroups they are confronted by the need to assimilate. Assimilation is not apart from the social problems among people of color, in toto. All people of color, both dark and light, male and female, want to succeed. From the brightest to the slowest of wit, regardless of skin color, all human beings desire success in life based on valuing themselves and the goals they want to attain. When legitimate avenues to success are cut off, people will resort to illegitimate and even harmful means. When avenues are cut off completely, people will seek escape from reality. Those who do not personally experience this pessimism will be completely baffled when trying to understand the self-destructive activities of others who may idealize light skin at their own expense. To some extent, all people of color who have migrated to the West have had legitimate avenues to success cut off by the racist stigma that is associated with their relatively dark skin; they have had to destroy a little of themselves to realize their goals. As a result, people of color in particular are being denied success by the obstacles of a skin color hierarchy. More and more, those who wear the label "Third world," are encountering difficulties vis-à-vis post-colonization in their attempts to assimilate both at home and abroad.

Some in the assimilated mainstream would probably be astonished to know that people of color idealize one another on the basis of having light skin. The time and effort invested by them to do away with discrimination might somehow make them appear less given to practices against which they have rallied. However, the idealization of light skin is a post-colonial issue that is deeply rooted and complex. It is so institutionalized throughout the world via Western influence that it is widely accepted that any person of color who has migrated is affected by it. To some extent, those who settle in the West give in to it once they arrive, regardless of their previous cultural experience or skin color. Thus, the largely Latino population in the state of Nevada could never have supported a Black man—such as Barack Obama—for president because his election would conflict with their forced and internalized colonial ideals. Only the non-colonized, such as post-colonial whites in the state of Iowa, can be free to assess the potential of a Black man to be president of the United States, because it is they who are among the group that set the standards.

For Latinos and other people of color, the idealization of light skin has a long and established history. Contributing to their manifestation of racism is the fact that for decades Europe has been portrayed as the ultimate social phenomenon. It has become a psychosocial objective directed at people of color—particularly the dark-skinned. There should be no doubt as to the accuracy of this assumption. Notwithstanding, to then characterize colonization in a narrow Western context does a disservice to the scientific method. It enables the otherwise absurd rhetoric of hierarchy within a single species, and, in fact, provides a conduit for the continued social, economic, and political domination of dark-skinned people regardless of race. However, deserving of sympathy, analyzing the role of people of color in the event of racism is a necessity. Hence, never previously suggested, it is imperative to analyze the role played by both them and other victims in the stigmatization of dark skin, if this stigma is ever to be overcome. While it is no doubt politically incorrect to cite victims or stray from the Western perpetrator model, avoidance of discussing other forms of racism would be tantamount to fraud. The role of people of color in the perpetuation of racism and Western ideals is one of the fundamental dynamics of oppression in the post-colonial, 21st-century era.

The Bleaching Syndrome

Among some people of color, the willingness to tolerate the racist denigration of dark skin has enabled the Bleaching Syndrome (Hall 1995). The Bleaching Syndrome is much more than a tendency toward light skin. It is a complex of behaviors that could ultimately lead to the complete disappearance of anything other than Western ideals. The Bleaching Syndrome is not peculiar to any one population, but is a worldwide matter of fact for all people of color. Universally, they have been either directly or indirectly influenced by colonial interests to bring about the same outcomes. Consequently, some among light-skinned people of color have been less stigmatized by their color through no fault of their own. The Bleaching Syndrome has evolved because these same members constantly have their group loyalties challenged and, more importantly, because light-skinned people of color have had more success in the post-colonial era. That would include not only skin color but the entire universe of social phenomena. In fact, of all the manifestations of the Bleaching Syndrome, the physical aspect of skin color is without a doubt the least important. Gene pools will alter skin color over time, given the effects of politics, geography, and economics. What people of color are or ultimately become is based solely on their strength of identity. Their ability to survive is inherent in their ability to revere who they are. If they cannot do this, little else matters.

Although the Bleaching Syndrome is a phenomenon for all people of color, its origin is obviously within the dominant Western culture, as the Third World manifestation of racism extended from Western psychological difficulty. For those people of color who migrate, however, the origin of the problem is irrelevant. Given the power differential, they cannot be concerned with solving their problems from the mainstream end. What is within their control is their community and what they think of themselves. They must be committed to community and self-image in eliminating the damage caused by the denigration of dark skin and other post-colonial influences.

Empowerment

One way to surely eliminate the Bleaching Syndrome and reduce psychological trauma is, for social scientists of color and other intellectuals to put more of their professional and personal energies into the empowerment of dark-skinned people, irrespective of race. The American Black Consciousness movement of the 1960 s was an effective strategy for African-Americans that inspired Latinos and others to become activists. It spurred the development of ethnic consciousness. By the 1970 s, as more dark-skinned people became activists, they began to realize just how far-reaching colonial influences could be. Some became pessimistic and disillusioned with the prospect of overcoming such a formidable obstacle. However, the real solution to the problem may exist above the fray.

As optimism begins to permeate the ranks of African, Latino, and sympathetic white Westerners, their consciousnesses may be both raised and united by a "multicultural" perspective. They may then pool their talents and resources to solve the denigration of dark skin, thus creating an equally formidable force to confront racist colonial residue. As a social threat to the status quo, this will undoubtedly cause some polarization. However, the "multicultural" effort is the only civil and moral alternative that is available within the emerging world-wide community. People of color who are ready must wage the struggle imme-diately and wholeheartedly, without reservation. Effective efforts in the form of political activism, product boycotts, and housing regulations could serve as a viable means of inspiring the West and the world it impacts. Indeed, the opposition will be rendered helpless as long as the struggle can be managed in a moral context that is commensurate with a universal code of ethics.

Under post-colonial influence, there is no single cure-all for the Bleaching Syndrome. It cannot be alleviated by governmental programs funded by tax dollars. What will eventually alleviate the Syndrome begins with the acknowl-edgement of its existence. That acknowledgement must come from both the dominant light-skinned and dominated darker-skinned population. Further-more, on the part of both light- and dark-skinned people of color, a will must manifest to internally value self and identity, as opposed to some externally derived ideals. Above all, a movement must eventually come about that will redefine the implications of dark skin color, not only in America and elsewhere in the West but in an increasingly diverse global community as well.

A New Rhetoric for Social Evolution

Ultimately to its credit, the West has begun to set rhetorical standards to enable harmony among the various skin color factions of the world. Perhaps more than any other civilization, the West encompasses a rich mixture of hues, languages, and religious philosophies. Unfortunately, what is to its credit has also caused problems. Increased diversity has led to competition among various groups for the control of resources. Different languages and religions, especially given recent migration to America, contribute to the competition, but the color of skin is by far the focal point. In an effort to control resources in their best interest, lighter-skinned groups have thus dominated the world to their benefit and that of their race, i.e.: skin color cohorts, which includes a light-skinned, non-European faction. Needless to say, the implications of skin color among people of color are a microcosm of Western civilization. Where descendants of the colonial mainstream could have afforded to be indifferent regarding the attitudes of people of color, people of color most of all cannot. Their existence is, in effect, one among many of the poor, less powerful peoples that is subjected to accusations of cultural inferiority suggested by their having dark skin. To enable quality of life and provide a better future for themselves and their families, people of color—if they are to remain viable—must join with others to redress the characterization of dark skin in a more positive and self-conducive context. Since their migration to the West, this has been all but an impossible task. The difficulty has been facilitated by the power imbalance between the two color opposites: the presence of color versus the absence of color. Human efforts to expose the intolerant mainstream and support the more tolerant alternative to unite for a new colorless world order would be of considerable significance.

Unfortunately, being dark-skinned in Western societies equates with the label "people of color." Being a person of color associates all persons so characterized with inferiority, denigration, and other obstacles to the quality of life that are not encountered by members of Eurocentric groups. In this context, skin color discrimination appears secondary to racism, given that people of color are not in a position to equal the social devastations brought by more powerful global Western forces. However, skin color discrimination, as a manifestation of 21st-century racism, is a "flip side" of white supremacy. Racist denigration of dark-skinned people, by people of color themselves, is as ignorant and unethical as racist denigration by the white Western mainstream. In the aftermath, people of color discriminate against persons with dark skin for the same reasons white Western racist populations discriminate against people of color: both have been convinced by racist ideology that certain capacities are limited by race genetics. Thus, the disparities between the West and other groups cannot only be rationalized but can be, in Western parlance, justified.

In this new 21st century, millennial moment of endings, not only are the implications of skin color being bandied about but, indeed, the entire world is poised for universal transformation. In the new millennium, an official end to racism and discrimination by race, gender, and similar such categories will come. Antiquated notions of race, as a biological concept, are becoming extinct with alarming rapidity. The ceaseless exploitation of social and political polarization has rendered race to be little more than a gigantic storehouse of raw emotion, destined for the archives of both real and imaginary colonial political objectives. With this understanding, it is now possible for people of color and Whites to begin the work of rewriting and redefining what is ideal and how selected ideals will impact the future of humanity. The antiquated notion of race as a biological concept has come to an end in the sense that miscegenation in the new millennium will continue to be universal. That fact is apparent, given that the relationship between phenotype and so-called race is changing drastically for Eurasians, Afrasians, and others. It is an interesting social evolution between the emerging importance of skin color and the waning significance of race. This Western influence has caused the world's varied population to be engaged in an unprecedented era of social evolution. In the current new era they are, in fact, the agents of social evolution. Thus, social science, as is presently organized, is losing its ability to assess this evolution, being obliged to serve, instead, the whims of an intellectual power structure that is driven by intellectual forces it cannot fully comprehend.

The 21st century is uniquely unprecedented in that it will witness the increasing miscegenation of mankind. The standard association of superiority with "race" will continue to decline until it is defunct. Accordingly, a new concept of humanity will emerge, one in which skin color will hopefully be less and less significant. Thus, the assumption that superiority is contingent on race or implied by skin color will be diminished as an obstacle to universal human growth and self-esteem. Subsequently, the end of race as the standard of Western ideals is evident in the growth of litigation brought on the basis of skin color in U.S. District Courts, such as *Walker v. the IRS* (1990). Furthermore, the influence of skin color over race is validated by various skin color studies including those contained in this volume that have been conducted by scholars who are sensitive to current trends. Their scientific method also forces Western society to correct itself. It raises the possibility of realistically and permanently changing the prescripts of human worth. Undoubtedly, if it can be done, it will be done.

Thus, the end of the 20th century is actually the beginning of a new era in the perception of humankind. The various modes of celebration enable the populous in preparation for what may be coming. Not long ago, the West had little idea of how radically its fundamental ideas about civilization would be overturned. In fact, given the new velocity of Western migration, it is logical to expect changes to be proportionately radical. It then goes without saying that such expectation is not mere speculation. However, at a critical point in history, which is yet to arrive, the new millennium will reveal a basis for such speculation. It will be rationalized in the utilization of two social science events that will manifest as megatrends: color miscegenation and intellectual miscegenation.

Megatrends

Heretofore, color miscegenation has been the primary megatrend. It would appear illogical on the surface. This is because the first and most fundamental objective of every living creature, even to the lowest primate, is to conserve its being. That notion extends to the cultural mindset of all in the Western and world populations. However, the strength of such a drive cannot be stated with any degree of certainty. Notwithstanding, perhaps the fundamental idealizations of light skin are not written in stone, but they are cultural habits that may be broken, in the spasms of intellectual debate, and then transcended. Accordingly, past notions about light skin have defined human worth, leading to a death extended from our moral lapses and a crime against humankind. However, science and biology, in fact, would suggest otherwise. Taken in the biological context, the freedom to engage in color miscegenation is a megatrend that is justifiable on both moral and biological grounds. The antebellum assumption of colonialists illuminates the point of how far power structures, with their collective obsessions, are prepared to go to dominate the mass mind-set, by presuming to affect the universal characteristics of human worth.

Among the most radical changes in the 21st century millennium is also the intellectual megatrend that no one color group will actually dominate human-ity—indeed, light skin as an ideal will cease to exist. Superiority will be irrelevant and less given to political solvency and more to the dictates of a multi-group perspective. Similarly, in the world there will be less intellectual homogeneity and tastes for good-bad, inferior-superior. This fact no doubt will extend to the attitudes and respect for multiracial and multicultural ways of thinking. However, the idealization of light skin color in some form may not, unfortunately, dominate, but may still survive. Those who celebrate the new millennium will continue to groan with discontent over past and present injus-tices that have been visited on dark-skinned people by the practices of racist ideals. Even so, the new millennium promises a trend toward total rebirth and worldwide regeneration. It will continue to be cultivated in the intellectual seeds that will be sown by those who can escape the insidious influences of color.

Yet, the questions remain of what lies ahead amid the end of light skin color as ideal. What could history be pointing to with its ruthless discarding of such a sacred Western concept? A clue may rest in the end of the tyranny of light skin as the standard racial criteria. Science has already seen technology end the tyranny of repetitive labor. Since that time, the West has led the world in charting the course of mankind in a new direction. Along the course of this new direction will come the human effort to reorganize social life, to reinvent the family, and to liberate dark-skinned people from the tyranny of their universal denigration. Unfortunately, absent their conscious and active parti-cipation, skin color among people of color and the prevailing human universe will triumph as a manifestation of racism well into the 21st century!

References

Hall, R. (1995). The Bleaching Syndrome: African Americans' response to cultural domina-tion vis-a-vis skin color. *Journal of Black Studies*, 26, 172–183.
Walker v. the Internal Revenue Service, 742 F. Supp. 670 (N.D. Ga. 1990)

Author Biographies

Nicole E. Belletti is a recent graduate of Bucknell University, majoring in Psychology, English, and French. During her time at Bucknell, Nicole participated in psychological research teams exploring inter-racial communication, obsessive-compulsive behaviors in young children, and the relationship between race and facial beauty, the subject of her honors thesis. In her thesis, Nicole used blended African American, Caucasian, and Asian faces to examine evaluations of facial beauty based on the race of the face being rated and the race of the rater. Currently, Nicole is a Child Care Counselor at KidsPeace, a non-profit organization for kids overcoming crisis. She plans to pursue a Ph.D. in clinical psychology.

Eduardo Bonilla-Silva is Research Professor of Sociology at Duke University. He received his Ph.D. from the University of Wisconsin. Dr. Bonilla-Silva has published three books: *White Supremacy and Racism in the Post Civil Rights Era, Racism Without Racists*, and *White Out*. His most recent work is on two book projects critical of the methods used by social analysts to assess racial matters (*Anything But Racism: How Social Analysts Limit the Significance of Racism* and *White Logic, White Methods: Racism and Methodology*) as well as another project examining the future of racial stratification in the United States (*We are all Americans! The Latin Americanization of Racial Stratification the USA*).

Alfiee M. Breland-Noble is a tenure track Assistant Professor in the department of Psychiatry and Behavioral Sciences at the Duke University Medical Center. Her research interests include improving treatment engagement for psychiatric illness in African American and other children of color and the diagnosis and treatment of adolescent depression in clinical trials. Currently, she is the principal investigator of The AAKOMA Project; a study examining readiness to engage in tmreatment for African-American adolescents with major depression. This project is currently funded via a National Institute of Mental Health (NIMH) five-year K01 career development award. She received her doctoral degree in counseling psychology from the University of Wisconsin-Madison, a Masters in Counseling from New York University and her Bachelor of Arts in

English from Howard University. Dr. Breland-Noble is currently completing a thesis for a Masters degree in Health Sciences (clinical trials) at the Duke School of Medicine. She has over 20 publications including works in the *Journal of the American Academy of Child and Adolescent Psychiatry, Psychiatric Annals and the Journal of Family Process.*

Keith C. Cheng is Associate Professor of Pathology, Biochemistry and Molecular Biology and Pharmacology at Penn State University School of Medicine. He is also Co-Director of the Penn State IBIOS Bioinformatics and Genomics graduate program (with John Carlson) and Director, Zebrafish Functional Genomics and Imaging Core. Dr. Cheng received his Ph.D. from University of Washington and Fred Hutchinson Cancer Research Center (1986); M.D. from New York University School of Medicine (1980); and B.A. from Harvard University (1976). Recently, Dr. Cheng discovered a new gene, the putative cation exchanger slc24a5, that appears to modulate vertebrate pigmentation via its effect on melanosome morphogenesis. Most interestingly, a variant found in the human homologue appears to be associated in a key way with the evolution of the light skin of the European branch of the human race. Most recently, Dr. Cheng has begun to use mouse models as a translational tool to find effective preventive and therapeutic treatments for inborn errors of metabolism.

David R. Dietrich is a student, Department of Sociology, at Duke University.

Brea Eaton, LPC, is a Middle School Counselor at Carter Middle School, in Clio, Michigan. Previously, she completed a Bachelor of Science degree in Clinical/Community Psychology from the University of Michigan-Flint (2000) and a Masters degree in Counseling from Michigan State University (2003). Clinically Mrs. Eaton is well-versed and experienced in the areas of foster care/adoption, anger management groups, the supervision of parental visits with their children, adjudicated persons and substance abuse treatment. In this regard, Ms. Eaton completed clinical training at the Dailey Life Center and Insight Recovery Services. While at Insight, she served as the Interim Clinical Director for Community Recovery Services working in conjunction with the Department of Corrections. As a school counselor, Mrs. Eaton's clinical work focuses on children dealing with divorce, anger management, study skills, and positive peer relationships. She has been a member of the Genesee Area Counseling Association for 5 years and is completing coursework to obtain the Certified Trauma Specialist (C.T.S.) designation through the TLC Institute.

Christina Gómez is Associate Professor in the Department of Sociology at Northeastern Illinois University in Chicago, Illinois. She received her Doctorate from Harvard University in the Department of Sociology and completed her undergraduate studies and MBA at the University of Chicago. She recently completed an edited book, *Mi Vida, Mi Voz: Latino College Students Tell Their*

Stories of Success, and is completing a book manuscript, *Latinos, Class, and the Boundaries of Whiteness*, which focuses on the racialization of Latinos in the United States. Her research focuses on identity construction, discrimination, and ethnic relations. She has been awarded various fellowships and grants including the Henry Luce Scholar Fellowship.

Ronald E. Hall is Associate Professor in the School of Social Work, Michigan State University, and an affiliated scholar with the Julian Somora Research Institute and the Asian Institute, Michigan State University. Dr. Hall received his Ph.D. from Atlanta University, MSW from the University of Michigan, and MCS from the University of Detroit. Having written his dissertation on skin color, in 1990 Dr. Hall testified as an expert witness to America's first skin color discrimination case between African Americans: *Morrow vs. IRS*. Dr. Hall later devised the Bleaching Syndrome to explain discrimination among people of color and has published numerous books and peer-reviewed papers on the subject. He has reviewed grant proposals on skin color for the National Science Foundation, peer-reviewed journals, and consulted with attorneys on skin color discrimination. In 2003, he won the Adele Mellen Prize for Distinguished Contribution to Scholarship for *Skin Color as a Post-Colonial Issue Among Asian-Americans*. He is associated with over a $1 million in research grant funds awarded to Michigan State University. His latest book is titled *Bleaching Beauty: Light Skin as Filipina Ideal* (2006).

Matthew S. Harrison is currently a Doctoral student in the Applied (Industrial/Organizational) Psychology program at The University of Georgia (UGA). A 2004 graduate of Emory University, where he earned his Bachelor of Arts degree in psychology, Harrison received his Master of Science degree from UGA's Applied (I/O) Psychology program in December 2005. His primary research focuses on workplace diversity. Most recently, his Master's thesis, *Colorism in the Job Selection Process: Are There Preferential Differences Within the Black Race?*, has received a wide-range of publicity, from being featured on UGA's homepage to http://www.BET.com. Numerous websites now feature his study, which has also been discussed on such popular syndicated radio shows as *The Michael Eric Dyson Show and The Tom Joyner Morning Show*. Mr. Harrison obtained his Ph.D. from UGA in May 2008.

Joni Hersch is Professor of Law and Economics at Vanderbilt University. She received her Ph.D. in Economics from Northwestern University. Dr. Hersch has published numerous articles on gender differences in labor market outcomes, the economics of home production, job risks, product safety regulation, and smoking risks and regulations. Having explored sex discrimination for decades, Dr. Hersch has recently begun to study discrimination on the basis of darker skin color in the U.S. labor market. The *American Economic Review* published her article "Skin Tone Effects among African Americans: Perceptions and Reality;" and her widely publicized paper

"Profiling the New Immigrant Worker: The Effects of Skin Color and Height" is currently under review. Dr. Hersch has developed an empirical model to determine whether new legal immigrants to the United States are discriminated against on the basis of darker skin color. Her research may be useful to plaintiffs who seek damages for skin color discrimination rather than racial discrimination.

Margaret Hunter is Assistant Professor in the Department of Sociology at Loyola Marymount University in Los Angeles. She holds a Ph.D. and M.A. in Sociology from the University of California, Los Angeles, and a B.A. from the University of Wisconsin, Madison. Her research areas include comparative racial and ethnic relations, skin color politics, feminist theory, and the sociology of knowledge. Her recent book *Race, Gender, and the Politics of Skin Tone* (Routledge 2005) compares the experiences of African American and Mexican American women with skin color discrimination. Her research on skin tone has been published in several journals including Gender & Society (2002) and *Sociological Inquiry* (1998). "Rethinking Epistemology, Methodology, and Racism: or, Is White Sociology Really Dead?" (*Race & Society 5* 2002) is Hunter's contribution to the debate about racism and knowledge construction in the discipline of sociology. She is currently working on an interview study analyzing the use of colorblind racial discourse among college students.

Keri Hurst and Melissa Willis are graduates of the Masters in Social Work program at Howard University

Joy King is currently serving as a Project Coordinator at the Program in Child Affective and Anxiety Disorders at Duke Child and Family Study Center. She serves as the research lab manager for The AAKOMA Project. She also coordinates the Cognitive Behavior Therapy – Relapse Prevention (CBT-RP) research study, a study that provides treatment for adolescents who are suicidal, depressed, and have problems related to substance abuse. Ms. King is a member of the diversity outreach team. She received her Bachelor of Arts in Psychology from Kent State University (2006).

Wendy Reynolds-Dobbs is a Doctoral candidate in the Applied (Industrial/ Organizational) Psychology program at The University of Georgia. In 2002, she earned her Bachelor of Arts degree in Psychology with a minor in Ethnic Studies from the University of California, San Diego. Ms. Reynolds-Dobbs received her Master of Science degree in Applied (I/O) Psychology from The University of Georgia in August 2005 and obtained her Ph.D. in May 2007. Currently, her research interests include the recruitment and retention of women and ethnic minorities in the workplace, career development and work experiences of women of color, and resistance to diversity initiatives in organizations.

Wendy D. Roth is an Assistant Professor of Sociology at the University of British Columbia. Her research focuses on how social processes challenge racial boundaries and transform classification systems. In 2007, she received the American Sociological Association Dissertation Award for her research on how migration to the mainland U.S. affects the racial identities of Dominicans and Puerto Ricans, and how their racial diversity affects these groups' socio-economic integration in the U.S. Roth's publications include articles on the racial identification of children from interracial marriages and the transmission of panethnic identities through migration. She is also a co-author of *Rampage: The Social Roots of School Shootings*.

Julissa Senices completed her internship in counseling psychology at the University of Miami-Counseling Center. She earned her Doctorate degree in counseling psychology at the Pennsylvania State University, State College, Pennsylvania. Her Bachelor's degree in psychology is from New York University. Dr. Senices has a wide range of professional experience within the field of psychology. Her interests have centered on diversity issues, eating disorders, and group dynamics. Her clinical experience includes adolescent and adult psychotherapy, as well as couples, families, and group psychother-apy. She has published articles on the concept of Hispanic Identity in the changing face of America. She has also taught a Master's level course on multicultural counseling.

Chastity Simmons received her undergraduate degree from Loyola University New Orleans and in May 2004 she received a Masters in Social Work from Howard University. Currently, she is a Social Worker for a private agency in Washington, DC. This agency ensures the well-being of children in foster care and works towards placing them in a permanent home. Her four years of experience in the social service field has afforded her the opportunity to work with a highly diverse population.

Kecia M. Thomas Professor of Psychology and Interim Director of the Institute for African American Studies at The University of Georgia is a scholar of industrial and organizational psychology. Formerly an undergraduate of Bucknell University, she earned her Ph.D. at Pennsylvania State University. Her research interests include the recruitment of non-traditional professionals to corporate organizations, impact of preferential treatment on beneficiaries, and influence of perceptions of procedural justice. She has written numerous journal articles and book chapters, as well as a book, *Diversity Dynamics in the Workplace* (Wadsworth 2005).

T. Joel Wade is Chair of the Psychology Department and Co-Director of the African American Studies Program at Bucknell University. Dr. Wade has earned a Ph.D. in social psychology, MA in social psychology, and BA in psychology. Dr. Wade has been a Carolina Minority Post-Doctoral Scholar in the Department of Psychology at the University of North Carolina at Chapel Hill. He was nominated as a potential Fellow at the Center for The Advanced Study in the Behavioral Sciences, Palo Alto, California. He was also awarded a Ford Foundation Minority Post-Doctoral Fellowship at the Institute for Research in Social Science, University of North Carolina at Chapel Hill. Wade has also received grants from the Ford Foundation. He is the author of numerous articles on skin color, and attractiveness. His research interests include self and person-perception from a biological perspective as it relates to attractiveness and self-esteem, and skin color. Current research foci include facial attractiveness, beauty-related halo effects, reactions to infidelity, and jealousy. Dr. Wade has taught courses in Social Psychology, Black Psychology, Introductory Psychology, Social Psychology Laboratory, and Race and Gender.

Keith B. Wilson is Associate Professor in the Department of Counselor Education, Counseling Psychology and Rehabilitation Services and Director of the Africana Research Center at Pennsylvania State University. Dr. Wilson received his Ph.D. from Ohio State University; M.Ed. from Kent State University; and B.A. from Wilberforce University. He has been honored with several service (e.g., Multicultural Resource Center, Diversity Recognition) and research awards (e.g., Outstanding Researcher Award, Presented by the Pennsylvania Counseling Association). Dr. Wilson's research interests are primarily centered around two areas: (1) Cross-cultural and multicultural issues among persons with disabilities in the Vocational Rehabilitation (VR) system in the United States and (2) privilege based on phenotype (hue/skin color) in the VR system and in the general population (i.e., Black and White Hispanics). Dr. Wilson's private counseling, psychotherapy, and consulting enterprise is an important extension of his teaching, research, and service.

Staci Young, LPC is a Children & Families Counselor at EVE, Inc. (End Violent Encounters), a domestic violence shelter within the state of Michigan. Previously, she completed her Bachelor of Arts in Psychology at Michigan State University in 2000 and a Masters in Counseling at Michigan State University in 2003. As a researcher, Ms. Young has studied domestic violence and its effects on children for the past 6 years and as a clinician, she completed internships at both Cristo Rey Community Center and EVE, Inc. She has published in the area of the effects of domestic violence on children. At Cristo Rey, her primary experience was in facilitating groups focusing on Substance Abuse and Anger Management. At EVE, Inc. she focused primarily on individual, group, and family counseling involving both women and children who were survivors of domestic violence. Since working at EVE, Inc. MS. Young has created a 10-week curriculum called Girls Are Powerful (GAP) for girls who are at-risk within the greater Lansing, MI area in collaboration with the Girl Scouts of Michigan Capital Council. Ms. Young has been a member of the American Counseling Association for 5 years.

Index

A

Acquired blindness, 14
Adenine, 10
Adjustee immigrants, 82
"Admixed" European-African
ancestry, 10–11
African Americans
attractiveness and halo
effects, 141
beauty, 136–140
employment, 143–144
enthusiasm, 143
intelligence perception, 141–142
judicial system, 144–145
marketplace theory, 137–138
media's representation, 52–53
negative portrayals, effect of, 53
mental health, 145
parenting skill, 142–143
Afro-Dominicans, 162
Afro-Puerto Rican, 162
Alanine *(Ala)*, 10
Ala111Thr, 10–12
Ala111Thr Allele of SLC24A5, world
distribution of, 12
American chattel system of slavery, 49
American job market, 158
Amerindian genetic factor
in diabetes, 195
500 amino-acid human golden
gene, 9
See also SLC24A5
Analysis of variance (ANOVA), 106
ANOVA, *see* Analysis of variance
(ANOVA)
Asian flack, 161
Asians/Latinos, racial attitudes, 161–162
Assimilation and idealized skin color,
240–241

Attractiveness and halo effects, African
Americans
beauty, 136–140
employment, 143–144
enthusiasm, 143
intelligence perception, 141–142
judicial system, 144–145
mental health, 145
parenting skill, 142–143
skin color halo effects,
141, 143
"Aztec Goddesses", 65

B

Beauty, African Americans, 136–140
See also Attractiveness and halo effects,
African Americans
BiDil, 15
Big-5 dimensions, 141
Black eumelanin, *see* Pigmentation
Black Indians, 34
"Black is beautiful", 136
Black Panthers and Brown
Berets, 65
Black Power Movement, 59
Black Racial Identity Attitude Scale-B Long
Form, 114
Black Wealth White Wealth, 69
Blanqueamiento (whitening),
151, 153
Bleaching syndrome, 25, 38–42, 73, 235,
237, 243
social ills, 40
Brown bag test, 71
Brown outs, role of skin color
and Latinas, 193–204
data and findings, 197–201
discussion, 201–202
phenotype, studies on, 195–196

Brown outs (*cont.*)
  skin color and literature, 194–195
  skin color stratification in Americas,
      196–197
Brown racism, 34

C
Cancer, risk of, 13–14
Cancer, susceptibility of, 13–14
Carmen Jones (film), 31
CCC, *see* Cutaneo-Chroma Correlate (CCC)
Cell biology, 4
Cellular process, golden zebrafish, 7
Civil Rights Act (1964), 54
Clark Study, findings, 57–58
Class dynamics, 152
Coefficients from logistic regression on
      likelihood of marriage skin color
      and independent variables, 200*t*
Collective black, 162–163, 166
Colonial subjects (Puerto Ricans), 162
Color, cost of, *see* Cost of color, payment
      for being black/brown
Color-blind racism, 64, 156, 166
Color complex, exporting, 72–75
Color consciousness, white young adults,
      125–134
  data analysis, 130–131
    analysis plan, 130
    results, 130–131
  limitations/future directions, 133
  manifestations of, 126–128
    caste system, 127
    research questions, 128
    skin-tone bias, 127
  methods, 128–130
    measures, IRF/MEI, 128–129
    procedures, 129–130
    subjects, 128
Color discrimination
  experiences with
      Dominican/ Puerto Rican
      non-migrants, 221–231
    in U.S., 227–231
  non-migrants' perceptions, by nationality
      and skin tone, 214*t*
Colorism
  among/within blacks, 57–58
  Caribbean societies and, 178
  children and, 180
  and media's representation, 51
    African American men, 53
    African American women, 52

Nicaraguan society and, 179
  skin color bias, 49
  See also Skin color
Color tests, *see* Brown bag test
Cost of color, payment for being
      black/brown
  education, 68–69
  employment, 66–68
  exporting color complex, 72–75
  housing, 69
  identity, 70–72
  spousal status, 69–70
Counts for most/least attractive face broken
      down by race, 107*t*
Cultural Identification Scale, 114
Cultural images valorizing Whiteness, 74
Cutaneo-Chroma Correlate (CCC), 105

D
dbSNP, *see* Single Nucleotide Polymorphism
      database (dbSNP)
The Debt (film), 30
Determinants, living thing, 5
Diabetes, Amerindian genetic factors, 195
Discrimination, employment treatment
      based on skin tone, 55–57
DNA, 5
Dominican non-migrant, experiences of
      color discrimination, 221–231
Double jeopardy situation, 57
"Double whammy", 173
  See also Skin color
Down These Mean Streets, 194
Dual Perspective (Norton, Dolores), 28

E
Education
  cost of color, 73–76
  racism, and, 19–20
Educational attainment of selected Asian
      and Latino Ethnic Groups, 2000,
      158*t*
EEOC, Equal Employment Opportunity
      Commission (EEOC)
Employment
  African Americans, 143–144
    See also Attractiveness and halo
        effects, African Americans
  cost of color, and, 73–76
  discriminatory treatment based on skin
      tone, 55–57
  racial discrimination in, 54–55
Empowerment, 242–243

Enthusiasm, African Americans, 143
Equal Employment Opportunity
          Commission (EEOC), 64–65, 67
Eurocentrism, 30
Eurogamy, 33
Exclusion and skin color, 240

F
Facial dimensions, 102*t*
Facial features, mean rankings, 110*t*
Fair Employment Council (FEC), 54
Fair skin women and intelligence, 141–142
Falero *vs.* Stryker Corporation, 32
FEC, *see* Fair Employment Council (FEC)
Felix *vs.* Manquez, 32
Female, racial features and facial
          attractiveness, 93–124
    discussion, 110–114
        attractiveness, 110–113
        facial features, 113–114
    facial dimensions for each face, 102*t*
    hypotheses, 101–105
    limitations and future research, 113–114
        appendix, 114–121
    method
        measures, 103–106
        participants, 103
        procedure, 105
        stimulus material, 103
    MFM, *see* Multiple Fitness Model
          (MFM)
    results, 106
        attractiveness, 106–108
        facial features, 110
        personality, 109
        racial identification, 109–110
        skin tone, 109
    scales, *see* Scales
    skin quality, 100–101, 113
    SSH, *see* Sexual Selection
          Hypothesis (SSH)
Filipina prototype, 26–27
Filipino, 27
"Full-blooded," Native Americans, 34

G
G. keras, horn, 6
G. kytos, cell, 6
G. melas, black, 6
G. soma, body, 6
'Generalized other,' concept of (George
          Mead), 28
Genes, 5–7, 9, 13–15, 18, 34, 94, 126

Genetic "hitch-hiking", 11
Genetic screens, 7
Genetics of human skin color and zebrafish
    Ala111Thr, 10
    cellular process, 7–8
    darkening of golden cells, 10
    golden, 7
    "HapMap" database, 10
    phenotype, 8
    reasons, light color of golden pigmented
          cells, 8
Genetic variations, light skin color
    in European, 12–13
    drug responsiveness, and, 15
Global attractiveness, 137
Globalization, 72, 216, 232
Good Morning America, 18
Guanine, 10

H
Halo effects, *see* Attractiveness and halo
          effects, African Americans
HapMap website, 15
*Haunting and the Sociological
          Imagination,* 35
Health implications of light skin color
    drugs, responsiveness to, 15
    education, 16
    income, 16
    job opportunity, 16
    psychological and psychiatric issues, skin
          color, 15
    skin cancer susceptibility, 13–14
Honorary whites, 154, 157–159, 163, 165,
          166–167
Housing, cost of color, 69

I
Identity, cost of color, 70–72
I Have a Dream speech, 47
Immigrant adaptation, study
          of, 69
Immigration, whitening population
          through, 155
Immunotherapy, 14
Impression Rating Form
          (IRF), 128–129
Indian facial features, 68
"Indios", 27
Intelligence perception, African Americans,
          141–142
    See also Attractiveness and halo effects,
          African Americans

Interviews, Latinos' perceptions of color
        discrimination
    Dominican/Puerto Rican non-migrant,
        221–231
IRF, *see* Impression Rating Form (IRF)

J
Jobs, front-office appearance, 67
Judeo-Christian Anglo tradition, 155
Judicial system, African Americans, 144–145
    See also Attractiveness and halo effects,
        African Americans

K
Keratinocytes, 6
    See also Pigmentation
King, Dr. Martin Luther, 47

L
Language, ('Black' and 'Chicano') 71
Latin Americanization, reason for
    changing demography, 155
    "multi-racial" movement, 156
    race relations, globalized, 156
        See also Race relations, Latin
            Americanization of
    racial retreat, 156
    reorganization, post-civil rights era,
        155–156
Latinos
    disabilities and VR acceptance/access,
        173–174
        See also Skin color
    migrants, attitudes toward
        discrimination, 206
    perceptions, color discrimination, *see*
        Sending-receiving society, Latinos
        perceptions
Latinos with disabilities, skin color and
    colorism, historical perspective, 177–178
    colorism, influence of, outside U.S.,
        178–180
    directions for future research, 186–187
    discussion, 182–184
    evidence to support colorism in
        U.S.(able-bodied Latinos),
        180–182
    implications, 187–188
    limitations of research, able-bodied
        population, 184
    literature review, vocational
        rehabilitation acceptance, 173–174
    strengths of research, 185–186

vocational rehabilitation, disabled
        people, 184–185
    VR acceptance/access, 173–174
Leu374Phe mutation, 12
Lightening of skin color
    SLC24A5, role of, 10–13
Lighter skin in northerly latitudes, biological
        reason, 11
Light skin
    European ancestry, 4
    health implications
        acquired blindness, 14
        immunotherapy, 14
        melanoma, 14
        skin cancer, 13
    northerly latitudes, biological reason, 11
    Scandinavians, 13
Light skin color, health implications of,
        see Health implications of light
        skin color
Linda Acupanda McGloin (1992), 26
Literary Heritage Project (U.S.), 194
Living thing, determinants, 5

M
Marketplace theory, African Americans,
        137–138
    self-perceived sexual attractiveness, 137
    skin color perception, 138
Marlowe-Crowne Social Desirability Scale
        (SD), 105
Marriage, interracial, 163–164
Marriage markets, discrimination in, 71–73
MATP, *see* Membrane-associated
        transporter protein (MATP)
Mean values and significance test by skin
        color, Latina sample, 198*t*
Media
    portrayals, effects of, 53–54
    representation, African Americans,
        52–53
    role, 49–50
    shaping our perceptions, 49–50
Megatrends, color/intellectual
        miscegenation, 245–246
MEI-R, *see* Multicultural/Multiracial
        Experience Inventory (MEI-R)
Melanocytes, 6
    See also Pigmentation
Melanoma, cancer of pigmented cells, 14
    immunotherapy, 14
Melanosomes, 6
    See also Pigmentation

Membrane-associated transporter protein
        (MATP), 12
Mental health, African Americans, 145
    See also Attractiveness and halo effects,
        African Americans
Mercury poisoning, skin bleaching
        creams, 74
Mestizo (mixed blood), 34, 74, 152, 155,
        195, 239
"Mestizo prototype", 195
MFM, *see* Multiple Fitness Model (MFM)
Miss Universe contest, outcomes, 238
Mulattoes, 49
Multicultural/Multiracial Experience
        Inventory (MEI-R), 129
Multigroup Ethnic Identity Measure, 114
Multiple Fitness Model (MFM), 98–99
    female facial attractiveness,
        features, 98

N

National Chicano Survey (1980), 195
National Human Genome Research
        Institute (NHGRI), 14, 17
National Survey of Black Americans
        (NSBA), 79
"Nature" and "nurture", 5
Needs, hierarchy of (Maslow), 40
Neighborhood integration, 163
Neutral immigrants, 162
New England Journal of Medicine, 15
New Immigrant Survey (2003), 78–83
    adjustee immigrants, 82
    descriptive statistics and correlations
        with skin color, 81*t*–82*t*
    histograms of skin color, 80
    scale (11-point), measurement of
        color, 79
    strata, sampling design, 79
New racism, 155
NHGRI, *see* National Human Genome
        Research Institute (NHGRI)
Nicaraguan society and colorism, 179
NIS-2003, *see* New Immigrant
        Survey (2003)
Non-migrants' perceptions of color
        discrimination, by nationality
        and skin tone, 214*t*
"Notions of beauty," 202
NSBA, *see* National Survey of Black
        Americans (NSBA)
Nubian Princesses, 65
"Nurturing environment", 27

O

Occupational status (2000), ethnic groups
    selected Asian ethnic groups, 160*t*
    selected Latino groups, 159*t*
OCPRW, *see* Office of the Commonwealth
        of Puerto Rico in Washington,
        D.C. (OCPRW)
Office of the Commonwealth of Puerto
        Rico in Washington, D.C.
        (OCPRW), 32
"One-drop" theory, 34
Orthologues, 9
Our Kind of People, 126

P

Paralogs, 9
Parenting skill, African Americans,
        142–143
    See also Attractiveness and halo effects,
        African Americans
Pathophysiology, concepts of, 4
People, 52
"People of color," 244
People of Color Racial Identity Attitude
        Scale, 114
Perceived attractiveness/skin tone/
        personality, rated as function
        of face, 108*t*
Perceptions, role of media, 49–50
    drawbacks, 50
Pigmentation
    cell biology of
        black eumelanin, 6
        melanin, 6
        melanocytes-G. melas, 6
    differences in, *see* Pigmentation
Pigmentocracy, 154, 155
Pinky, 31
5-point Likert scale, 103
Political refugees, 162
Porosity, 154
Portrayals of media, effects
        of, 53–54
Power imbalance
    presence of color *vs.* absence
        of color, 244
"Progressive whitening," 179
    See also Skin color
Psychological/psychiatric issues
    skin color, associated with, 15
Puerto Rican non-migrant, experiences
        of color discrimination,
        221–231

R
Race
    biology and today's manifestations
        demystifying skin color and race, 3–23
        manifestations of racism in 21st
            century, 25–44
    costs of
        being black and brown, 65–76
        skin color bias in workplace, media's
            role and implications, 47–62
        skin color/immigrant wages/
            discrimination, 77–90
    pervasiveness of
        attractiveness and halo effects,
            evaluation of African Americans,
            135–150
        brown outs, role of skin color and
            Latinas, 193–204
        interracial interactions on color
            consciousness among white young
            adults, 125–134
        Latin Americanization of U.S. race
            relations, 151–170
        Latinos' perceptions of color
            discrimination through
            sending-receiving society
            comparison, 205–234
        racial characteristics and female facial
            attractiveness perception, 93–124
        skin color and Latinos with
            disabilities, 171–191
Race and Politics, 161
Race and skin color, demystifying
    cell biology of pigmentation, 6–7
    demystifying skin color and race, 17–18
    education, 19–20
    health implications of light skin color,
        13–16
    historical context, 4–5
    microbes, discovery of, 4
    National Human Genome Research
        Institute, 17
    racism, origin, 5–6
    role for zebrafish and genetics of human
        skin color, 7–10
    skin pigmentation/science/race, 18–19
    SLC24A5 in lightening of skin color
        in Europeans, 10–13
    sociology of SLC24A5 story, 16–17
Race relations, Latin Americanization of,
    151–170
    collective racial attitudes, 162–163
    consequences, 166–167

    data, 157–159
    interracial marriage, 163–164
    prediction of changes, 154, 166
    racial attitudes, Asians/Latinos, 161–162
    racial stratification in United States,
        153–155
    reason for, 155–156
        See also Latin Americanization,
            reason for
    residential segregation among racial
        strata, 164–165
    self-reports, Latino, 160–161
    subjective standing of racial strata,
        159–160
    three racial strata, social interaction
        among members, 163
Racial attitudes, Asians/Latinos,
    161–162
Racial democracy, regions of, 209
Racial discrimination
    employment selection, in, 54–55
    housing patterns, in, 181–182
        See also Skin color
    levels of, 71
Racial-identity theories, 48
Racial phenotypicality bias, 131
Racial self-classification, Latin America
    origin Latino ethnic groups
    (2000), 161*t*
Racial strata, subjective standing
    of, 159–160
Racial tipping point, 165
Racism, reconceptualizing, 237–238
Racism (21st century), manifestations
    of, 25–44
    beauty and women of color, 36–38
    bleaching syndrome, 25, 38–42
    dual perspective (Norton, Dolores), 28
    Eurocentrism, 30
    Filipina prototype, 26
    "Filipino", 27
    "indios", 27
    nurturing environment, 27
    "significant others", 27
    skin color
        African Americans, 30–32
        Asian Americans, 33–34
        Hispanic Americans, 32–33
        Native Americans, 34–36
    society, ideals of, 25–26
    Spanish colonials, in Philippines, 26
Reconceptualizing racism, 237–238
    Miss Universe contest, outcomes, 238

Regression coefficients and betas for models of (LN) hourly wages on skin color, 199*t*

Representation of media, African Americans, 50–52

S

Scales
 Black Racial Identity Attitude Scale-B Long Form, 114
 Cutaneo-Chroma Correlate (CCC), 105
 Marlowe-Crowne Social Desirability Scale (SD), 105
 Multicultural/Multiracial Experience Inventory (MEI-R), 129
 People of Color Racial Identity Attitude Scale, 114
 5-point Likert scale, 103
 11-point scale, 79
 scale of skin color, 79*f*

School Daze, 64

Science, 17

Self-actualization (Maslow), 29

Sending-receiving society, Latinos perceptions, 205–234
 belief in color discrimination, 214–221
 colorism at home/abroad, 207–210
 experiences, *see* Color discrimination
 interviews, *see* Interviews, Latinos' perceptions of color discrimination
 methodology, 210–213
 Puerto Rico-unemployed medical technician, 226
 sending societies, in, 213–214

SEP, *see* Socioeconomic position (SEP)

Sexism, 183
 See also Skin color

Sexual attractiveness, African Americans men/woman, 137–138

Sexual Selection Hypothesis (SSH), 97–100
 female facial attractiveness, 93–124
 recent studies, 97–98
 symmetry, 97

Sickle cell trait, 18

"Significant others", 27

Similarity Attraction Theory (Byrne), 58

Single Nucleotide Polymorphism database (dbSNP), 15

Skin bleaching creams, harmful effects
 harmful ingredients, 74
 mercury poisoning, 74

Skin color
 African Americans, 30–32
 Asian Americans, 33–34
 assimilation and idealized, 240–241
 attractiveness, *see* Attractiveness and halo effects, African Americans
 bias/colorism, 49
 brown outs, role of Latinas and, 193–204
 descriptive statistics and correlations, 81*t*–82*t*
 discrimination
  productivity characteristics, effect of, 89
 earnings, and, 199–200
 effect on education, 68–69
 exclusion and, 240
 halo effects, African Americans, 143
 hierarchies, 68
 Hispanic Americans, 32–33
 histograms of, 80
 idealization, 235–237
 immigrant wages and discrimination, 77–90
  diversity-visa principals, 78
  employment-visa principals, 78
  wage equation, *see* Wage equation estimates
 and literature, 194–195
 marriage, and, 201–202
 mean values and significance test, Latina sample, 198*t*
 Native Americans, and, 34–36
 perception, 138
 and race, misconceptions, 4
 regression coefficients and betas for models of (LN) hourly wages, 199*t*
 scale (11-point) measurement, 79
 stratification in Americas, 196–197

Skin (light or dark) and racism, 240–241

Skin pigmentation, science/race, 18

Skin quality, 100–101, 113

SLC24A5, 9, 12
 and light-skinned East Asians, 13
 and SriLankans, 13
 See also 500 amino-acid human golden gene

SLC24A5, sociology of, 16–17

SLC45A2 (AIM1-antigen in melanoma 1), 12
 See also Membrane-associated transporter protein (MATP)

Smiling discrimination, 155–156

Social environment, 6

Social evolution, new rhetoric for, 243–245
Socioeconomic indicators, 65
Socioeconomic position (SEP), 133
Sodium, calcium exchanger, 9
"Spanish", 27
Spanish colonials, in Philippines, 26
Spatial assimilation theory, 69
Spousal status, cost of color, 69–70
Statistical Package for Social Sciences, SPSS
        14.0 (SPSS Inc), 130

T
"Third world", 242
Threonine *(Thr)*, 10
Tracy Walker *vs.* Internal Revenue Service
        (IRS), 31
Tribalism, 5
Triple discrimination, 194
"Triple jeopardy situation", 57
"Triple whammy", 173
        See also Skin color
"Twoness", 28

U
*Understanding Human Behavior in the Social
        Environment,* 41
Underwhite mutation in mice, 12
Urban Inequality, Boston Social Survey
        Data, 197
U.S. Literary Heritage Project, 194

V
Visa principals, diversity/employment, 78
VR services and disabled people, 184–185
        See also Skin color
VR system, 172–177, 183, 184, 187–188

W
Wage equation estimates
        additional variables, inclusion of, 84–85
        coefficients on skin color in log wage
                equations, 85*t*
        interpretations, 86–88
Wage regressions (U.S.), 88
Walker *vs.* the IRS (1990), 245
Watson *vs.* Fort Worth, 54
White aesthetics, 74
"White Secret", 193, 196
Women
        beauty and color, 36–38
        intelligence and fair skin, African
                Americans, 141–142
Workplace, skin color bias
        African Americans, media's
                representation, 50–51
        colorism among/within blacks, 57–59
        colorism and media's representation, 53
                African American men, 53
                African American women, 52–53
        colorism/skin color bias, 49
        employment discriminatory treatment,
                55–57
        employment selection, in, 54–55
        media's portrayals, effects of, 53–54
        media's role, 47–62
        shaping our perceptions, role
                of media, 49–50
World News Tonight, 18

Z
Zebrafish and genetics of human skin
        color, 7–10